grog grog
GAH!

1st panel
Scar's
toupee

The disbelief over "toupee"!!!

I mentioned on the inside flap of volume 13 that as I was nodding off I wrote some crazy notes on a Post-it...and guess what? I did it again! "Scar's toupee."

—Hiromu Arakawa, 2010

Born in Hokkaido (northern Japan), Hiromu Arakawa first attracted national attention in 1999 with her award-winning manga *Stray Dog*. Her series *Fullmetal Alchemist* debuted in 2001 in Square Enix's monthly manga anthology *Shonen Gangan*.

FULLMETAL ALCHEMIST
VOL. 25

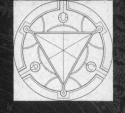

VIZ Media Edition

Story and Art by Hiromu Arakawa

Translation/Akira Watanabe
English Adaptation/Jake Forbes
Touch-up Art & Lettering/Wayne Truman
Design/Julie Behn
Editor/Alexis Kirsch

Printed in the U.S.A.

Published by VIZ Media, LLC
P.O. Box 77010
San Francisco, CA 94107

10 9 8 7 6 5 4 3 2 1
First printing, June 2011

www.viz.com

RATED T FOR TEEN

PARENTAL ADVISORY
FULLMETAL ALCHEMIST is rated T for Teen and is recommended for ages 13 and up. Contains mildly strong language, tobacco/alcohol use and fantasy violence.
ratings.viz.com

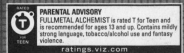

鋼の錬金術師

FULLMETAL ALCHEMIST

HIROMU ARAKAWA

荒川弘

25

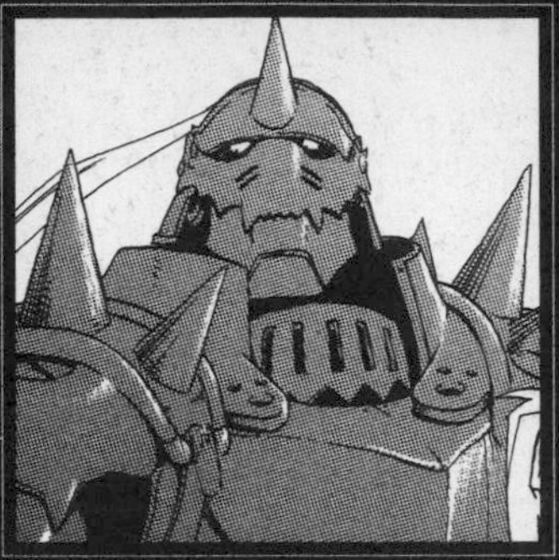

アルフォンス・エルリック

Alphonse Elric

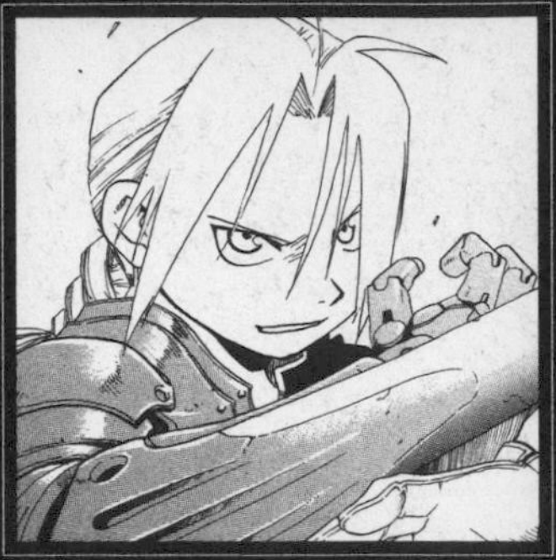

エドワード・エルリック

Edward Elric

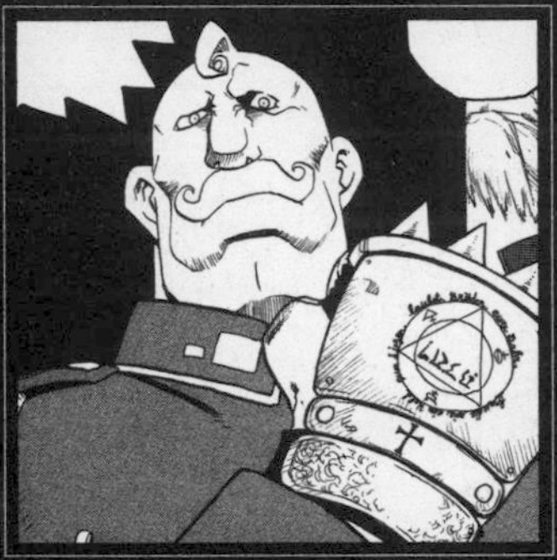

アレックス・ルイ・アームストロング

Alex Louis Armstrong

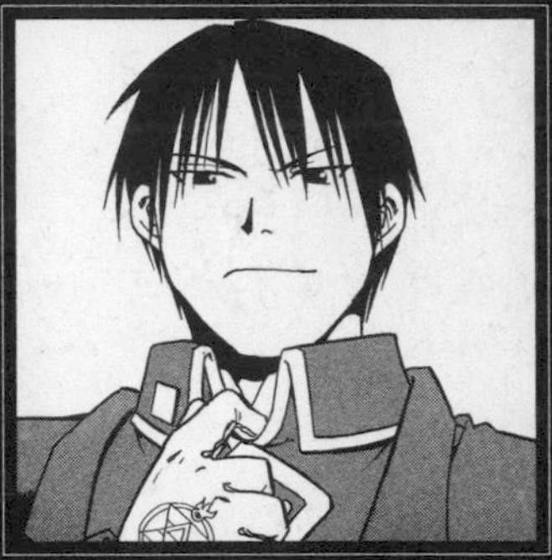

ロイ・マスタング

Roy Mustang

OUTLINE
FULLMETAL ALCHEMIST

Using a forbidden alchemical ritual, the Elric brothers attempted to bring their dead mother back to life. But the ritual went wrong, consuming Edward Elric's leg and Alphonse Elric's entire body. At the cost of his arm, Edward was able to graft his brother's soul into a suit of armor. Equipped with mechanical "auto-mail" to replace his missing limbs, Edward becomes a state alchemist in hopes of finding a way to restore their bodies. Their search embroils them in a deadly conspiracy that threatens to take the innocence, if not the lives, of everyone involved.

As the "Day of Reckoning" looms, Central City has become a warzone! On one side, the Homunculi and the military leaders who have sold out their country for power; on the other, a rag-tag alliance of rebel soldiers loyal to Major General Armstrong of Briggs and Roy Mustang, Ishbalan refugees and, of course, the Elric family. With the Fuhrer-President missing and morale amongst Central's loyal soldiers low, the Briggs soldiers managed to capture Central HQ, but now Bradley is back and the tides are turning against our heroes. Meanwhile, in the Homunculi's lair, deep beneath Central City, Hohenheim confronts his old nemesis, The Dwarf in the Flask, while Ed, Mustang, Scar and their friends are in the fight of their lives against a squad of super-soldiers. . .

鋼の錬金術師
FULLMETAL ALCHEMIST

CHARACTERS
FULLMETAL ALCHEMIST

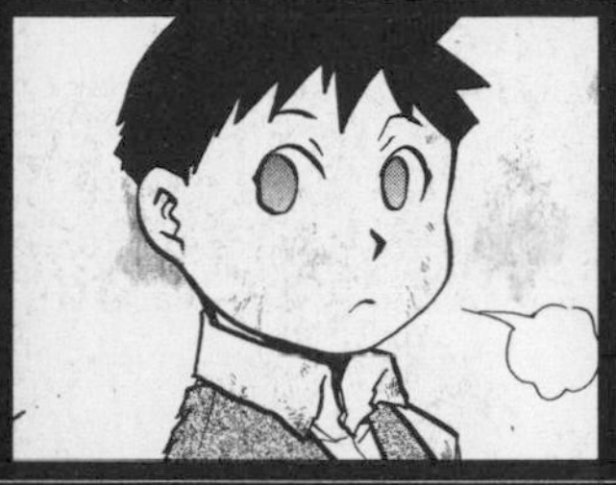

□ セリム・ブラッドレイ(プライド)

Selim Bradley (Pride)

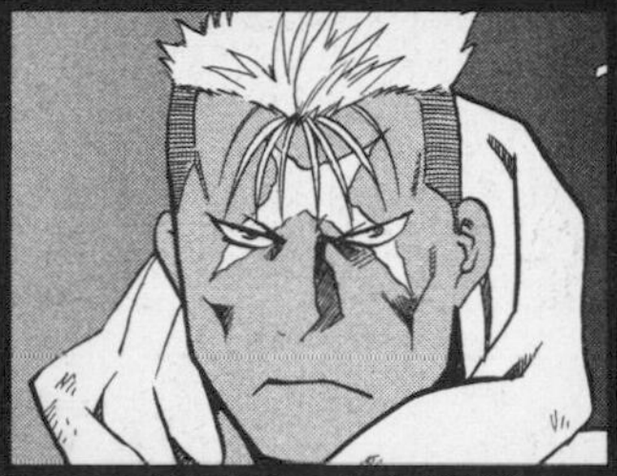

□ スカー

Scar

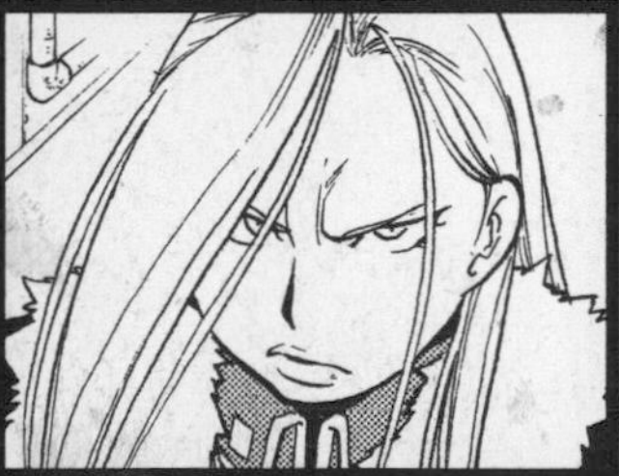

□ オリヴィエ・ミラ・アームストロング

Olivier Mira Armstrong

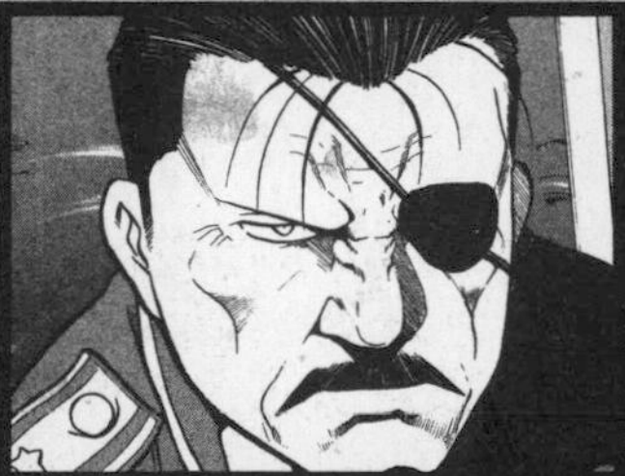

□ キング・ブラッドレイ

King Bradley

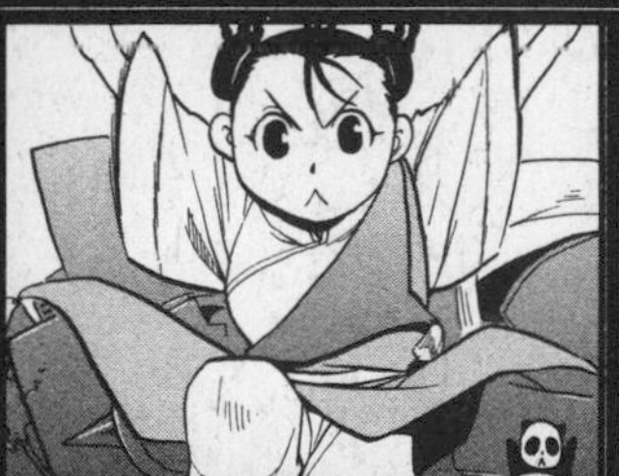

□ メイ・チャン

May Chang

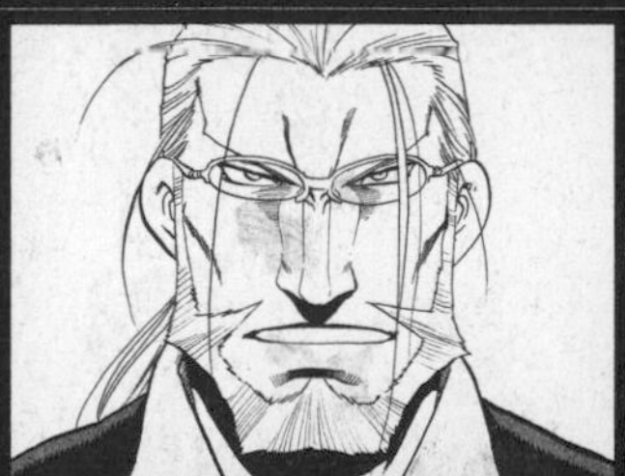

□ ヴァン・ホーエンハイム

Van Hohenheim

CONTENTS

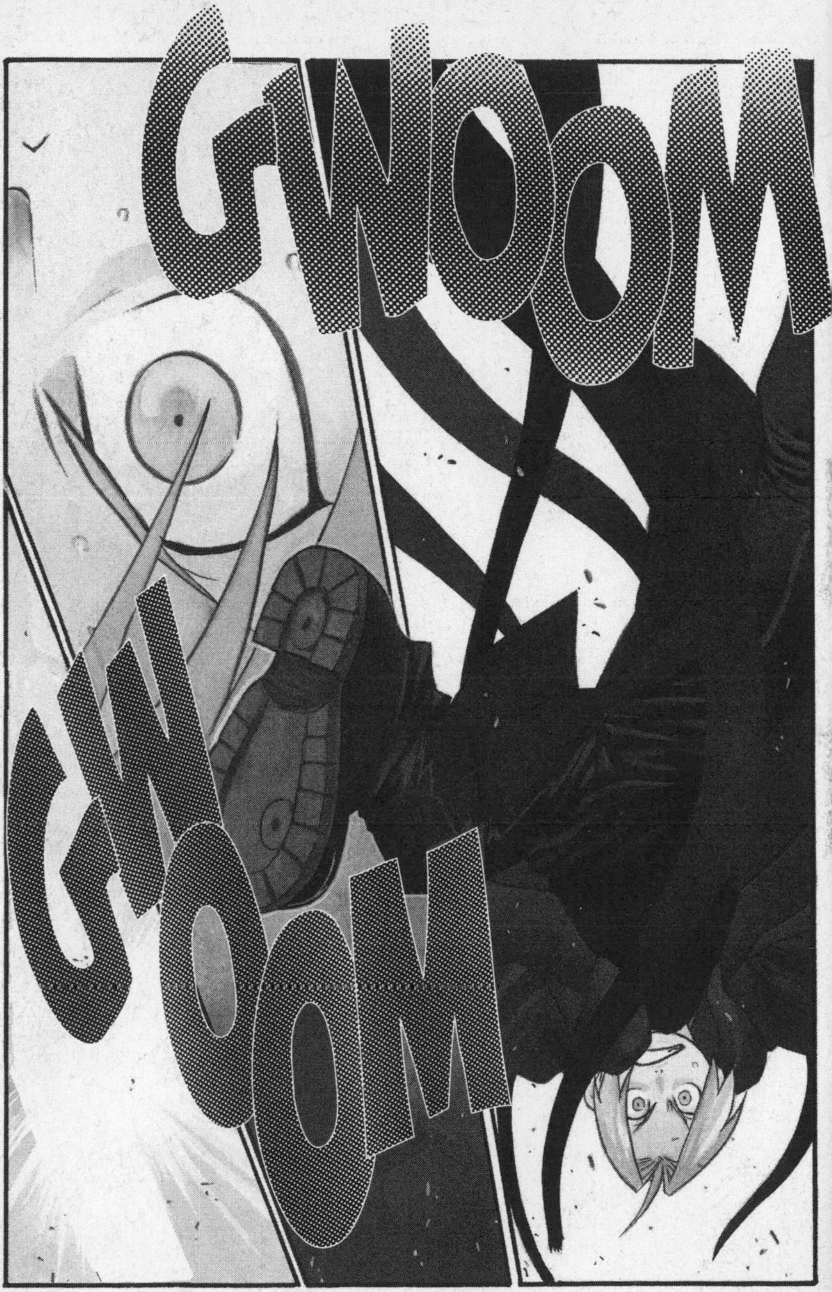
GWOOM
GWOOM

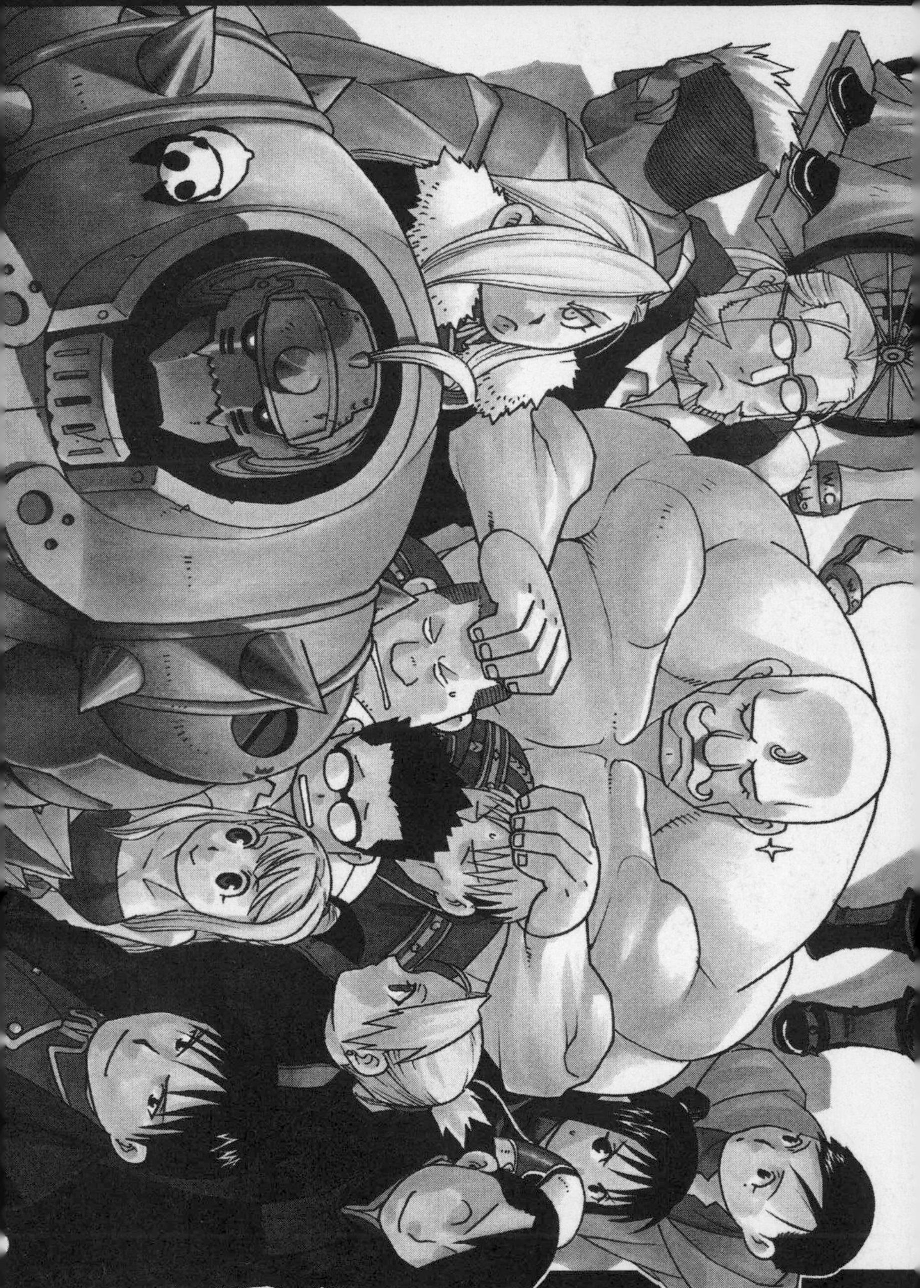

Chapter 100
Holding the Gate

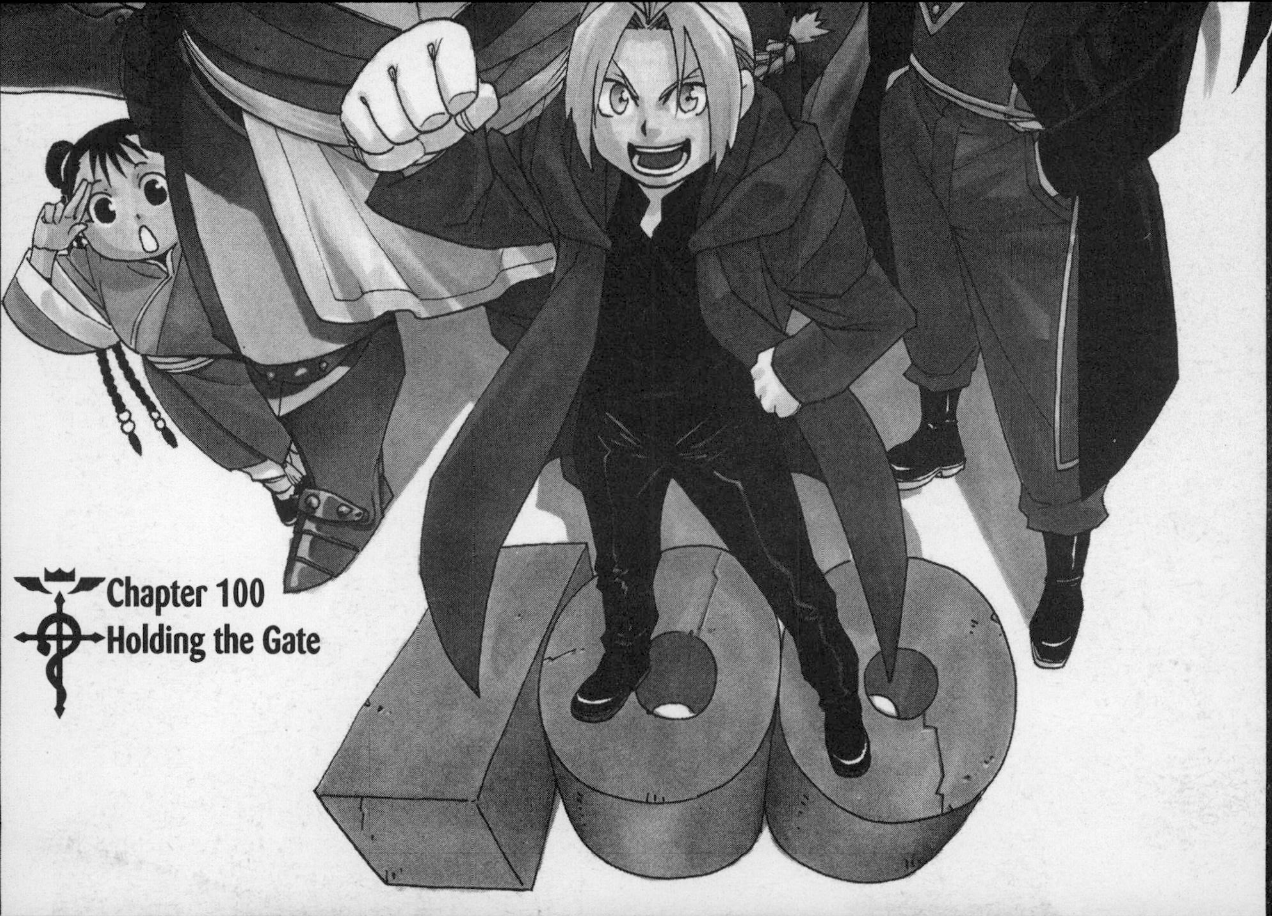

FULLMETAL
ALCHEMIST

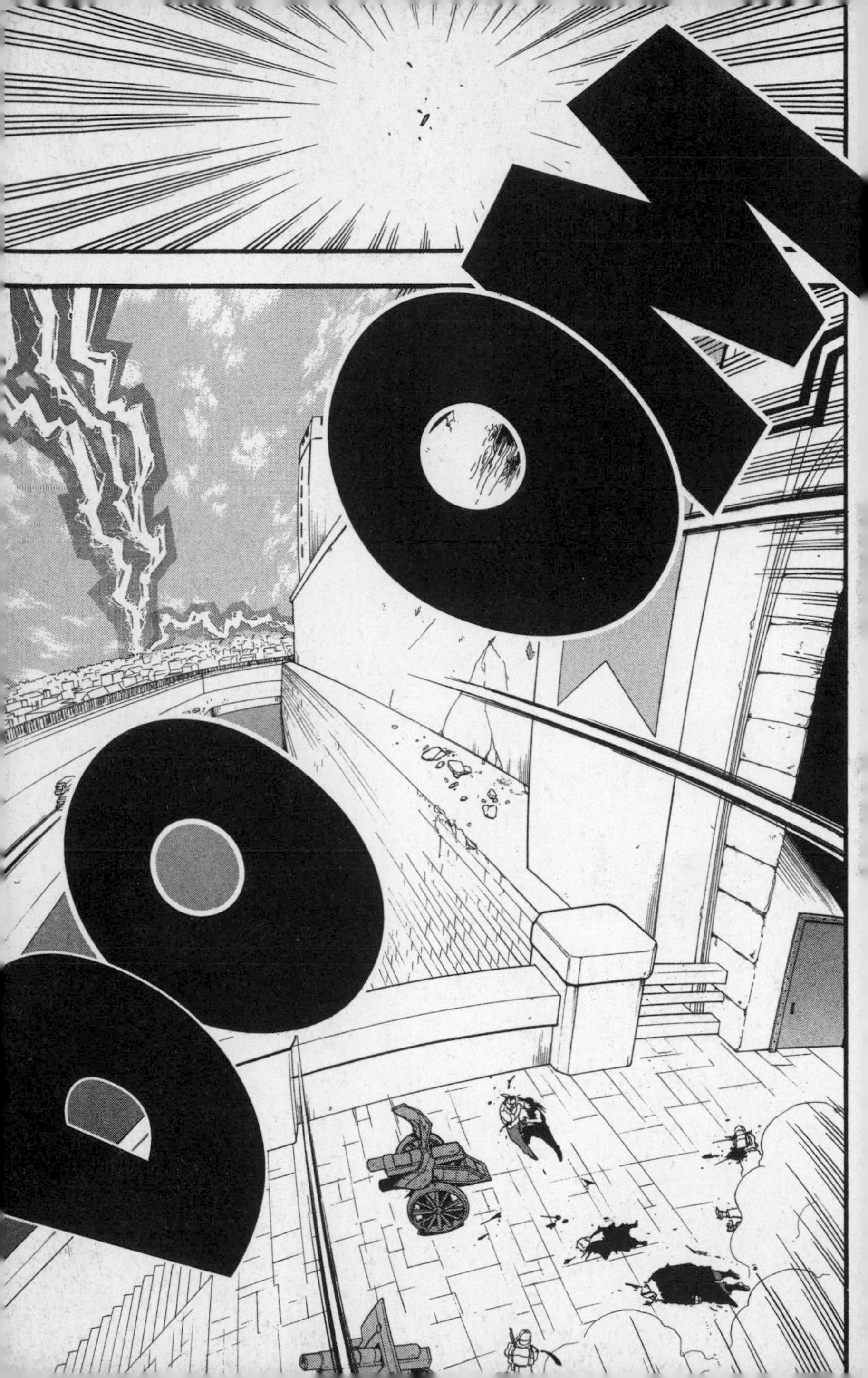
DOOM

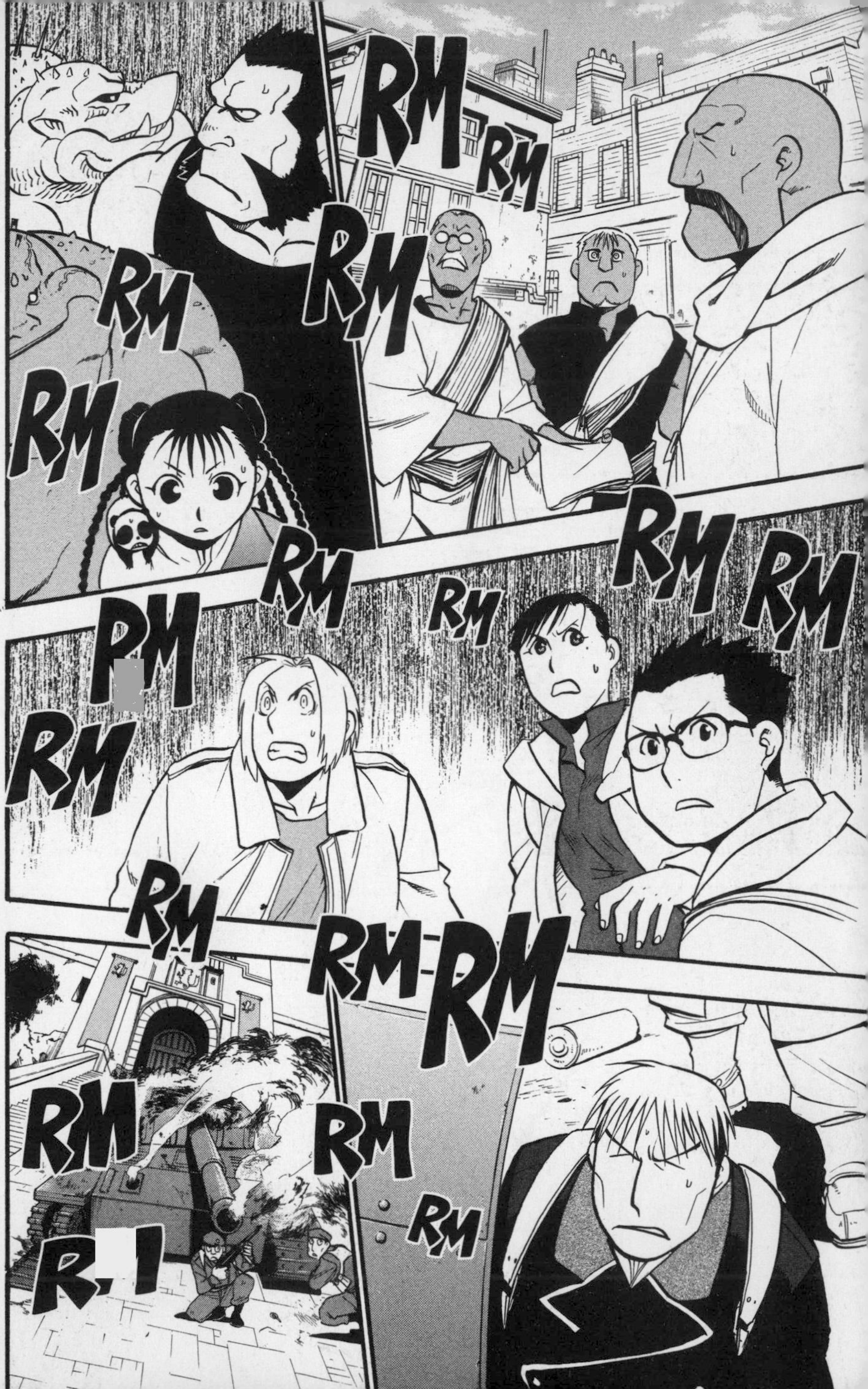
RM
RM
RM
RM
RM
RM
RM
RM
RM
RM
RM
RM
RM-RM
RM
RM
RM
RM

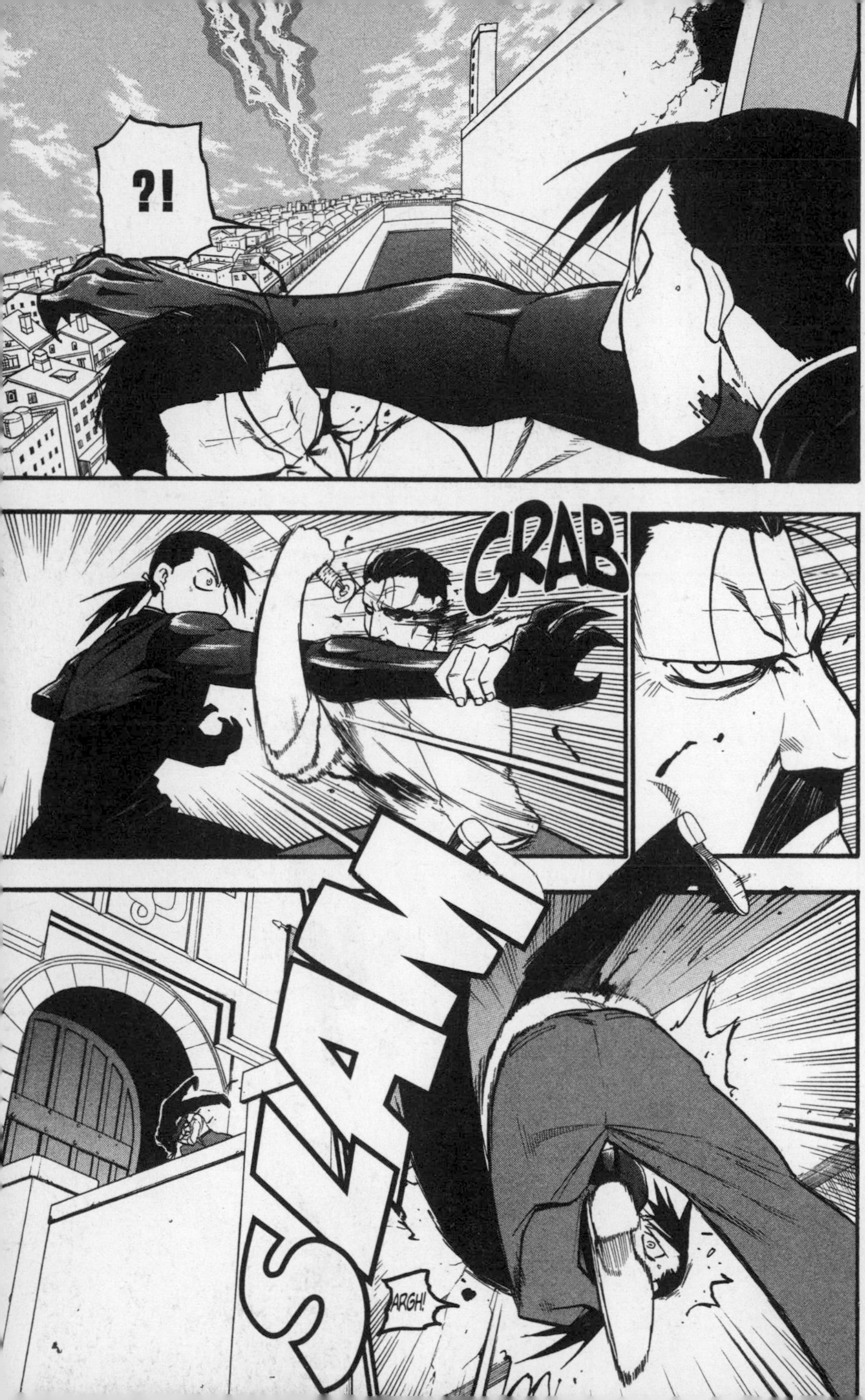

?!
GRAB
SLAM
ARGH!

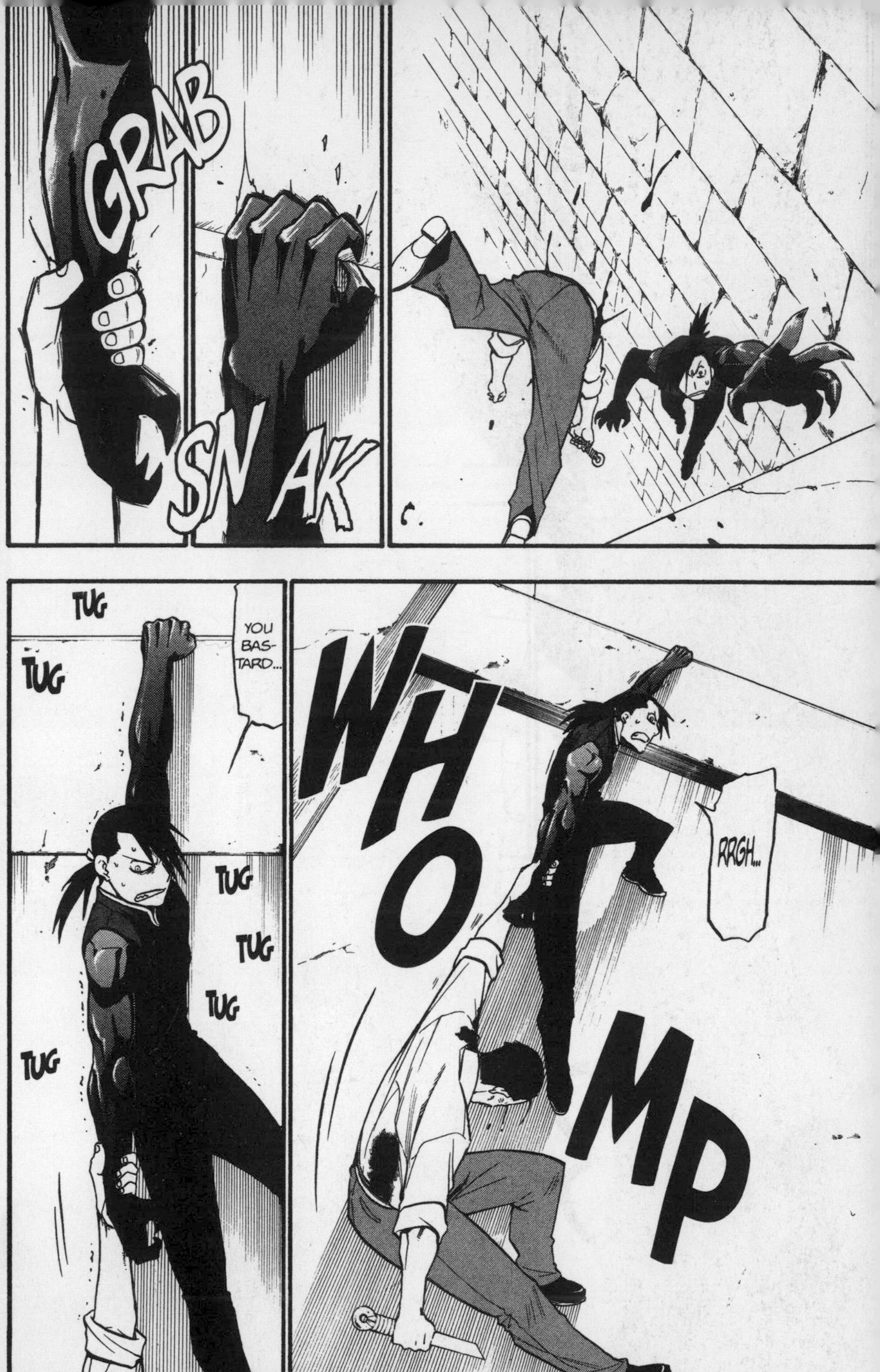
SNAK
GRAB
WHOMP
RRGH...
YOU BAS-TARD...
TUG
TUG
TUG
TUG
TUG
TUG

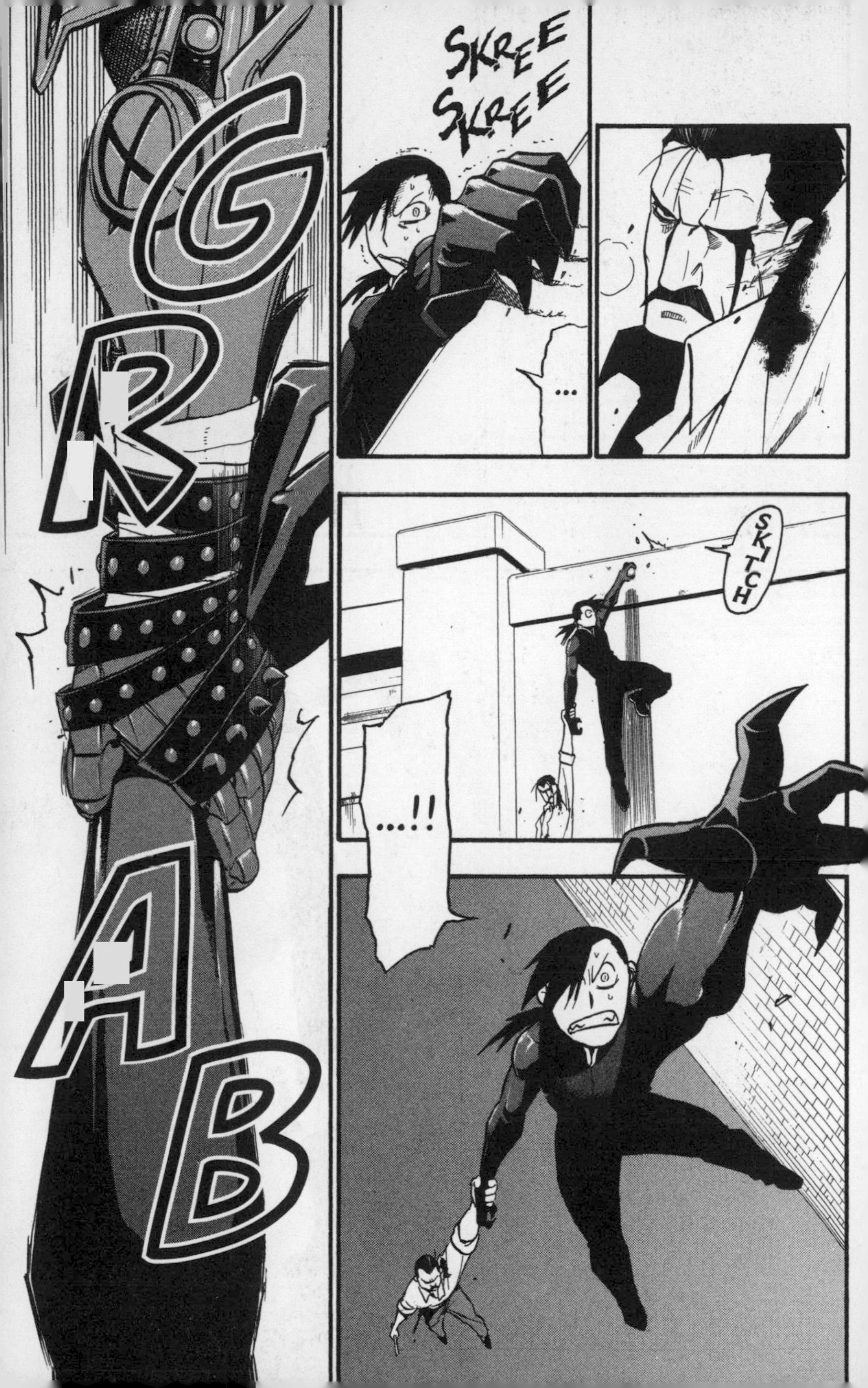
SKREE SKREE
...
SKITCH
...!!
GRAB

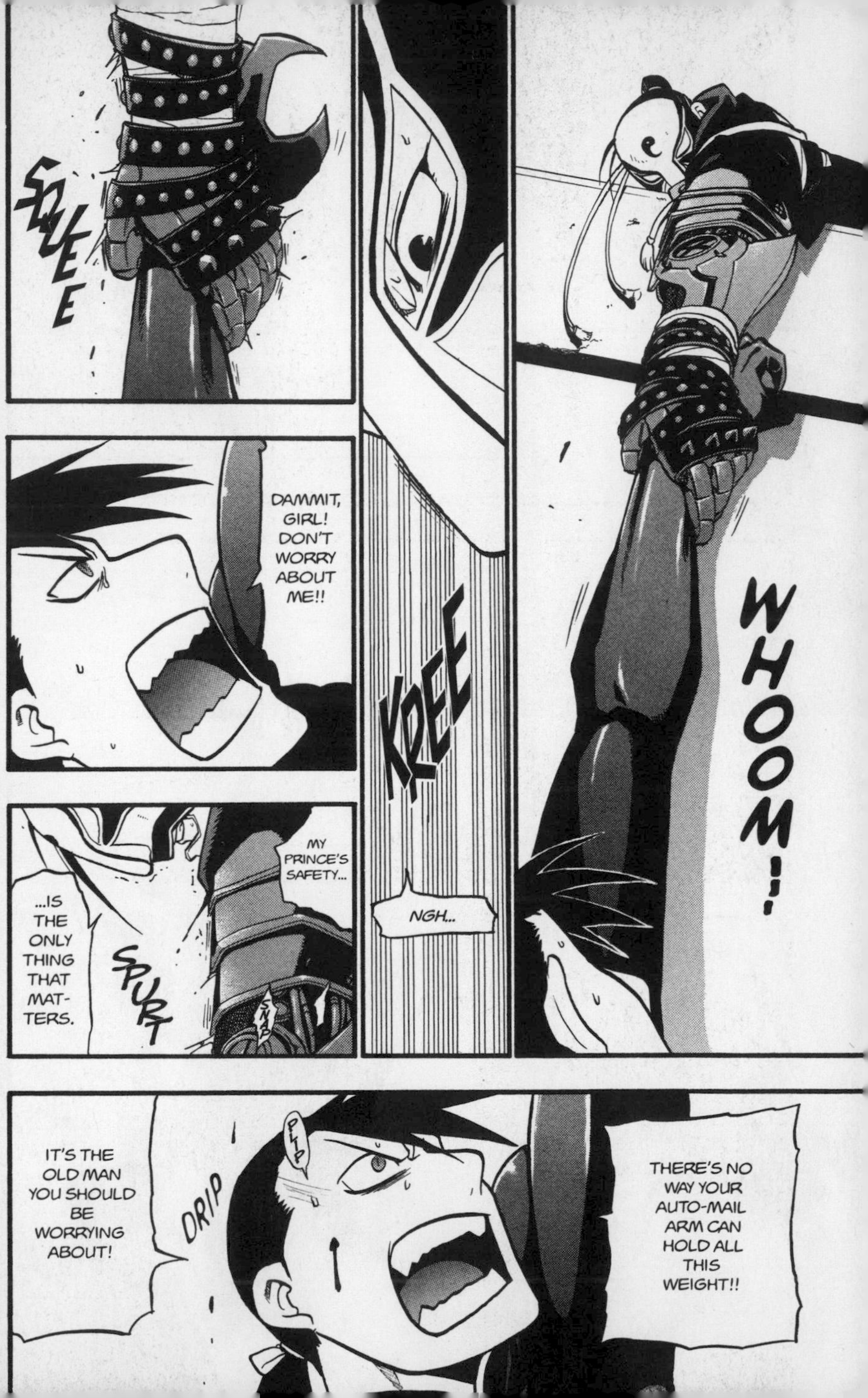
WHOOM!!
KREE
NGH...
SQUEEE
DAMMIT, GIRL! DON'T WORRY ABOUT ME!!
MY PRINCE'S SAFETY...
...IS THE ONLY THING THAT MAT-TERS.
SPURT
SNAP
THERE'S NO WAY YOUR AUTO-MAIL ARM CAN HOLD ALL THIS WEIGHT!!
PLIP
IT'S THE OLD MAN YOU SHOULD BE WORRYING ABOUT!
DRIP

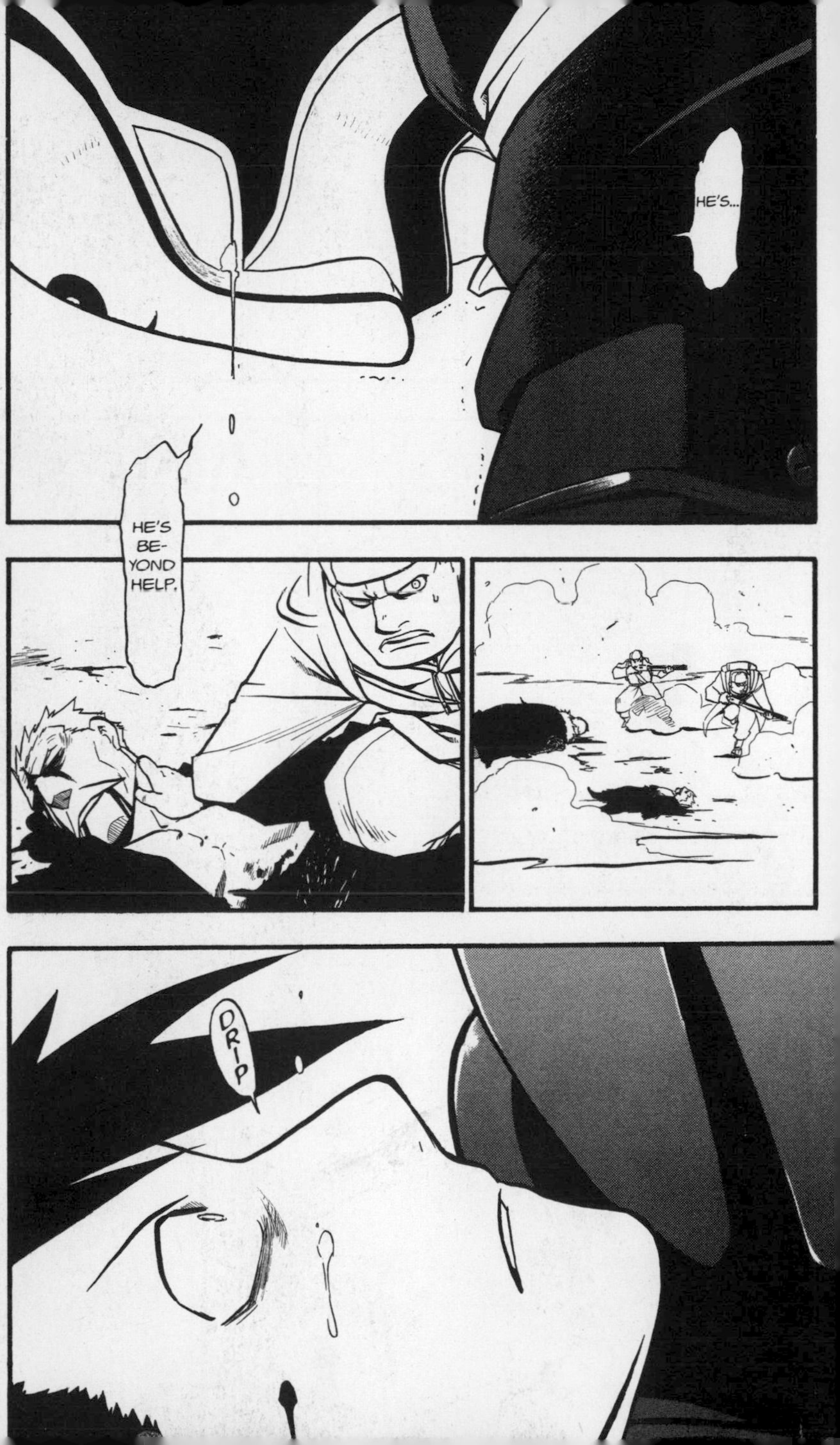
HE'S...
HE'S BE-YOND HELP.
DRIP

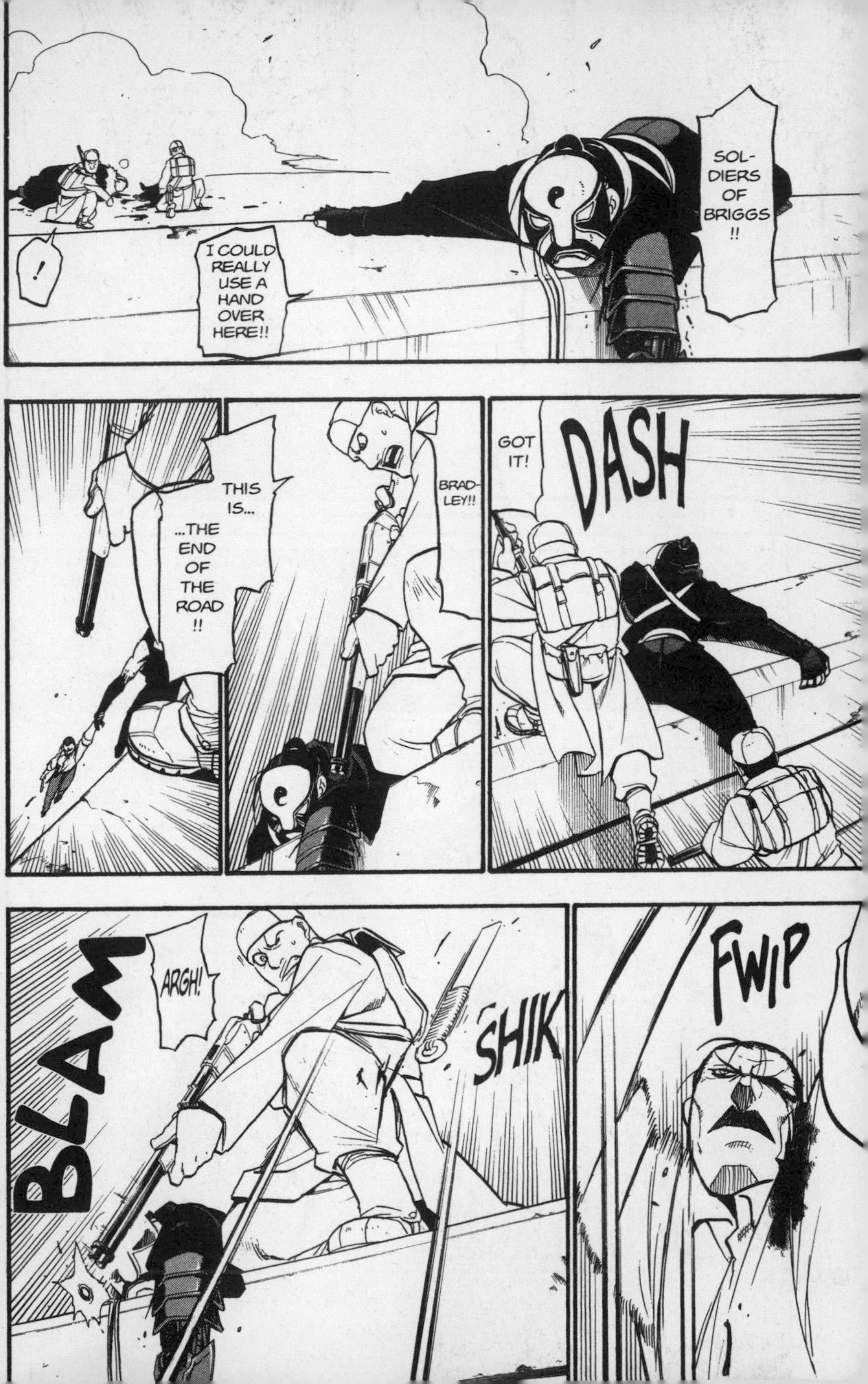
SOL-DIERS OF BRIGGS !!
I COULD REALLY USE A HAND OVER HERE!!
!
DASH
GOT IT!
BRAD-LEY!!
THIS IS...
...THE END OF THE ROAD !!
FWIP
SHIK
ARGH!
BLAM

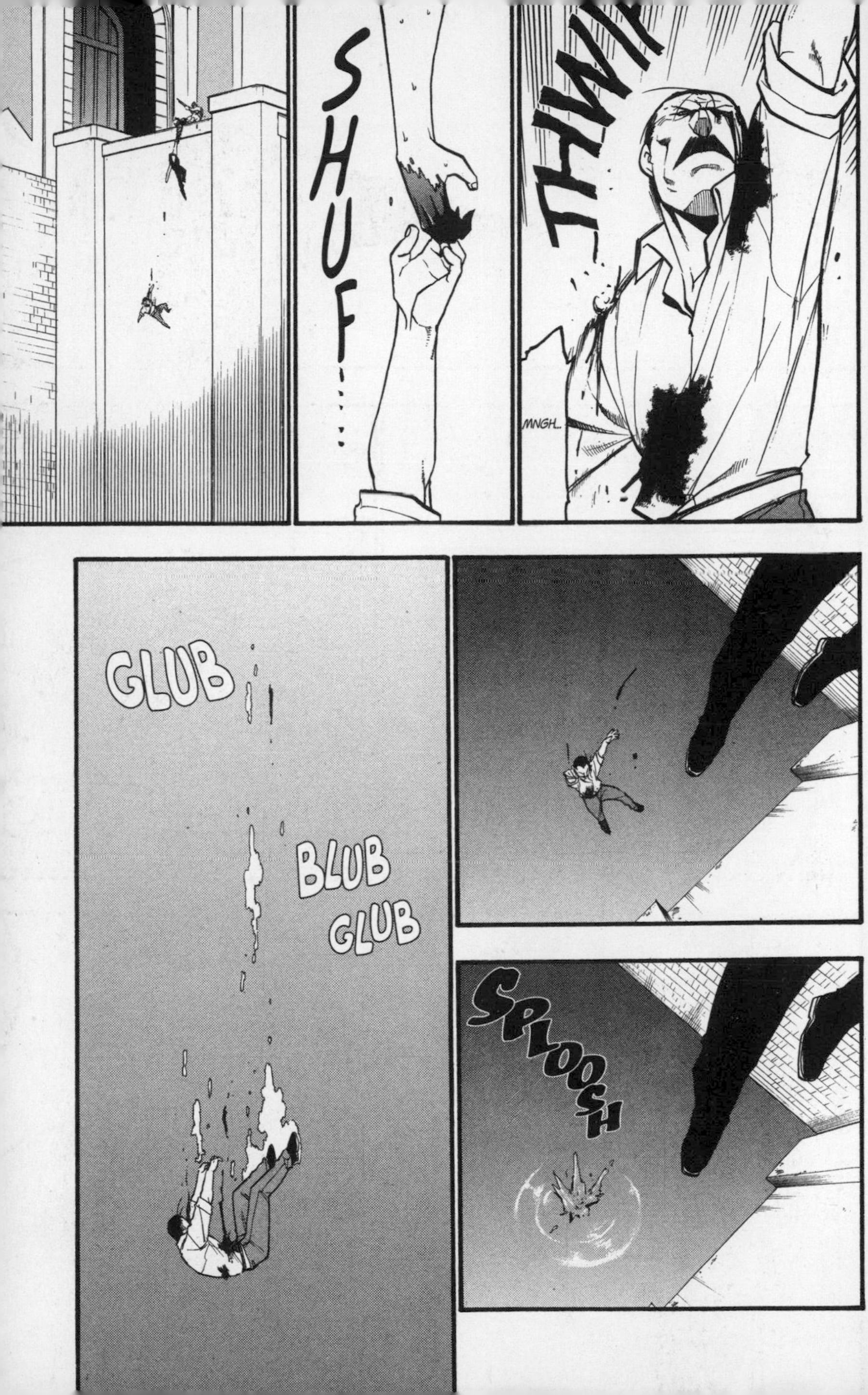
THWI
MNGH..
SHUF...
SPLOOSH
GLUB
BLUB
GLUB

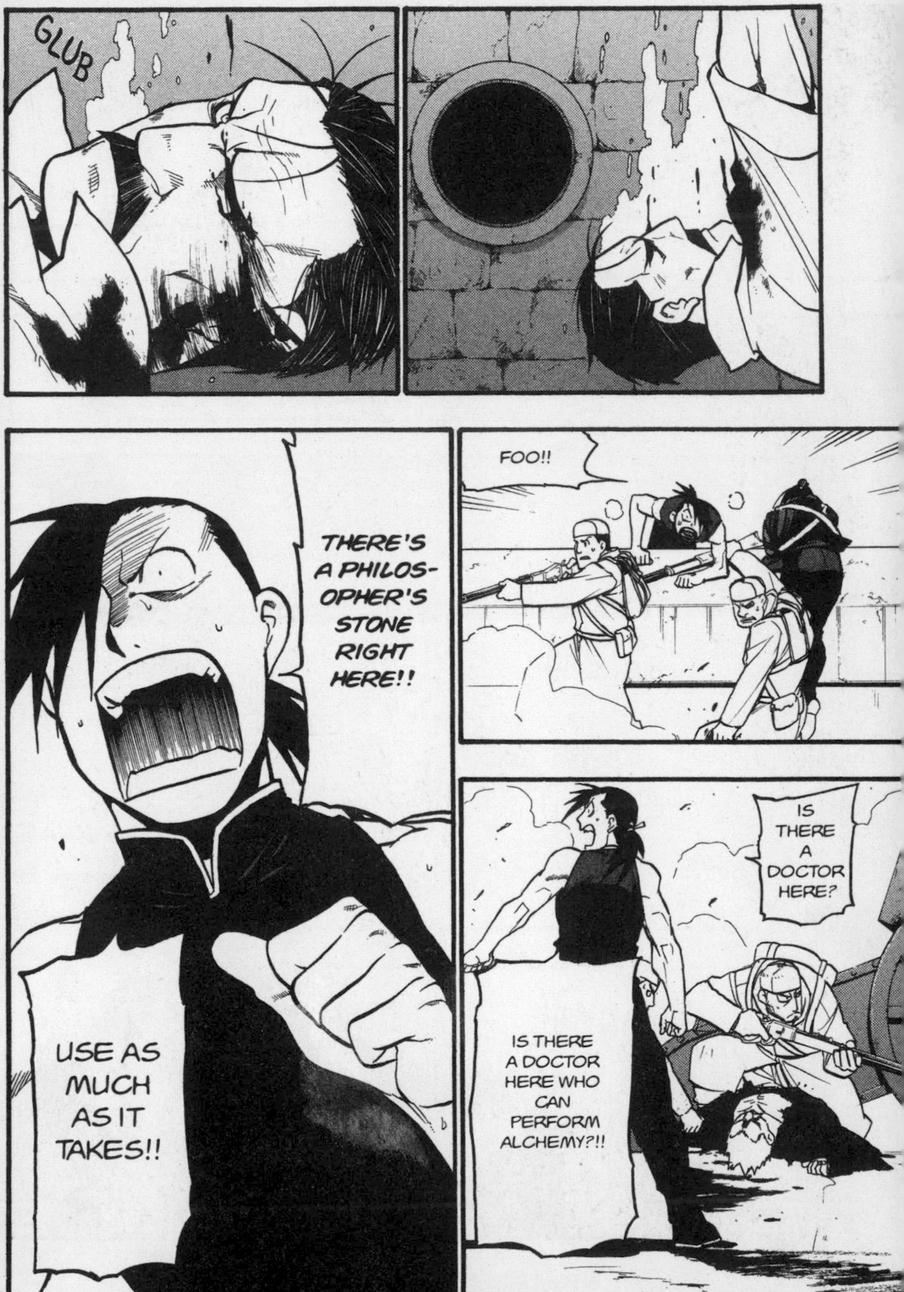
GLUB
FOO!!
IS THERE A DOCTOR HERE?
IS THERE A DOCTOR HERE WHO CAN PERFORM ALCHEMY?!!
THERE'S A PHILOSOPHER'S STONE RIGHT HERE!!
USE AS MUCH AS IT TAKES!!

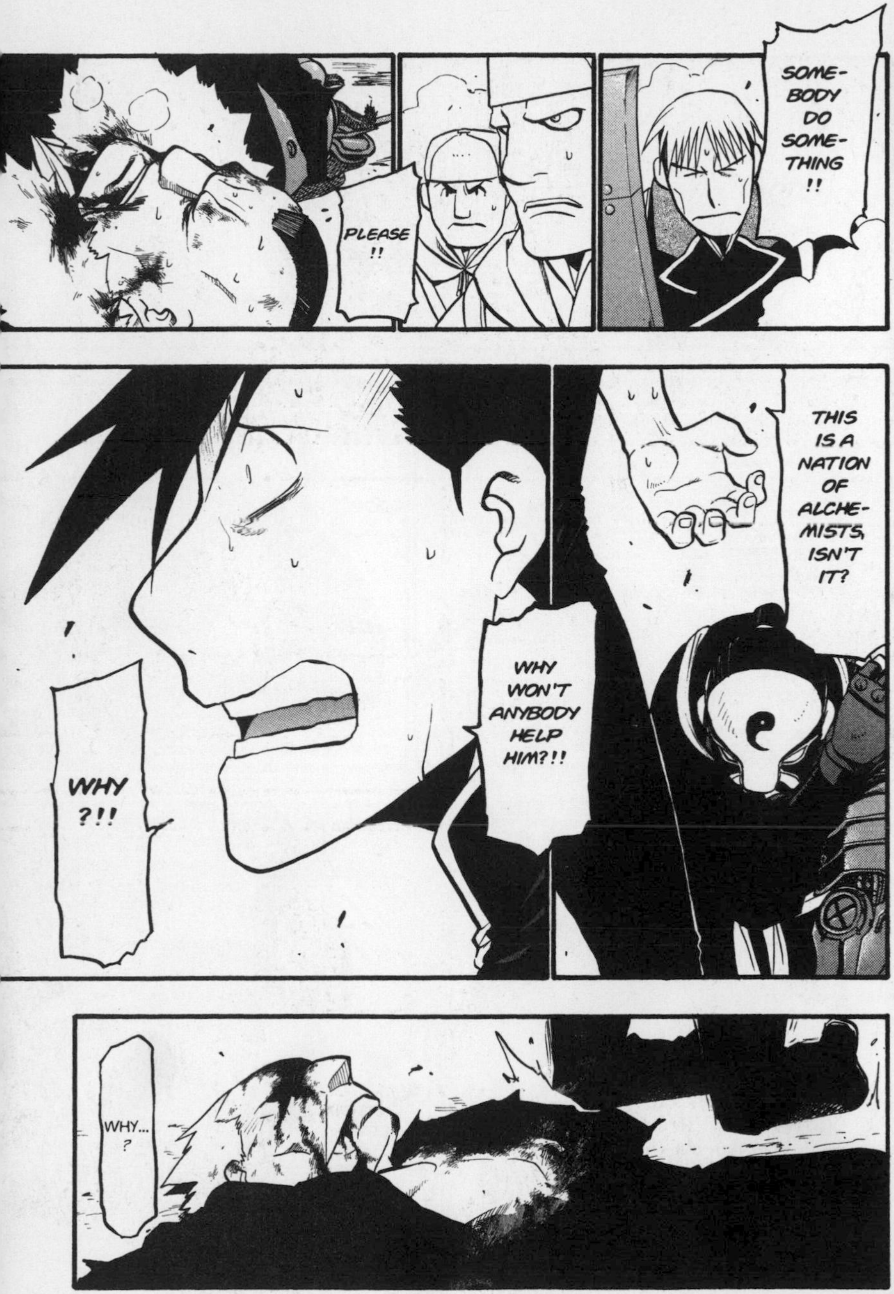
SOMEBODY DO SOMETHING!!
PLEASE!!
THIS IS A NATION OF ALCHEMISTS, ISN'T IT?
WHY WON'T ANYBODY HELP HIM?!!
WHY?!!
WHY...?

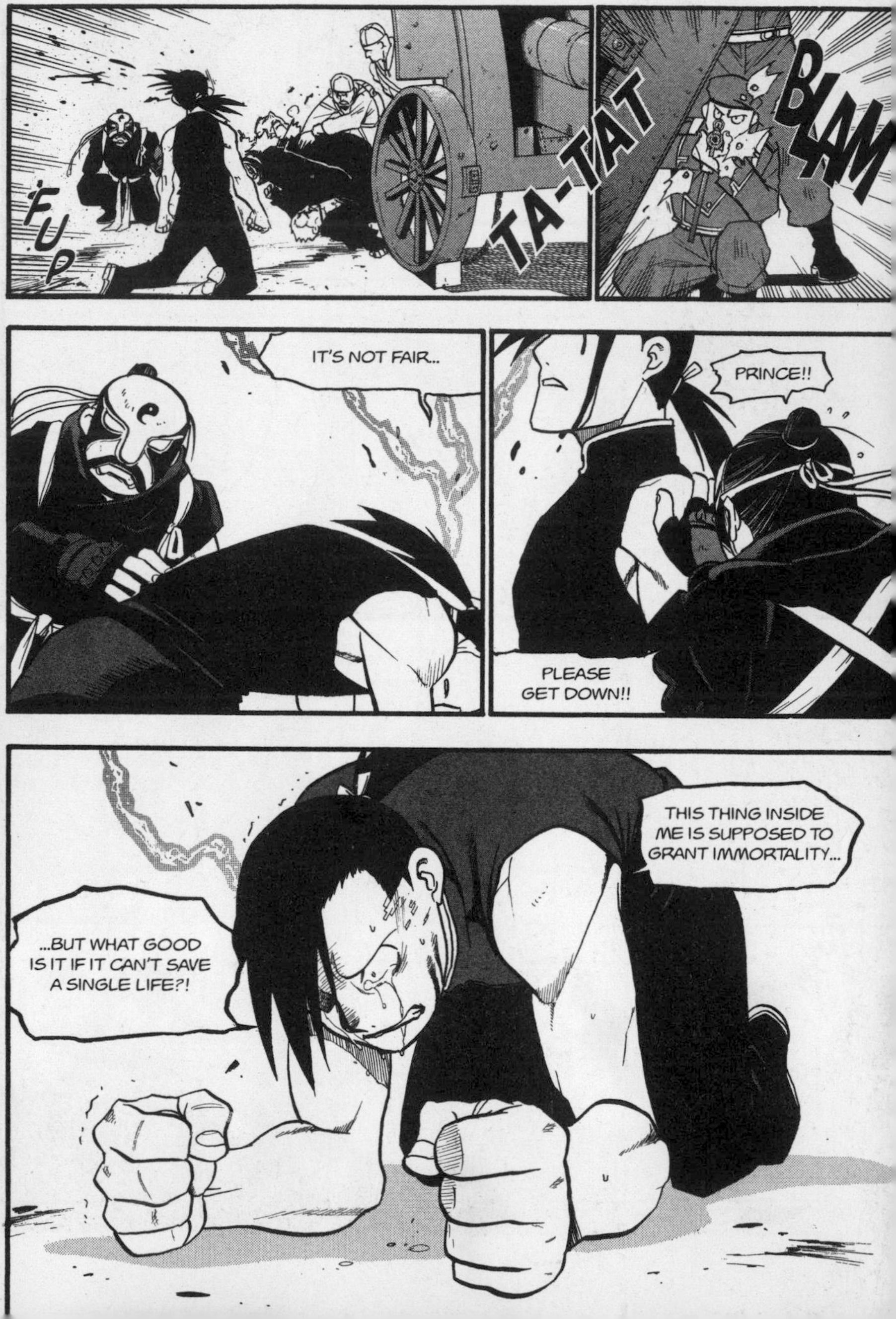
BLAM
TA-TAT
FUP
PRINCE!!
PLEASE GET DOWN!!
IT'S NOT FAIR...
THIS THING INSIDE ME IS SUPPOSED TO GRANT IMMORTALITY...
...BUT WHAT GOOD IS IT IF IT CAN'T SAVE A SINGLE LIFE?!

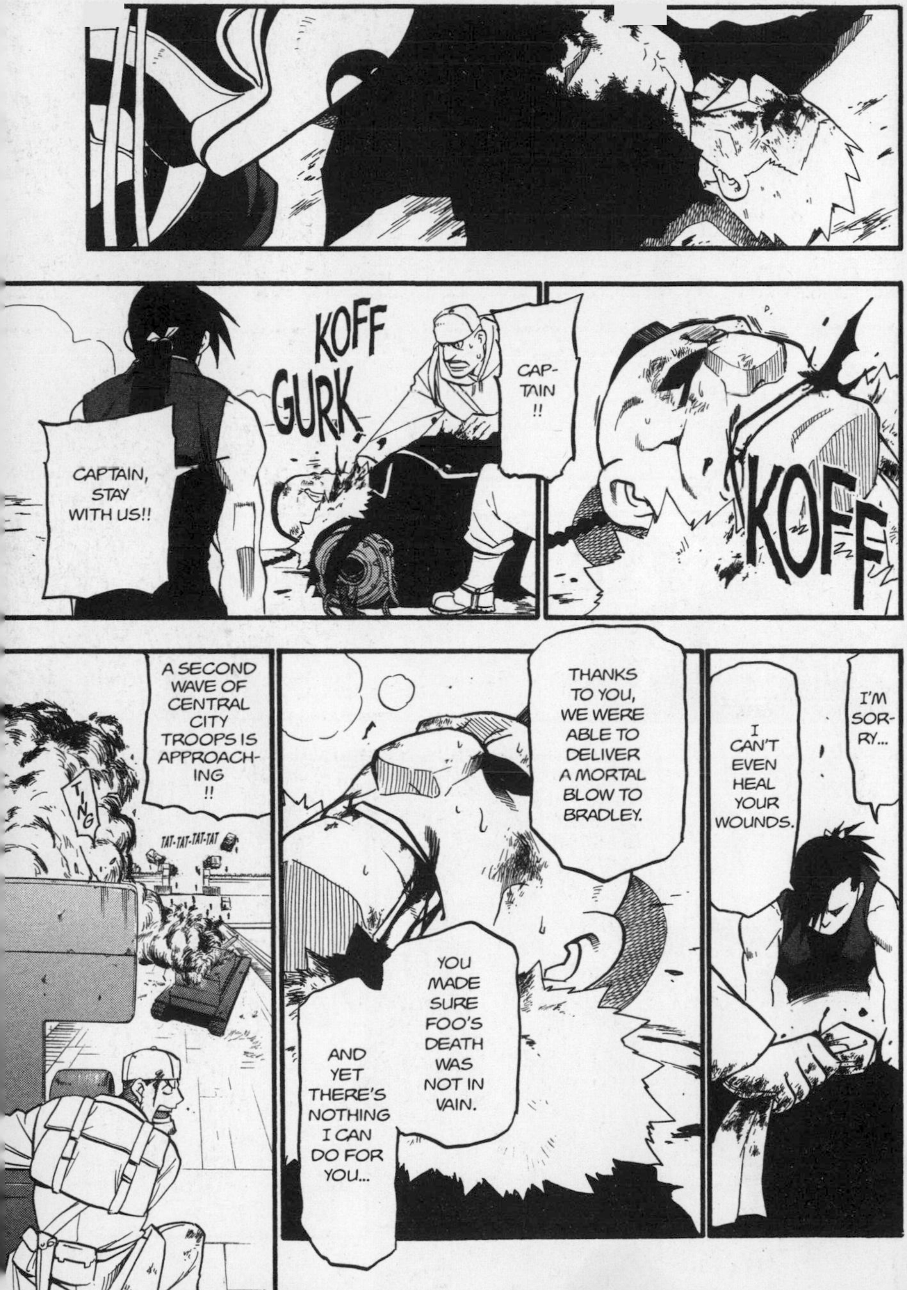
KOFF
CAP-TAIN !!
KOFF GURK
CAPTAIN, STAY WITH US!!
I'M SOR-RY...
I CAN'T EVEN HEAL YOUR WOUNDS.
THANKS TO YOU, WE WERE ABLE TO DELIVER A MORTAL BLOW TO BRADLEY.
YOU MADE SURE FOO'S DEATH WAS NOT IN VAIN.
AND YET THERE'S NOTHING I CAN DO FOR YOU...
A SECOND WAVE OF CENTRAL CITY TROOPS IS APPROACH-ING !!
TING
TAT-TAT-TAT-TAT

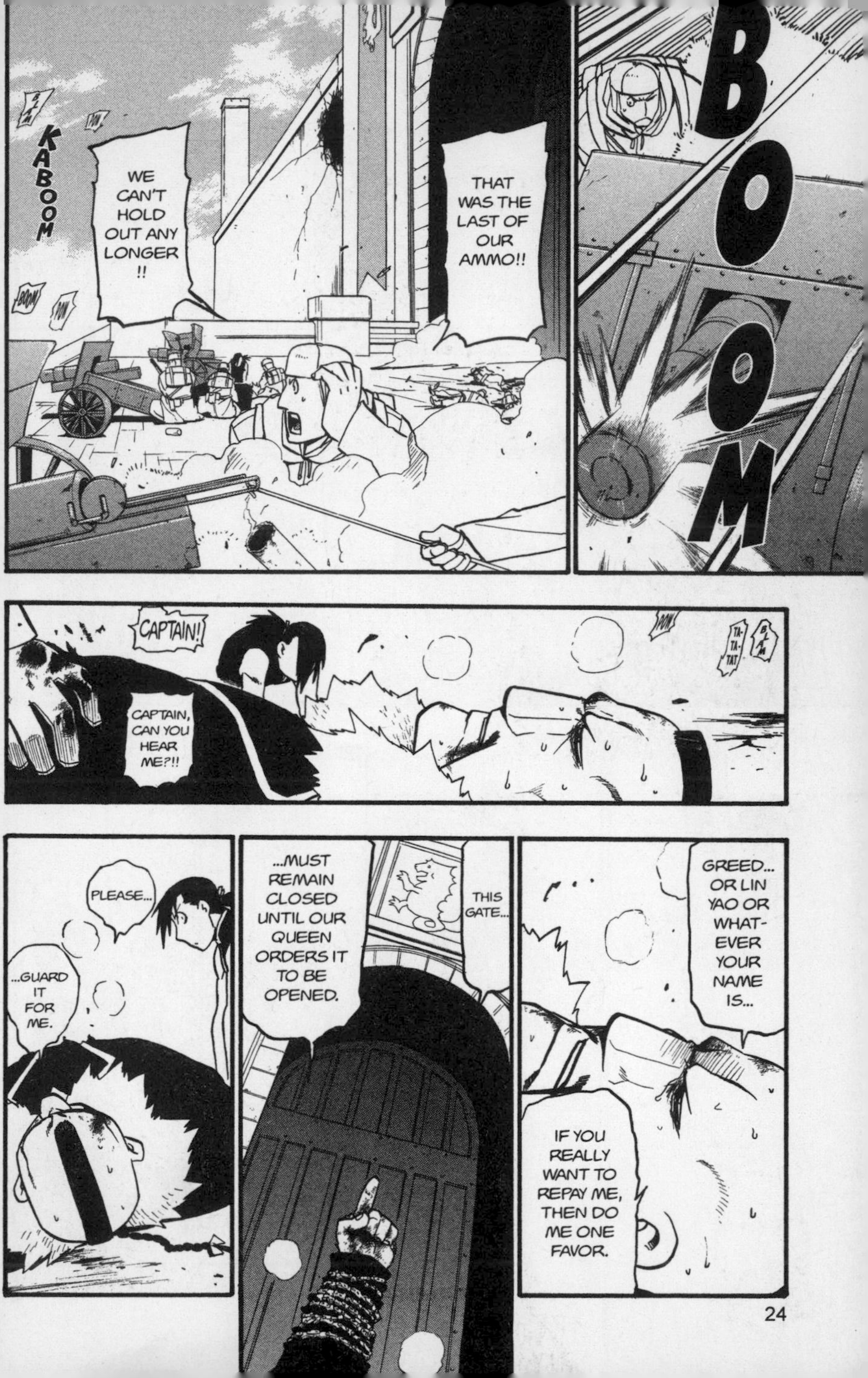
BOOM
THAT WAS THE LAST OF OUR AMMO!!
WE CAN'T HOLD OUT ANY LONGER!!
KABOOOM
BOOM
TA-TA-TAT
BLAM
CAPTAIN!
CAPTAIN, CAN YOU HEAR ME?!!
GREED... OR LIN YAO OR WHATEVER YOUR NAME IS...
IF YOU REALLY WANT TO REPAY ME, THEN DO ME ONE FAVOR.
THIS GATE...
...MUST REMAIN CLOSED UNTIL OUR QUEEN ORDERS IT TO BE OPENED.
PLEASE...
...GUARD IT FOR ME.

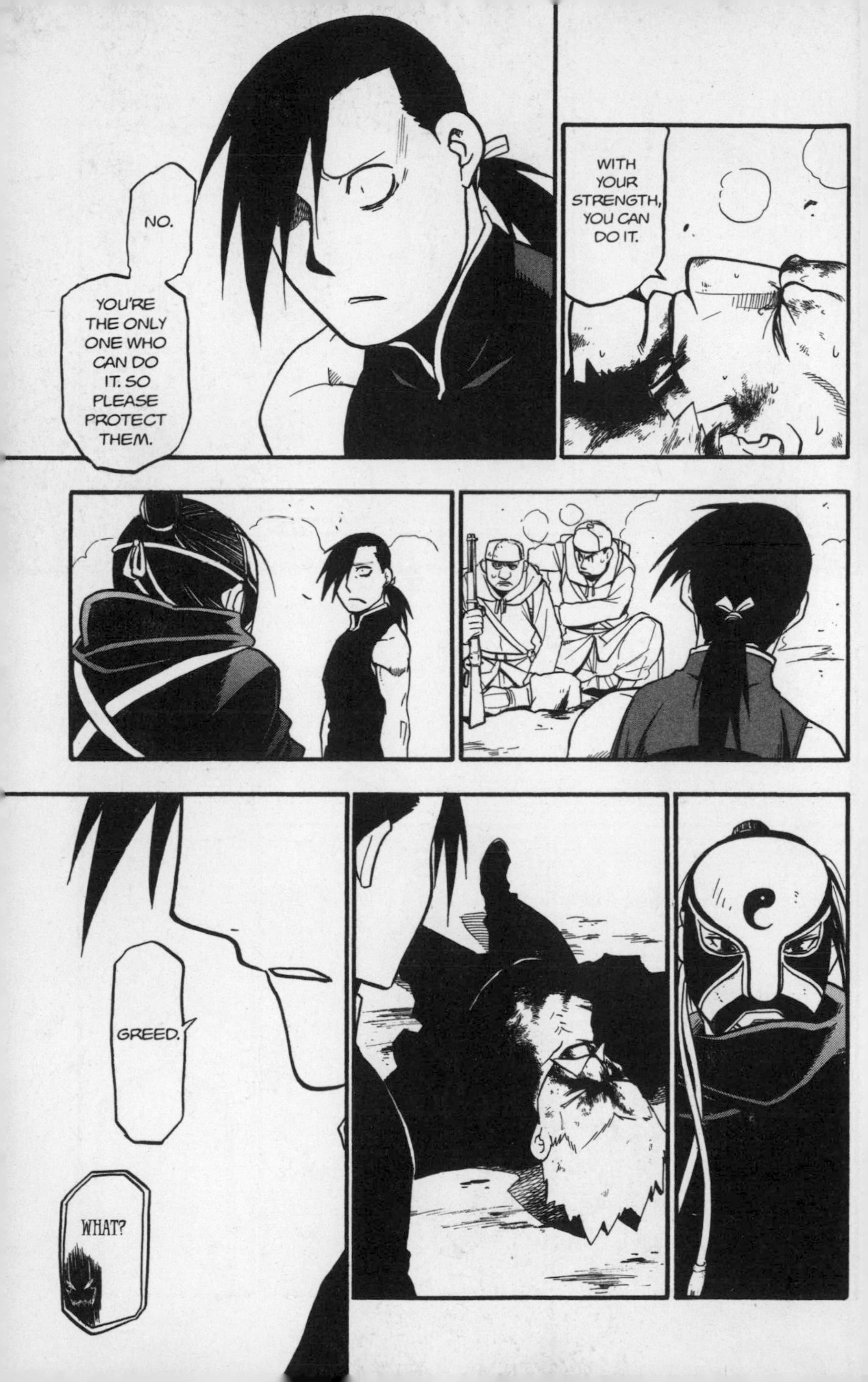
WITH YOUR STRENGTH, YOU CAN DO IT.
NO.
YOU'RE THE ONLY ONE WHO CAN DO IT. SO PLEASE PROTECT THEM.
GREED.
WHAT?

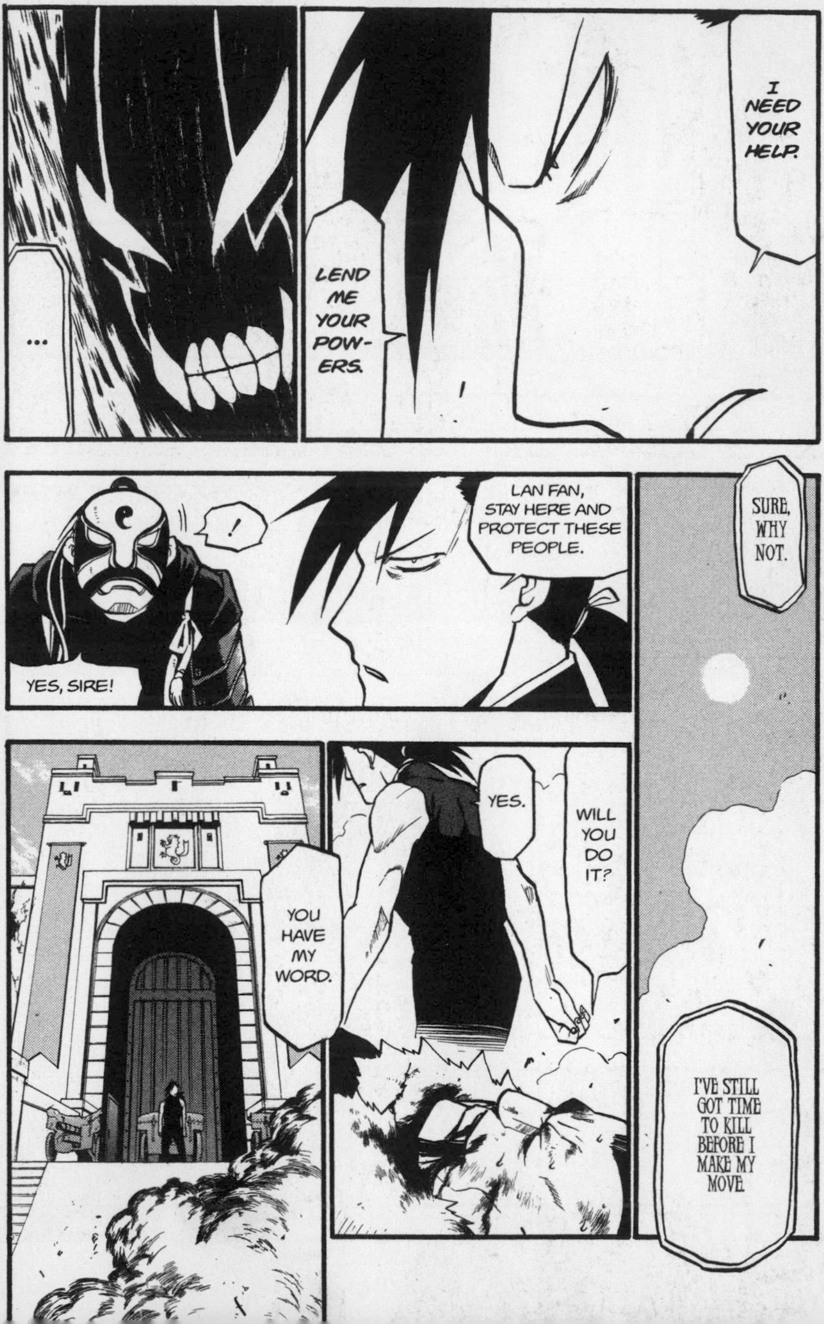
I NEED YOUR HELP.
LEND ME YOUR POW-ERS.
...
SURE, WHY NOT.
I'VE STILL GOT TIME TO KILL BEFORE I MAKE MY MOVE.
LAN FAN, STAY HERE AND PROTECT THESE PEOPLE.
!
YES, SIRE!
WILL YOU DO IT?
YES.
YOU HAVE MY WORD.

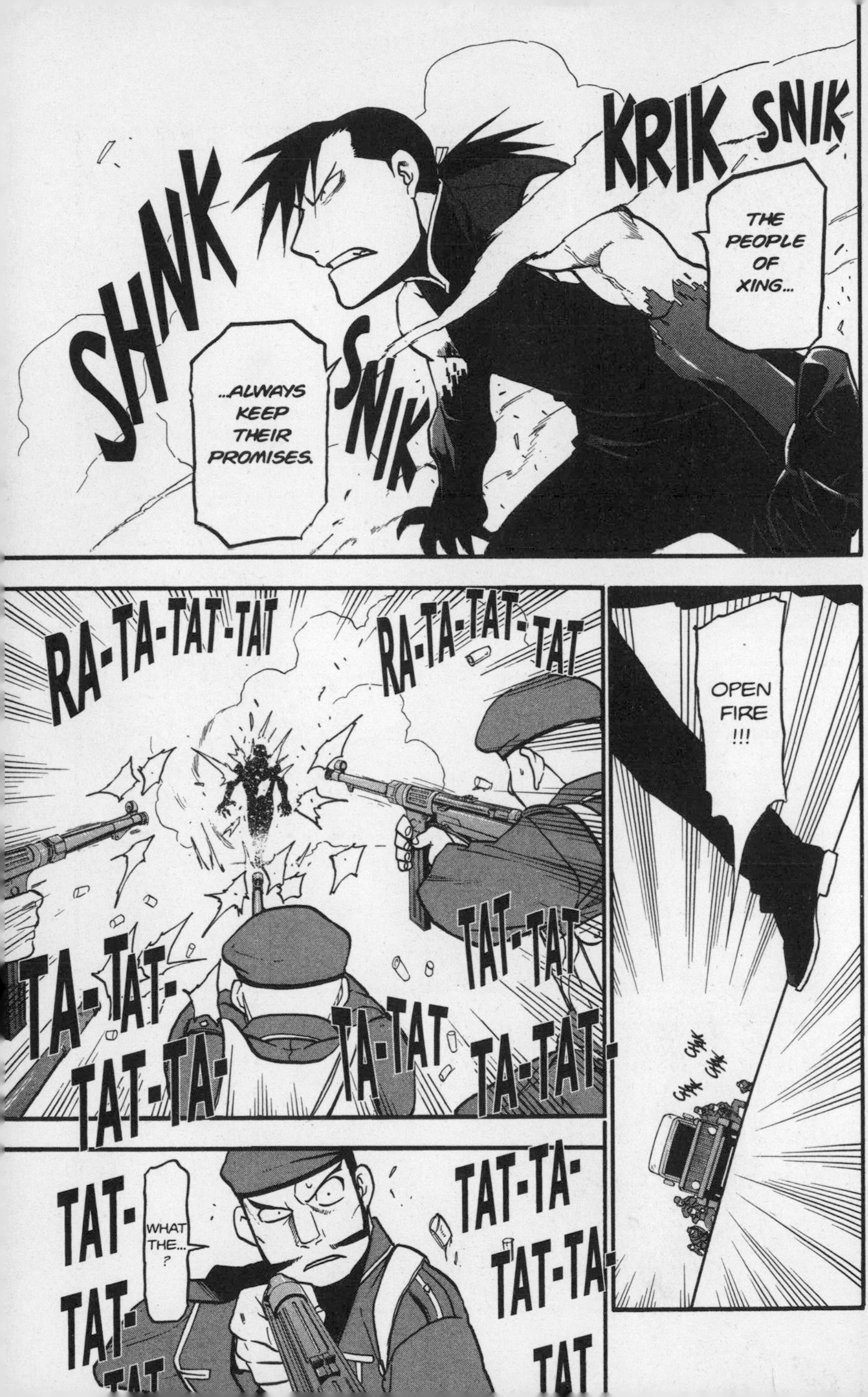
KRIK SNIK
THE PEOPLE OF XING...
SNIK
...ALWAYS KEEP THEIR PROMISES.
SHNK
OPEN FIRE!!!
CHAK CHAK CHAK CHAK
RA-TA-TAT-TAT
RA-TA-TAT-TAT
TAT-TAT
TA-TAT-
TA-TAT
TA-TAT-TAT-TA-
TAT-TA-TAT-TA-TAT
WHAT THE...?
TAT-TAT-

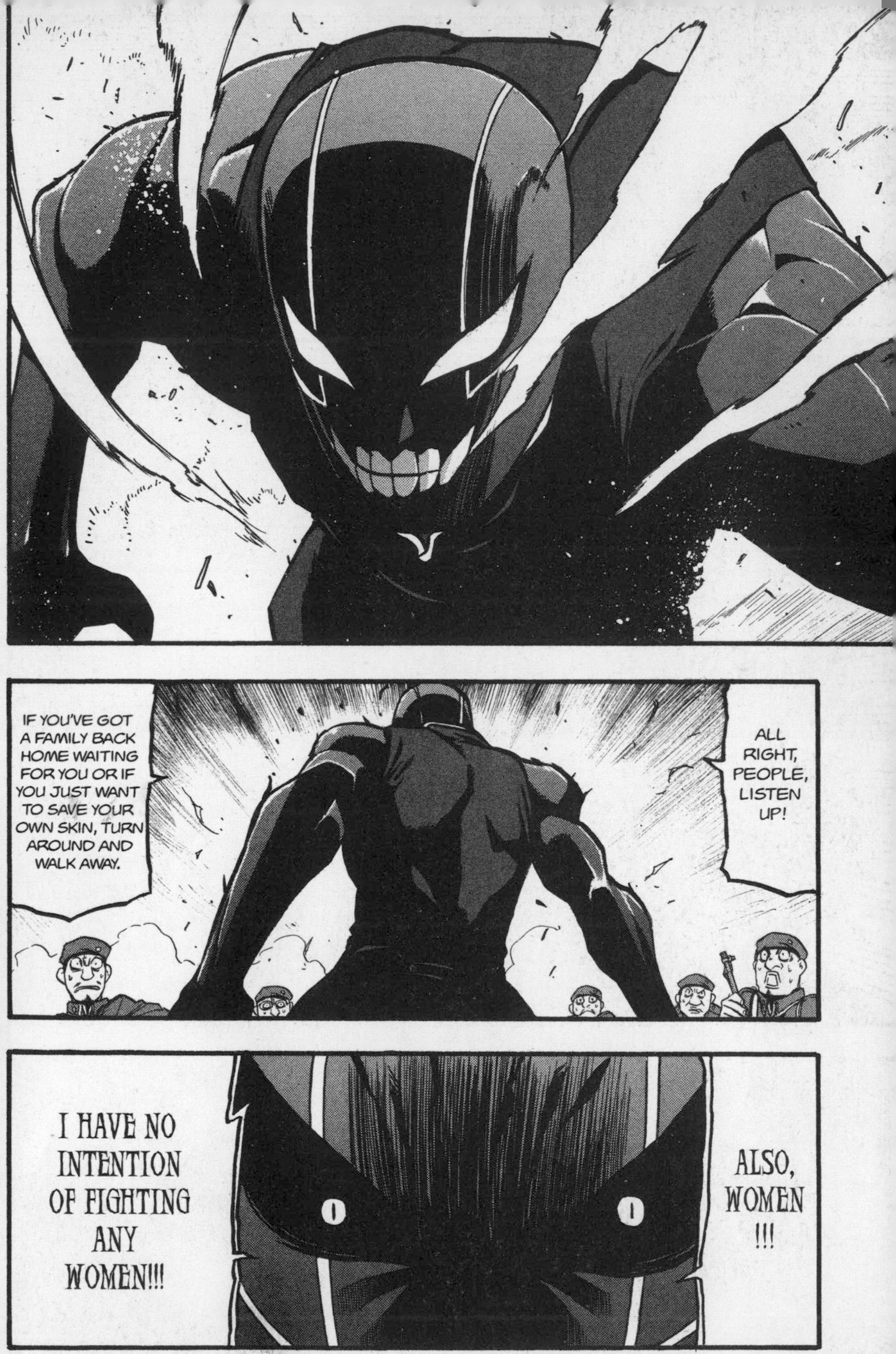
ALL RIGHT, PEOPLE, LISTEN UP!
IF YOU'VE GOT A FAMILY BACK HOME WAITING FOR YOU OR IF YOU JUST WANT TO SAVE YOUR OWN SKIN, TURN AROUND AND WALK AWAY.
ALSO, WOMEN!!!
I HAVE NO INTENTION OF FIGHTING ANY WOMEN!!!

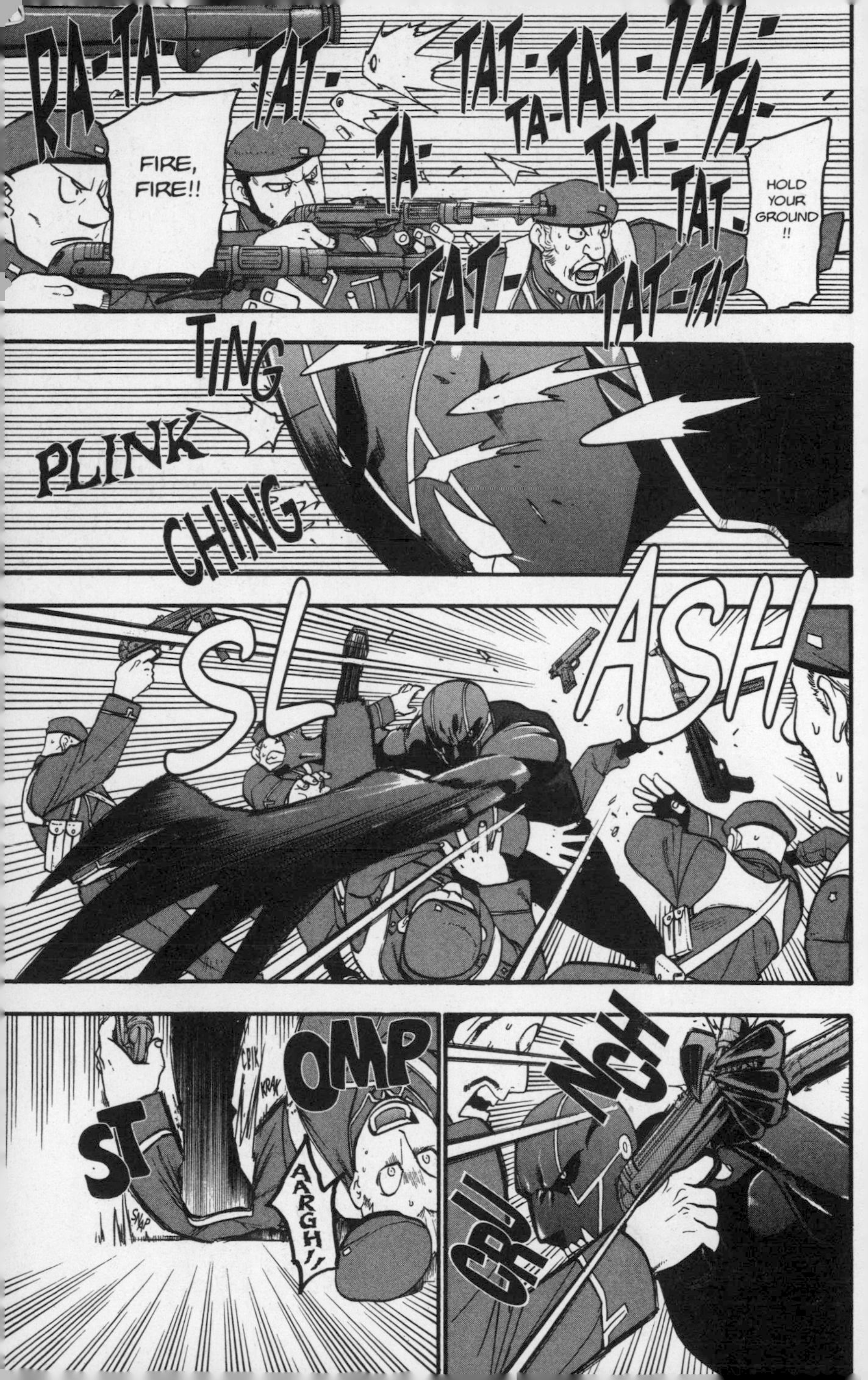

HOLD YOUR GROUND !!
TAT-TA-TAT-TAT-TAT-TAT
TAT-TA-TAT-TAT-TAT
RA-TA-TAT-TA-TA-TAT
FIRE, FIRE!!
TING
PLINK
CHING
SLASH
CRUNCH
STOMP
CRIK
KRAK
AARGH!!
SNAP

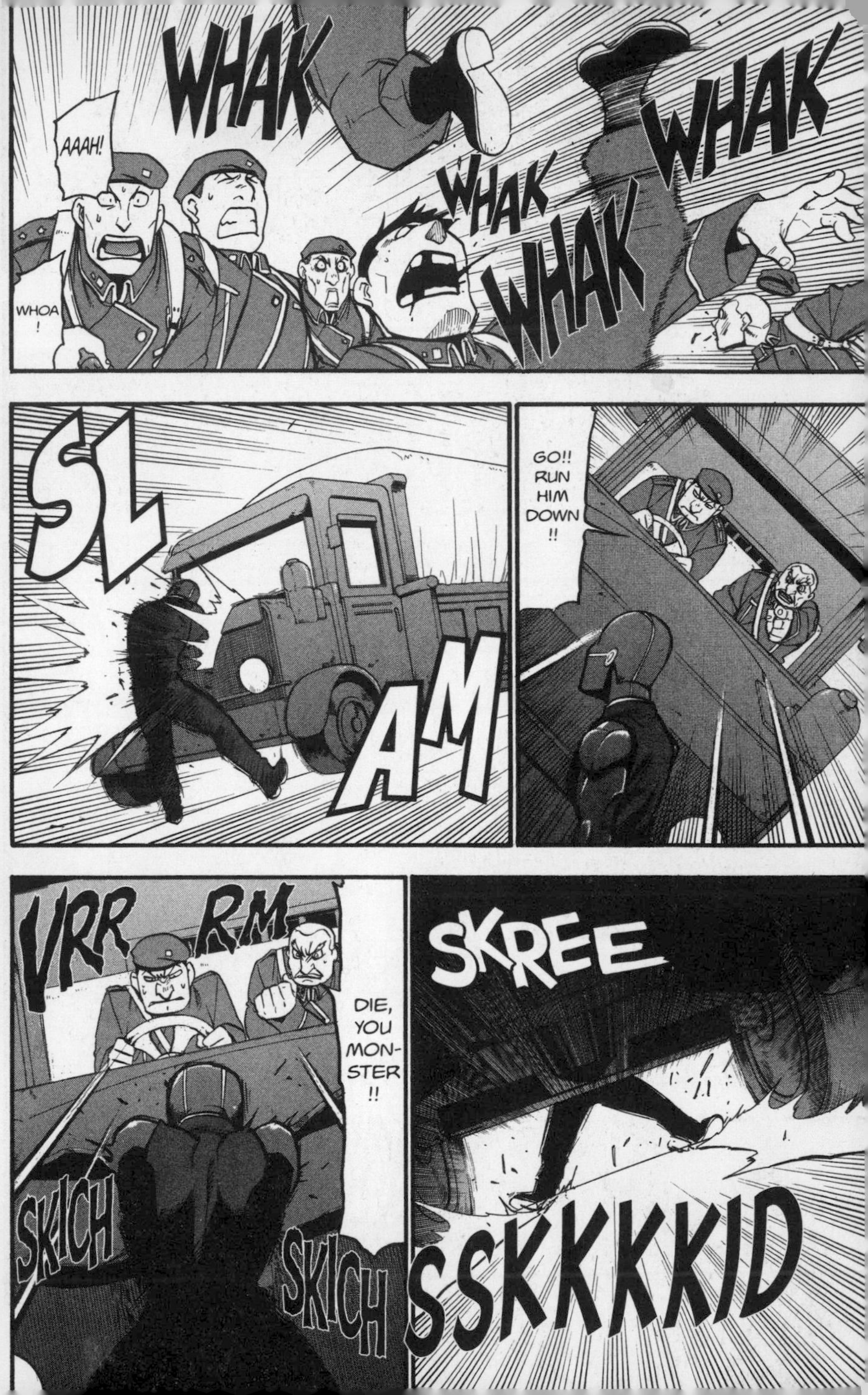
WHAK
WHAK
WHAK
WHAK
WHAK
AAAH!
WHOA!
GO!! RUN HIM DOWN!!
SL AM
SKREE
SSKKKID
VRR RM
DIE, YOU MON-STER!!
SKICH
SKICH

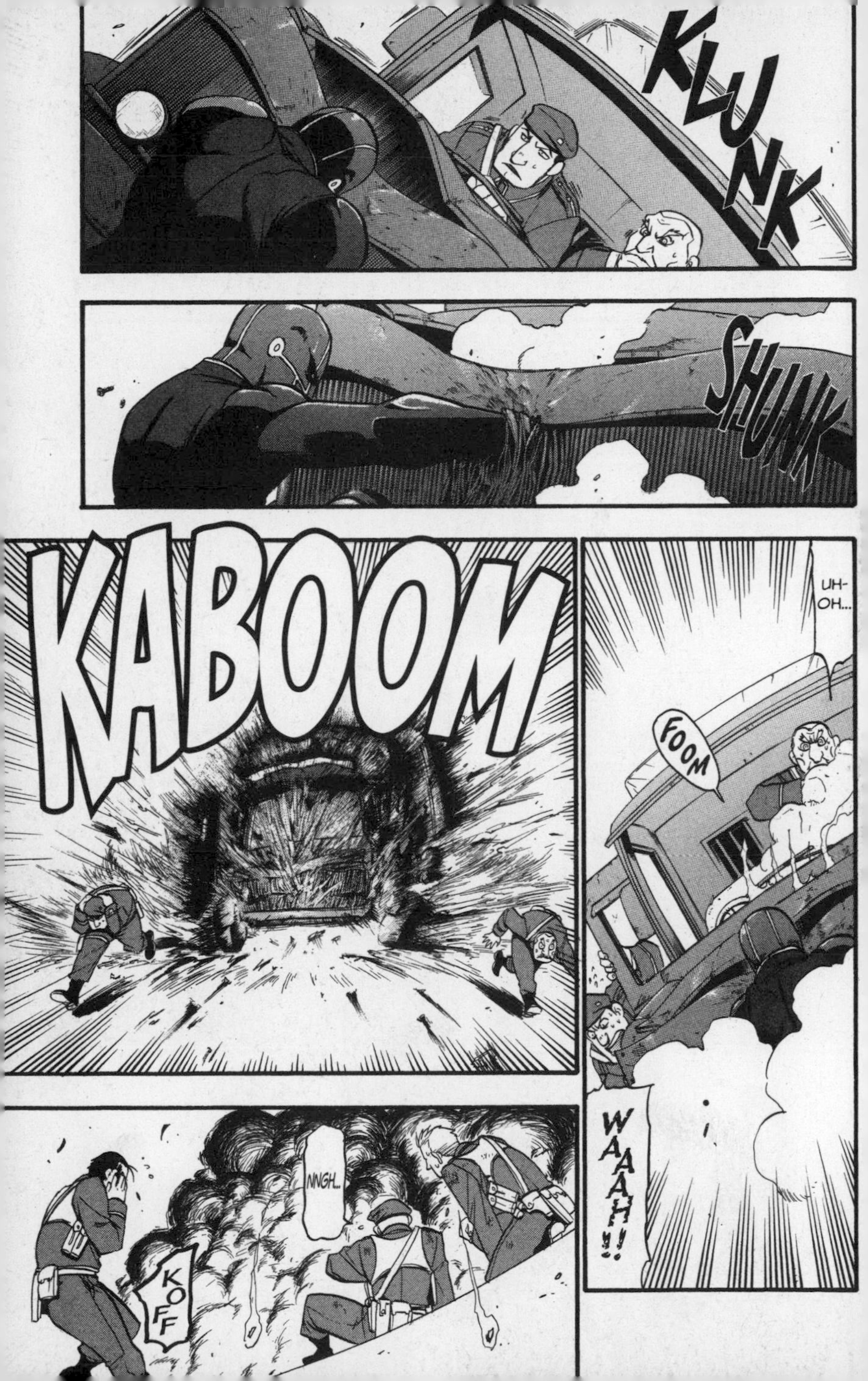
KLUNK
SHUNK
UH-OH...
FOOM
WAAAH!!
KABOOM
NNGH..
KOFF

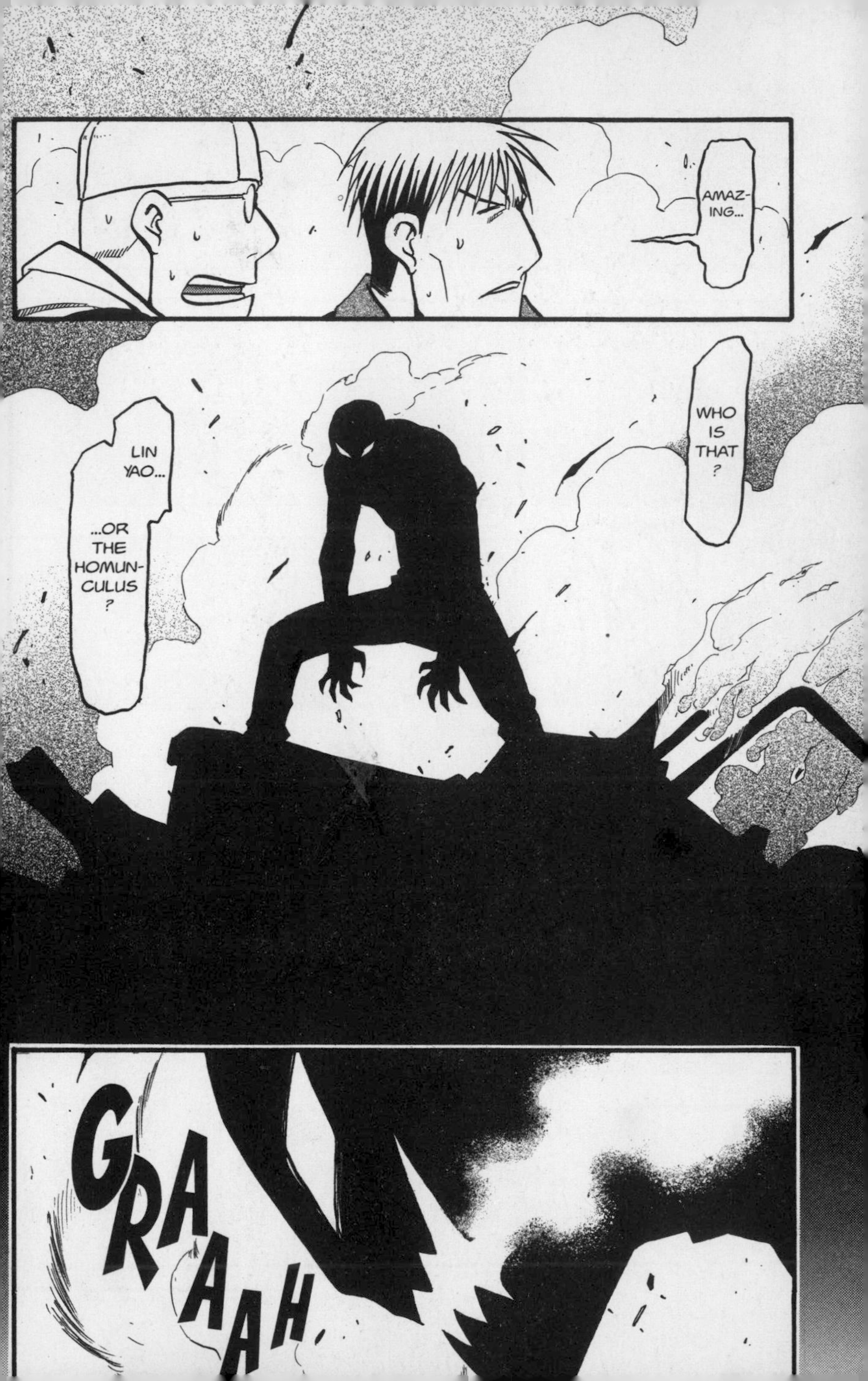
AMAZ-ING...
WHO IS THAT?
LIN YAO...
...OR THE HOMUN-CULUS?
GRAAAH

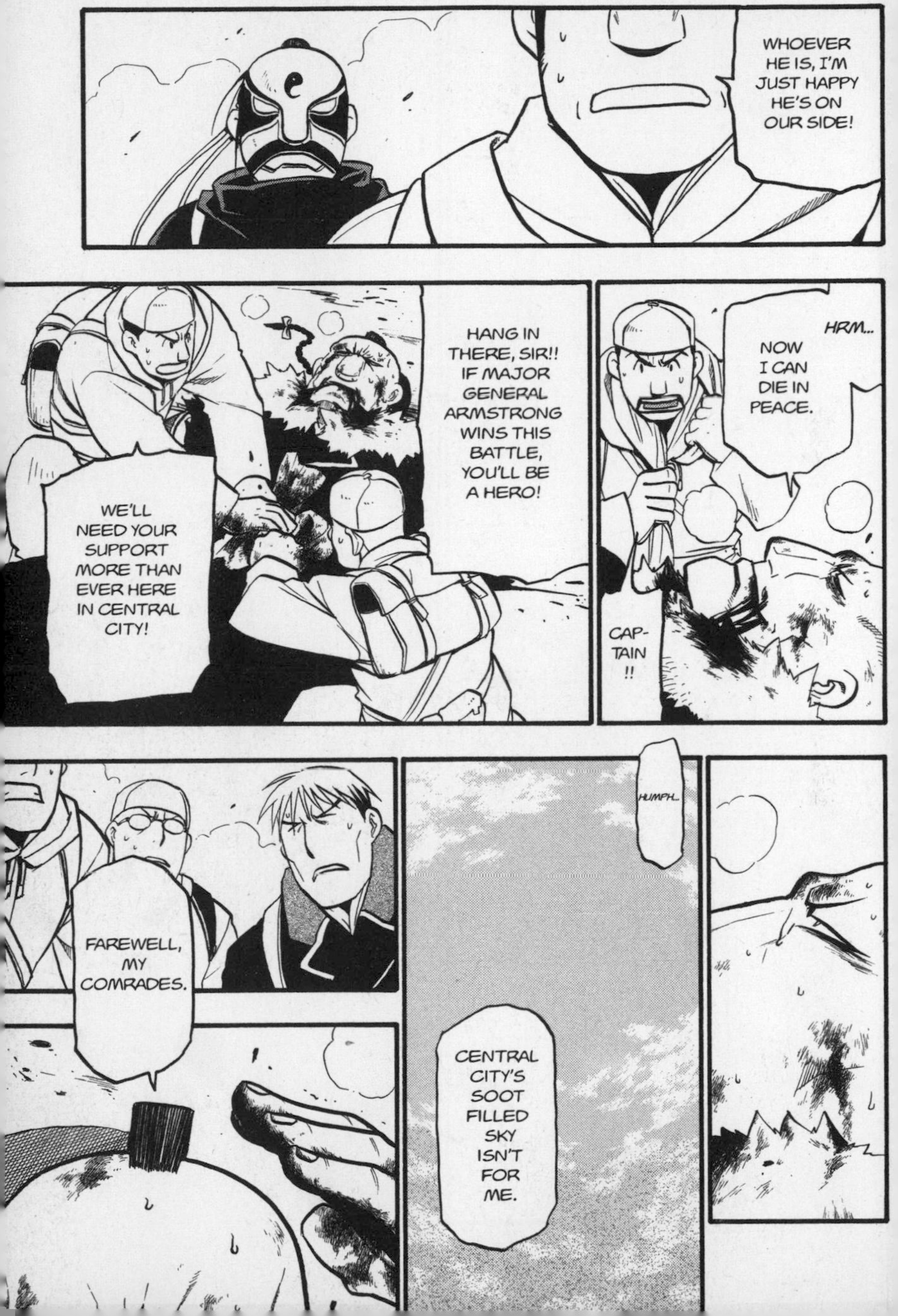
WHOEVER HE IS, I'M JUST HAPPY HE'S ON OUR SIDE!
HRM...
NOW I CAN DIE IN PEACE.
CAP-TAIN !!
HANG IN THERE, SIR!! IF MAJOR GENERAL ARMSTRONG WINS THIS BATTLE, YOU'LL BE A HERO!
WE'LL NEED YOUR SUPPORT MORE THAN EVER HERE IN CENTRAL CITY!
HUMPH...
CENTRAL CITY'S SOOT FILLED SKY ISN'T FOR ME.
FAREWELL, MY COMRADES.

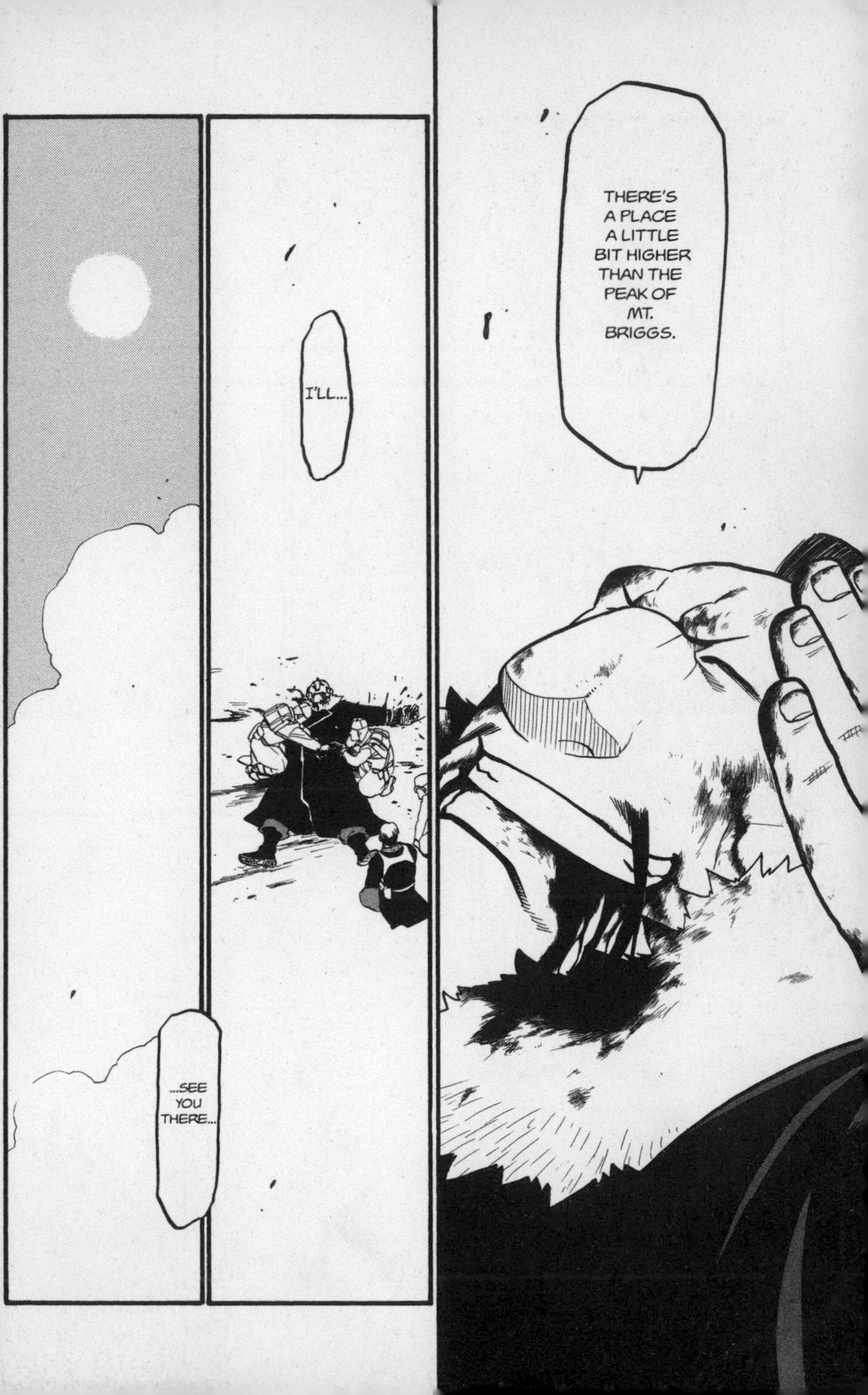
THERE'S A PLACE A LITTLE BIT HIGHER THAN THE PEAK OF MT. BRIGGS.
I'LL...
...SEE YOU THERE...

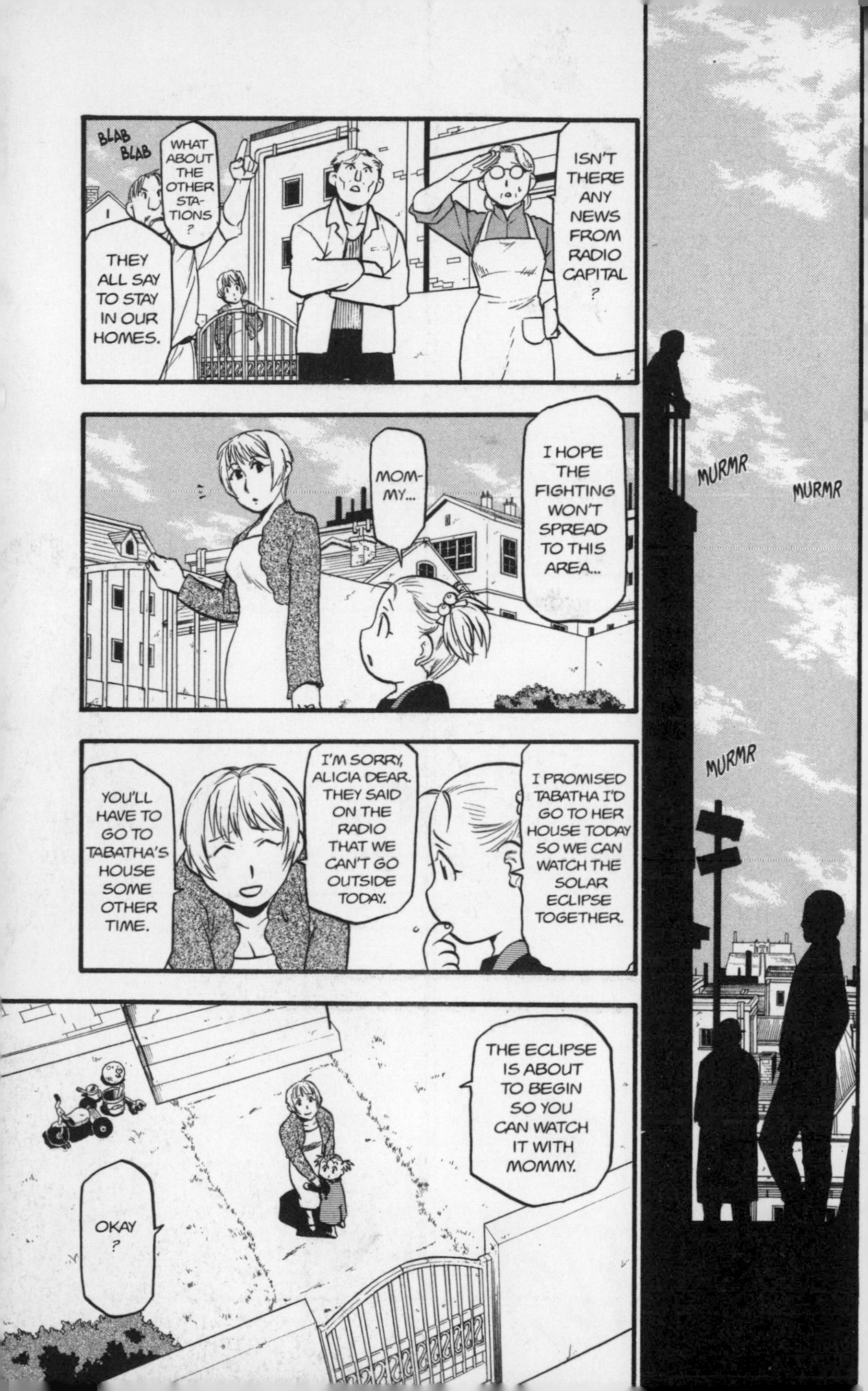
MURMR
MURMR
MURMR
ISN'T THERE ANY NEWS FROM RADIO CAPITAL?
WHAT ABOUT THE OTHER STATIONS?
BLAB BLAB
THEY ALL SAY TO STAY IN OUR HOMES.
I HOPE THE FIGHTING WON'T SPREAD TO THIS AREA...
MOMMY...
I PROMISED TABATHA I'D GO TO HER HOUSE TODAY SO WE CAN WATCH THE SOLAR ECLIPSE TOGETHER.
I'M SORRY, ALICIA DEAR. THEY SAID ON THE RADIO THAT WE CAN'T GO OUTSIDE TODAY.
YOU'LL HAVE TO GO TO TABATHA'S HOUSE SOME OTHER TIME.
THE ECLIPSE IS ABOUT TO BEGIN SO YOU CAN WATCH IT WITH MOMMY.
OKAY?

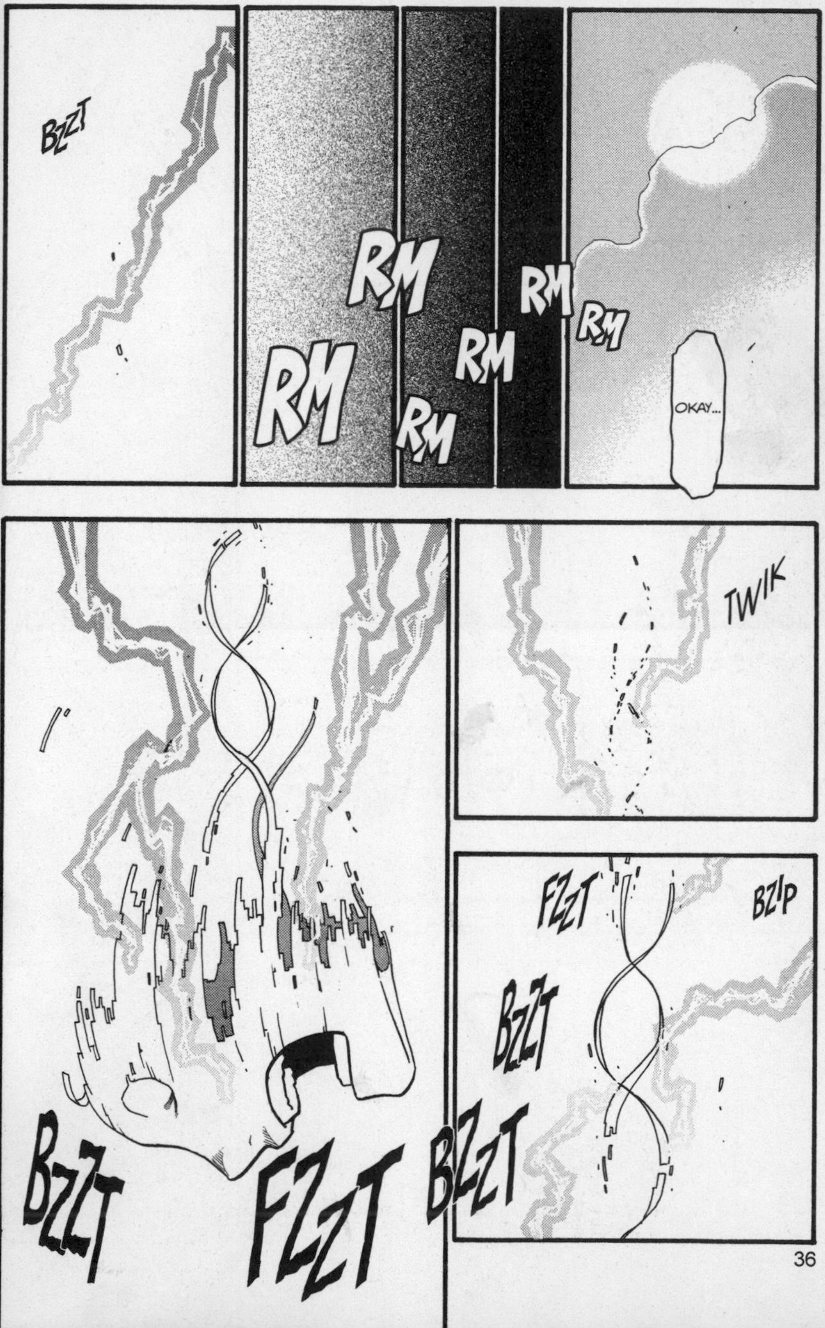
OKAY...
RM
RM
RM
RM
RM
RM
BZZT
TWIK
BZIP
FZZT
BZZT
BZZT
FZZT
BZZT

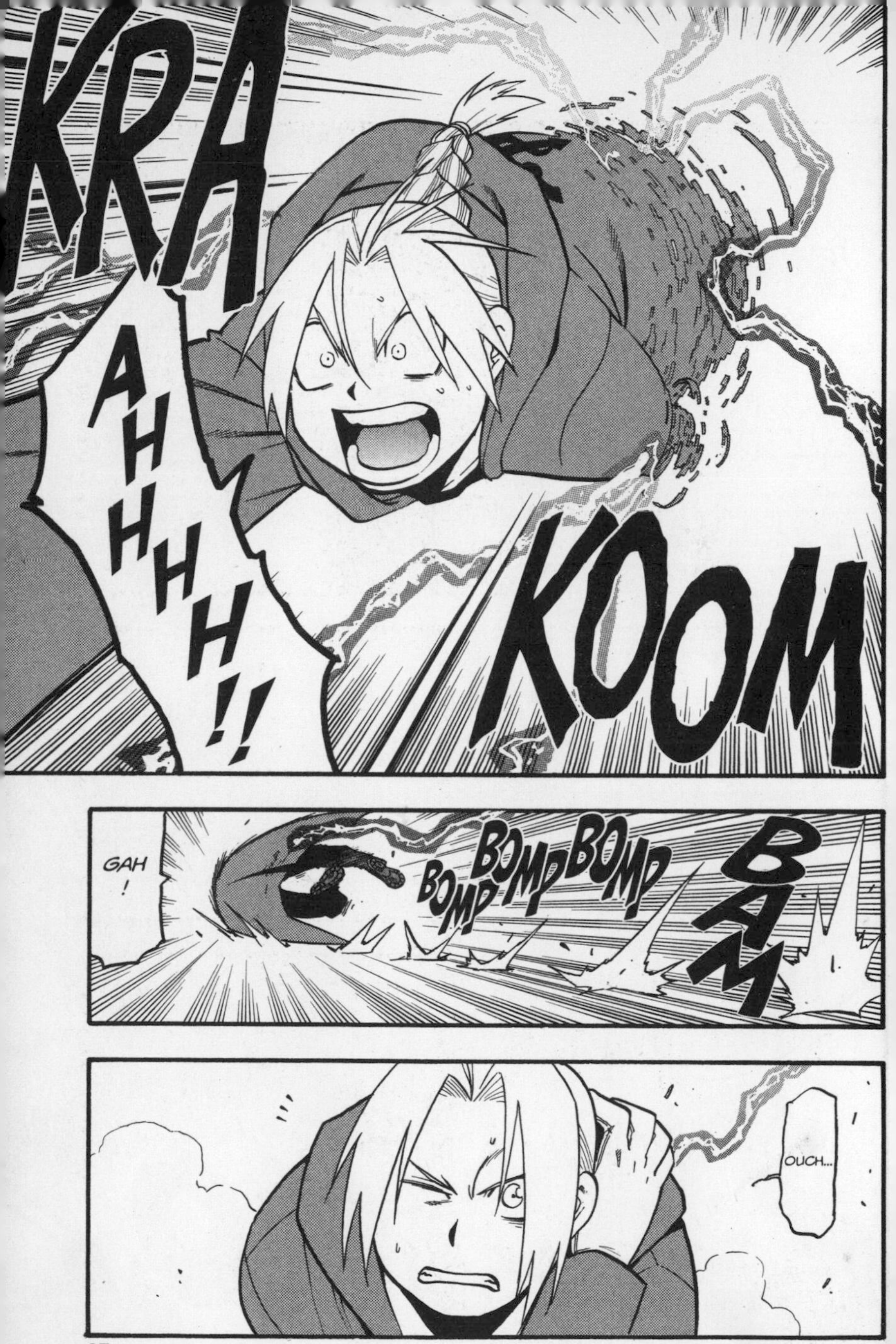
KRA
AHHHH!!
KOOM
BAM
BOMP BOMP BOMP BOMP
GAH!
OUCH...

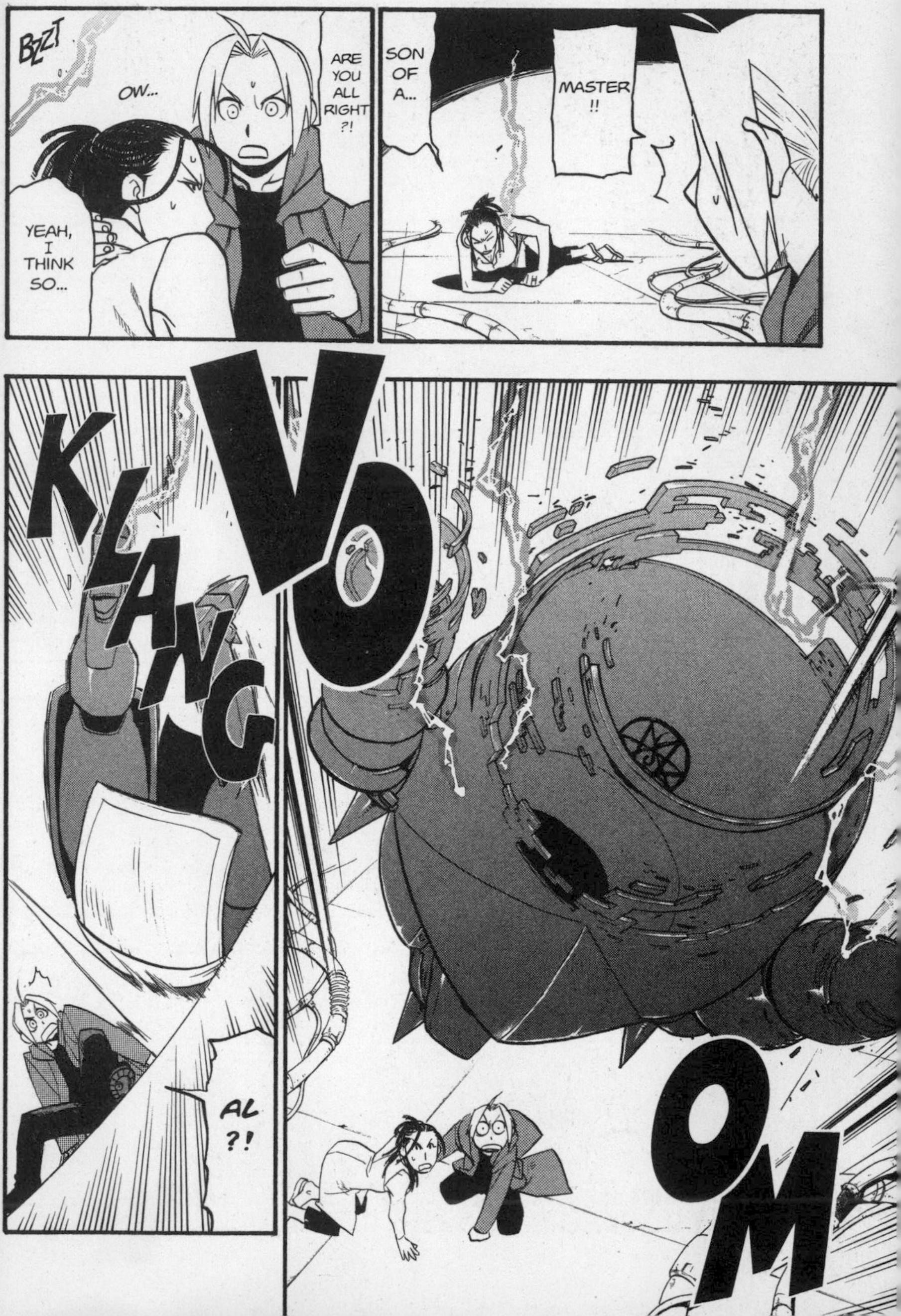
SON OF A...
MASTER!!
BZZT
OW...
ARE YOU ALL RIGHT?!
YEAH, I THINK SO...
VOOM
KLANG
AL?!

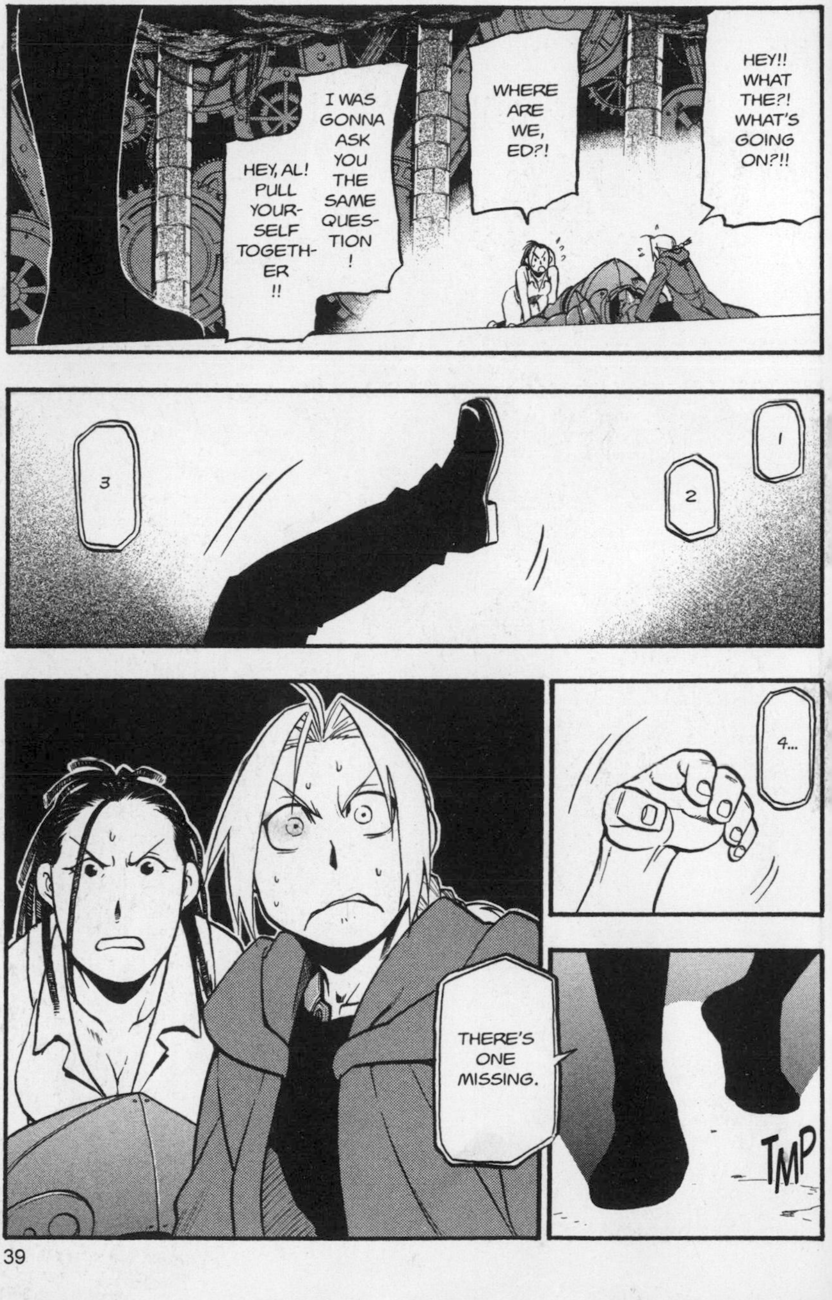
HEY!! WHAT THE?! WHAT'S GOING ON?!!
WHERE ARE WE, ED?!
I WAS GONNA ASK YOU THE SAME QUESTION!
HEY, AL! PULL YOURSELF TOGETHER!!
1
2
3
4...
TMP
THERE'S ONE MISSING.

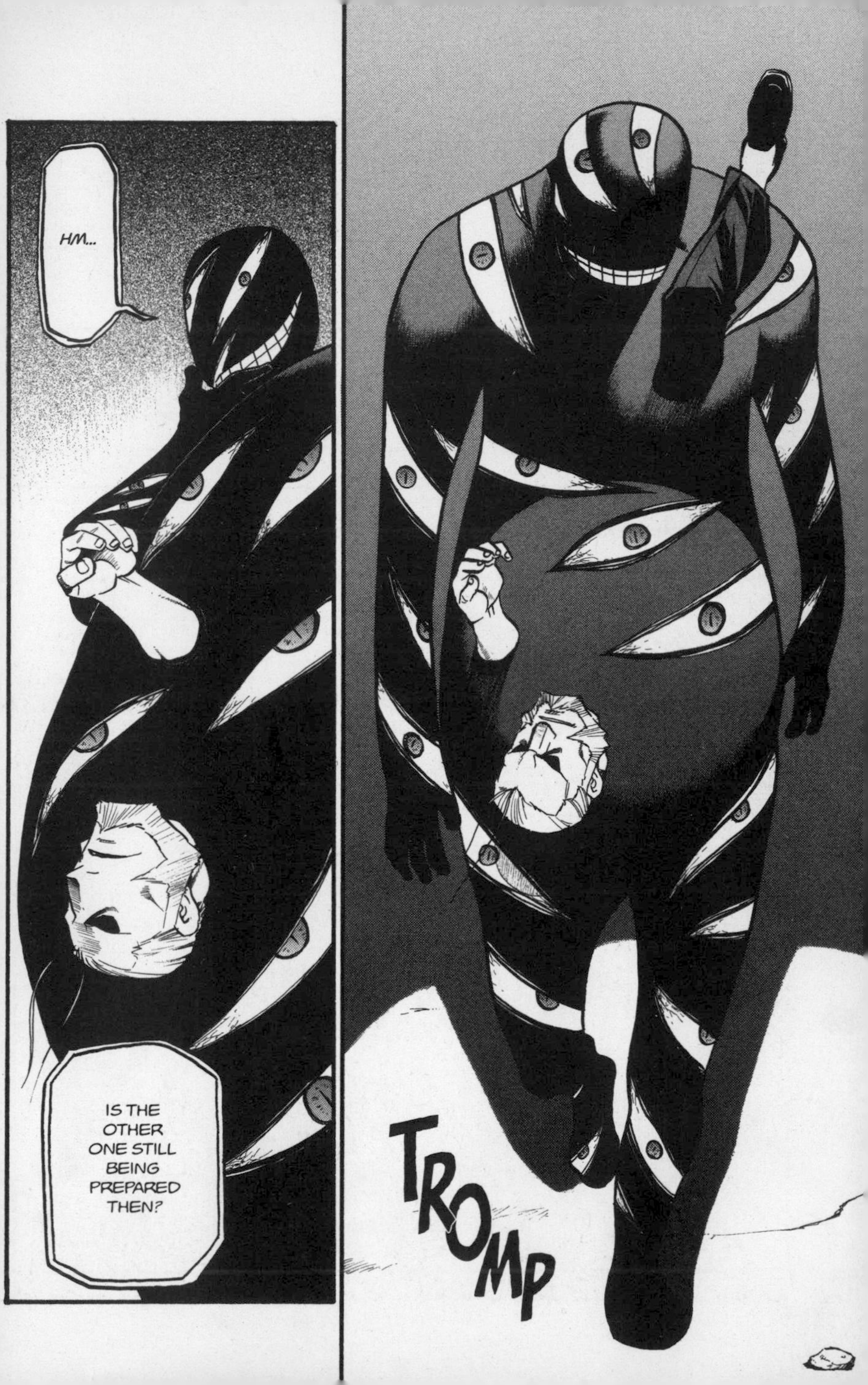
TROMP
HM...
IS THE OTHER ONE STILL BEING PREPARED THEN?

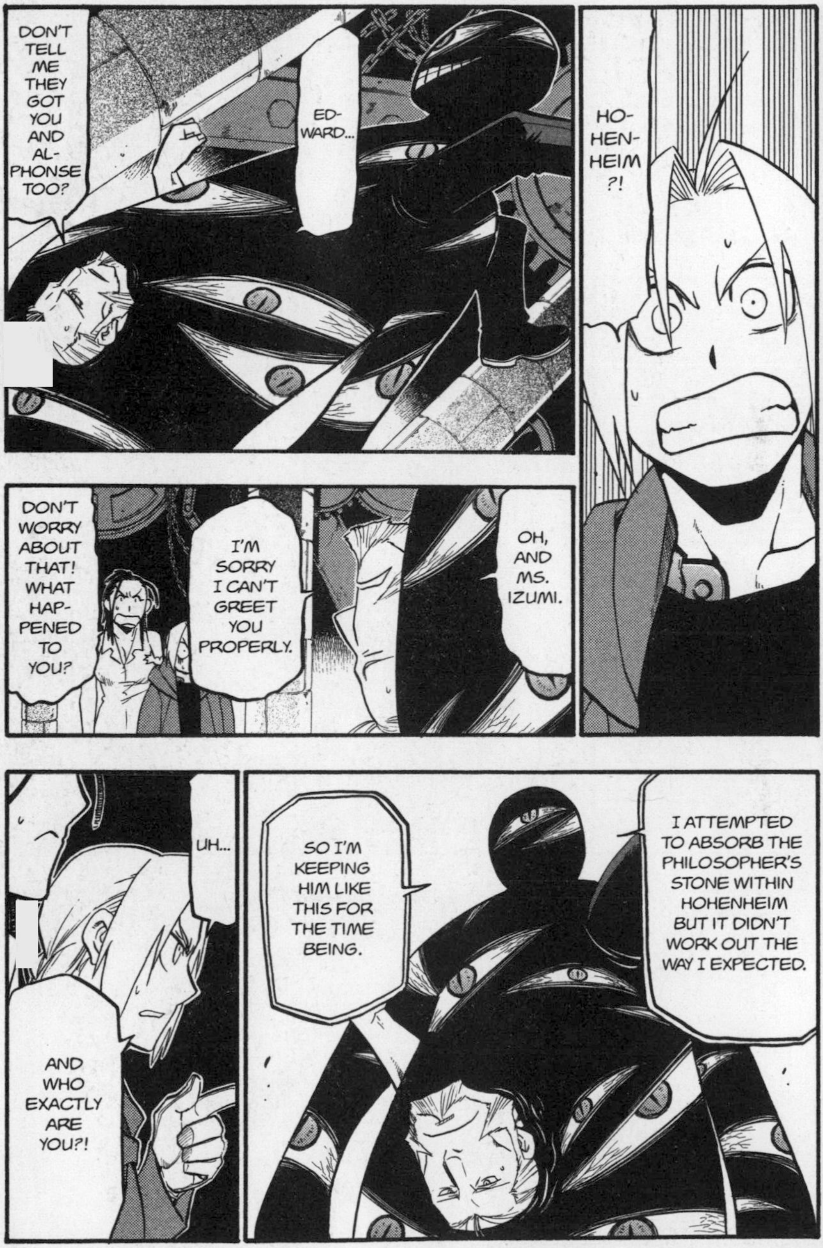
HO-HEN-HEIM?!
ED-WARD...
DON'T TELL ME THEY GOT YOU AND AL-PHONSE TOO?
OH, AND MS. IZUMI.
I'M SORRY I CAN'T GREET YOU PROPERLY.
DON'T WORRY ABOUT THAT! WHAT HAP-PENED TO YOU?
I ATTEMPTED TO ABSORB THE PHILOSOPHER'S STONE WITHIN HOHENHEIM BUT IT DIDN'T WORK OUT THE WAY I EXPECTED.
SO I'M KEEPING HIM LIKE THIS FOR THE TIME BEING.
UH...
AND WHO EXACTLY ARE YOU?!

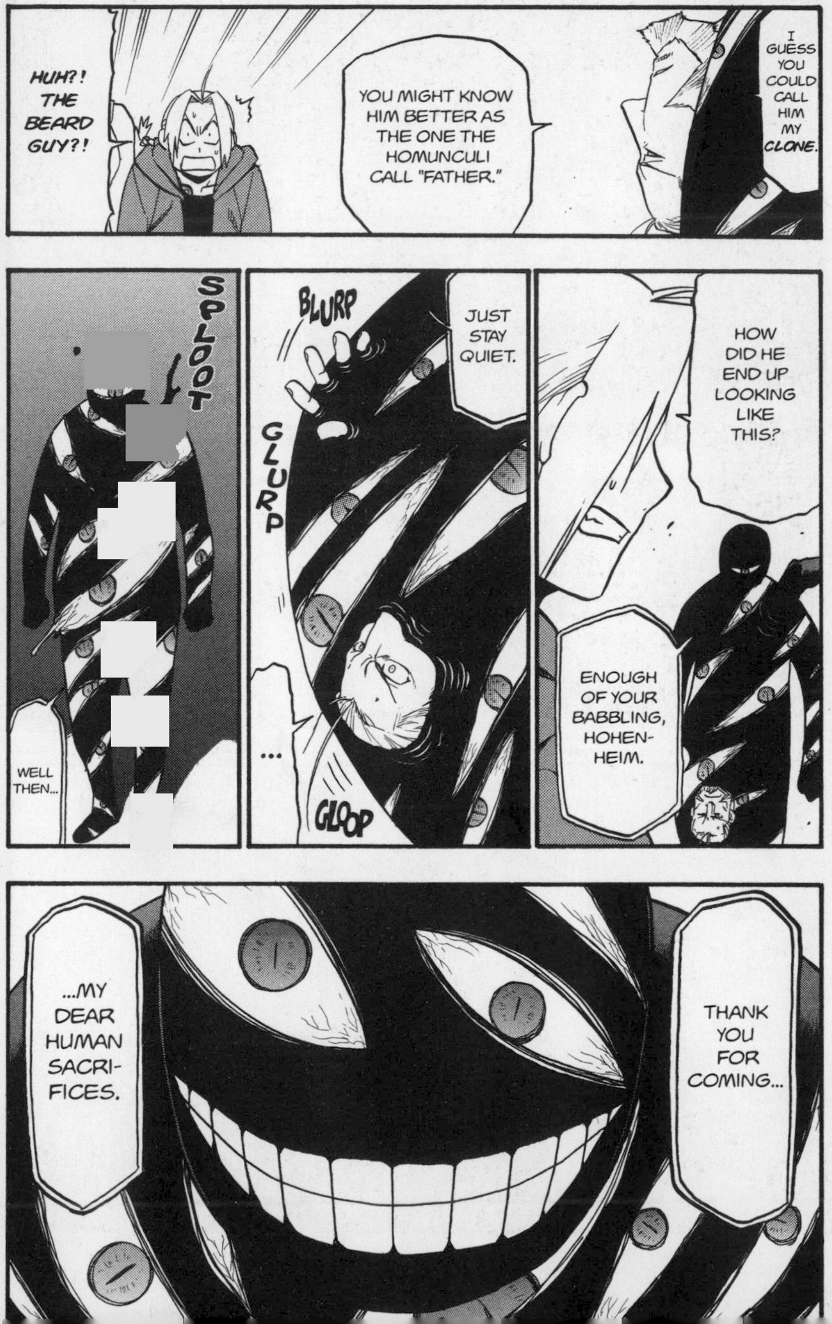
I GUESS YOU COULD CALL HIM MY CLONE.
YOU MIGHT KNOW HIM BETTER AS THE ONE THE HOMUNCULI CALL "FATHER."
HUH?! THE BEARD GUY?!
HOW DID HE END UP LOOKING LIKE THIS?
ENOUGH OF YOUR BABBLING, HOHENHEIM.
JUST STAY QUIET.
BLURP
GLURP
...
GLOOP
SPLOOT
WELL THEN...
THANK YOU FOR COMING...
...MY DEAR HUMAN SACRIFICES.

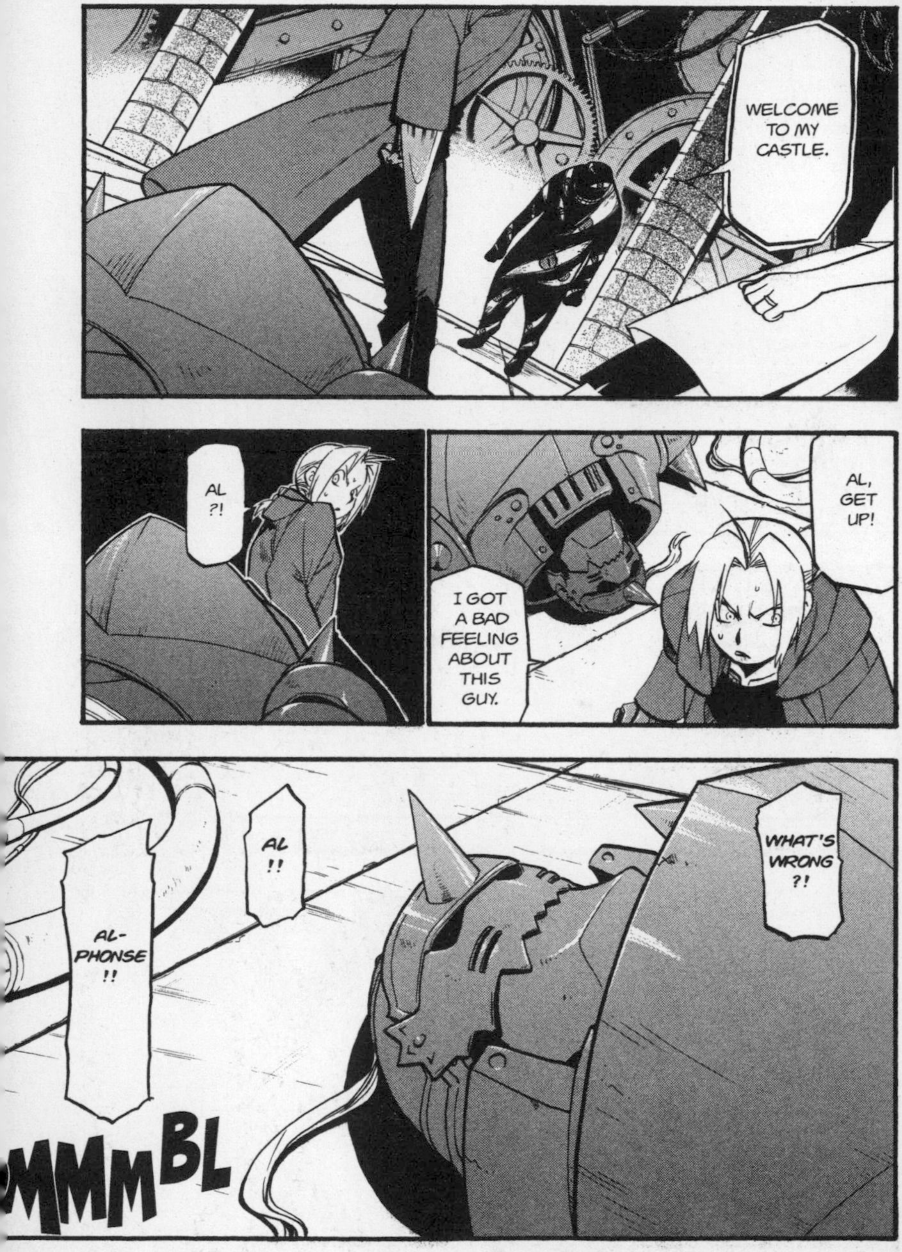
WELCOME TO MY CASTLE.
AL, GET UP!
I GOT A BAD FEELING ABOUT THIS GUY.
AL ?!
WHAT'S WRONG ?!
AL !!
AL-PHONSE !!
MMMMBL

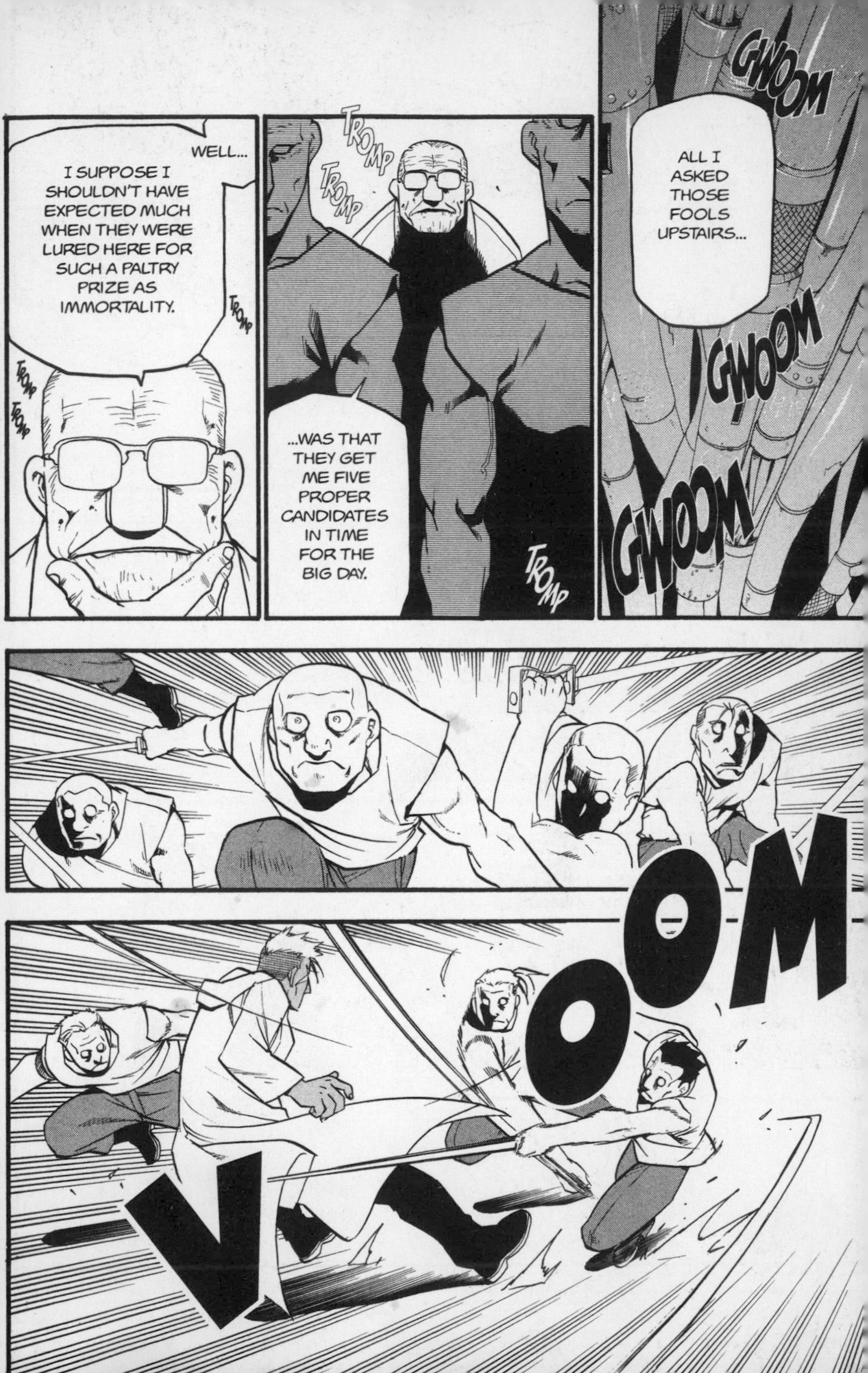
GWOOM
ALL I ASKED THOSE FOOLS UPSTAIRS...
GWOOM
GWOOM
TROMP
TROMP
...WAS THAT THEY GET ME FIVE PROPER CANDIDATES IN TIME FOR THE BIG DAY.
TROMP
WELL...
I SUPPOSE I SHOULDN'T HAVE EXPECTED MUCH WHEN THEY WERE LURED HERE FOR SUCH A PALTRY PRIZE AS IMMORTALITY.
TROMP
TROMP
TROMP
VOOM

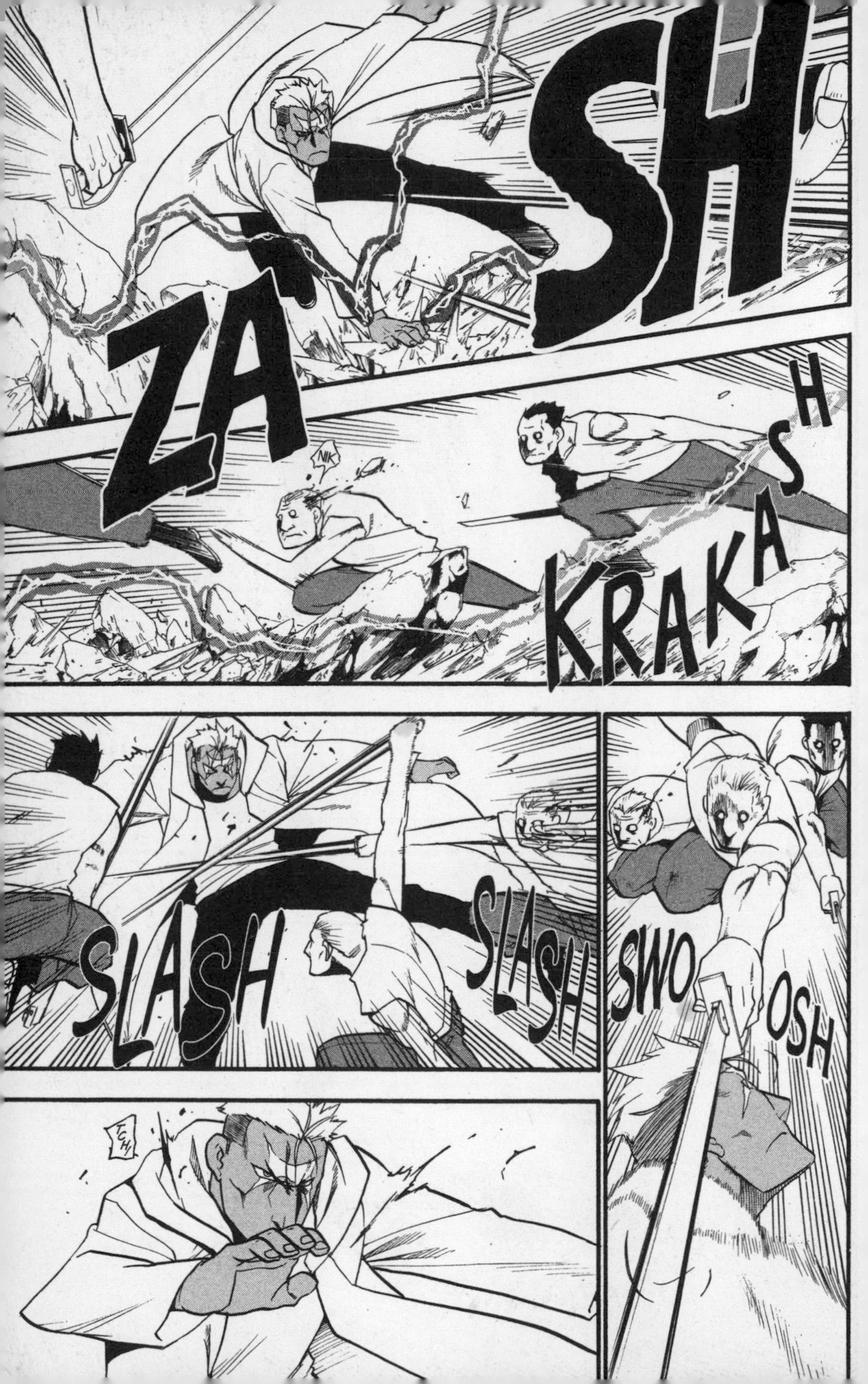
ZASH
KRAKASH
NIK
SWOOSH
SLASH
SLASH
TCH!

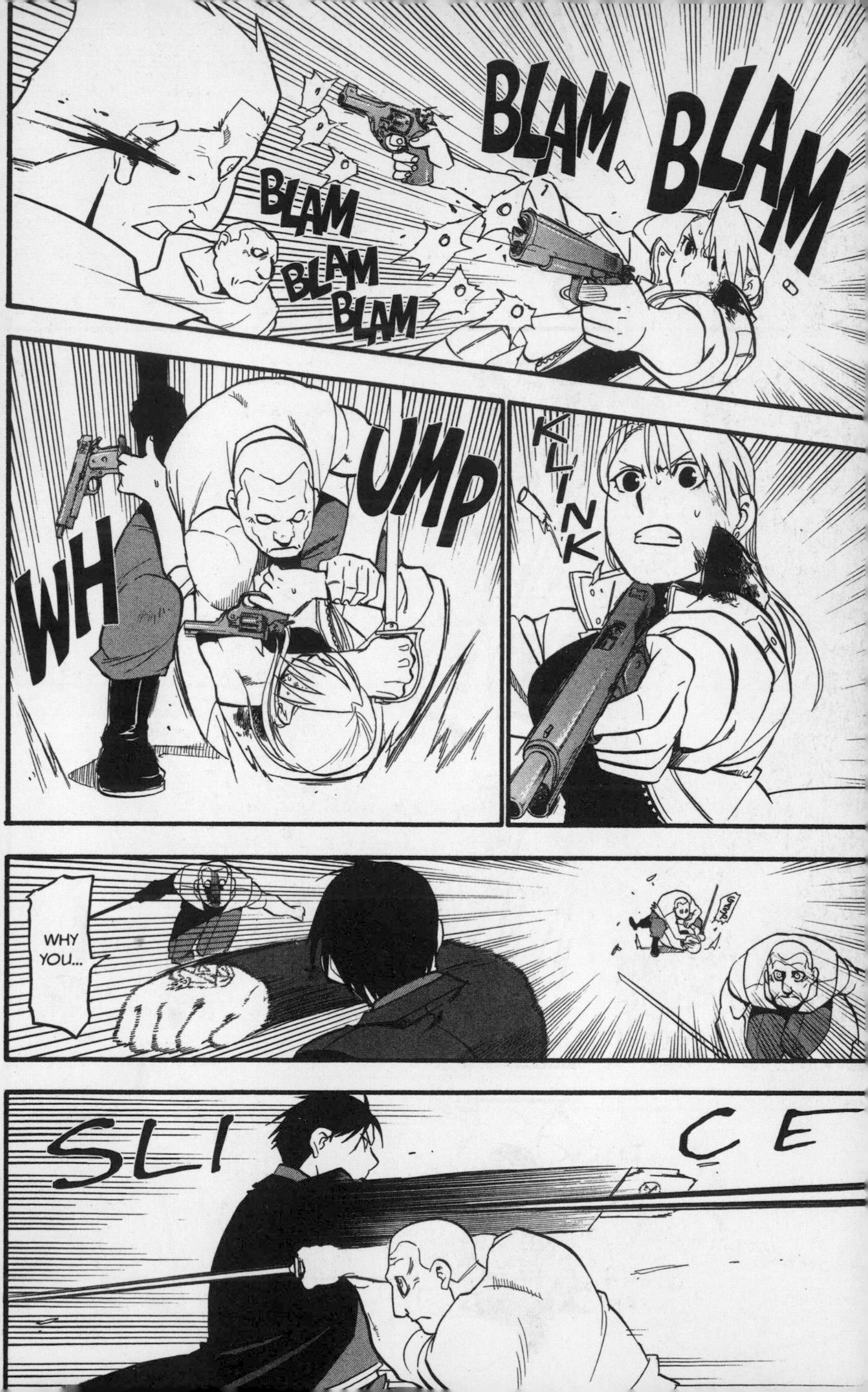
BLAM BLAM
BLAM
BLAM
BLAM
KLINK
WH UMP
WHY YOU...
SLI CE

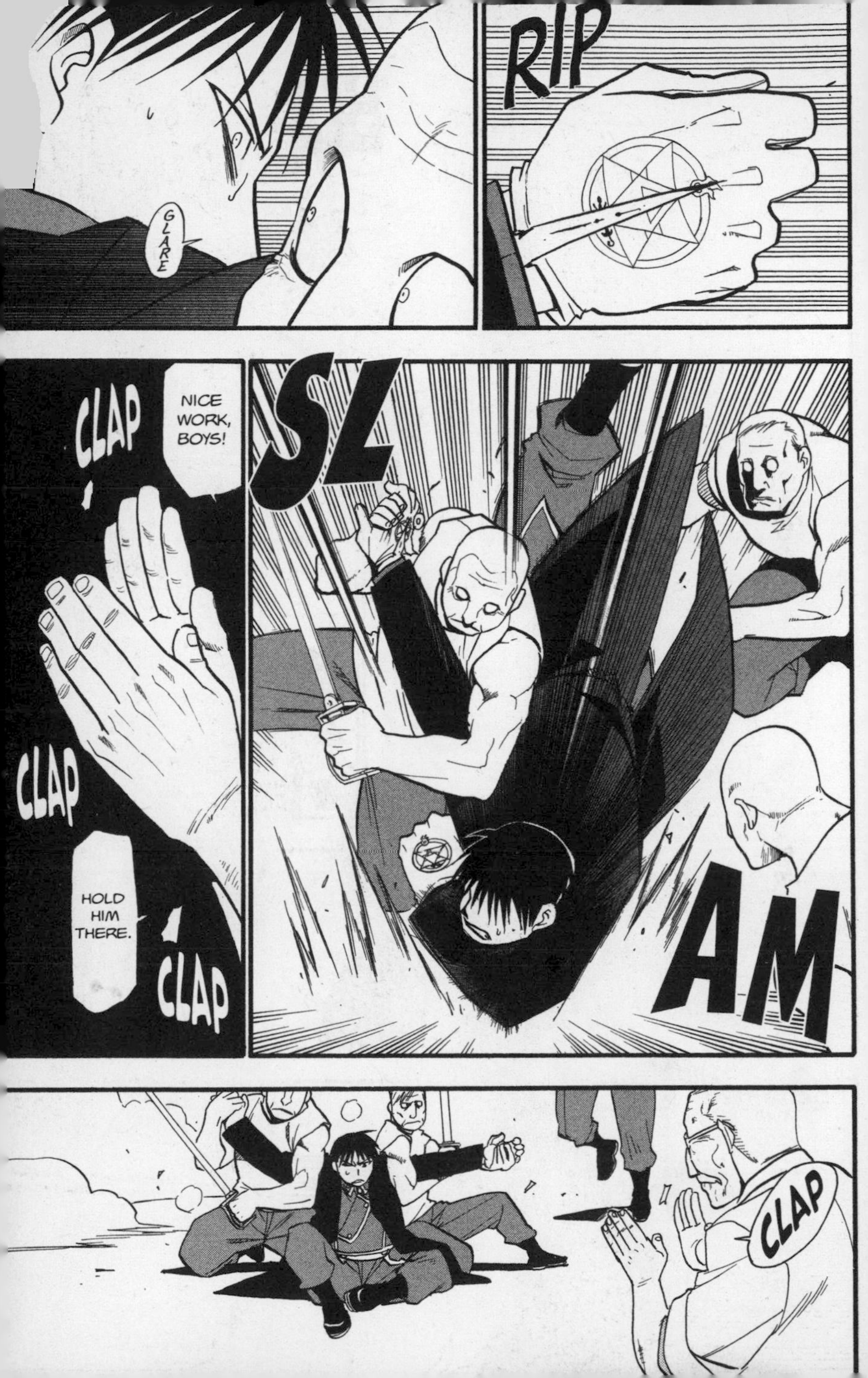
RIP
GLARE
SL
AM
CLAP
NICE WORK, BOYS!
CLAP
HOLD HIM THERE.
CLAP
CLAP

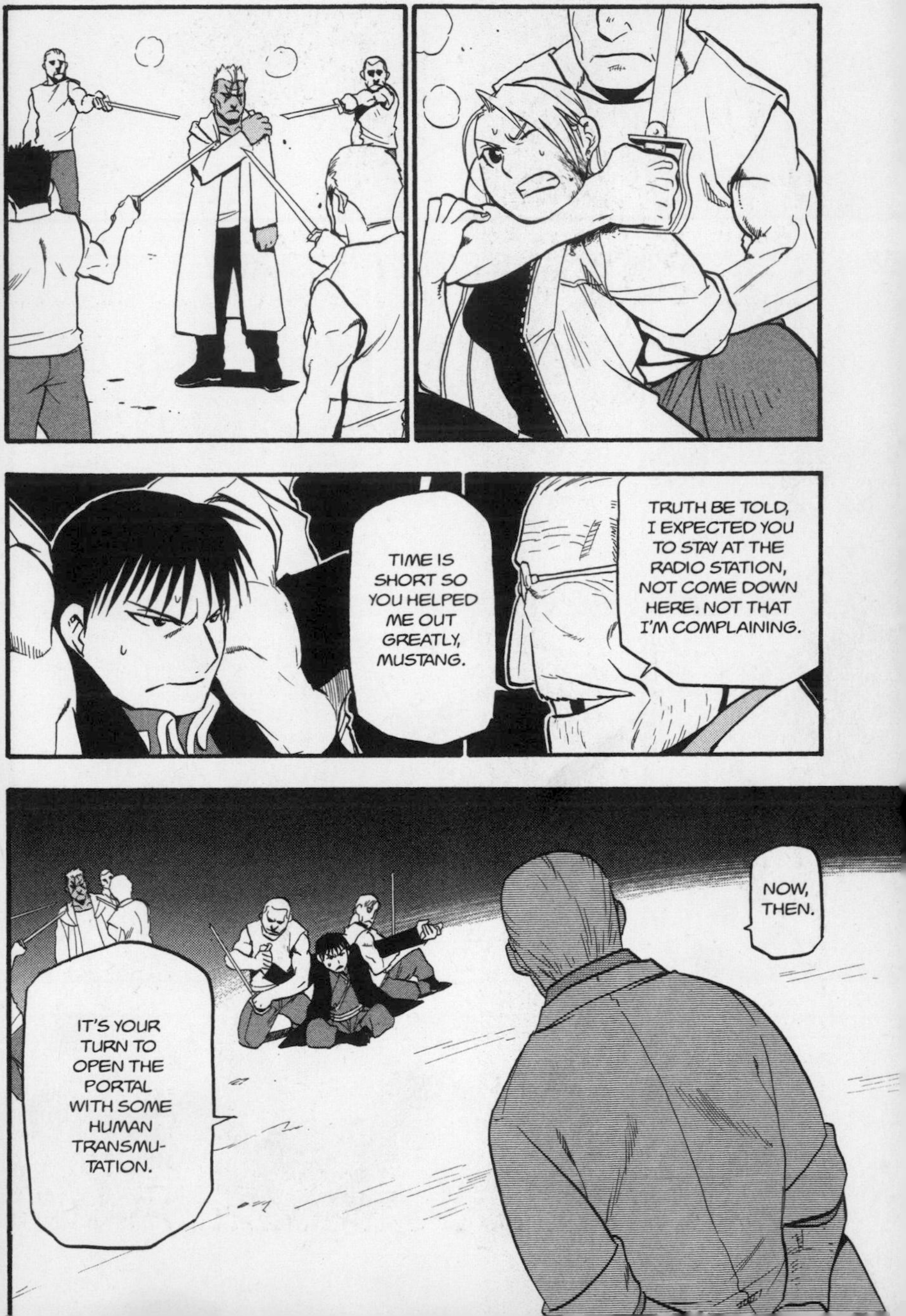
TRUTH BE TOLD, I EXPECTED YOU TO STAY AT THE RADIO STATION, NOT COME DOWN HERE. NOT THAT I'M COMPLAINING.
TIME IS SHORT SO YOU HELPED ME OUT GREATLY, MUSTANG.
NOW, THEN.
IT'S YOUR TURN TO OPEN THE PORTAL WITH SOME HUMAN TRANSMU-TATION.

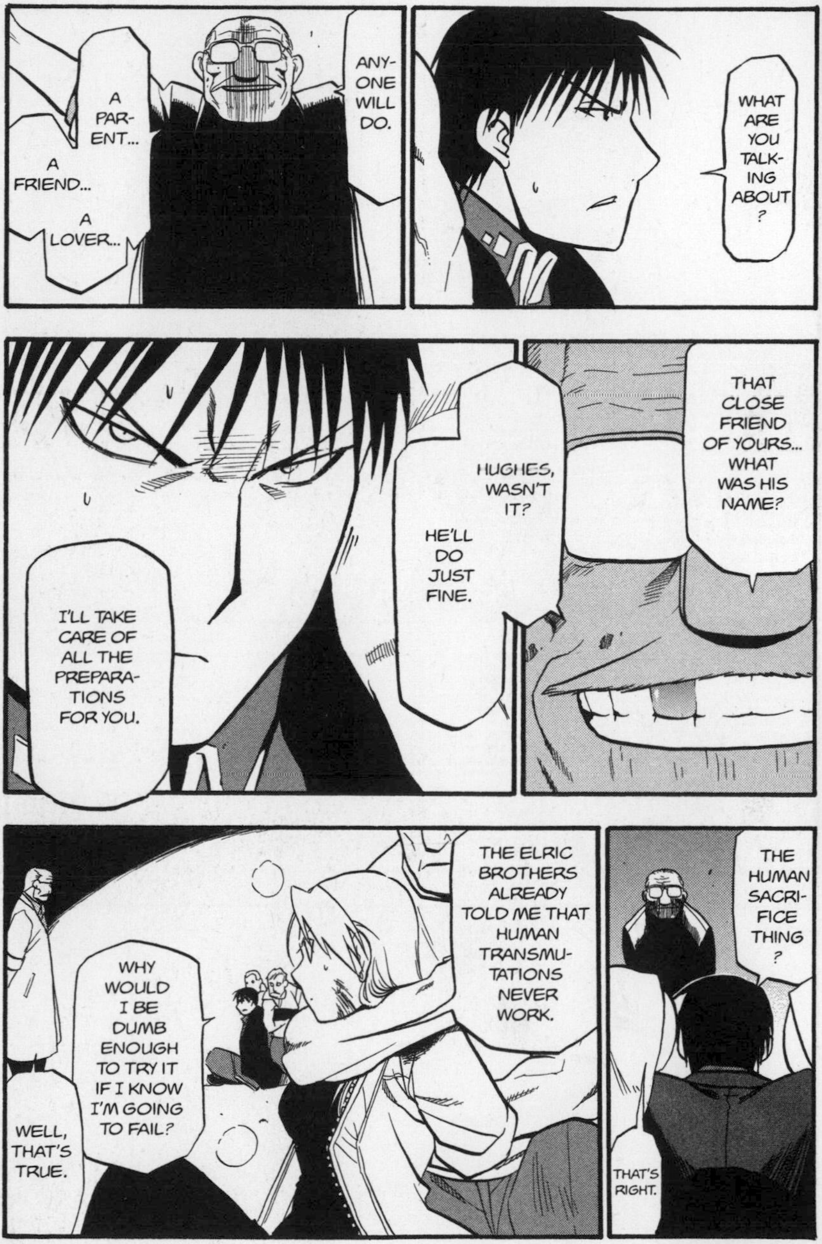
WHAT ARE YOU TALKING ABOUT?
ANYONE WILL DO.
A PARENT...
A FRIEND...
A LOVER...
THAT CLOSE FRIEND OF YOURS... WHAT WAS HIS NAME?
HUGHES, WASN'T IT?
HE'LL DO JUST FINE.
I'LL TAKE CARE OF ALL THE PREPARATIONS FOR YOU.
THE HUMAN SACRIFICE THING?
THAT'S RIGHT.
THE ELRIC BROTHERS ALREADY TOLD ME THAT HUMAN TRANSMUTATIONS NEVER WORK.
WHY WOULD I BE DUMB ENOUGH TO TRY IT IF I KNOW I'M GOING TO FAIL?
WELL, THAT'S TRUE.

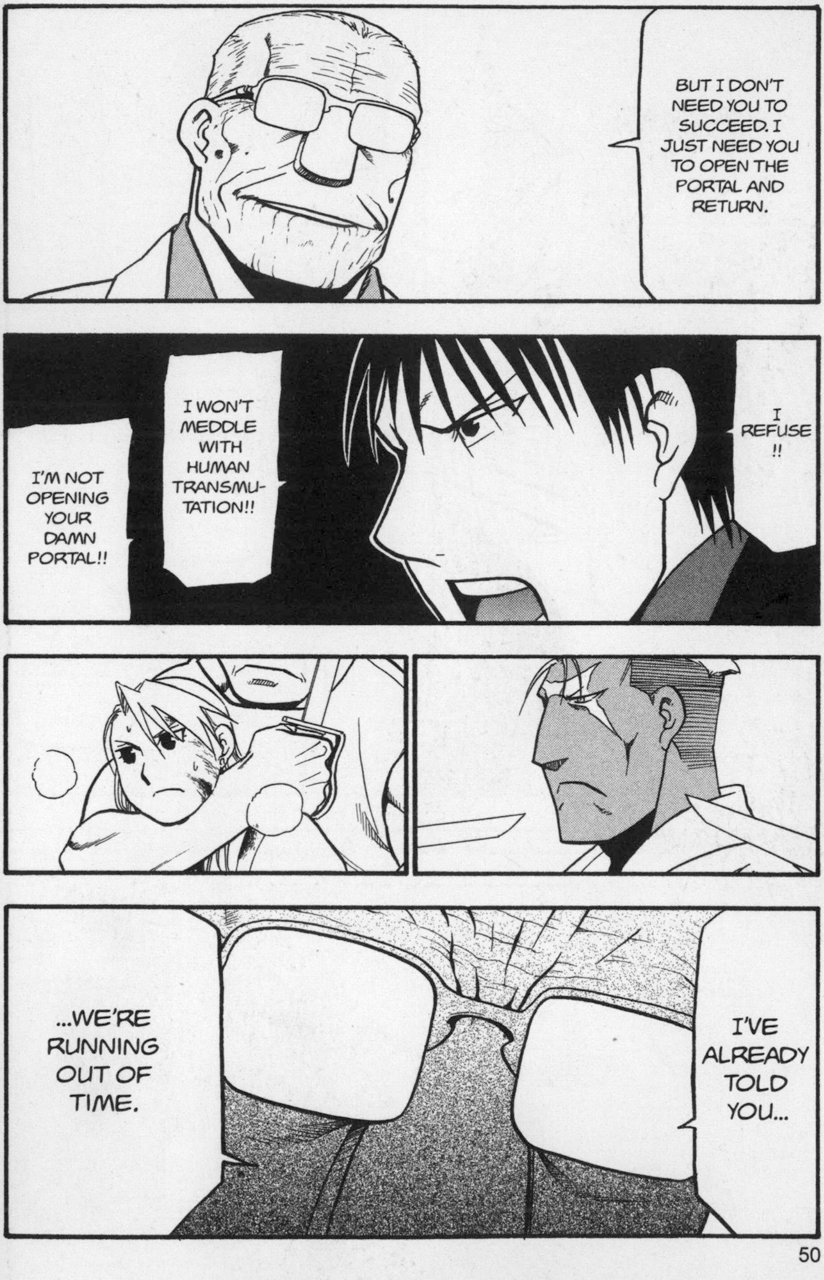
BUT I DON'T NEED YOU TO SUCCEED. I JUST NEED YOU TO OPEN THE PORTAL AND RETURN.
I REFUSE!!
I WON'T MEDDLE WITH HUMAN TRANSMUTATION!!
I'M NOT OPENING YOUR DAMN PORTAL!!
I'VE ALREADY TOLD YOU...
...WE'RE RUNNING OUT OF TIME.

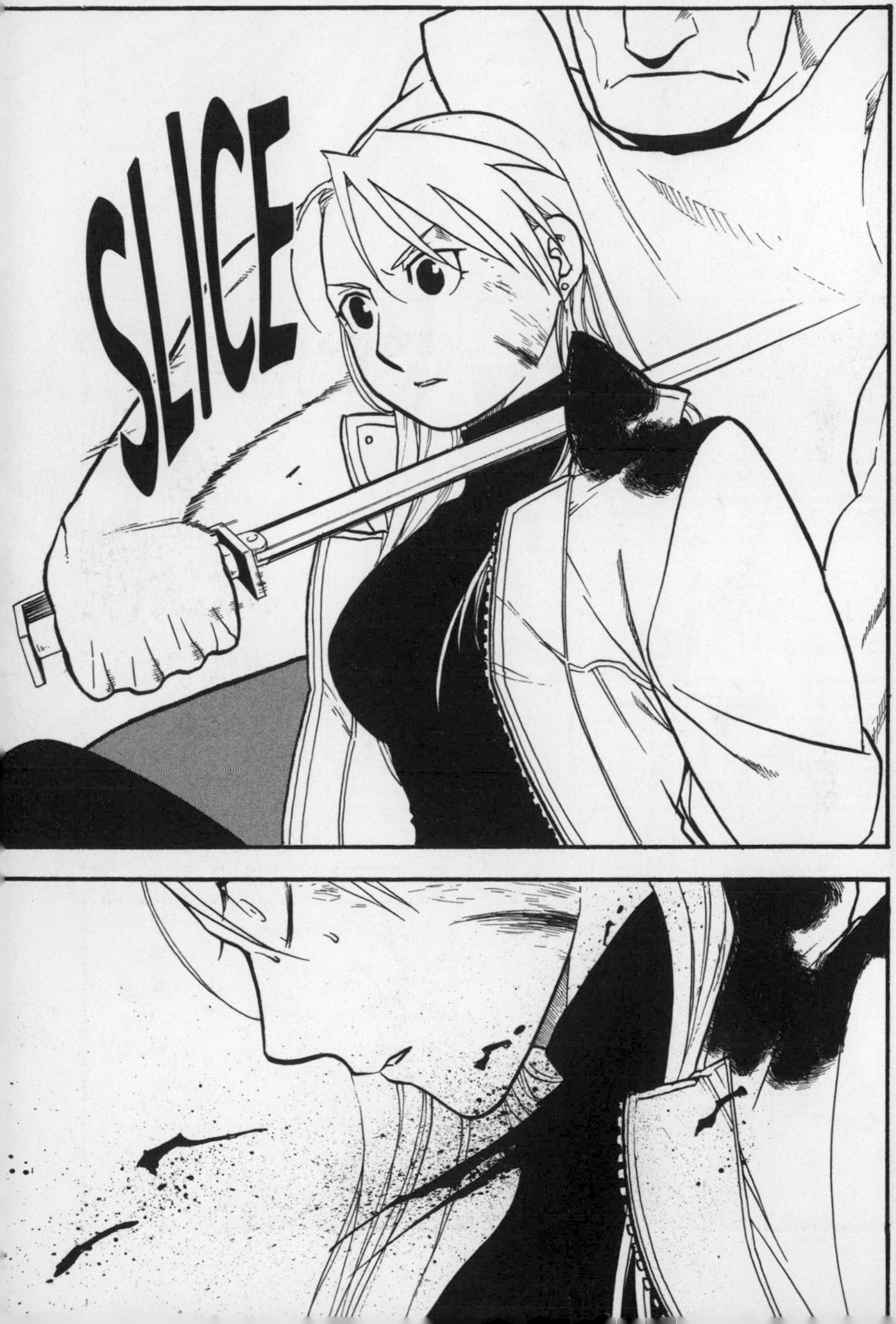
SLICE

LIEUTENANT!!!

NOW, THEN ...

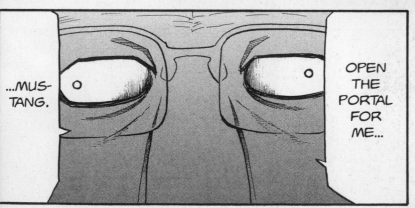

...MUS-TANG.

OPEN THE PORTAL FOR ME...

FULLMETAL
ALCHEMIST

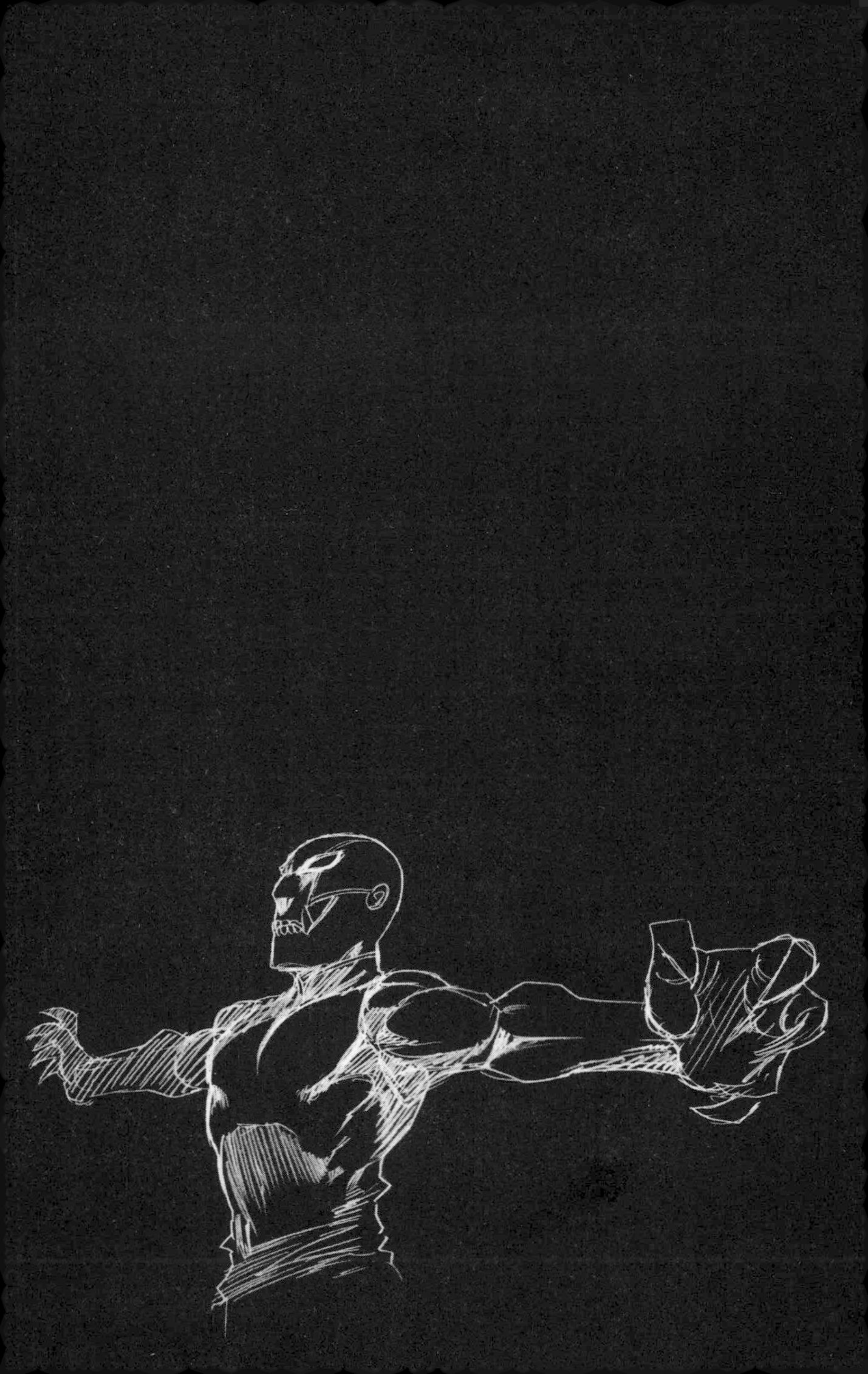

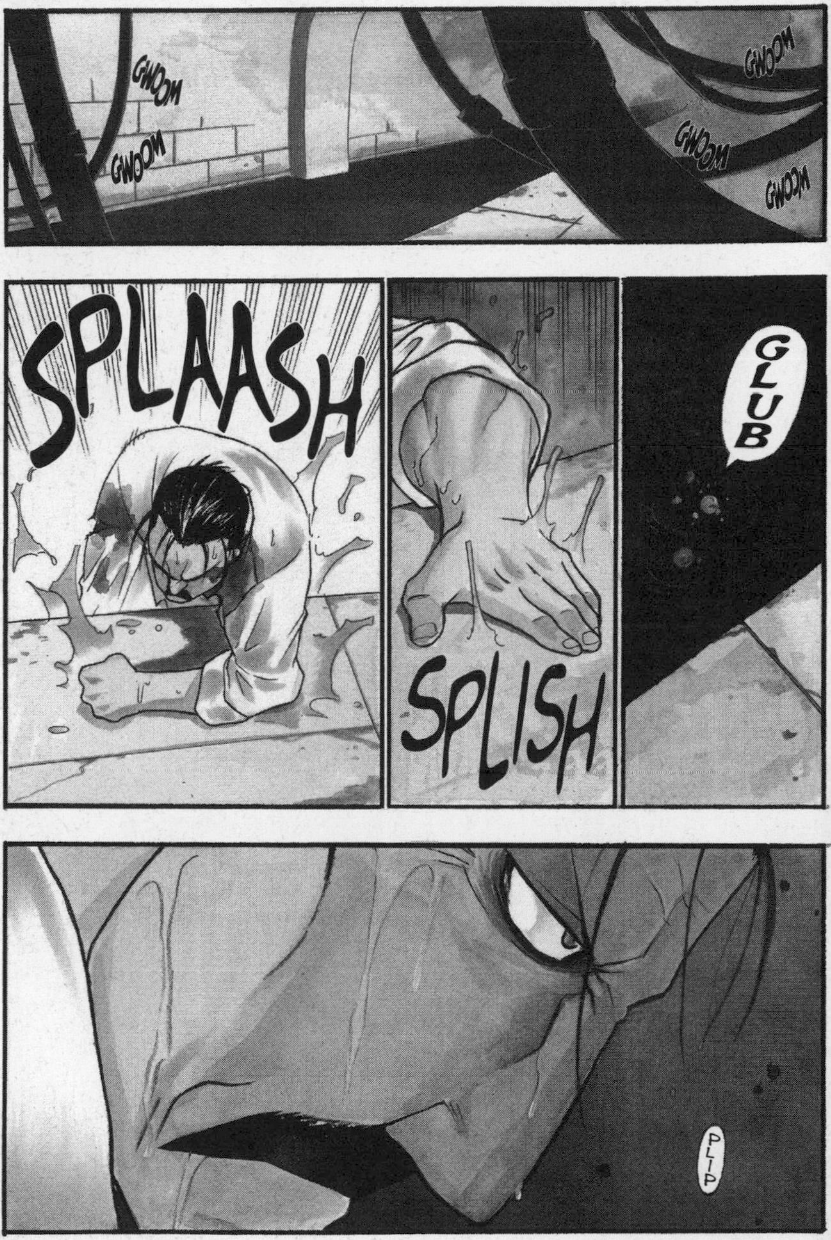
GWOOM
GWOOM
GWOOM
GWOOM
GWOOM
GLUB
SPLISH
SPLAASH
PLIP

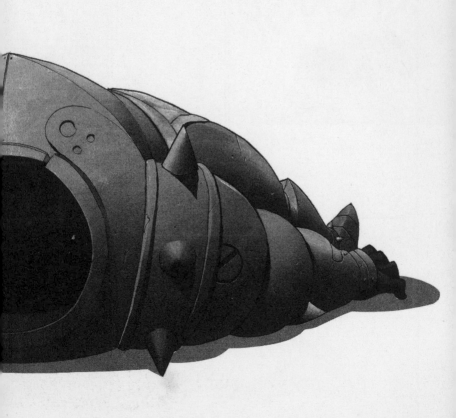

Chapter 101
The Fifth Human Sacrifice

FULLMETAL
ALCHEMIST

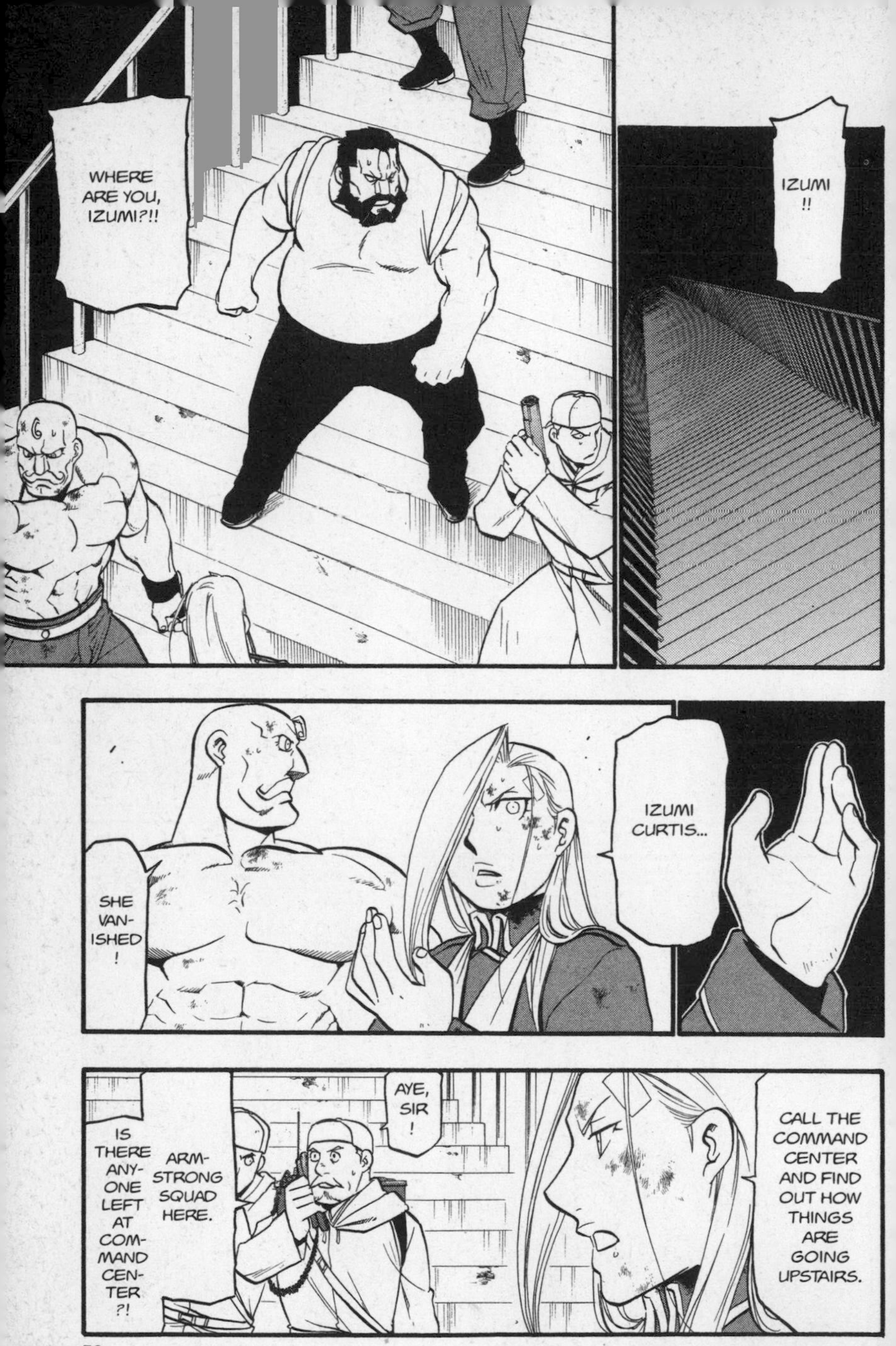
IZUMI !!
WHERE ARE YOU, IZUMI?!!
IZUMI CURTIS...
SHE VANISHED!
CALL THE COMMAND CENTER AND FIND OUT HOW THINGS ARE GOING UPSTAIRS.
AYE, SIR!
ARMSTRONG SQUAD HERE.
IS THERE ANYONE LEFT AT COMMAND CENTER?!

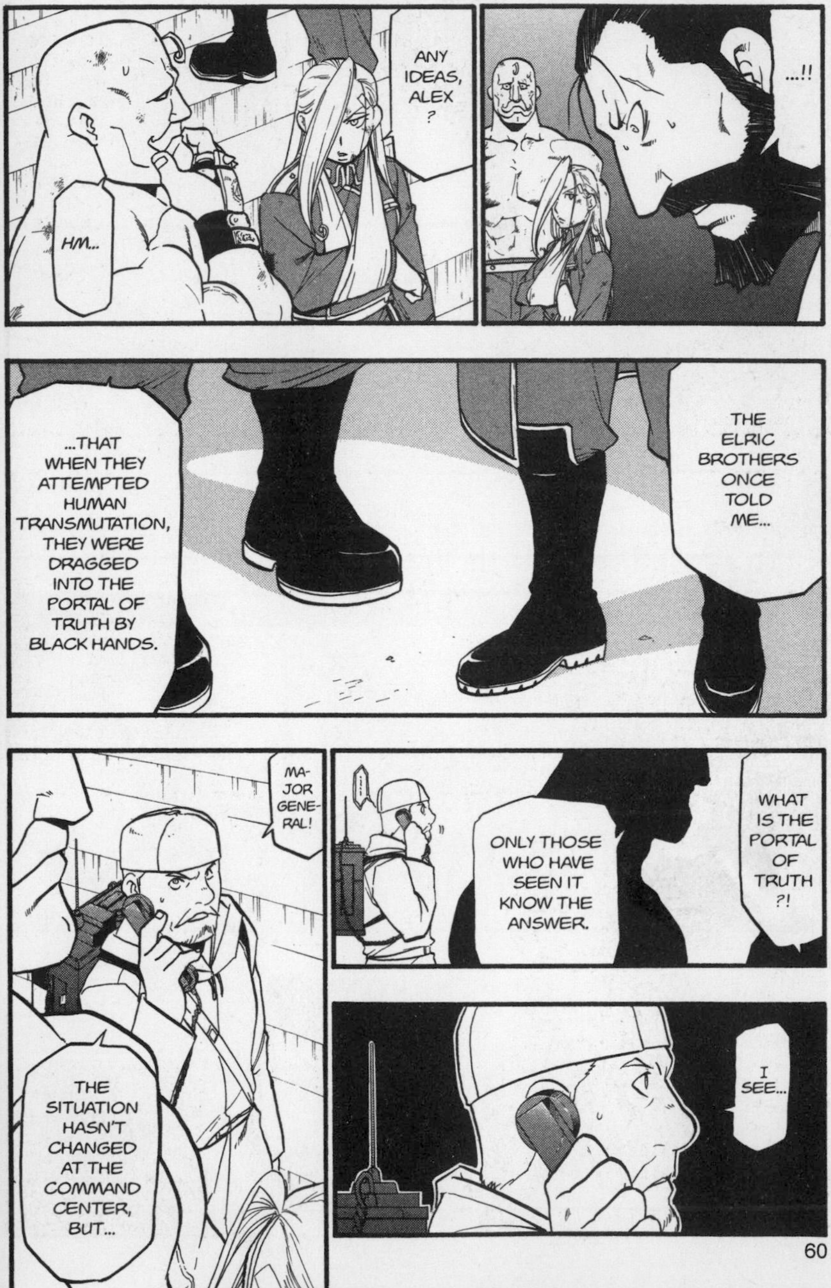
...!!
ANY IDEAS, ALEX?
HM...
THE ELRIC BROTHERS ONCE TOLD ME...
...THAT WHEN THEY ATTEMPTED HUMAN TRANSMUTATION, THEY WERE DRAGGED INTO THE PORTAL OF TRUTH BY BLACK HANDS.
WHAT IS THE PORTAL OF TRUTH?!
ONLY THOSE WHO HAVE SEEN IT KNOW THE ANSWER.
I SEE...
MAJOR GENERAL!
THE SITUATION HASN'T CHANGED AT THE COMMAND CENTER, BUT...

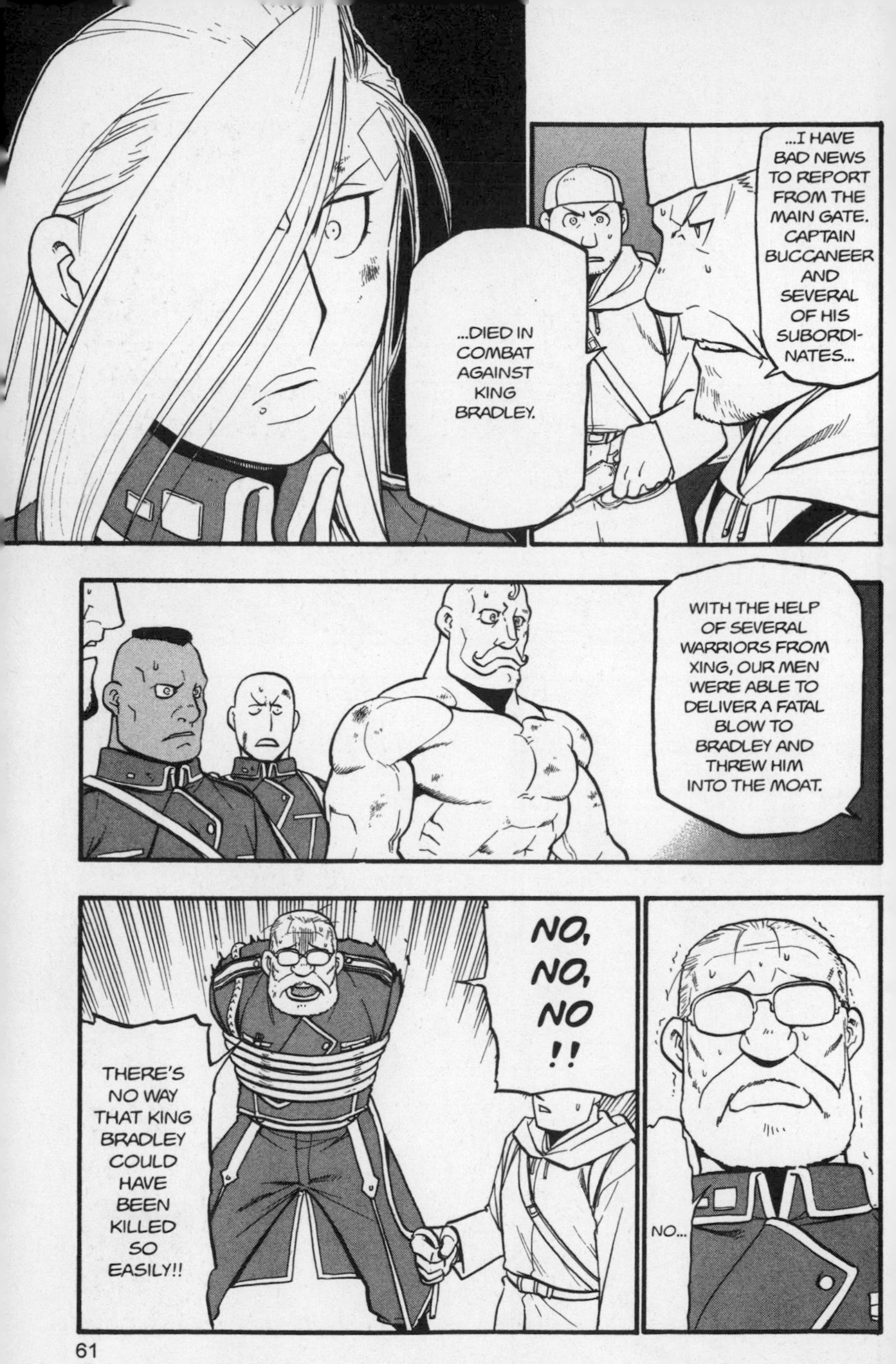
...I HAVE BAD NEWS TO REPORT FROM THE MAIN GATE. CAPTAIN BUCCANEER AND SEVERAL OF HIS SUBORDI-NATES...
...DIED IN COMBAT AGAINST KING BRADLEY.
WITH THE HELP OF SEVERAL WARRIORS FROM XING, OUR MEN WERE ABLE TO DELIVER A FATAL BLOW TO BRADLEY AND THREW HIM INTO THE MOAT.
NO...
NO, NO, NO!!
THERE'S NO WAY THAT KING BRADLEY COULD HAVE BEEN KILLED SO EASILY!!

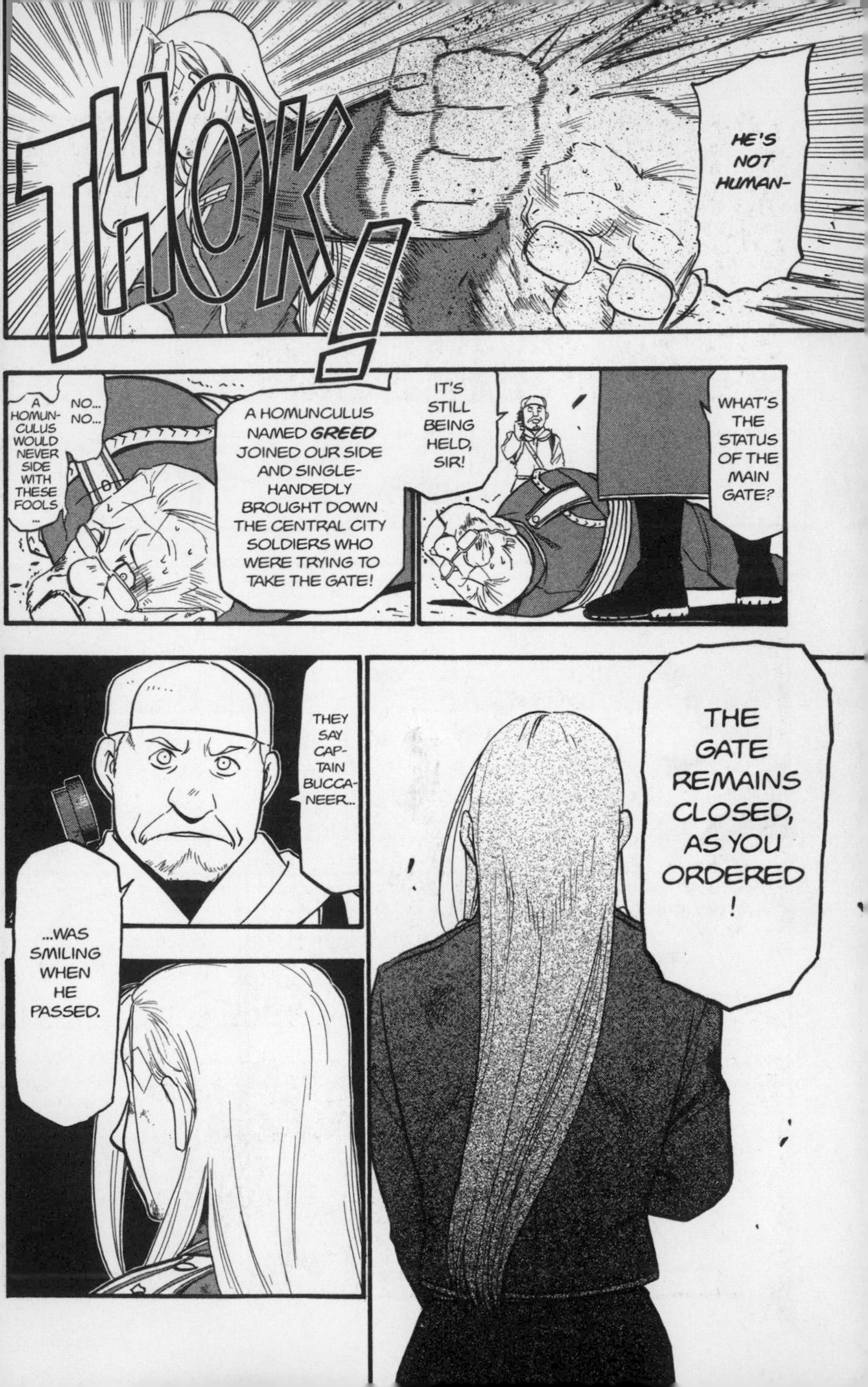
HE'S NOT HUMAN-
THOK!
WHAT'S THE STATUS OF THE MAIN GATE?
IT'S STILL BEING HELD, SIR!
A HOMUNCULUS NAMED **GREED** JOINED OUR SIDE AND SINGLE-HANDEDLY BROUGHT DOWN THE CENTRAL CITY SOLDIERS WHO WERE TRYING TO TAKE THE GATE!
NO... NO...
A HOMUNCULUS WOULD NEVER SIDE WITH THESE FOOLS...
THE GATE REMAINS CLOSED, AS YOU ORDERED!
THEY SAY CAPTAIN BUCCANEER...
...WAS SMILING WHEN HE PASSED.

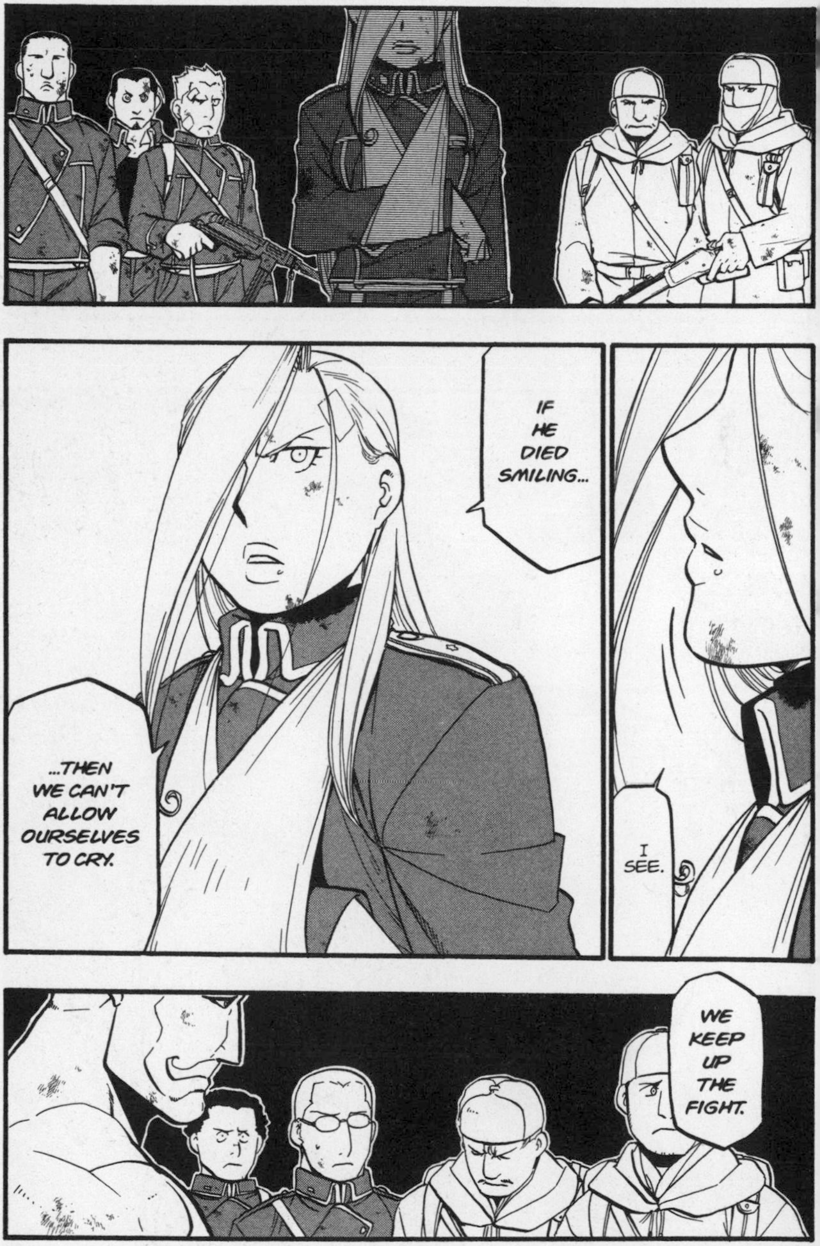
I SEE.
IF HE DIED SMILING...
...THEN WE CAN'T ALLOW OURSELVES TO CRY.
WE KEEP UP THE FIGHT.

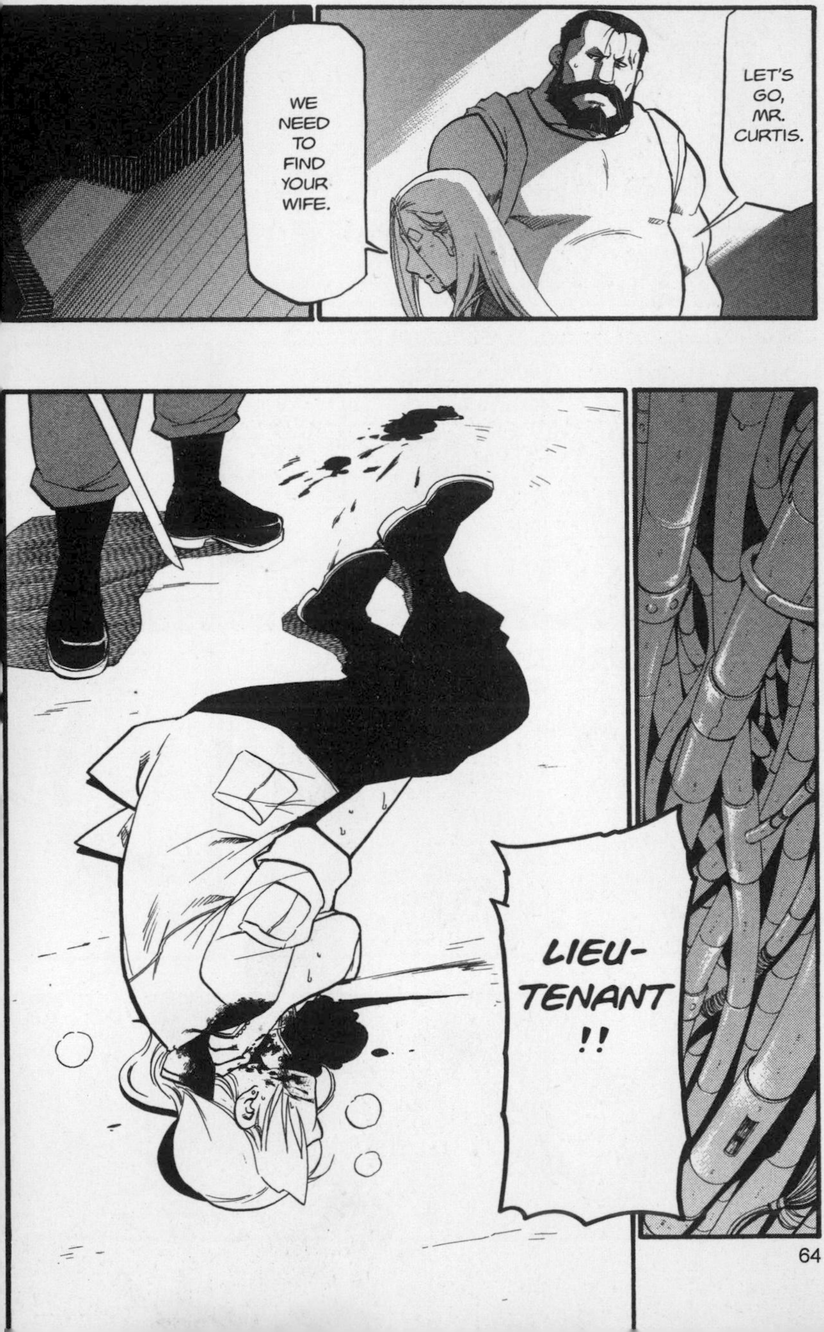
LET'S GO, MR. CURTIS.
WE NEED TO FIND YOUR WIFE.
LIEU-TENANT!!

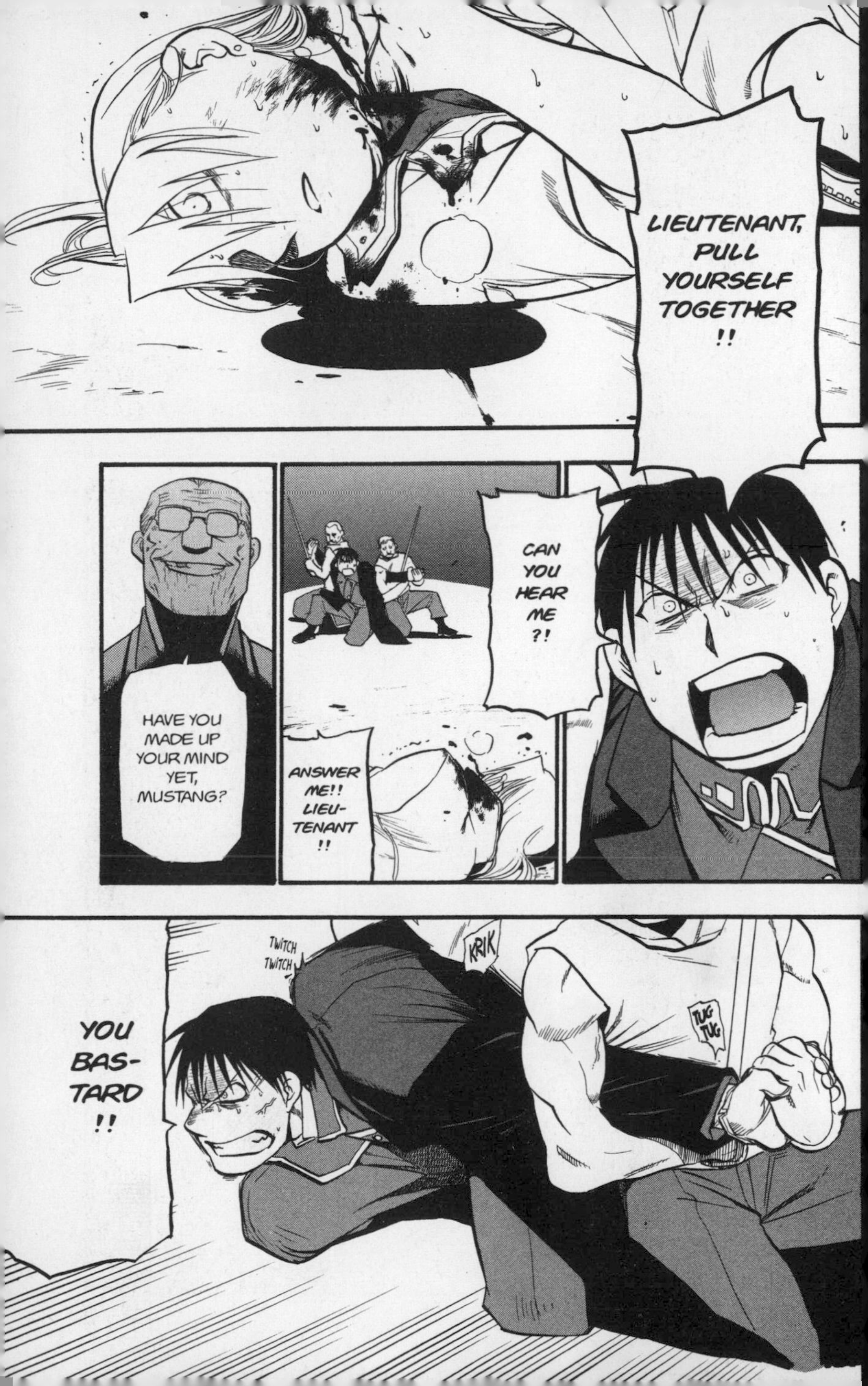
LIEUTENANT, PULL YOURSELF TOGETHER!!
CAN YOU HEAR ME?!
ANSWER ME!! LIEU-TENANT!!
HAVE YOU MADE UP YOUR MIND YET, MUSTANG?
TUG TUG
KRIK
TWITCH TWITCH
YOU BAS-TARD!!

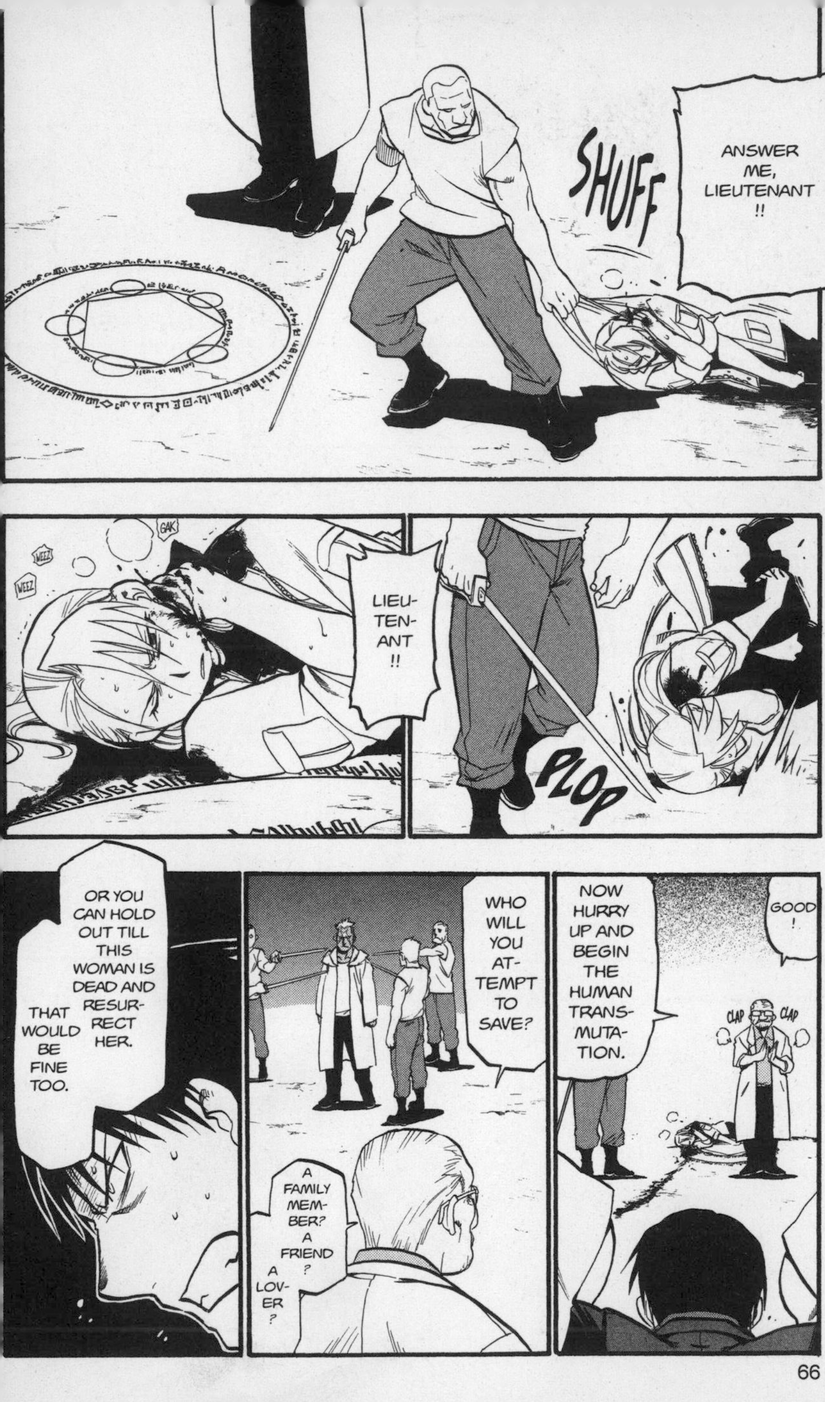
SHUFF
ANSWER ME, LIEUTENANT !!
LIEU-TEN-ANT !!
PLOP
GAK
WEEZ
WEEZ
GOOD !
NOW HURRY UP AND BEGIN THE HUMAN TRANS-MUTA-TION.
CLAP CLAP
WHO WILL YOU AT-TEMPT TO SAVE?
A FAMILY MEM-BER? A FRIEND ? A LOV-ER ?
OR YOU CAN HOLD OUT TILL THIS WOMAN IS DEAD AND RESUR-RECT HER.
THAT WOULD BE FINE TOO.

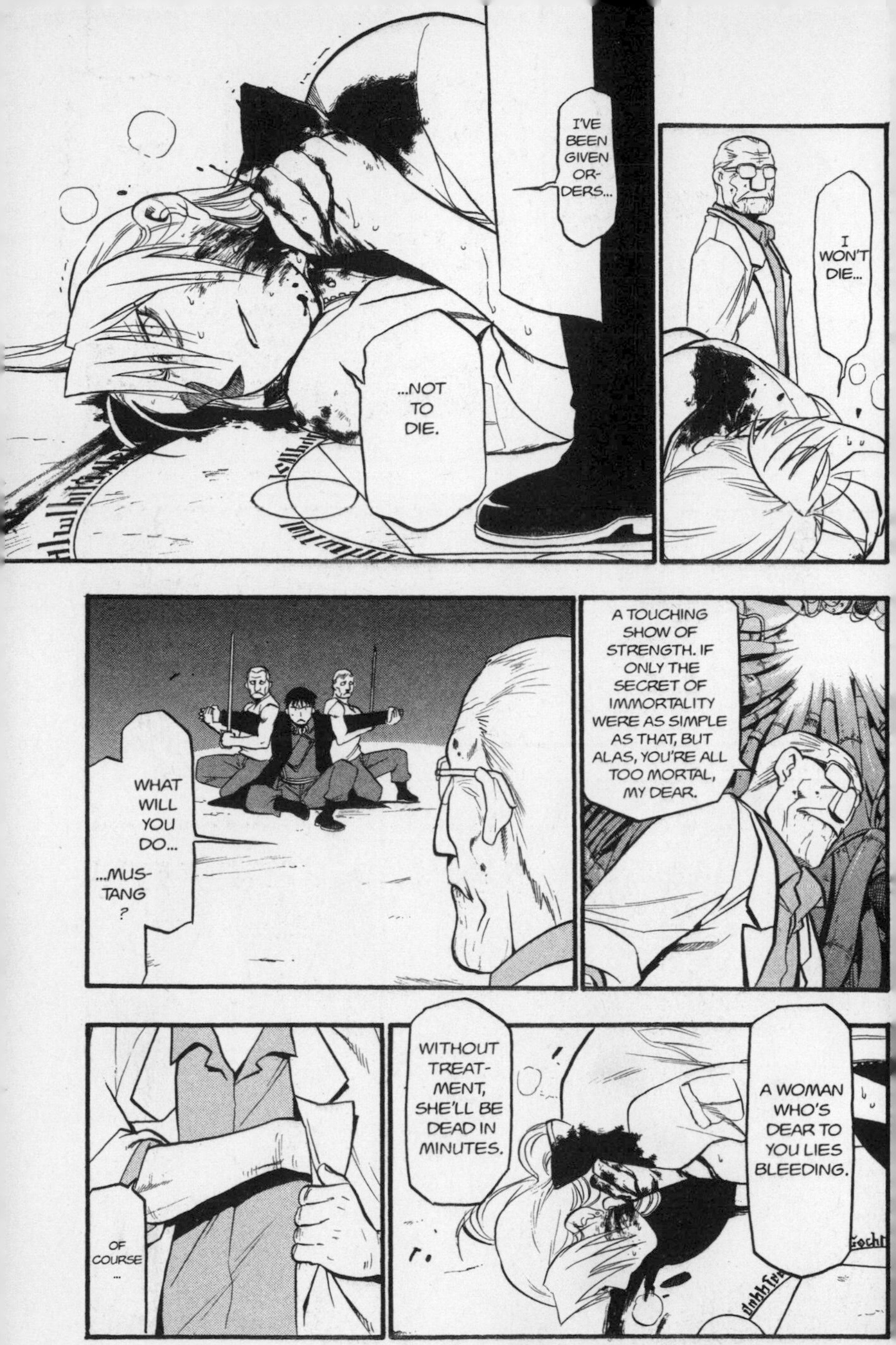
I WON'T DIE...
I'VE BEEN GIVEN ORDERS...
...NOT TO DIE.
A TOUCHING SHOW OF STRENGTH. IF ONLY THE SECRET OF IMMORTALITY WERE AS SIMPLE AS THAT, BUT ALAS, YOU'RE ALL TOO MORTAL, MY DEAR.
WHAT WILL YOU DO...
...MUSTANG?
A WOMAN WHO'S DEAR TO YOU LIES BLEEDING.
WITHOUT TREATMENT, SHE'LL BE DEAD IN MINUTES.
OF COURSE...

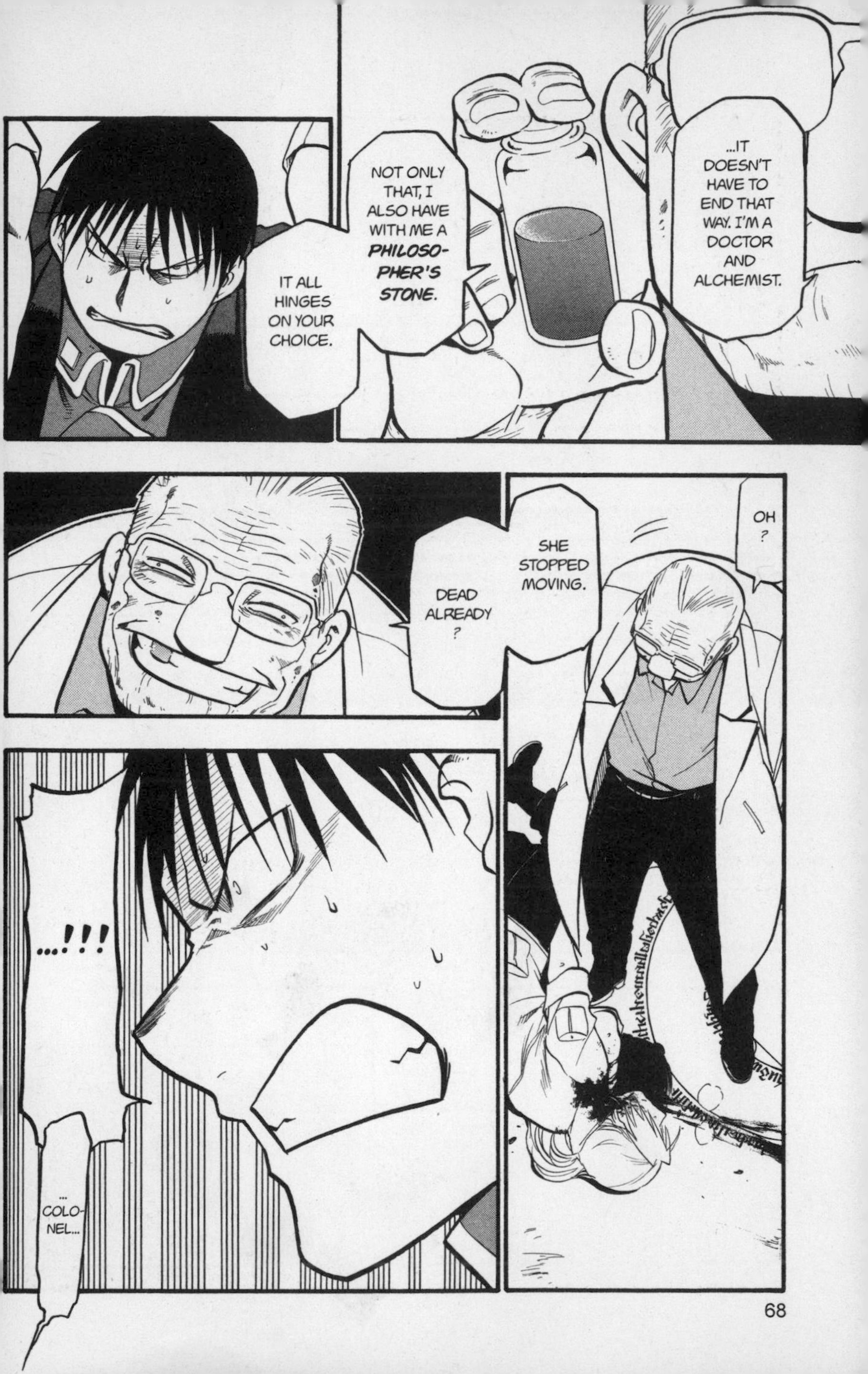
...IT DOESN'T HAVE TO END THAT WAY. I'M A DOCTOR AND ALCHEMIST.
NOT ONLY THAT, I ALSO HAVE WITH ME A **PHILOSOPHER'S STONE**.
IT ALL HINGES ON YOUR CHOICE.
OH?
SHE STOPPED MOVING.
DEAD ALREADY?
...!!!
...COLONEL...

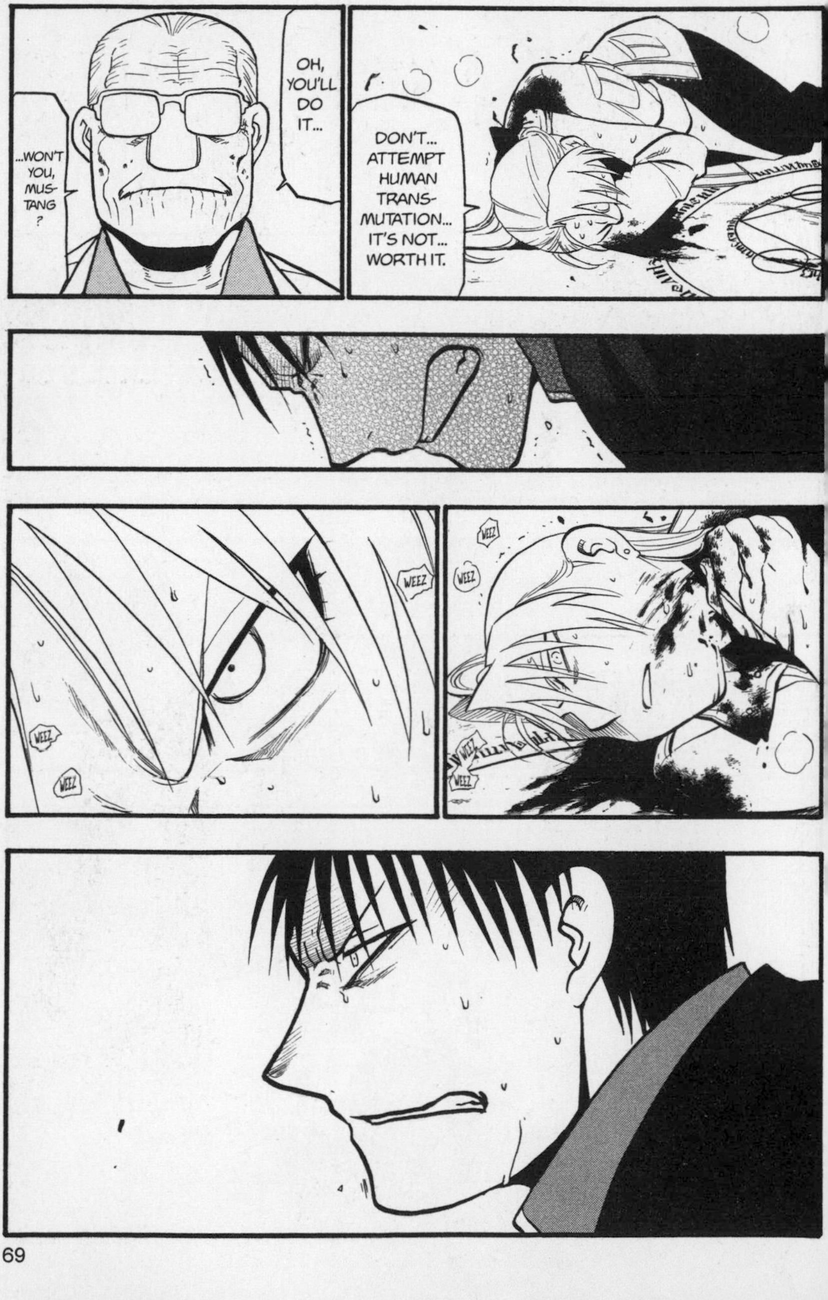
DON'T... ATTEMPT HUMAN TRANS-MUTATION... IT'S NOT... WORTH IT.
OH, YOU'LL DO IT...
...WON'T YOU, MUS-TANG?
WEEZ
WEEZ
WEEZ
WEEZ
WEEZ
WEEZ
WEEZ

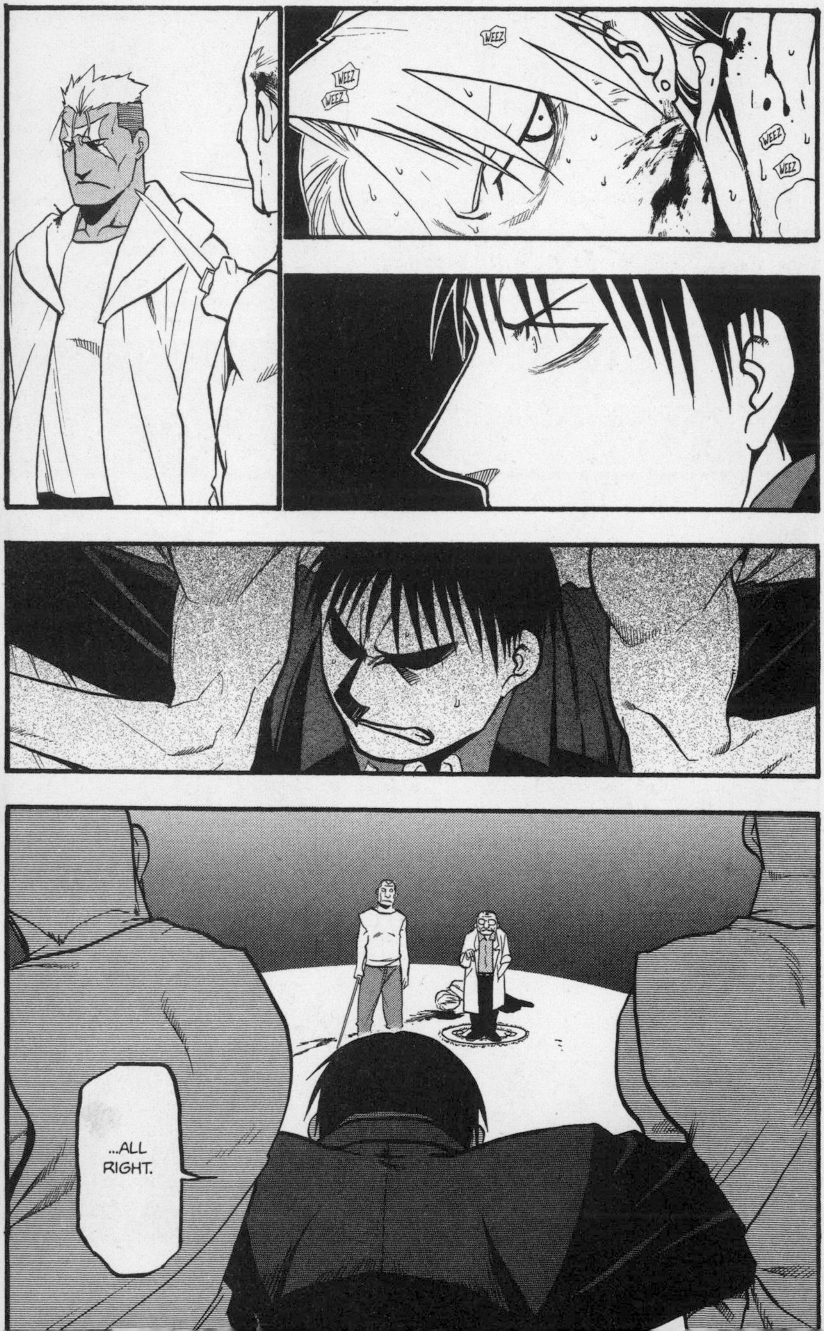
WEEZ
WEEZ
WEEZ
WEEZ
WEEZ
...ALL RIGHT.

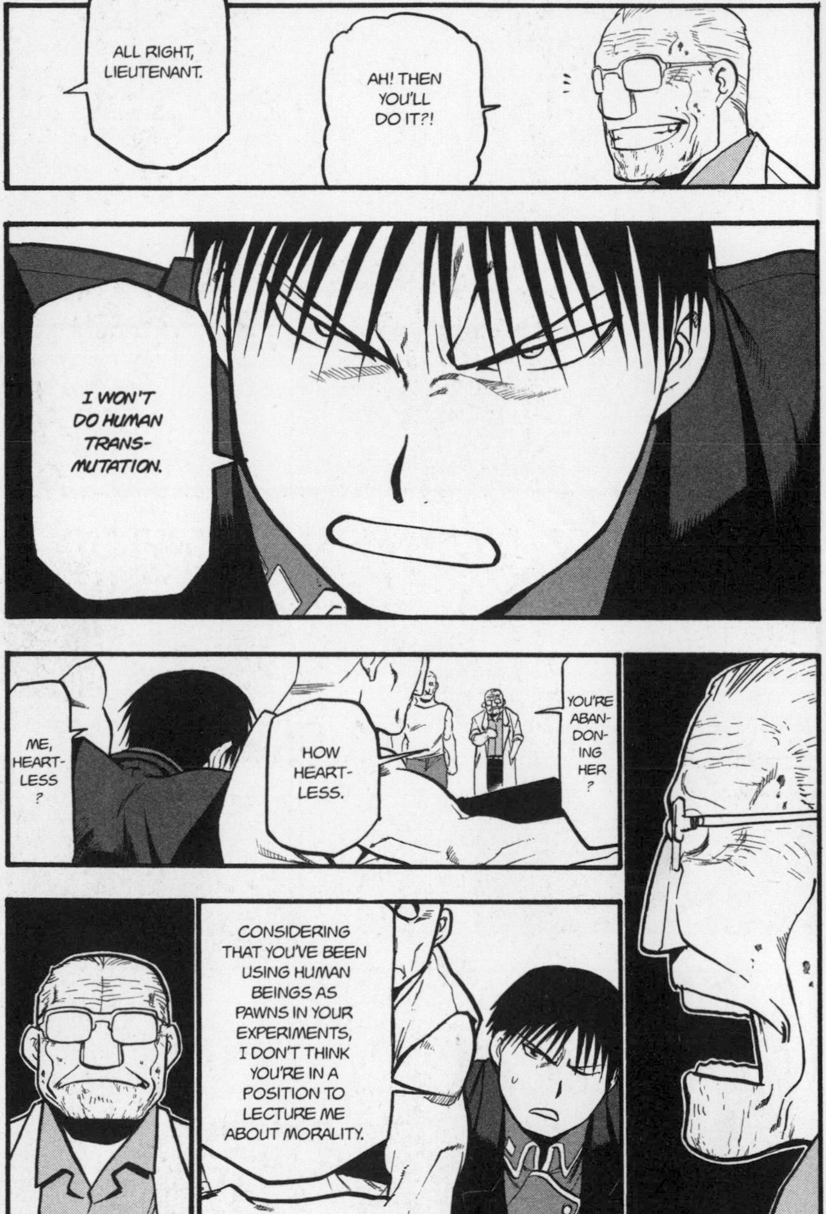
AH! THEN YOU'LL DO IT?!
ALL RIGHT, LIEUTENANT.
I WON'T DO HUMAN TRANSMUTATION.
YOU'RE ABANDONING HER?
HOW HEARTLESS.
ME, HEARTLESS?
CONSIDERING THAT YOU'VE BEEN USING HUMAN BEINGS AS PAWNS IN YOUR EXPERIMENTS, I DON'T THINK YOU'RE IN A POSITION TO LECTURE ME ABOUT MORALITY.

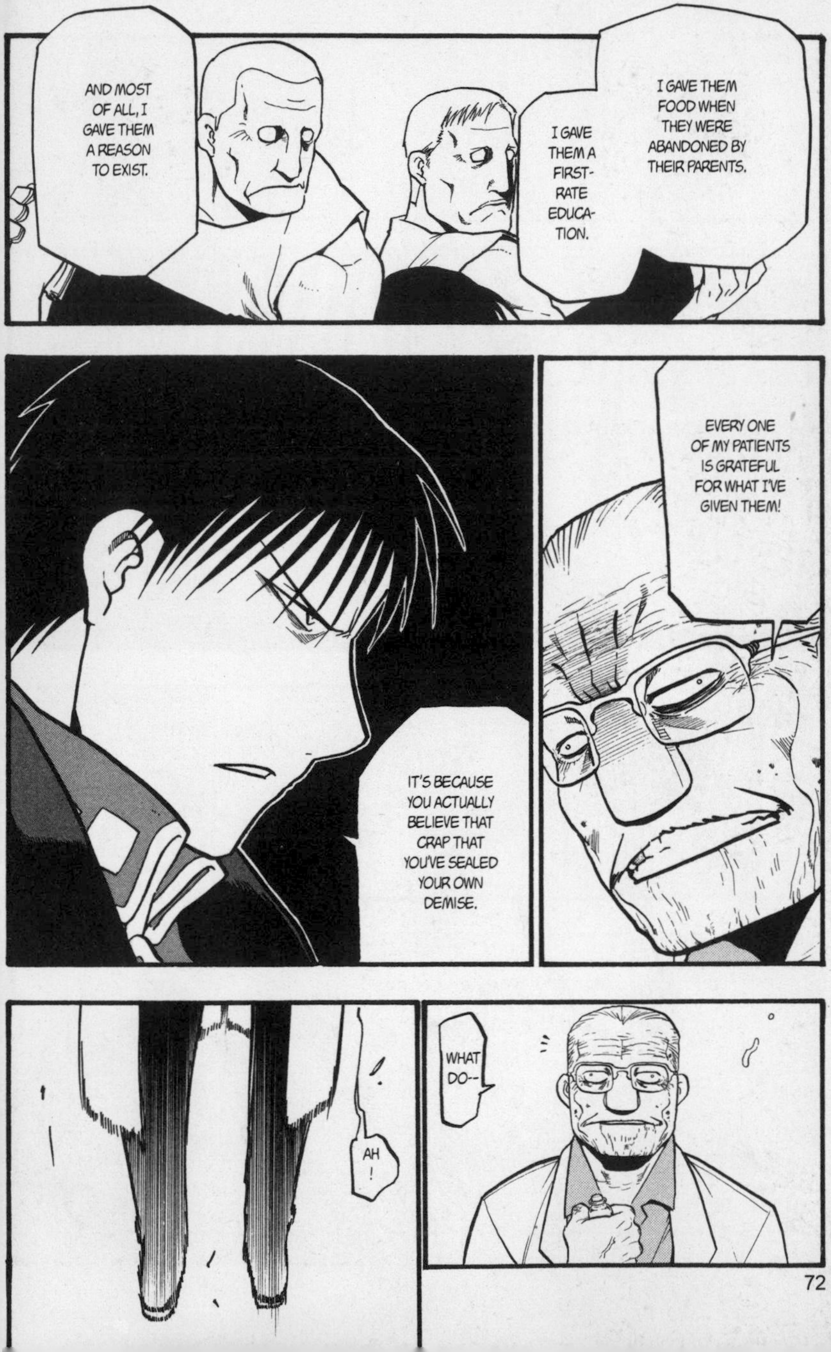
I GAVE THEM FOOD WHEN THEY WERE ABANDONED BY THEIR PARENTS.
I GAVE THEM A FIRST-RATE EDUCATION.
AND MOST OF ALL, I GAVE THEM A REASON TO EXIST.
EVERY ONE OF MY PATIENTS IS GRATEFUL FOR WHAT I'VE GIVEN THEM!
IT'S BECAUSE YOU ACTUALLY BELIEVE THAT CRAP THAT YOU'VE SEALED YOUR OWN DEMISE.
WHAT DO--
AH!

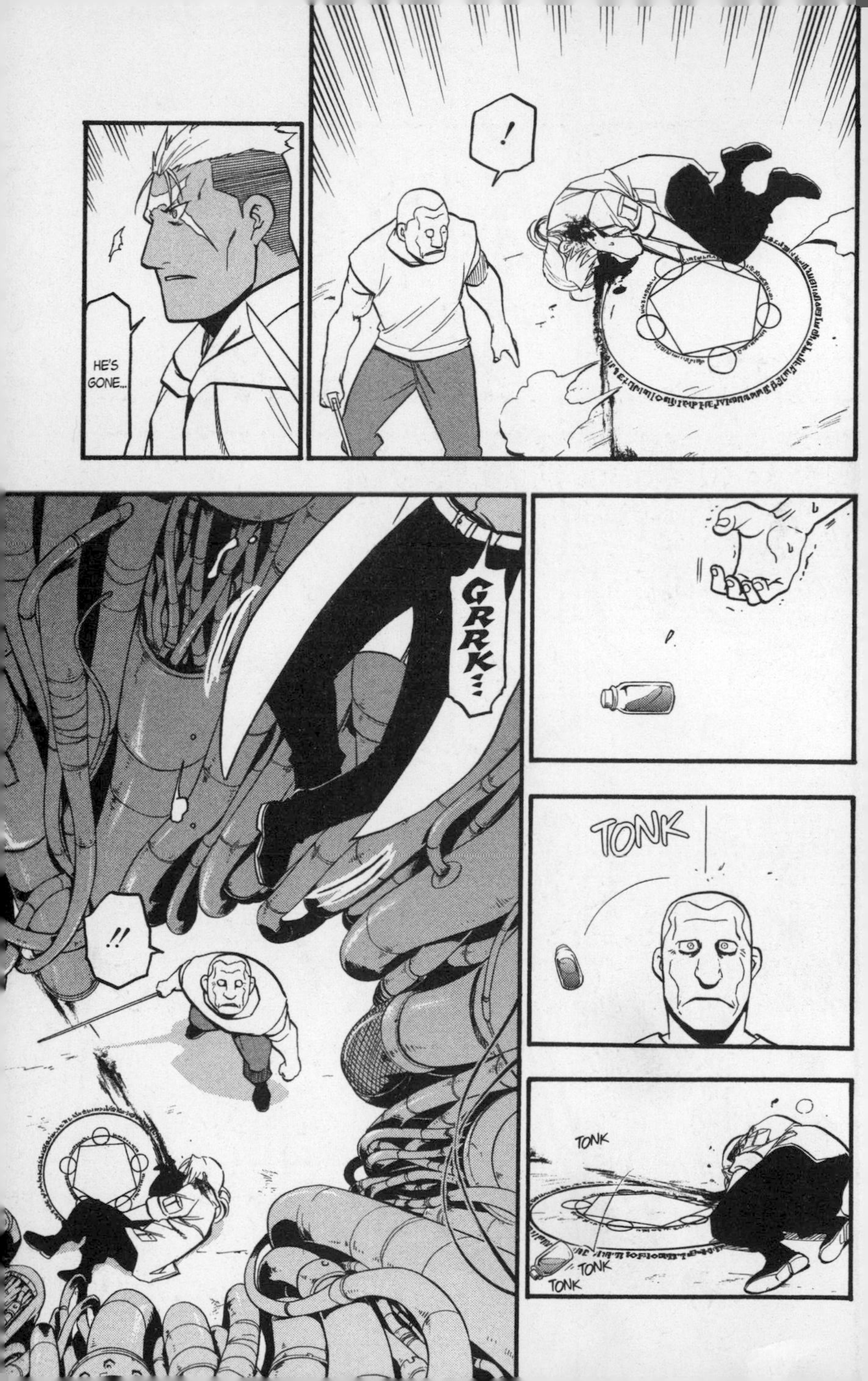
!
HE'S GONE...
TONK
TONK
TONK
TONK
GRRK!!
!!

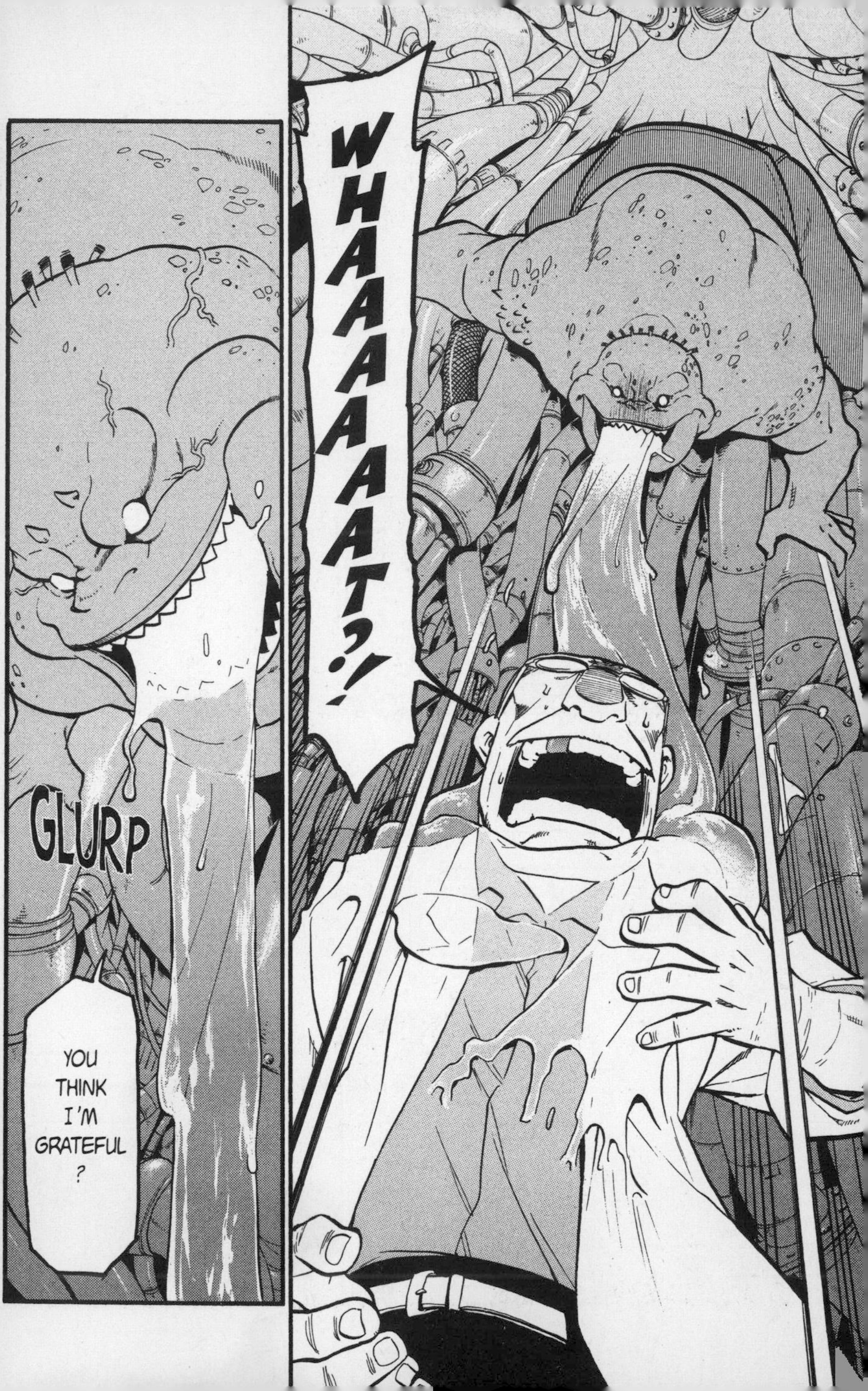
WHAAAAAAT?!
GLURP
YOU THINK I'M GRATEFUL?

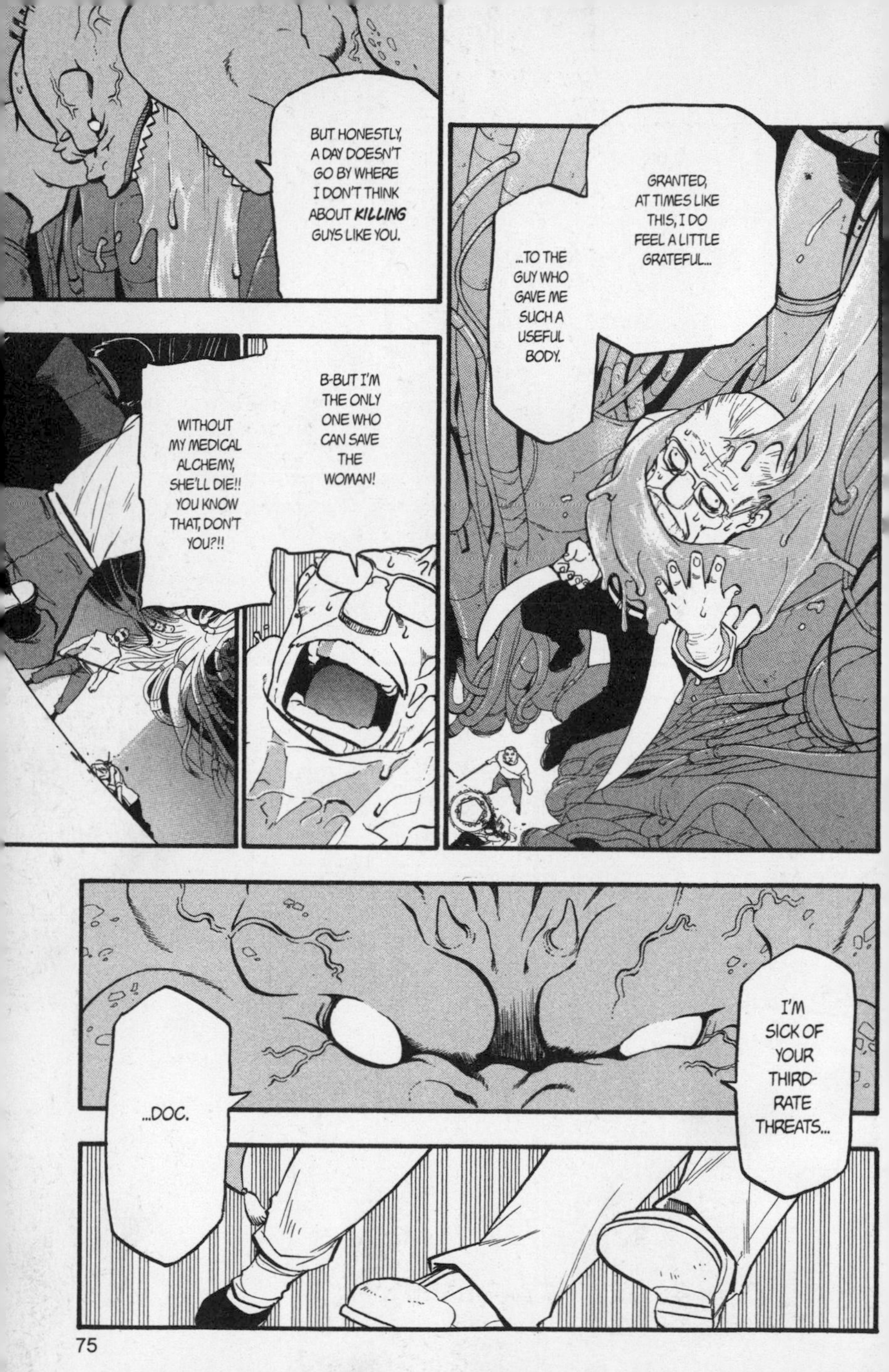
BUT HONESTLY, A DAY DOESN'T GO BY WHERE I DON'T THINK ABOUT **KILLING** GUYS LIKE YOU.
GRANTED, AT TIMES LIKE THIS, I DO FEEL A LITTLE GRATEFUL...
...TO THE GUY WHO GAVE ME SUCH A USEFUL BODY.
B-BUT I'M THE ONLY ONE WHO CAN SAVE THE WOMAN!
WITHOUT MY MEDICAL ALCHEMY, SHE'LL DIE!! YOU KNOW THAT, DON'T YOU?!!
I'M SICK OF YOUR THIRD-RATE THREATS...
...DOC.

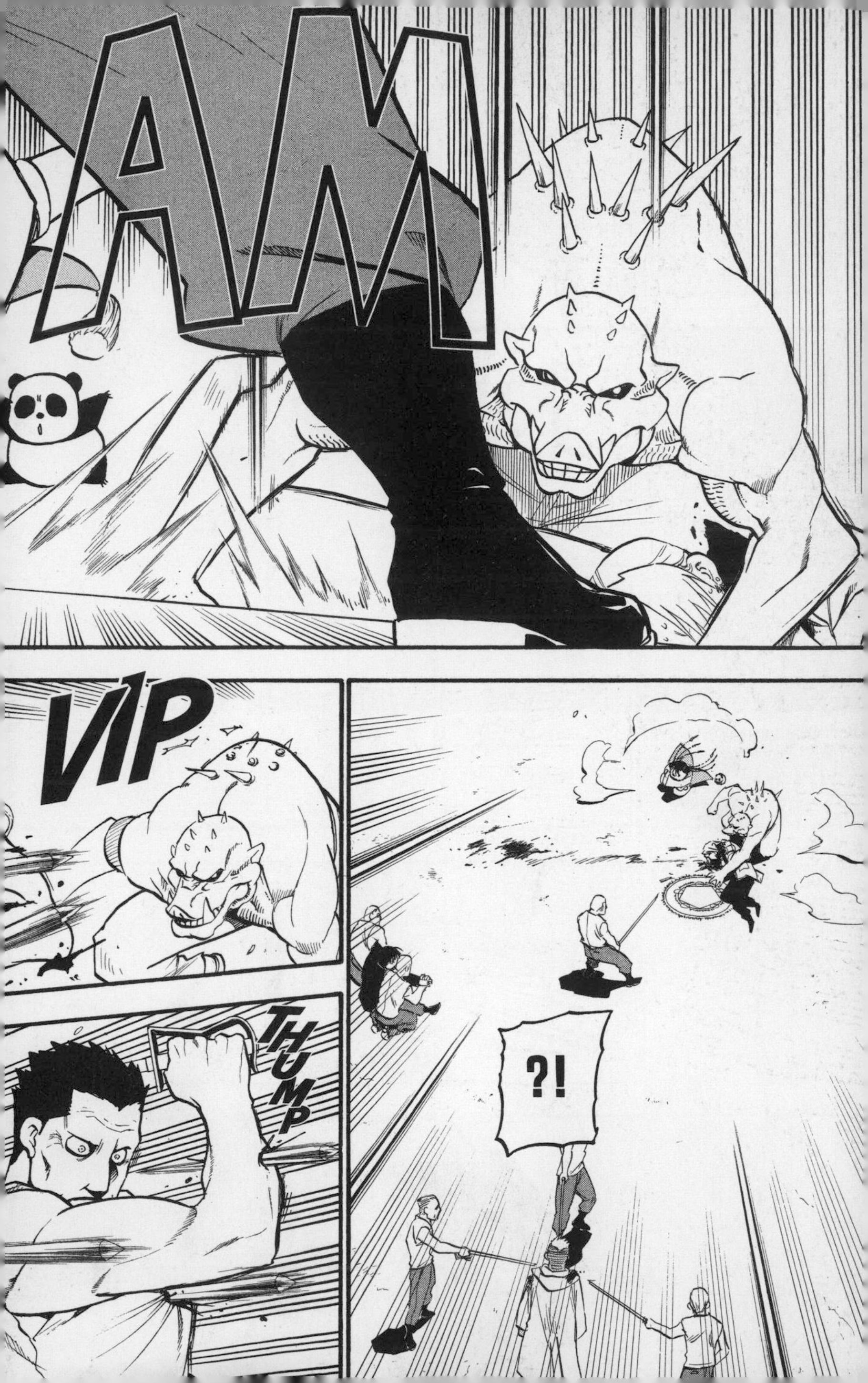

AAM
?!
VIP
THUMP

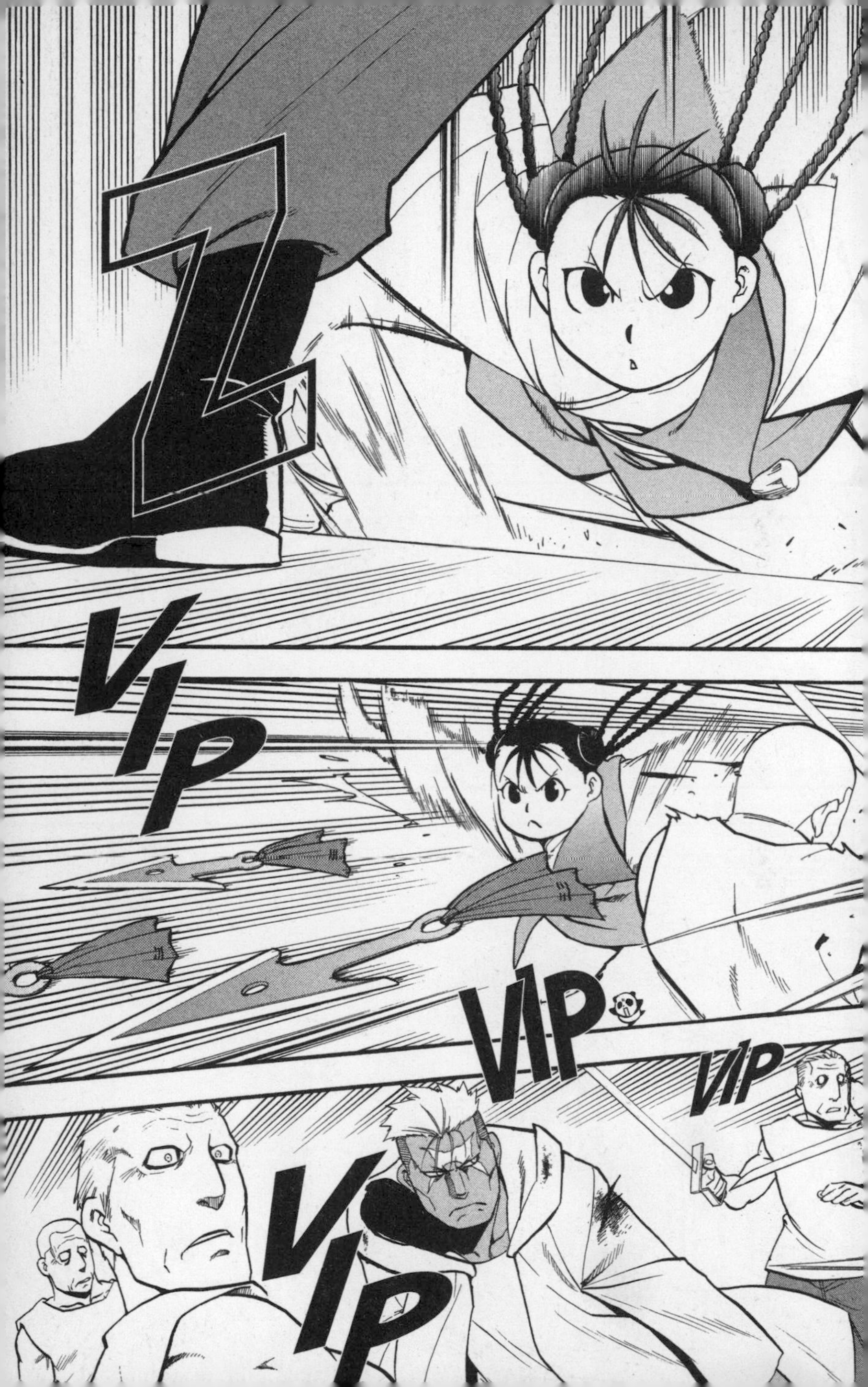
Z
VIP
VIP
VIP
VIP

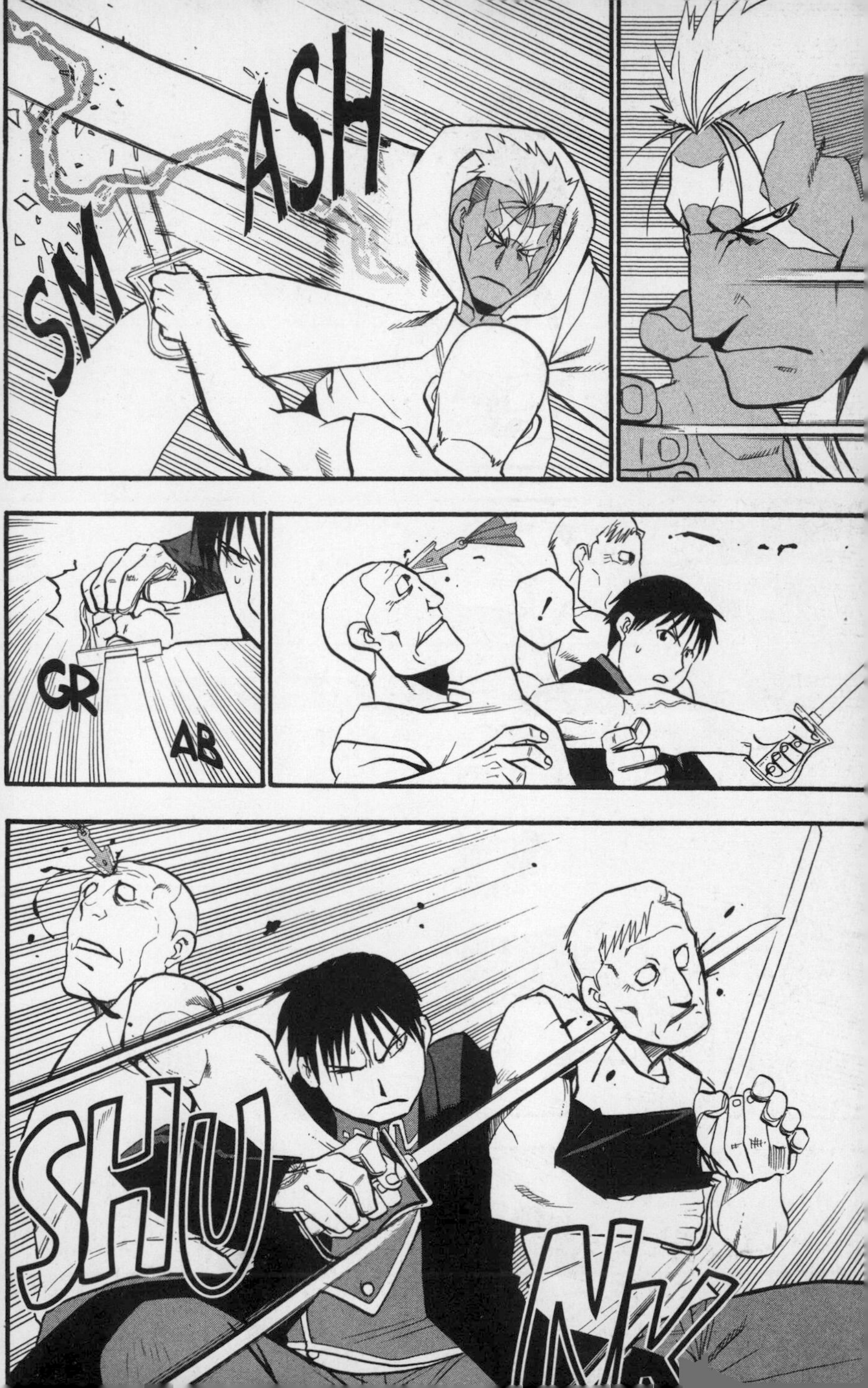
SMASH
!
GRAB
SHUNK

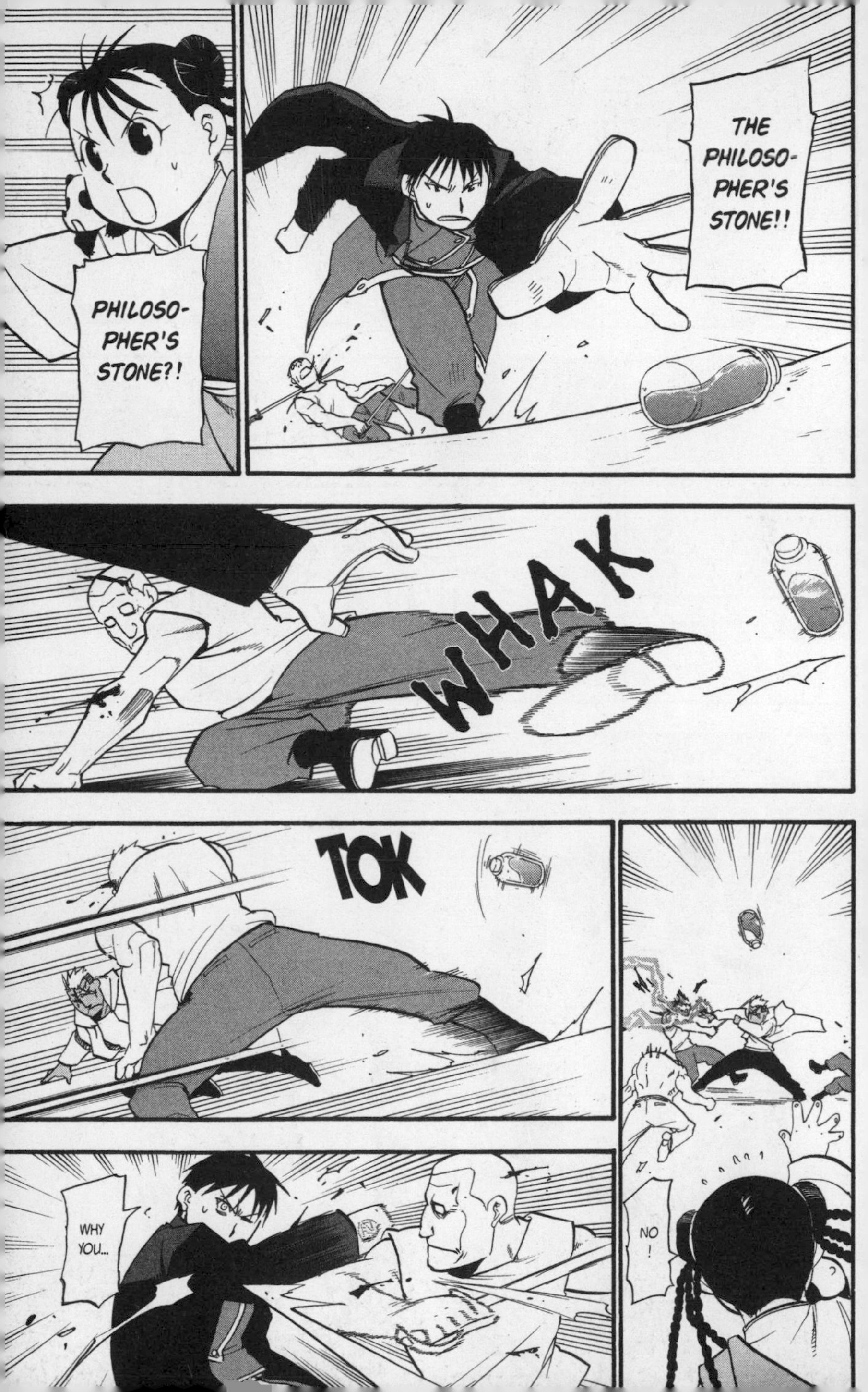
THE PHILOSOPHER'S STONE!!
PHILOSOPHER'S STONE?!
WHAK
NO!
TOK
WHY YOU...

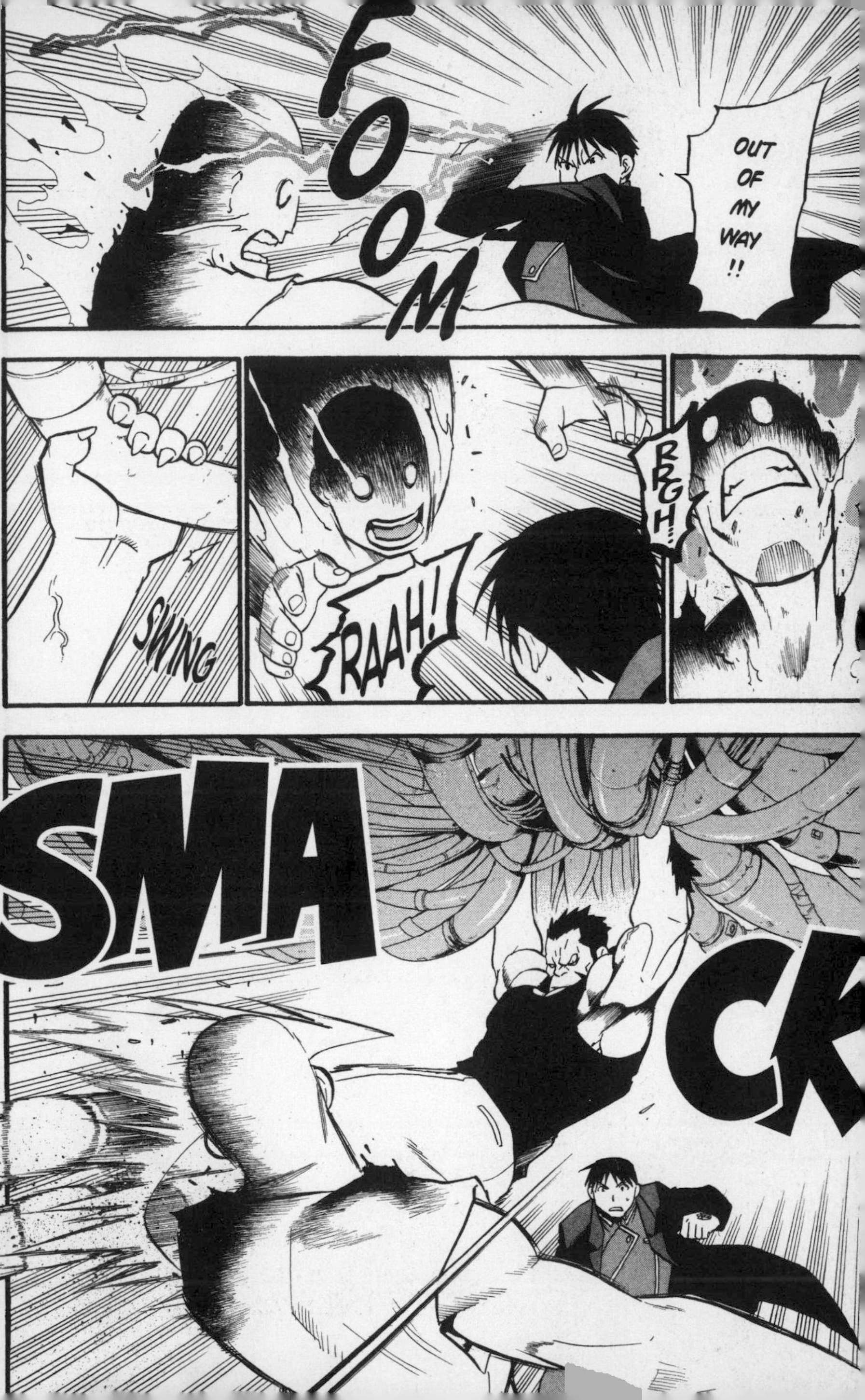
OUT OF MY WAY !!
FOOM
RRGH!!
RAAH!
SWING
SMACK

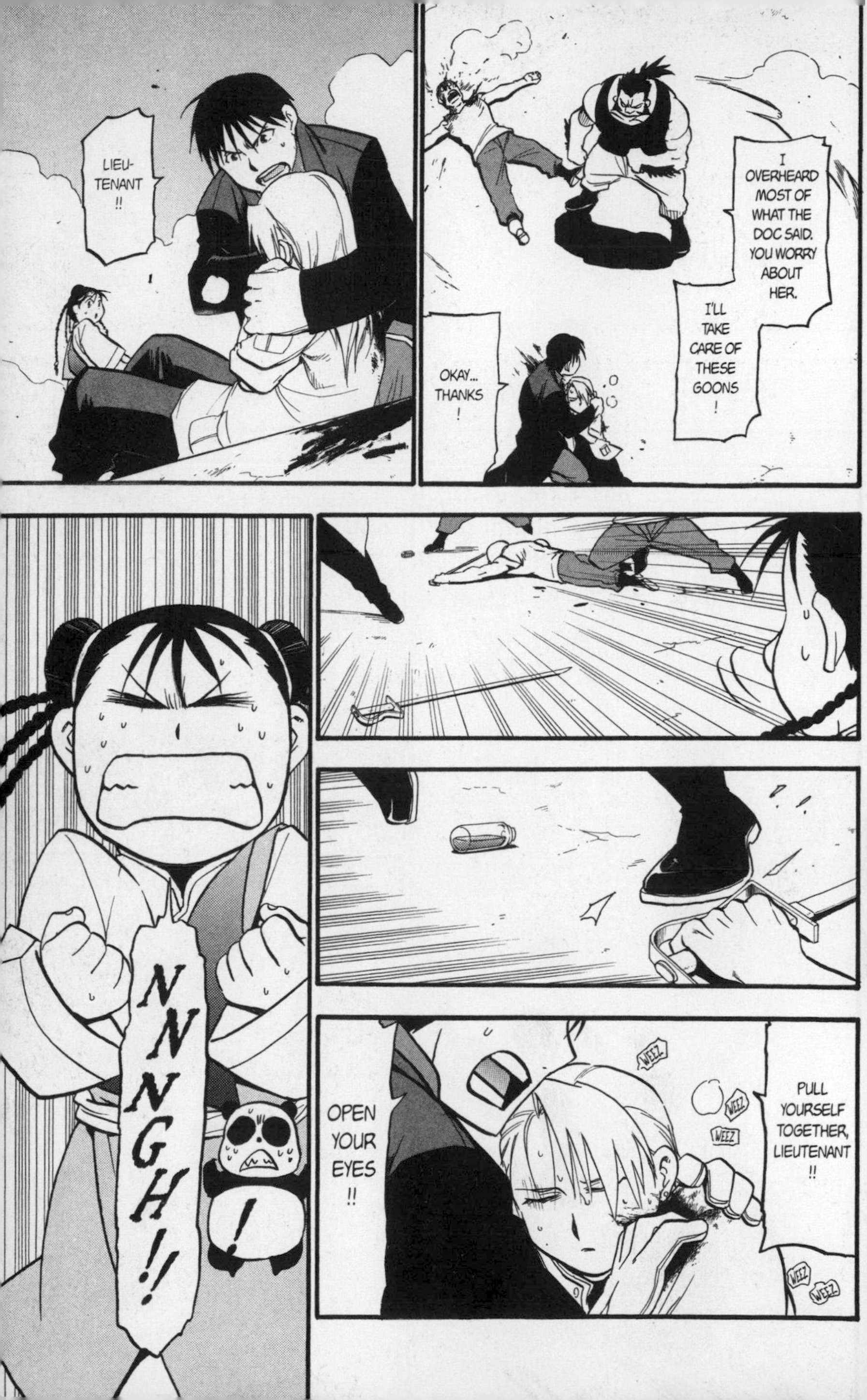
I OVERHEARD MOST OF WHAT THE DOC SAID. YOU WORRY ABOUT HER.
I'LL TAKE CARE OF THESE GOONS!
OKAY... THANKS!
LIEU-TENANT!!
PULL YOURSELF TOGETHER, LIEUTENANT!!
WEEZ
WEEZ
WEEZ
WEEZ
WEEZ
OPEN YOUR EYES!!
NNNGH!!!

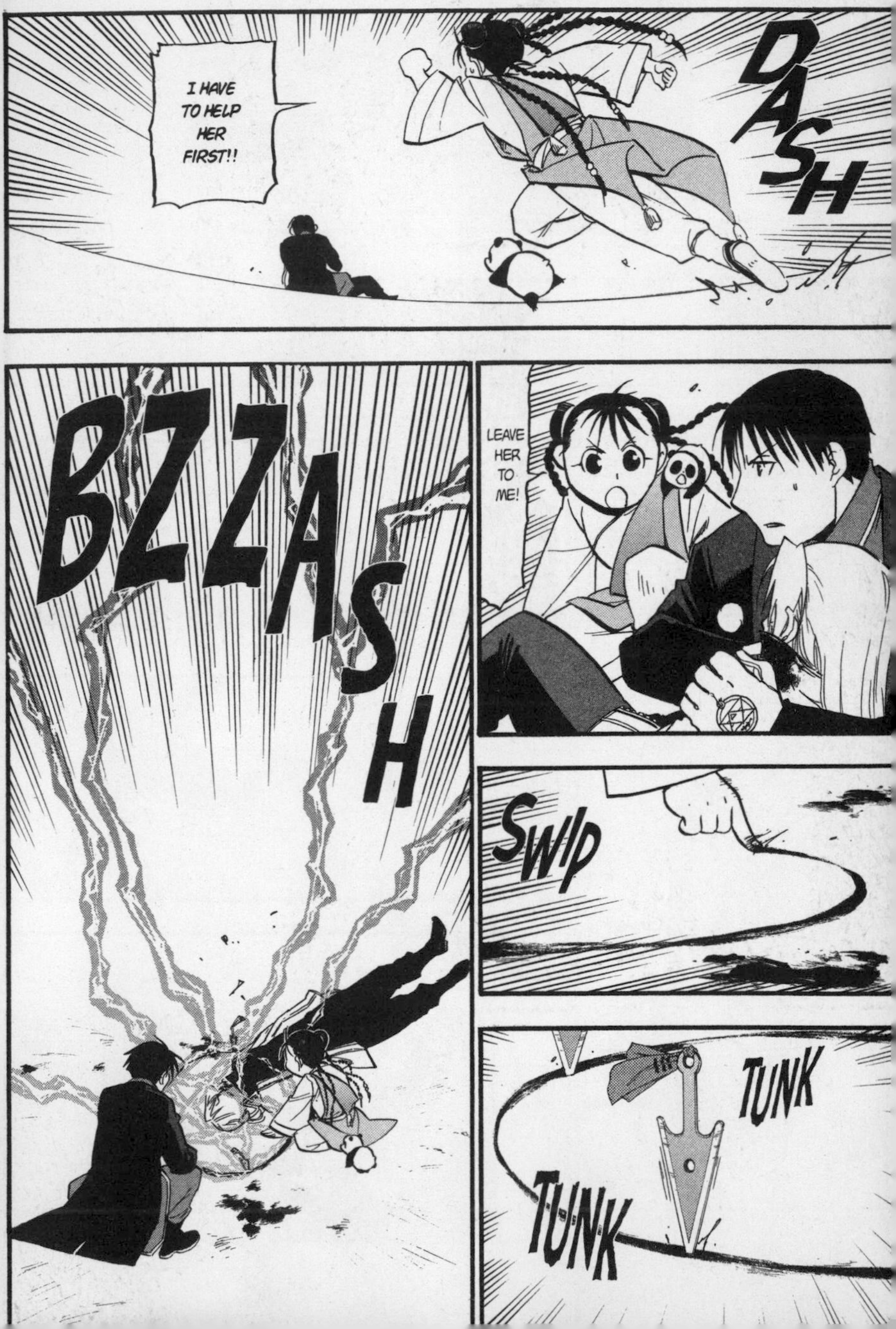
DASH
I HAVE TO HELP HER FIRST!!
LEAVE HER TO ME!
SWIP
TUNK
TUNK
BZZASH

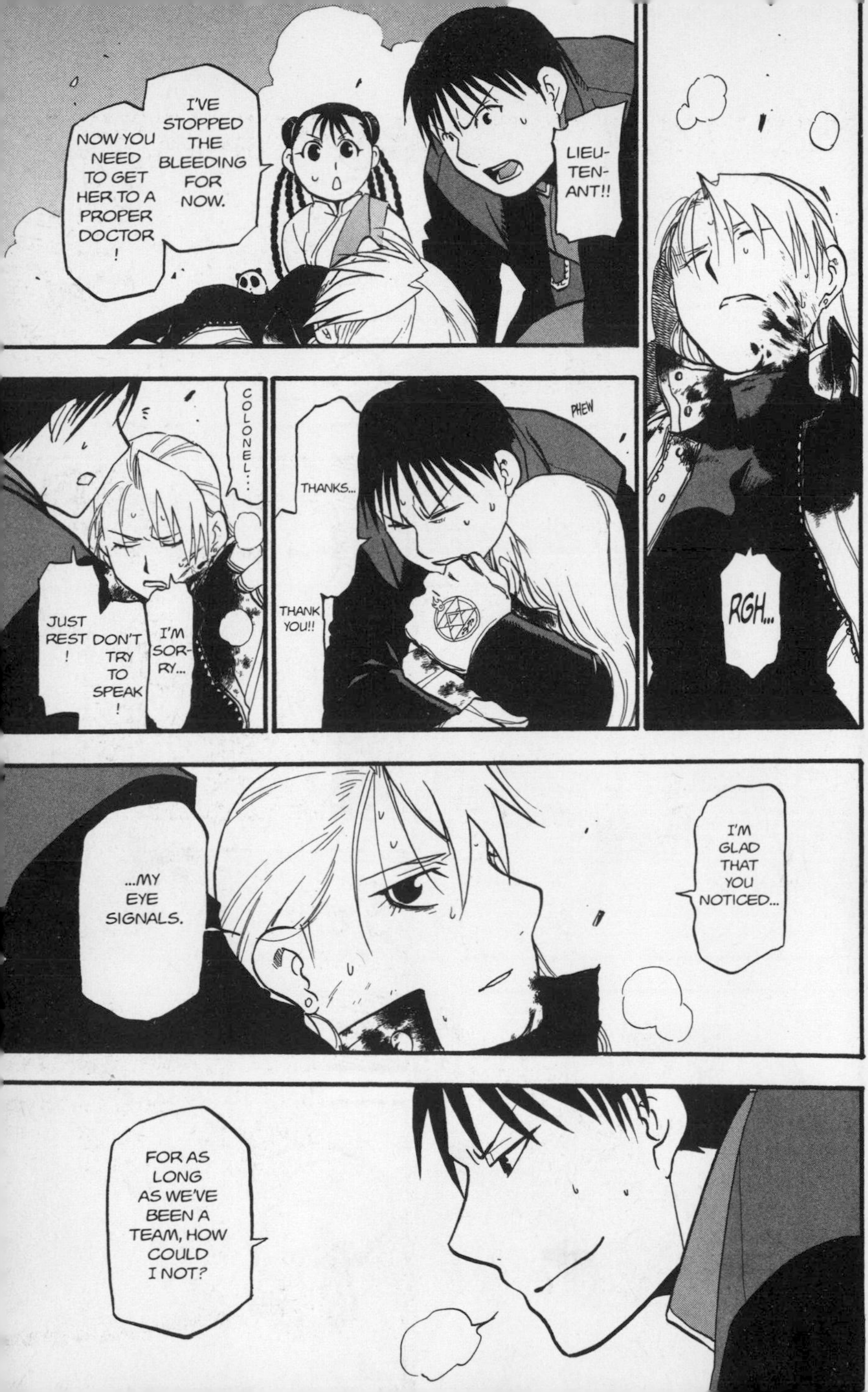
RGH...
LIEU-TEN-ANT!!
I'VE STOPPED THE BLEEDING FOR NOW.
NOW YOU NEED TO GET HER TO A PROPER DOCTOR!
PHEW
THANKS...
THANK YOU!!
COLONEL...
I'M SOR-RY...
DON'T TRY TO SPEAK!
JUST REST!
I'M GLAD THAT YOU NOTICED...
...MY EYE SIGNALS.
FOR AS LONG AS WE'VE BEEN A TEAM, HOW COULD I NOT?

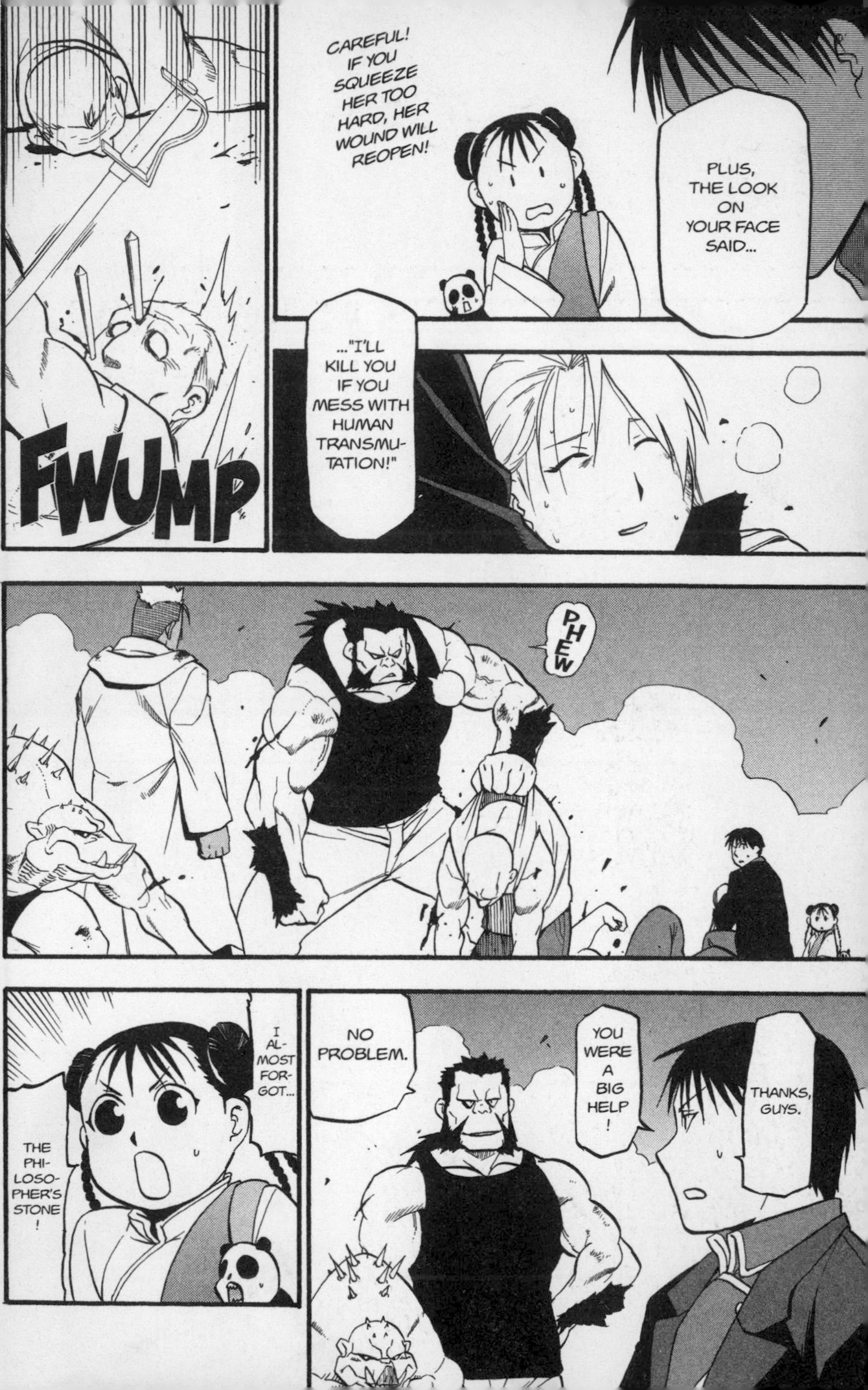
PLUS, THE LOOK ON YOUR FACE SAID...
CAREFUL! IF YOU SQUEEZE HER TOO HARD, HER WOUND WILL REOPEN!
..."I'LL KILL YOU IF YOU MESS WITH HUMAN TRANSMUTATION!"
FWUMP
PHEW
THANKS, GUYS.
YOU WERE A BIG HELP!
NO PROBLEM.
I ALMOST FORGOT...
THE PHILOSOPHER'S STONE!

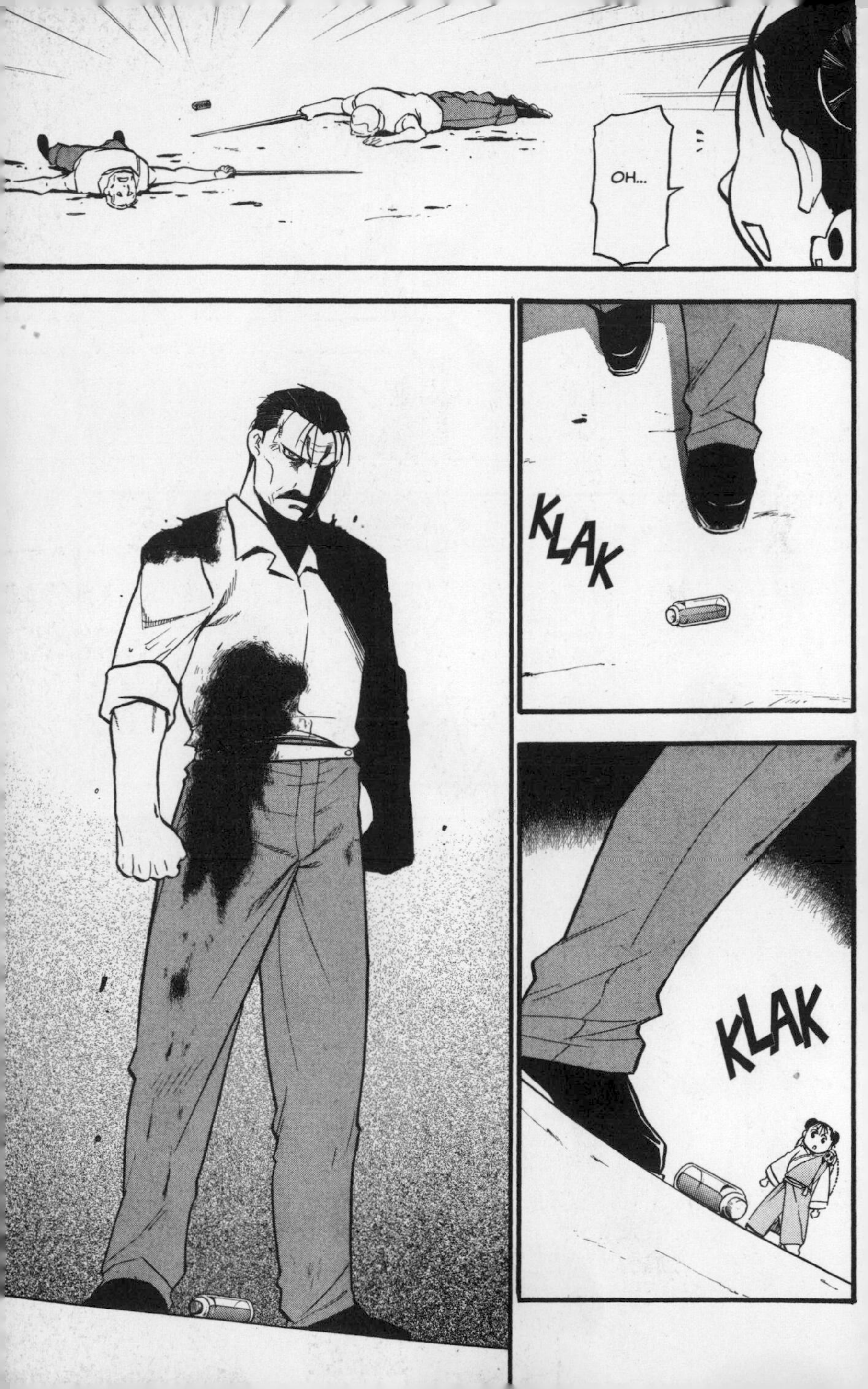
OH...
KLAK
KLAK

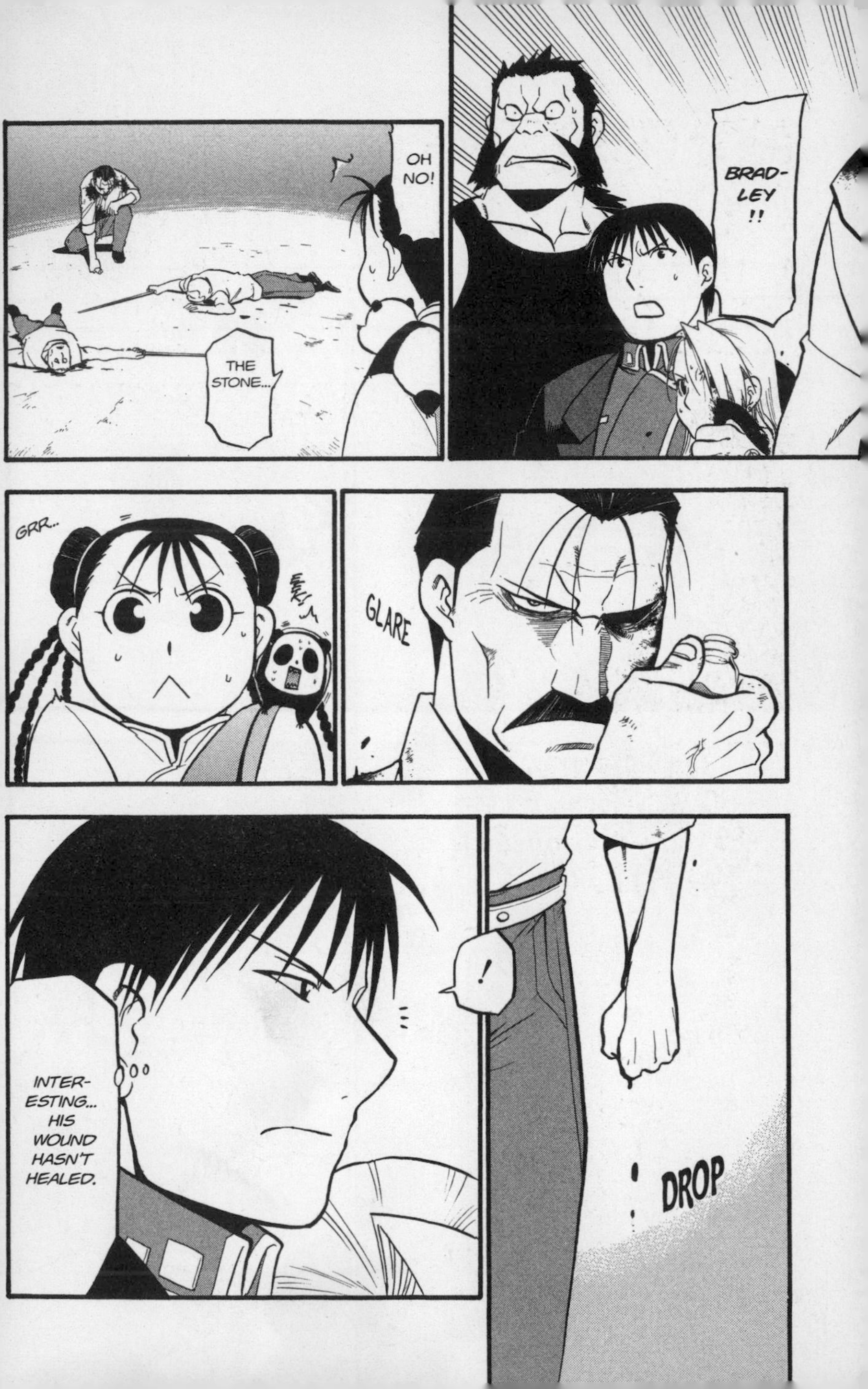
BRAD-LEY!!
OH NO!
THE STONE...
GLARE
GRR...
DROP
!
INTER-ESTING... HIS WOUND HASN'T HEALED.

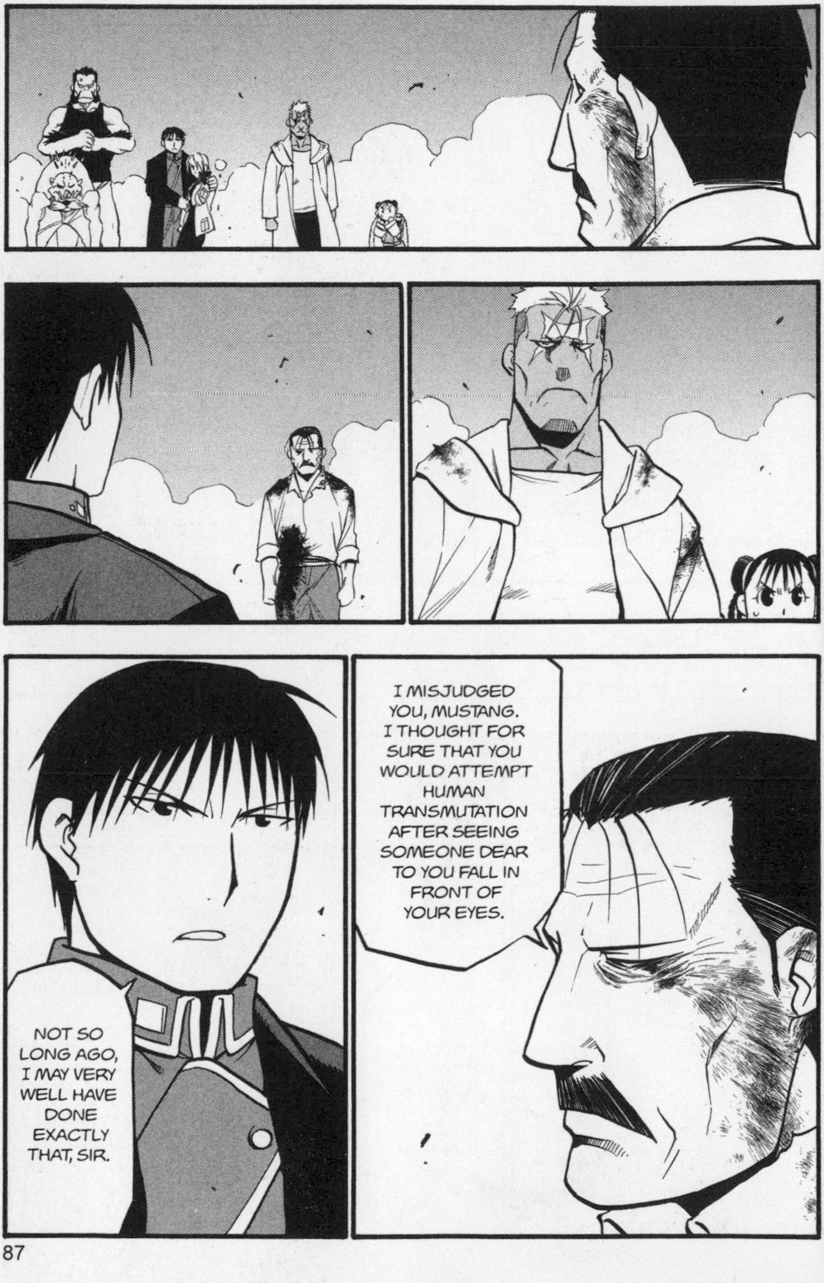
I MISJUDGED YOU, MUSTANG. I THOUGHT FOR SURE THAT YOU WOULD ATTEMPT HUMAN TRANSMUTATION AFTER SEEING SOMEONE DEAR TO YOU FALL IN FRONT OF YOUR EYES.
NOT SO LONG AGO, I MAY VERY WELL HAVE DONE EXACTLY THAT, SIR.

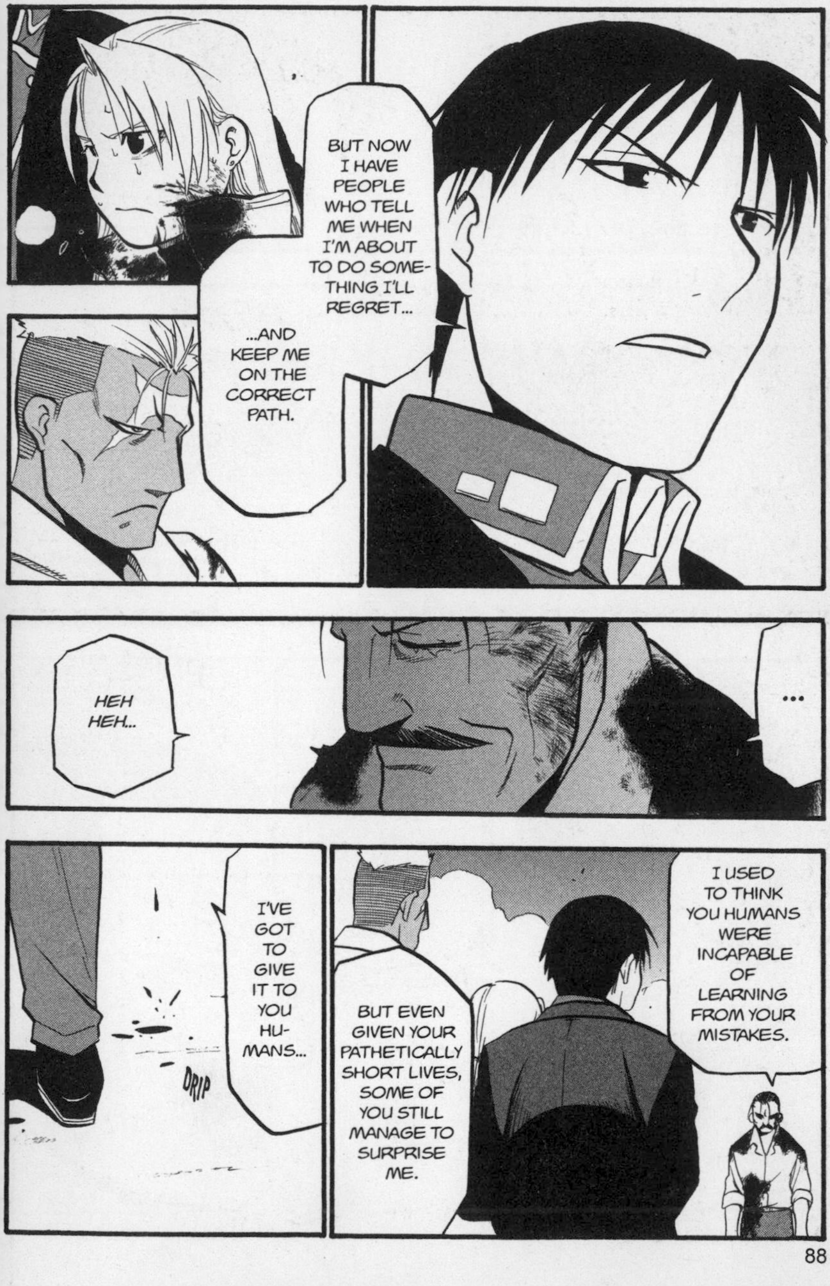
BUT NOW I HAVE PEOPLE WHO TELL ME WHEN I'M ABOUT TO DO SOMETHING I'LL REGRET...
...AND KEEP ME ON THE CORRECT PATH.
...
HEH HEH...
I USED TO THINK YOU HUMANS WERE INCAPABLE OF LEARNING FROM YOUR MISTAKES.
BUT EVEN GIVEN YOUR PATHETICALLY SHORT LIVES, SOME OF YOU STILL MANAGE TO SURPRISE ME.
I'VE GOT TO GIVE IT TO YOU HUMANS...
DRIP

YOUR REFUSAL TO BEHAVE AS EXPECTED IS REALLY UPSETTING.

WHAT'S WRONG?

...

IT'S COMING FROM DIRECTLY BENEATH US!

I FEEL IT...

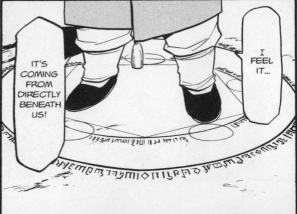

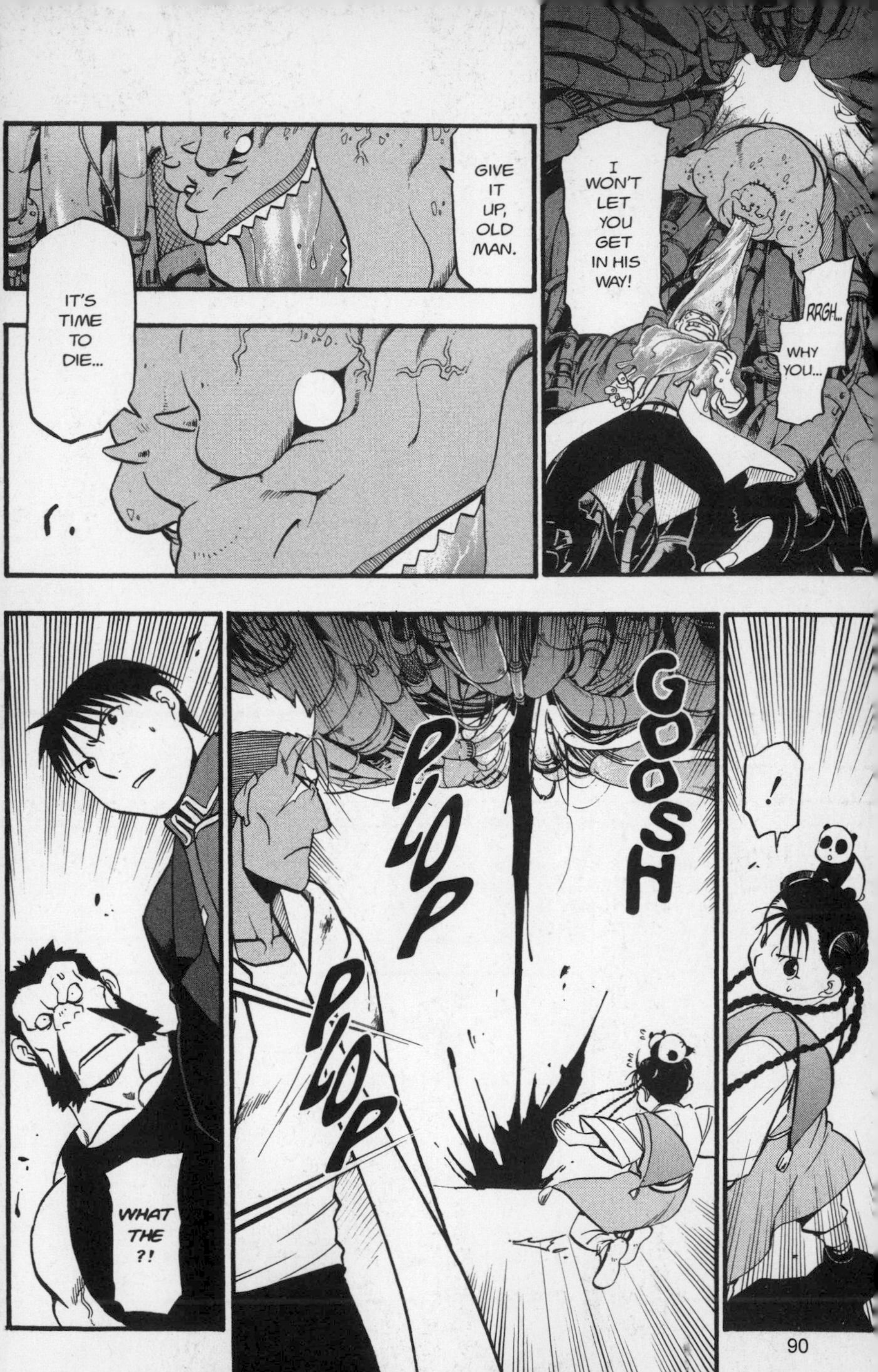
I WON'T LET YOU GET IN HIS WAY!
RRGH...
WHY YOU...
GIVE IT UP, OLD MAN.
IT'S TIME TO DIE...
!
GOOSH
PLOP
PLOP
WHAT THE ?!

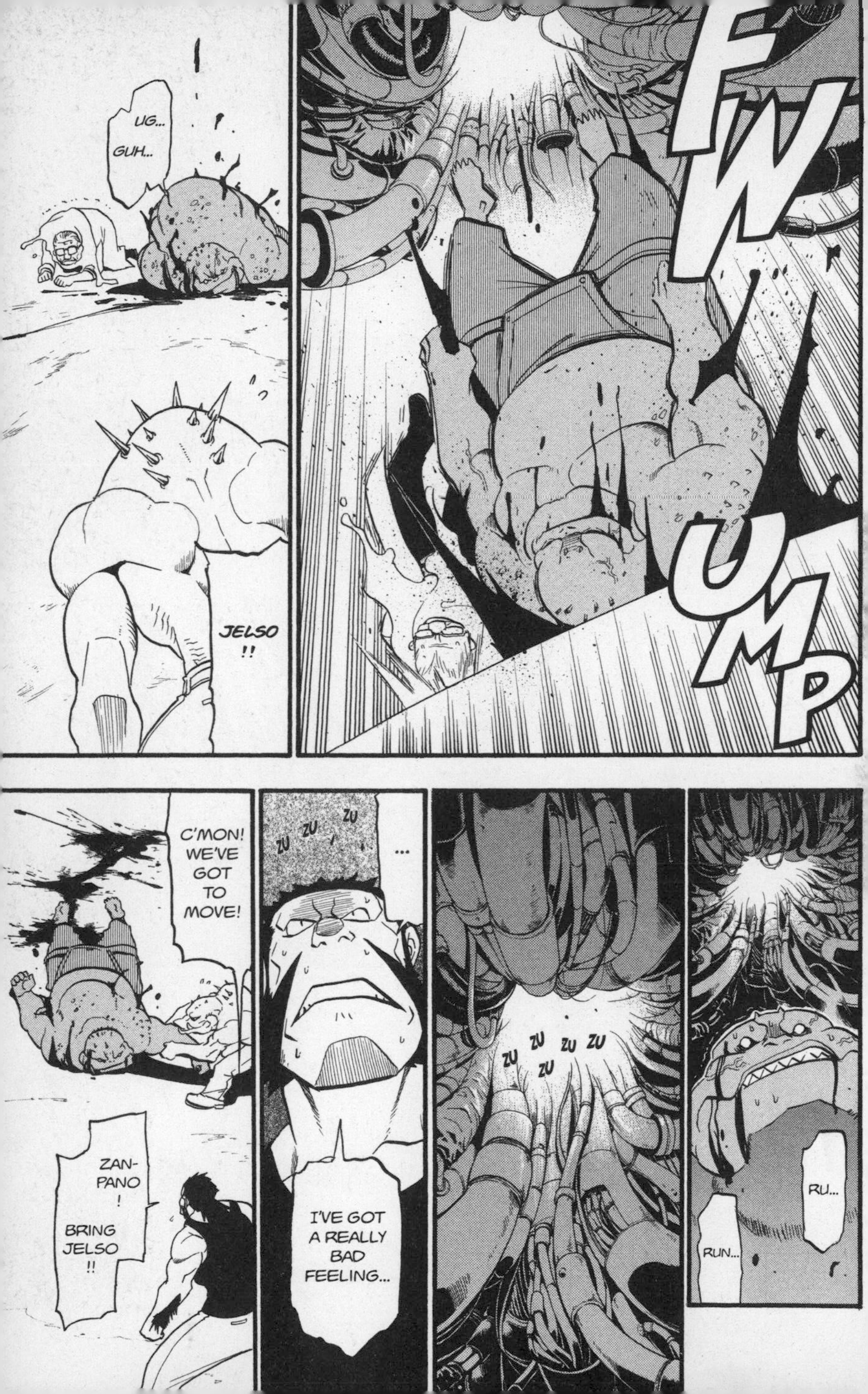
FWUMP
UG... GUH...
JELSO !!
RU...
RUN...
ZU ZU ZU ZU ZU
ZU ZU ZU
...
I'VE GOT A REALLY BAD FEELING...
C'MON! WE'VE GOT TO MOVE!
ZAN-PANO! BRING JELSO !!

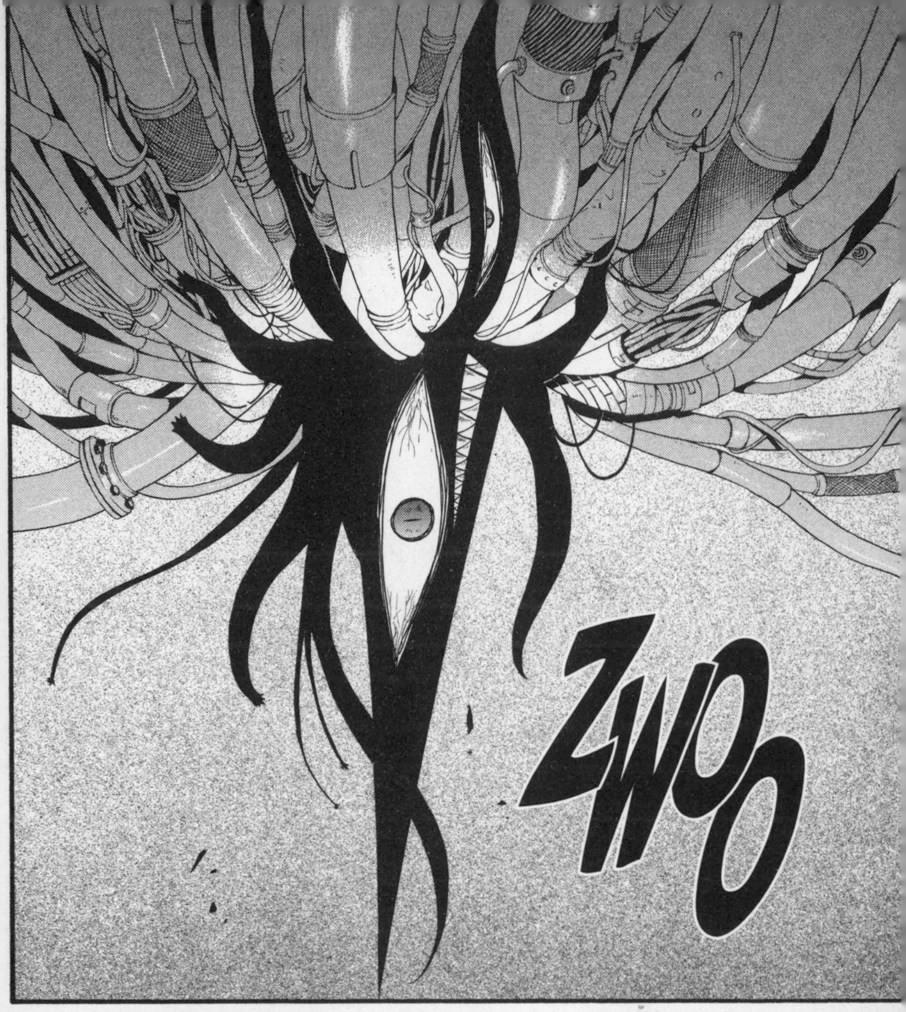
ZWOO

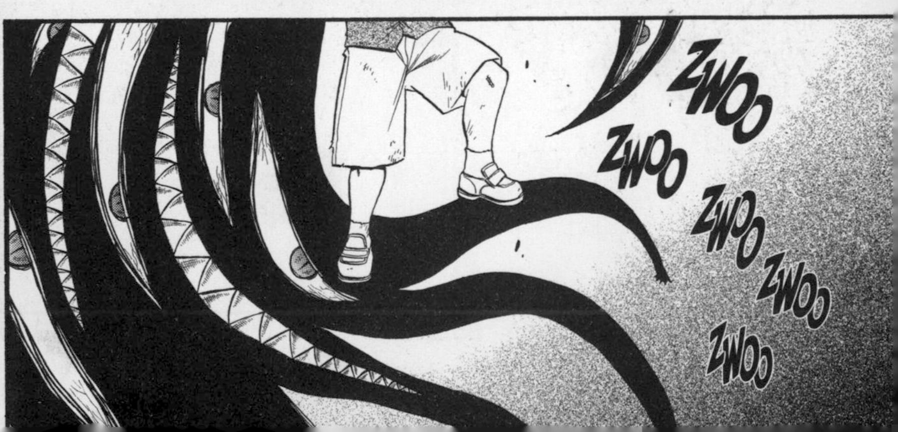
ZWOO
ZWOO
ZWOO
ZWOO
ZWOO

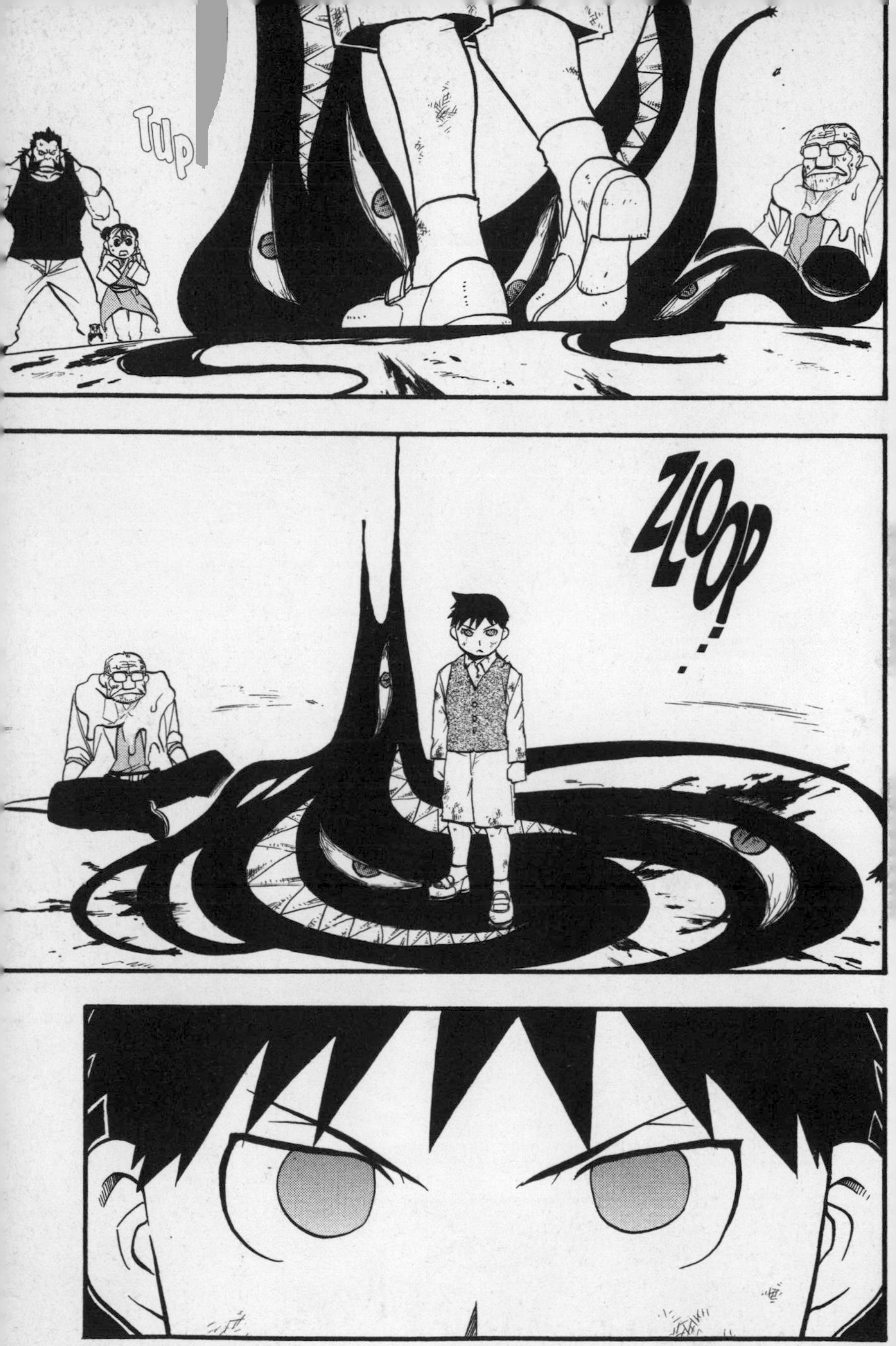
TUP
ZLOOP

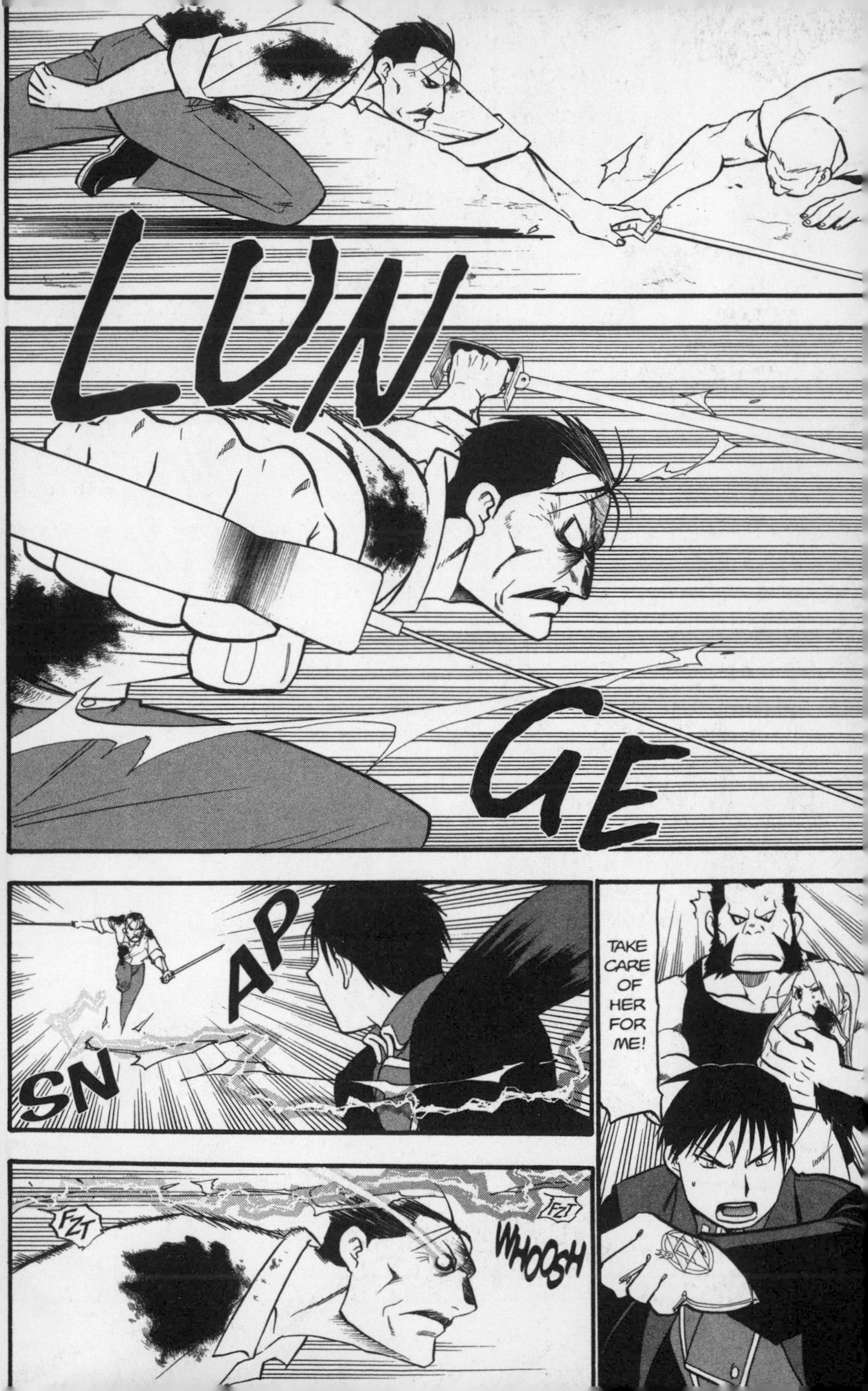
LUNGE
TAKE CARE OF HER FOR ME!
SNAP
FZT
WHOOSH
FZT

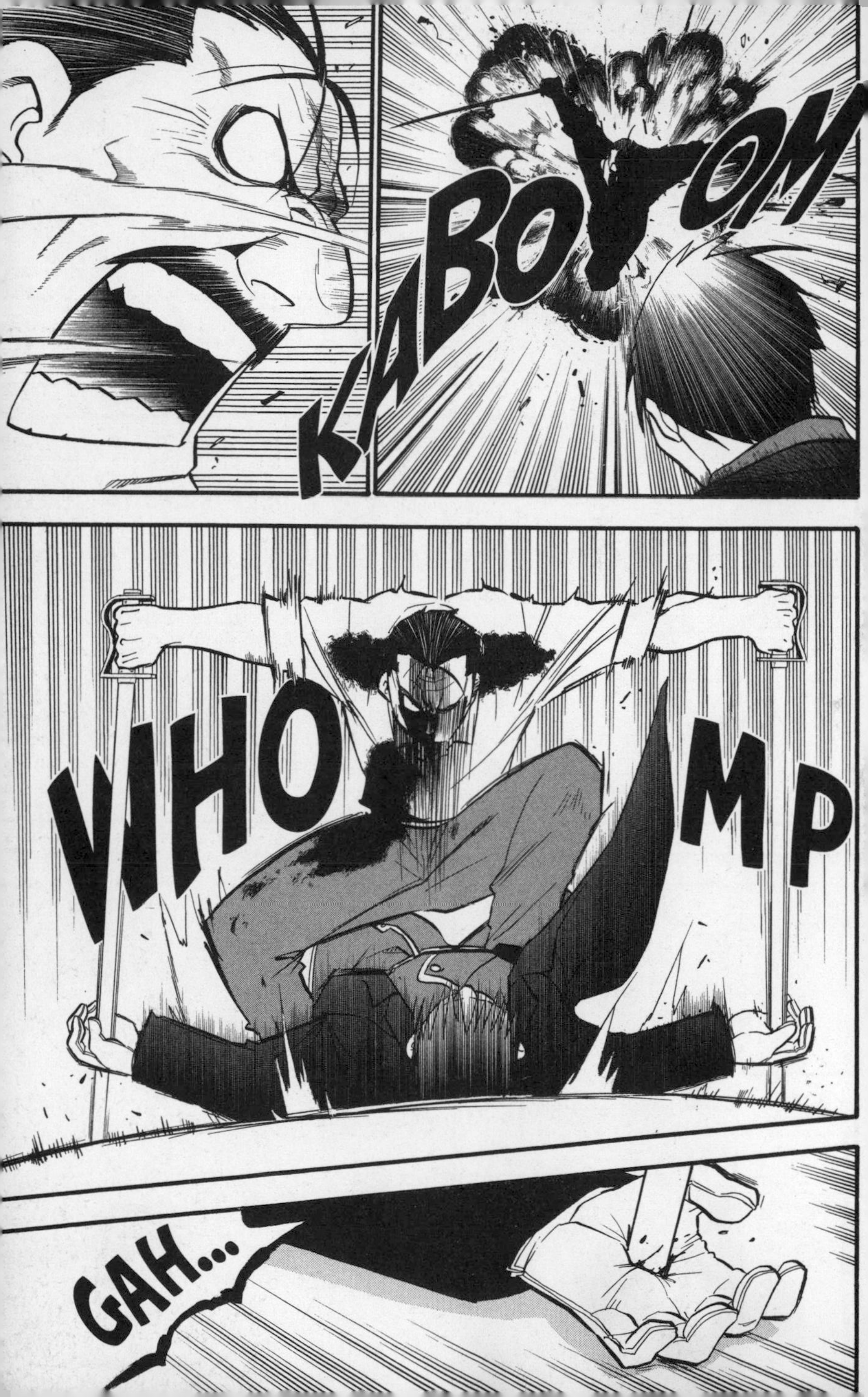
KABOOM
WHOMP
GAH...

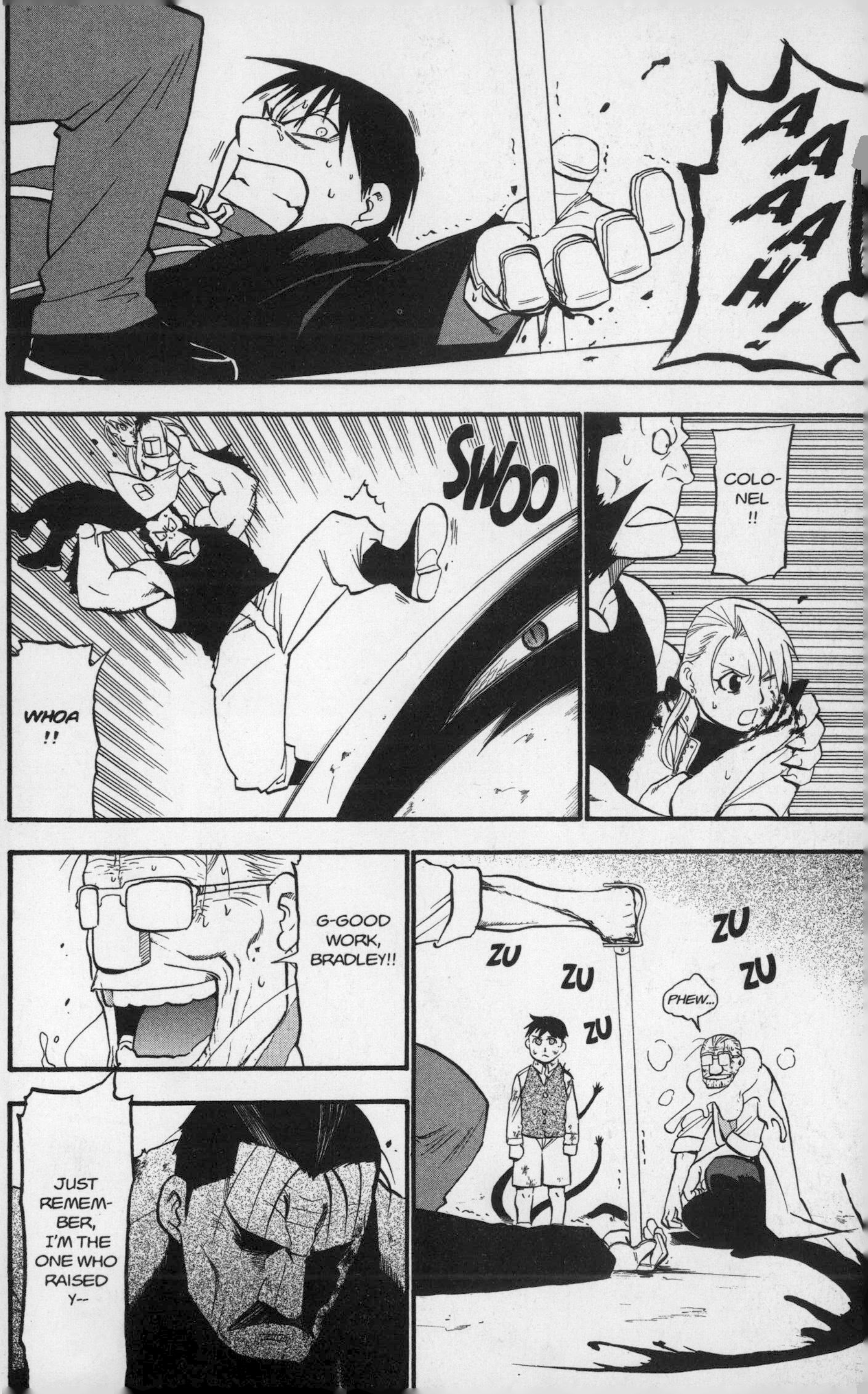
AAAAH!!
COLO-NEL!!
SWOO
WHOA!!
ZU
ZU
ZU
ZU
ZU
PHEW...
G-GOOD WORK, BRADLEY!!
JUST REMEM-BER, I'M THE ONE WHO RAISED Y--

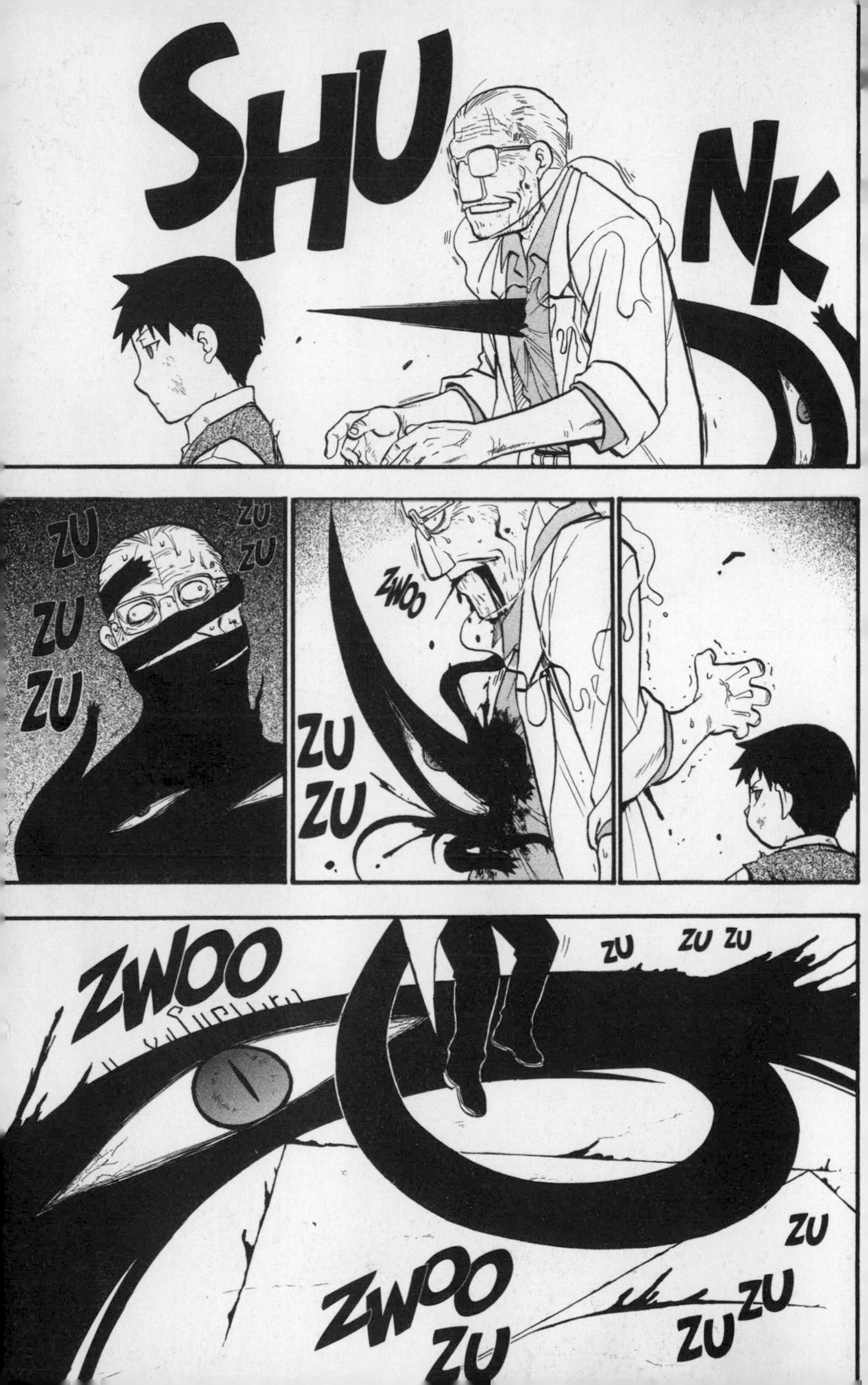
SHUNK
ZWOO
ZU ZU
ZU ZU
ZU
ZU ZU ZU
ZU ZU
ZU
ZWOO
ZU
ZU ZU
ZWOO ZU

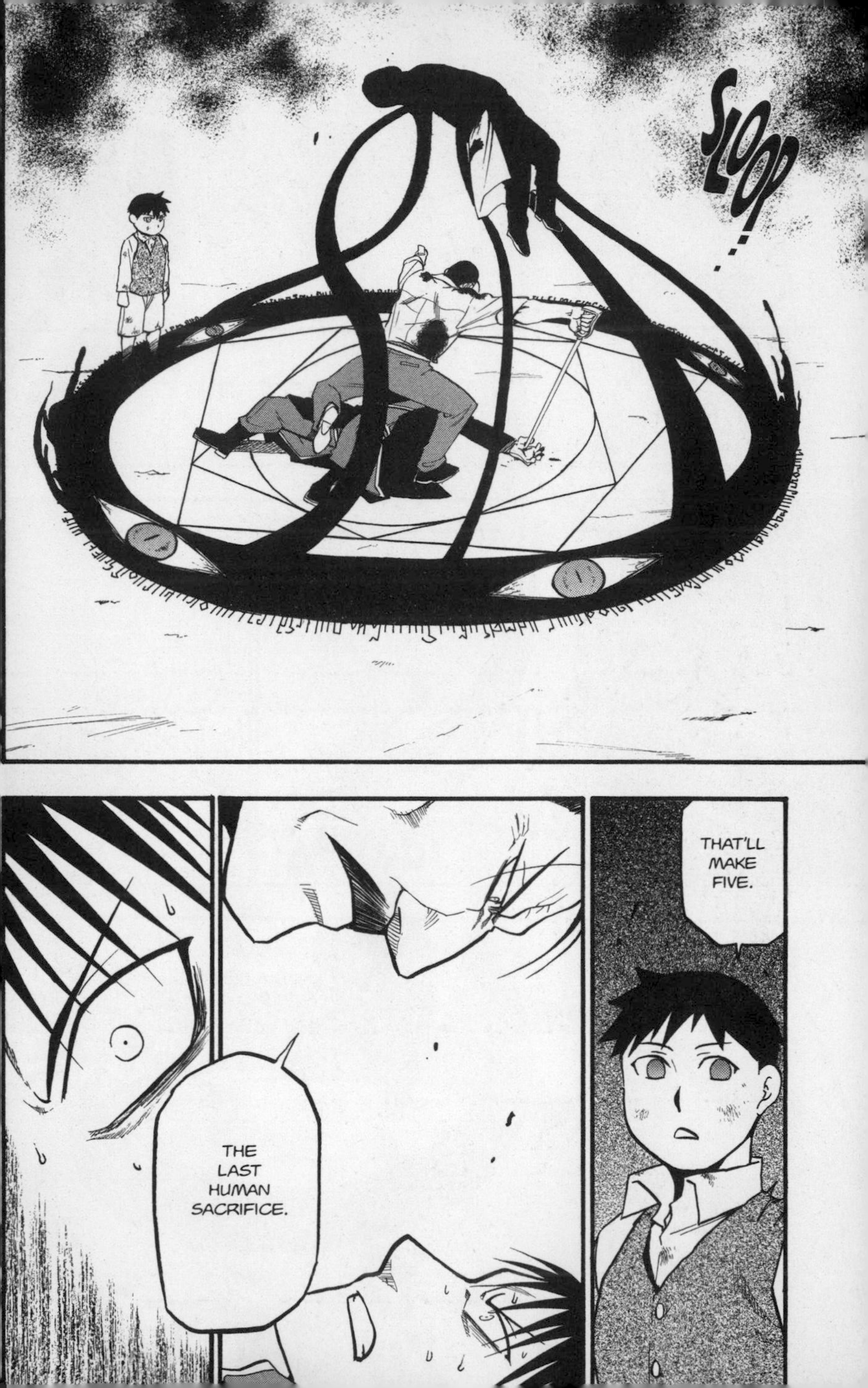
SLOOP...
THAT'LL MAKE FIVE.
THE LAST HUMAN SACRIFICE.

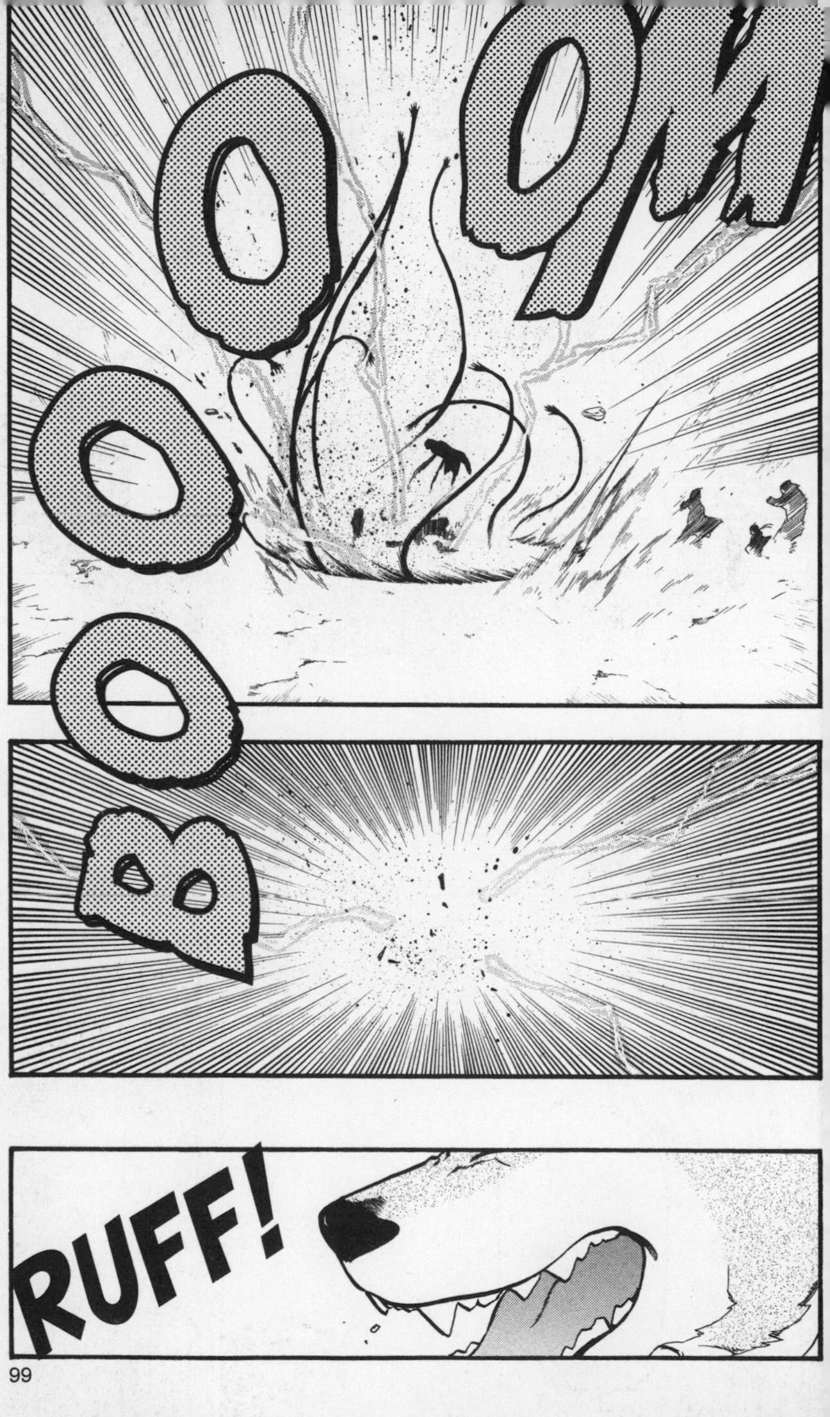
BOOOOM
RUFF!

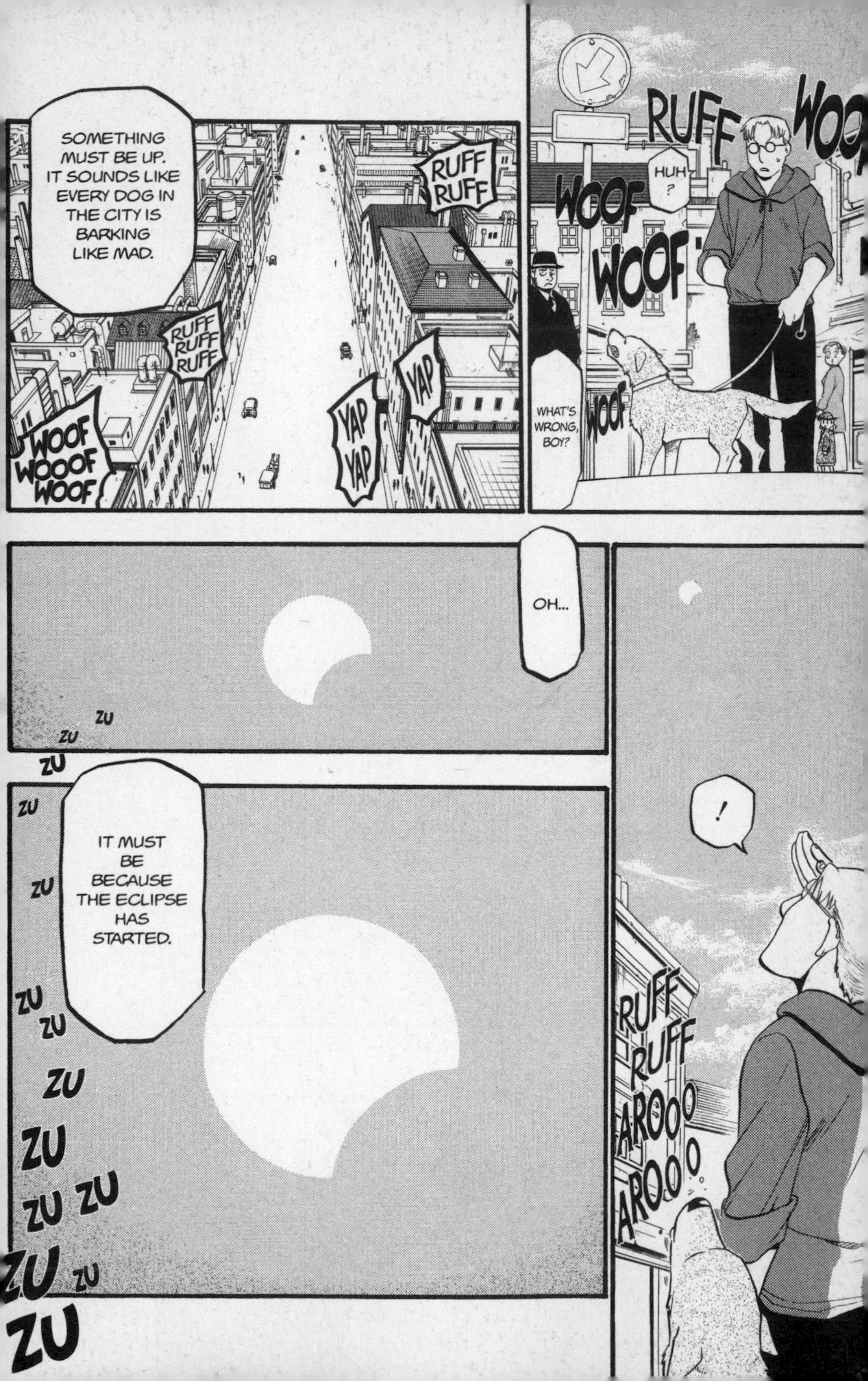
RUFF
WOO
HUH?
WOOF
WOOF
WOOF
WHAT'S WRONG, BOY?
SOMETHING MUST BE UP. IT SOUNDS LIKE EVERY DOG IN THE CITY IS BARKING LIKE MAD.
RUFF RUFF
RUFF RUFF RUFF
YAP
YAP YAP
WOOF WOOOF WOOF
OH...
!
RUFF RUFF AROOO AROOO
ZU ZU ZU
IT MUST BE BECAUSE THE ECLIPSE HAS STARTED.
ZU ZU ZU ZU ZU ZU ZU ZU ZU ZU ZU

**FULLMETAL
ALCHEMIST**

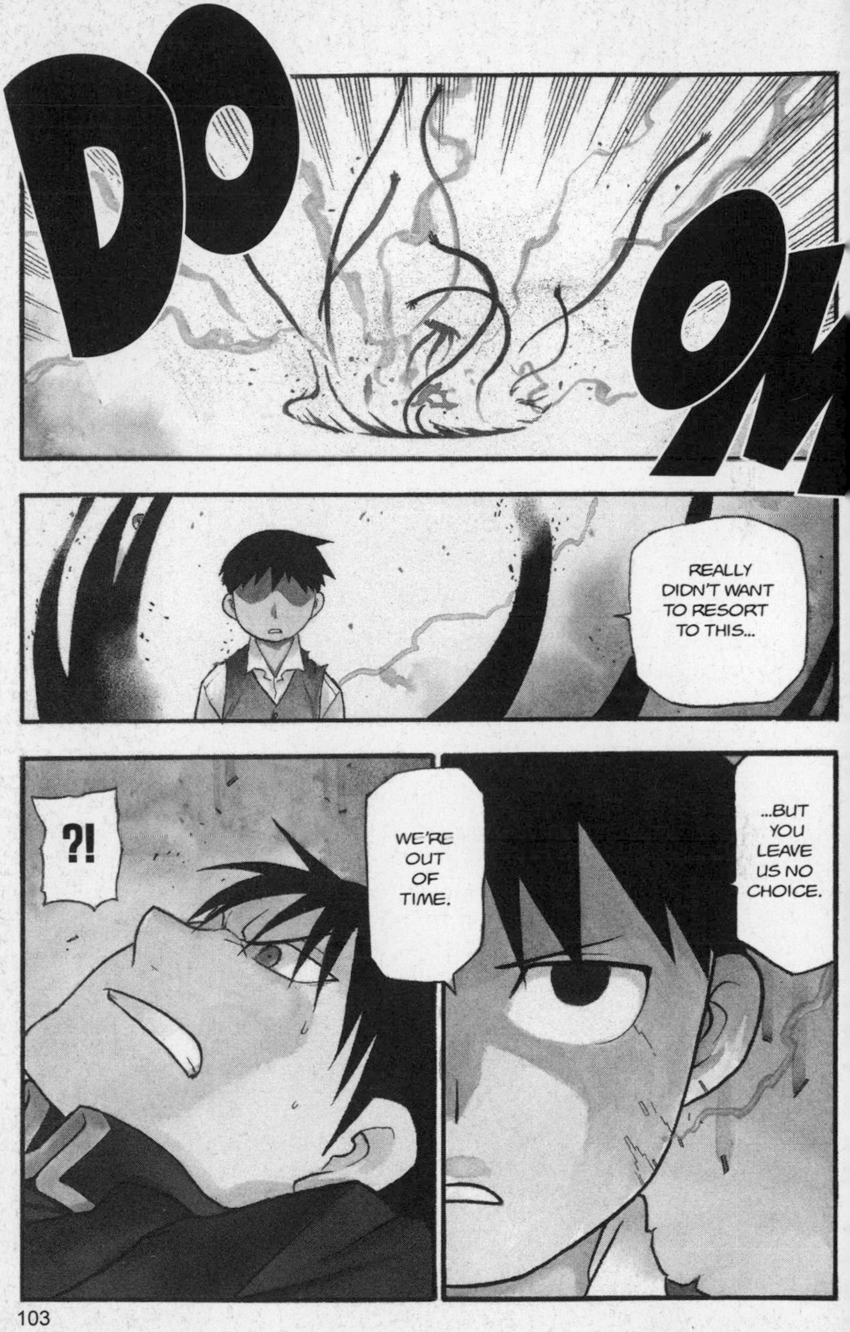
DOOOM
REALLY DIDN'T WANT TO RESORT TO THIS...
...BUT YOU LEAVE US NO CHOICE.
WE'RE OUT OF TIME.
?!

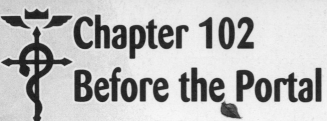

Chapter 102
Before the Portal

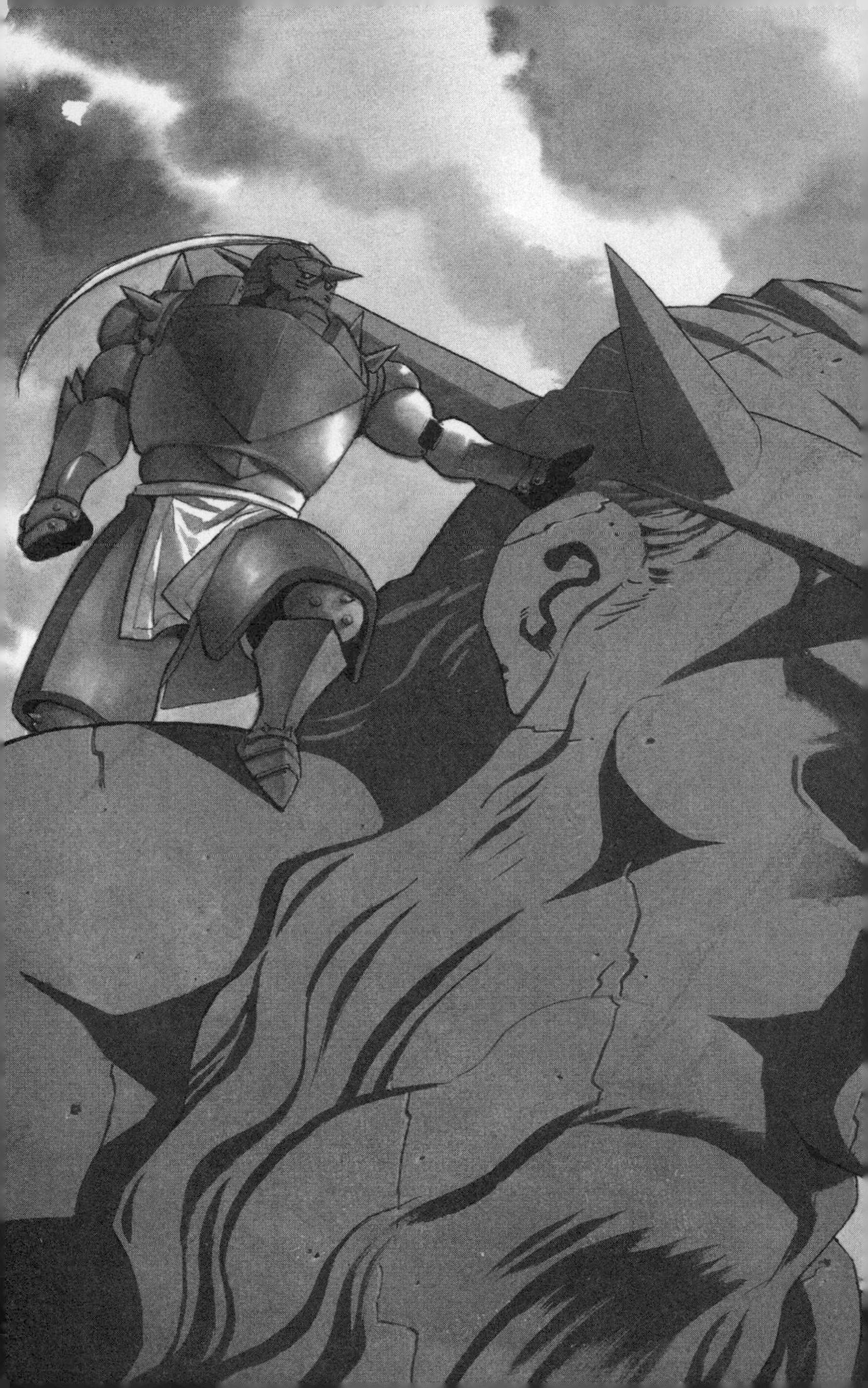

FULLMETAL
ALCHEMIST

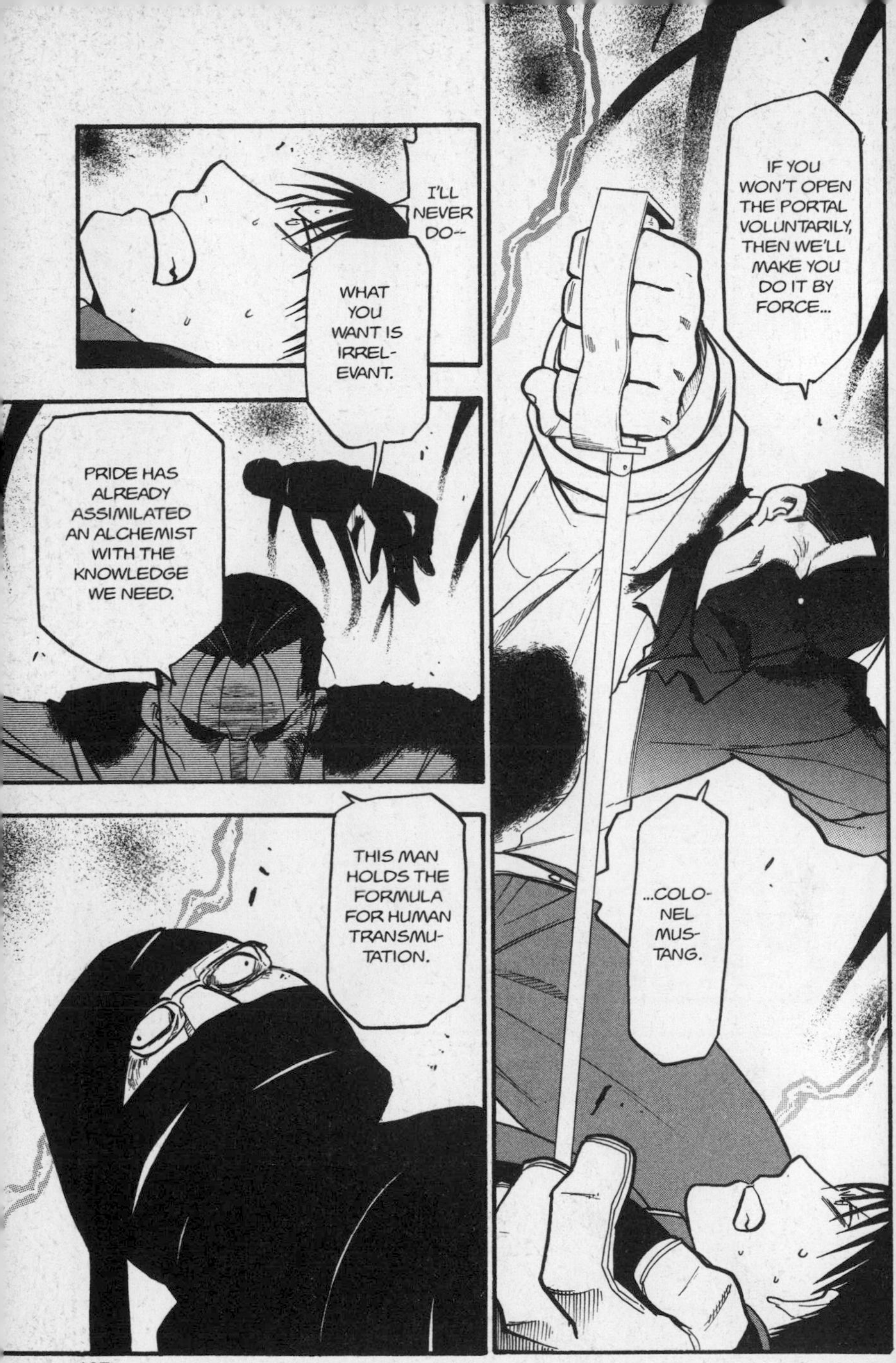
I'LL NEVER DO--
WHAT YOU WANT IS IRREL-EVANT.
PRIDE HAS ALREADY ASSIMILATED AN ALCHEMIST WITH THE KNOWLEDGE WE NEED.
THIS MAN HOLDS THE FORMULA FOR HUMAN TRANSMU-TATION.
IF YOU WON'T OPEN THE PORTAL VOLUNTARILY, THEN WE'LL MAKE YOU DO IT BY FORCE...
...COLO-NEL MUS-TANG.

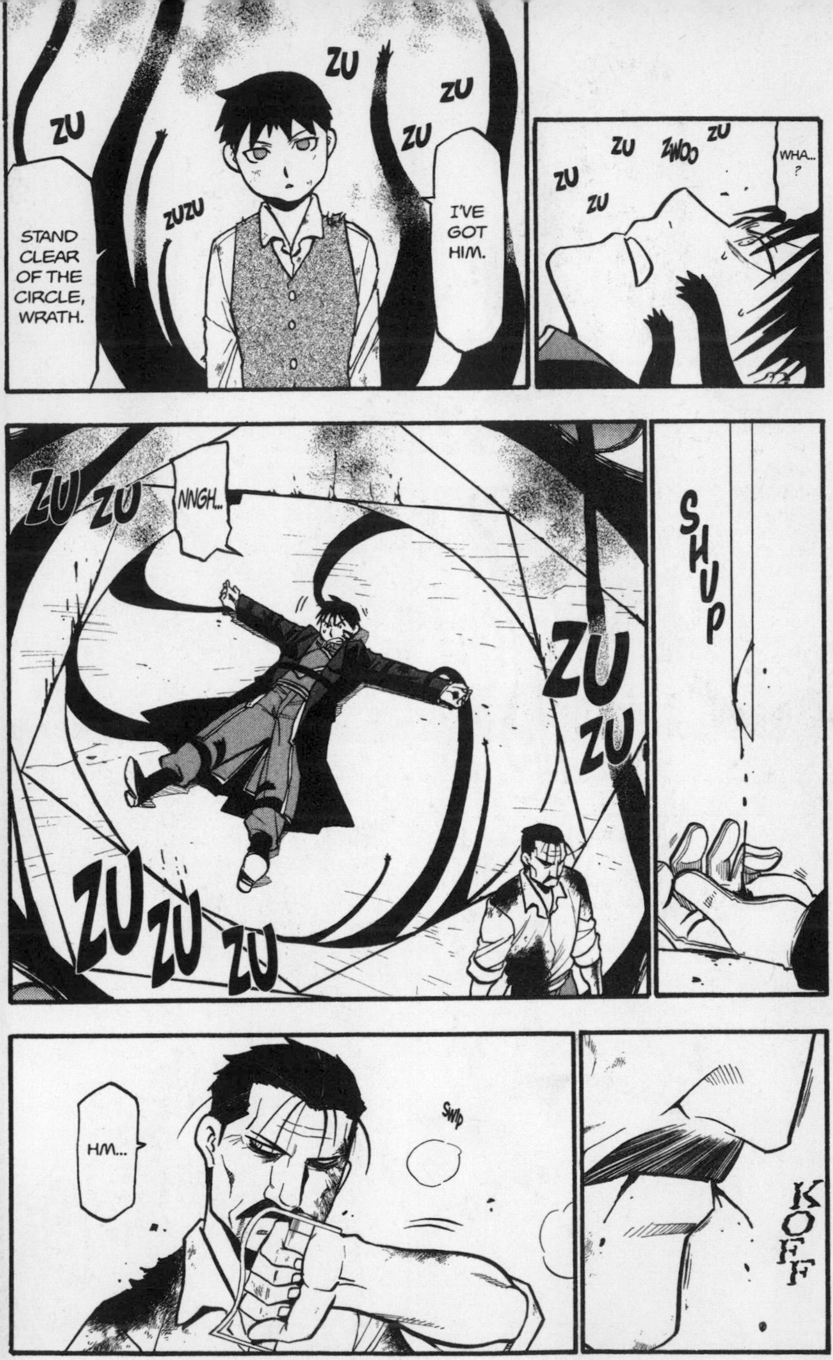
WHA... ?
ZU
ZWOO
ZU
ZU
ZU
ZU
ZU
ZU
ZU
ZUZU
I'VE GOT HIM.
STAND CLEAR OF THE CIRCLE, WRATH.
SHUP
ZU
ZU
NNGH...
ZU
ZU
ZU
ZU
ZU
KOFF
SWIP
HM...

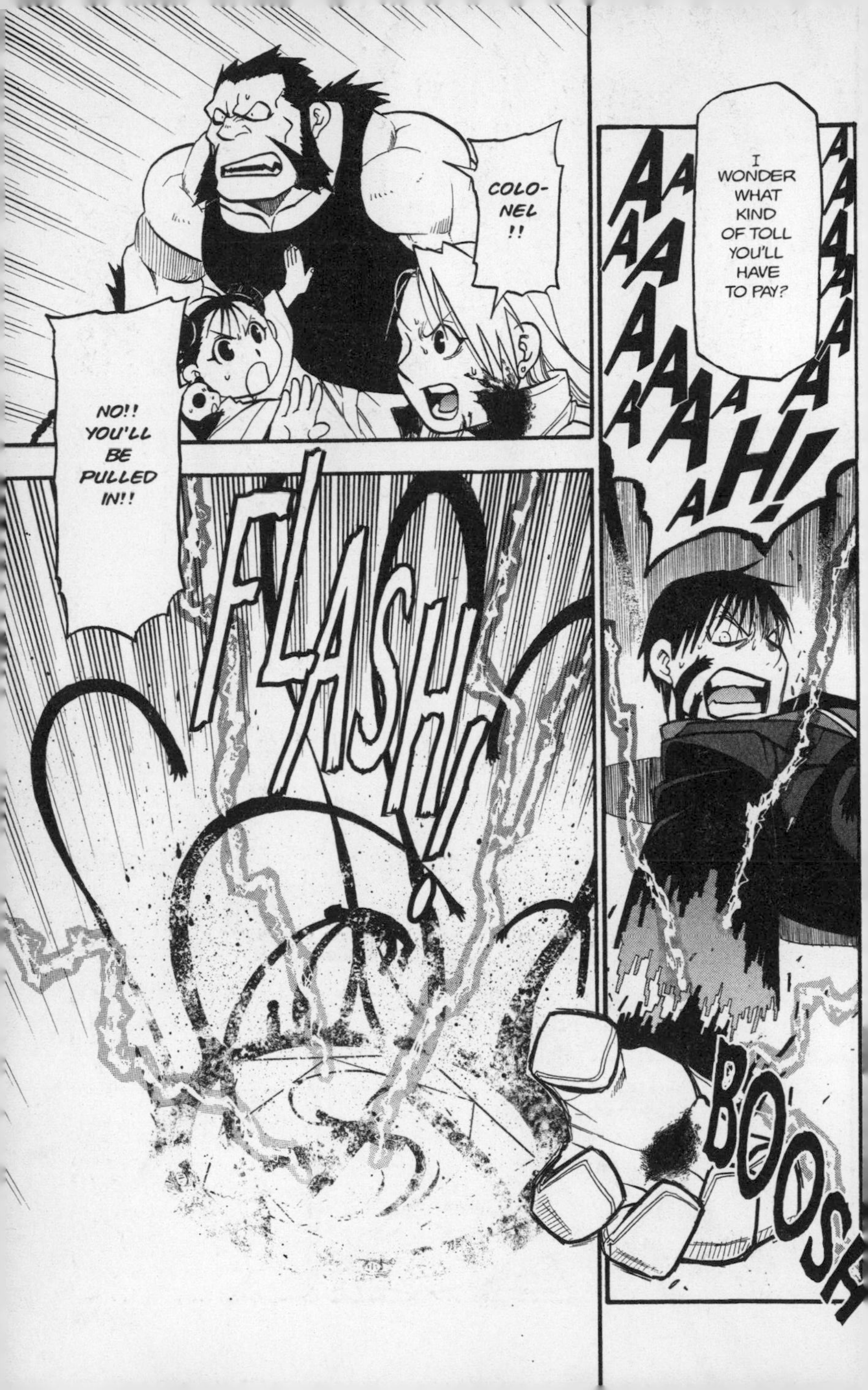
I WONDER WHAT KIND OF TOLL YOU'LL HAVE TO PAY?
AAAAAAAAH!
BOOSH
COLONEL!!
NO!! YOU'LL BE PULLED IN!!
FLASH

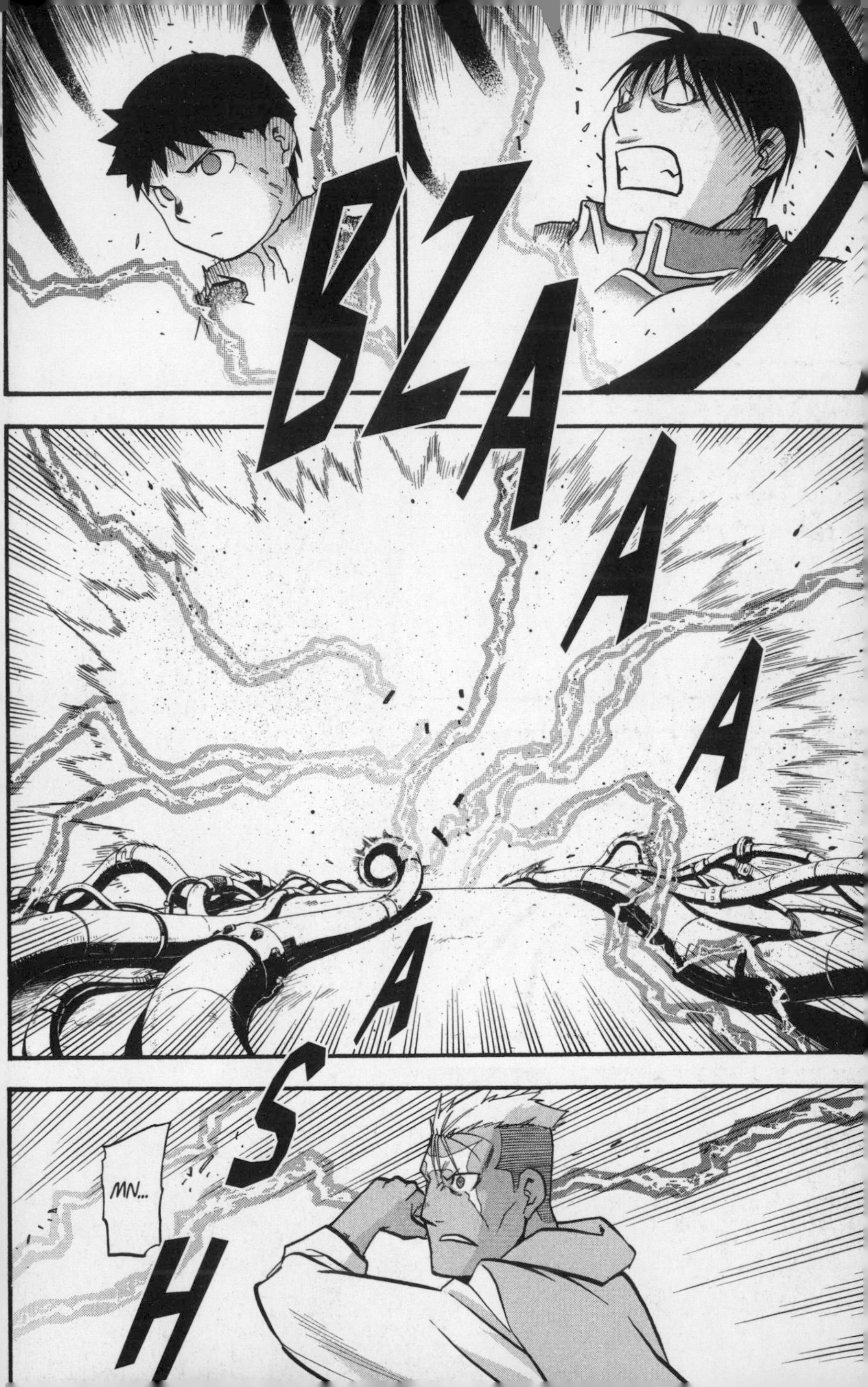
BZAAAAASH
MN...

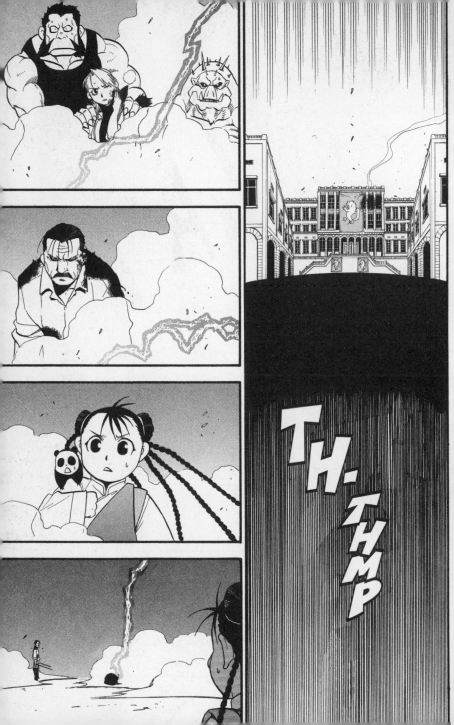

TH.
THMP

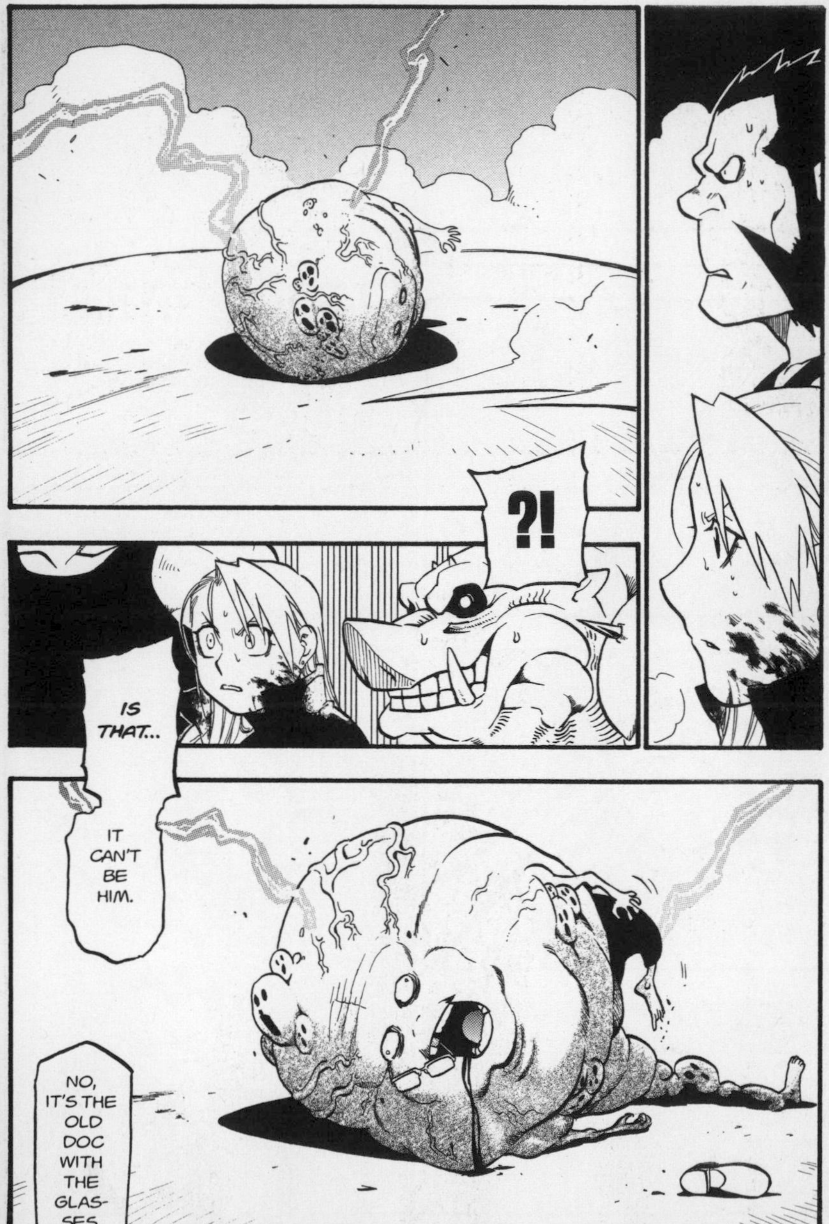

?!
IS THAT...
IT CAN'T BE HIM.
NO, IT'S THE OLD DOC WITH THE GLAS-SES.

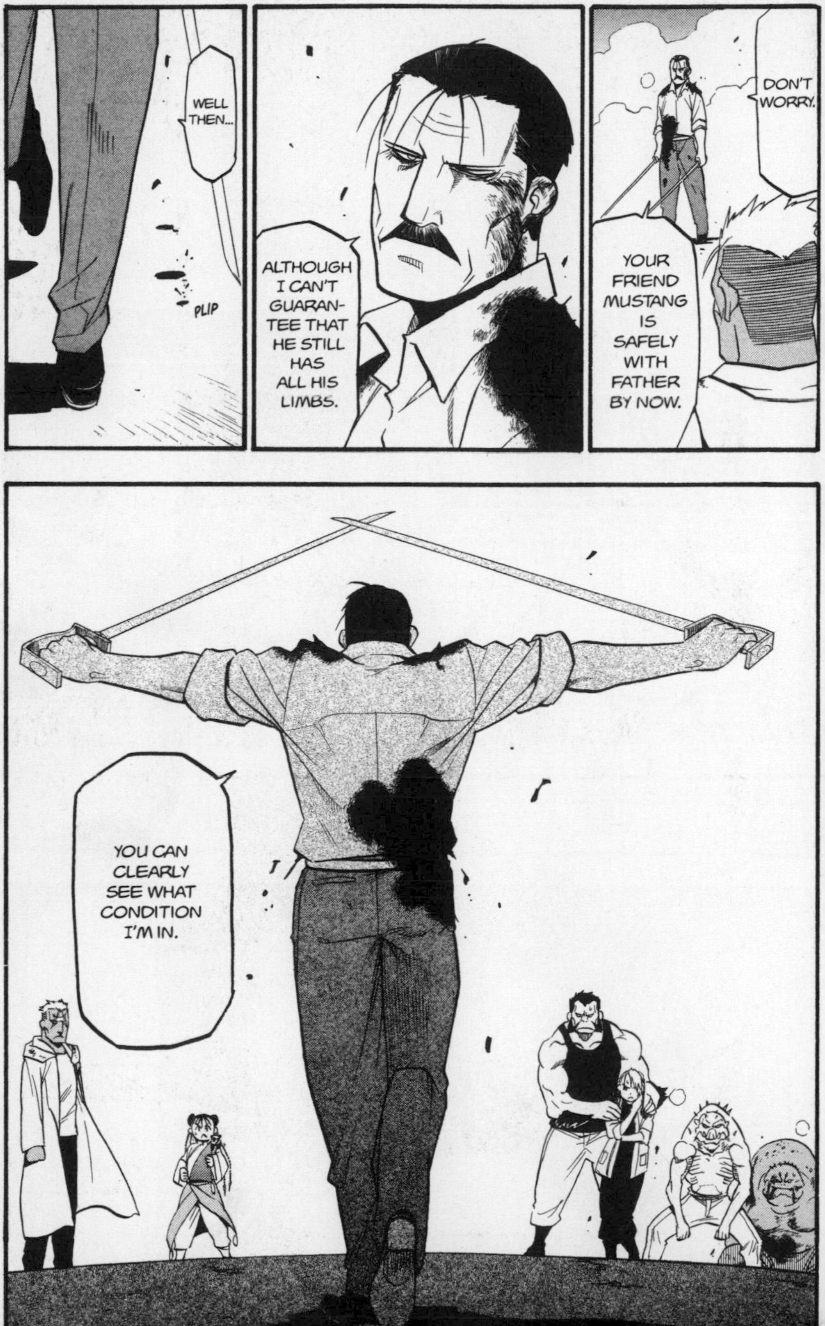
DON'T WORRY.
YOUR FRIEND MUSTANG IS SAFELY WITH FATHER BY NOW.
ALTHOUGH I CAN'T GUARAN-TEE THAT HE STILL HAS ALL HIS LIMBS.
WELL THEN...
PLIP
YOU CAN CLEARLY SEE WHAT CONDITION I'M IN.

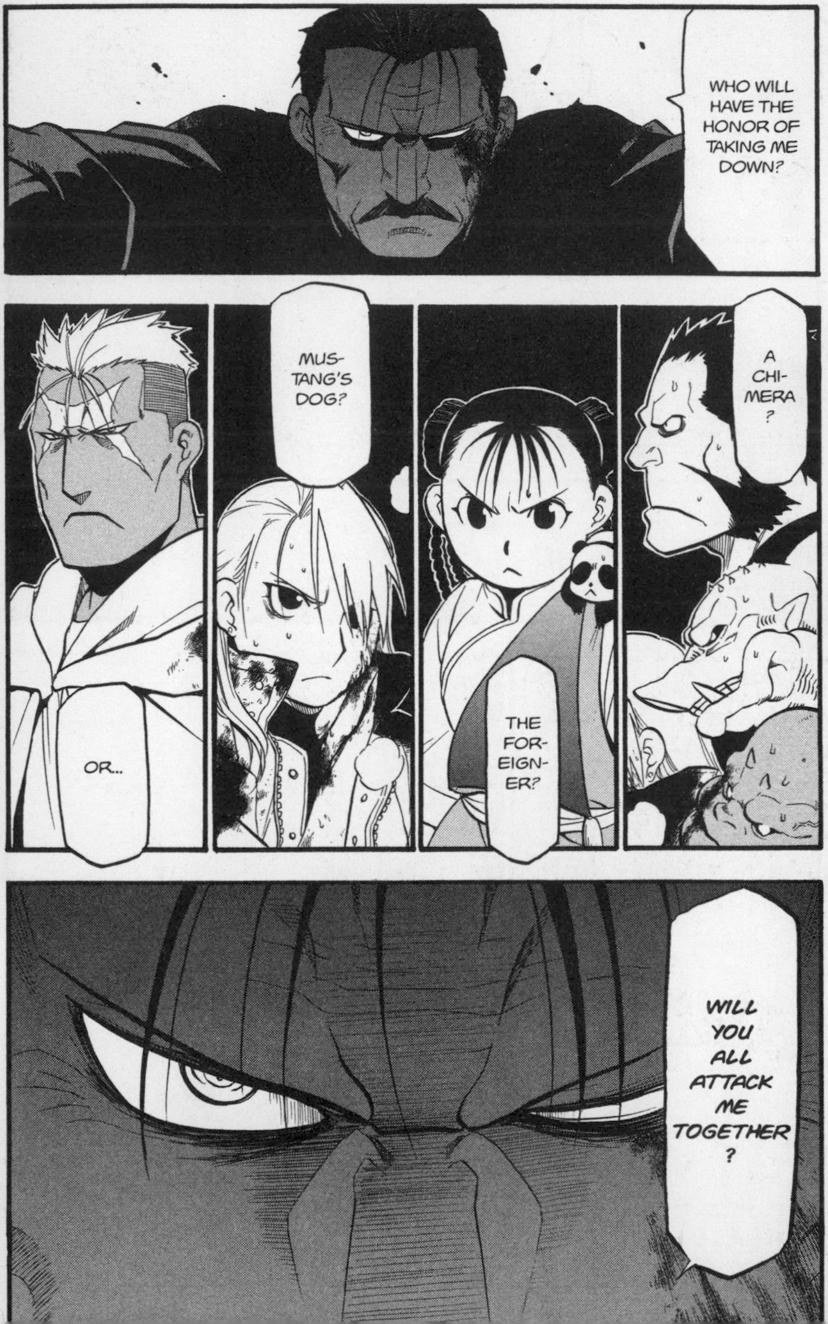
WHO WILL HAVE THE HONOR OF TAKING ME DOWN?
A CHIMERA?
THE FOREIGNER?
MUSTANG'S DOG?
OR...
WILL YOU ALL ATTACK ME TOGETHER?

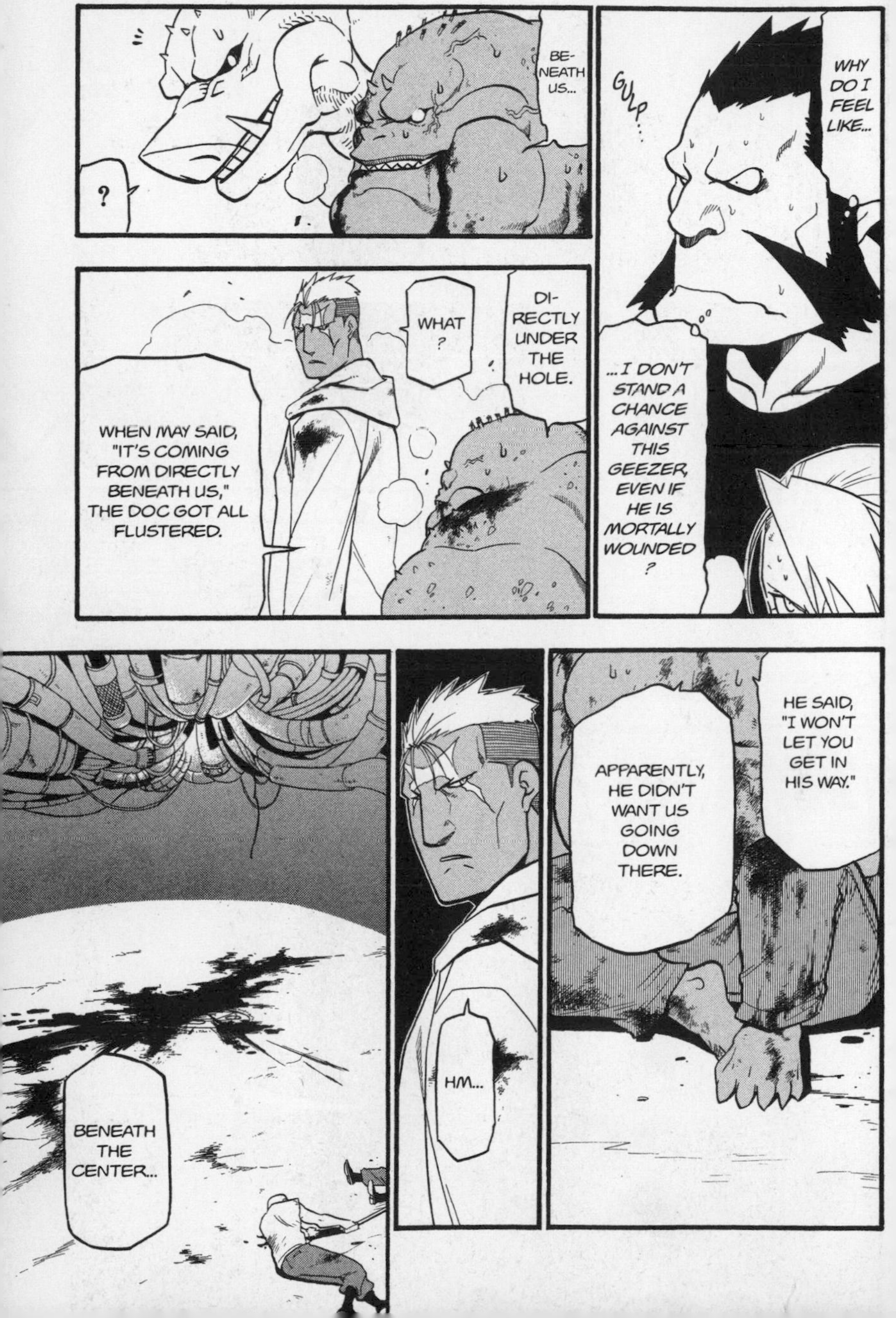
WHY DO I FEEL LIKE...
GULP...
...I DON'T STAND A CHANCE AGAINST THIS GEEZER, EVEN IF HE IS MORTALLY WOUNDED?
BE-NEATH US...
?
DI-RECTLY UNDER THE HOLE.
WHAT?
WHEN MAY SAID, "IT'S COMING FROM DIRECTLY BENEATH US," THE DOC GOT ALL FLUSTERED.
HE SAID, "I WON'T LET YOU GET IN HIS WAY."
APPARENTLY, HE DIDN'T WANT US GOING DOWN THERE.
HM...
BENEATH THE CENTER...

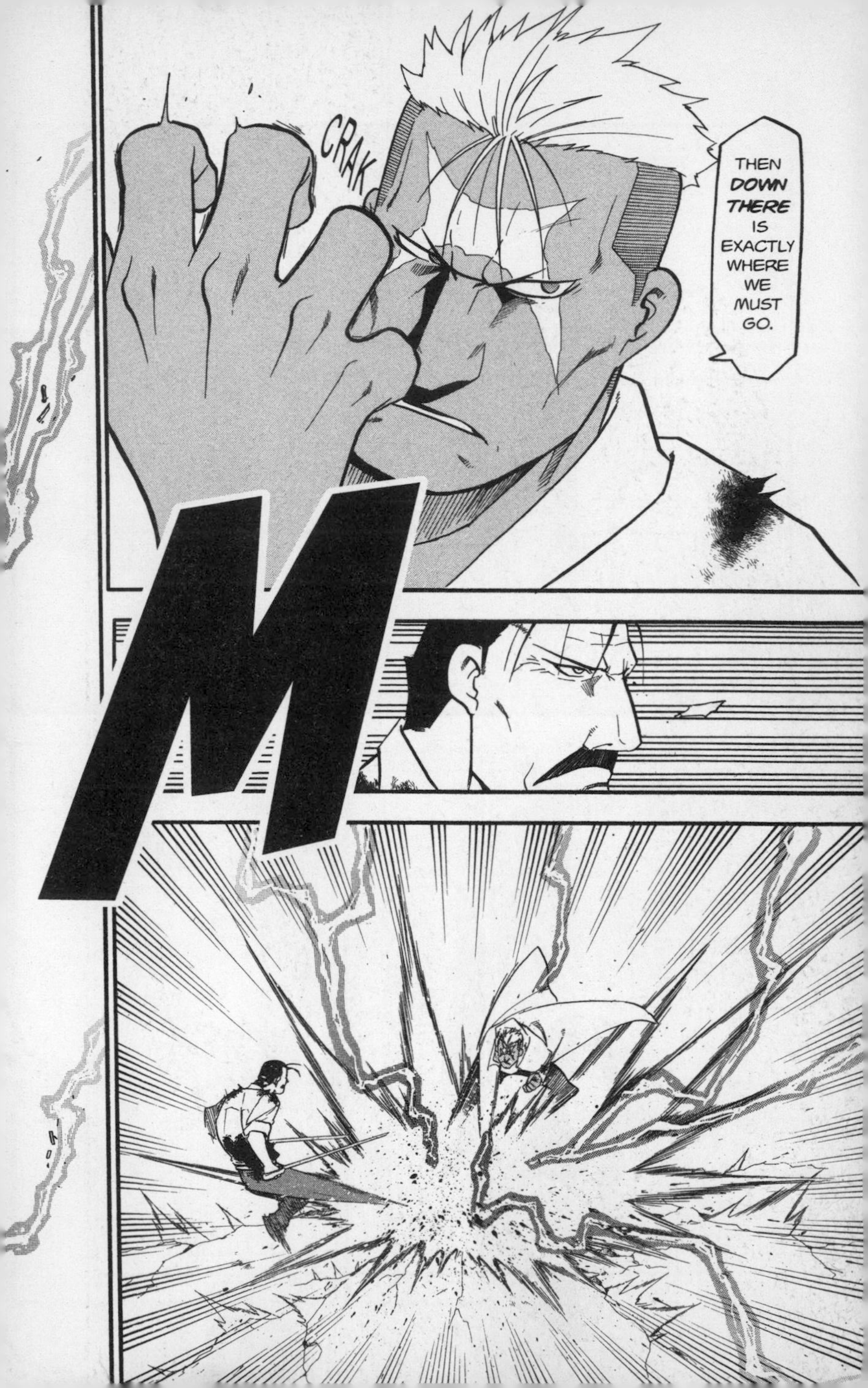
CRAK
THEN DOWN THERE IS EXACTLY WHERE WE MUST GO.
M

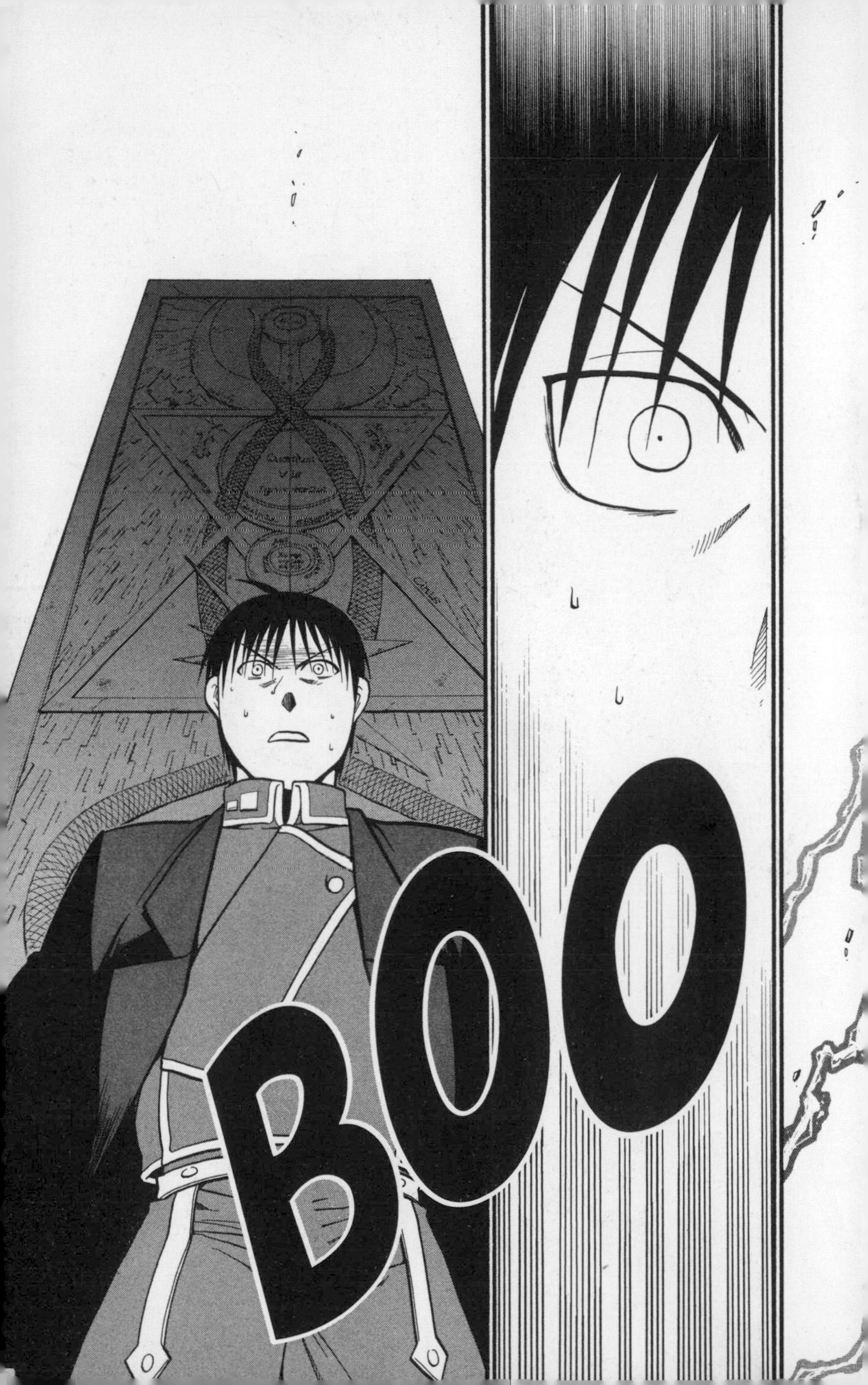
BOO

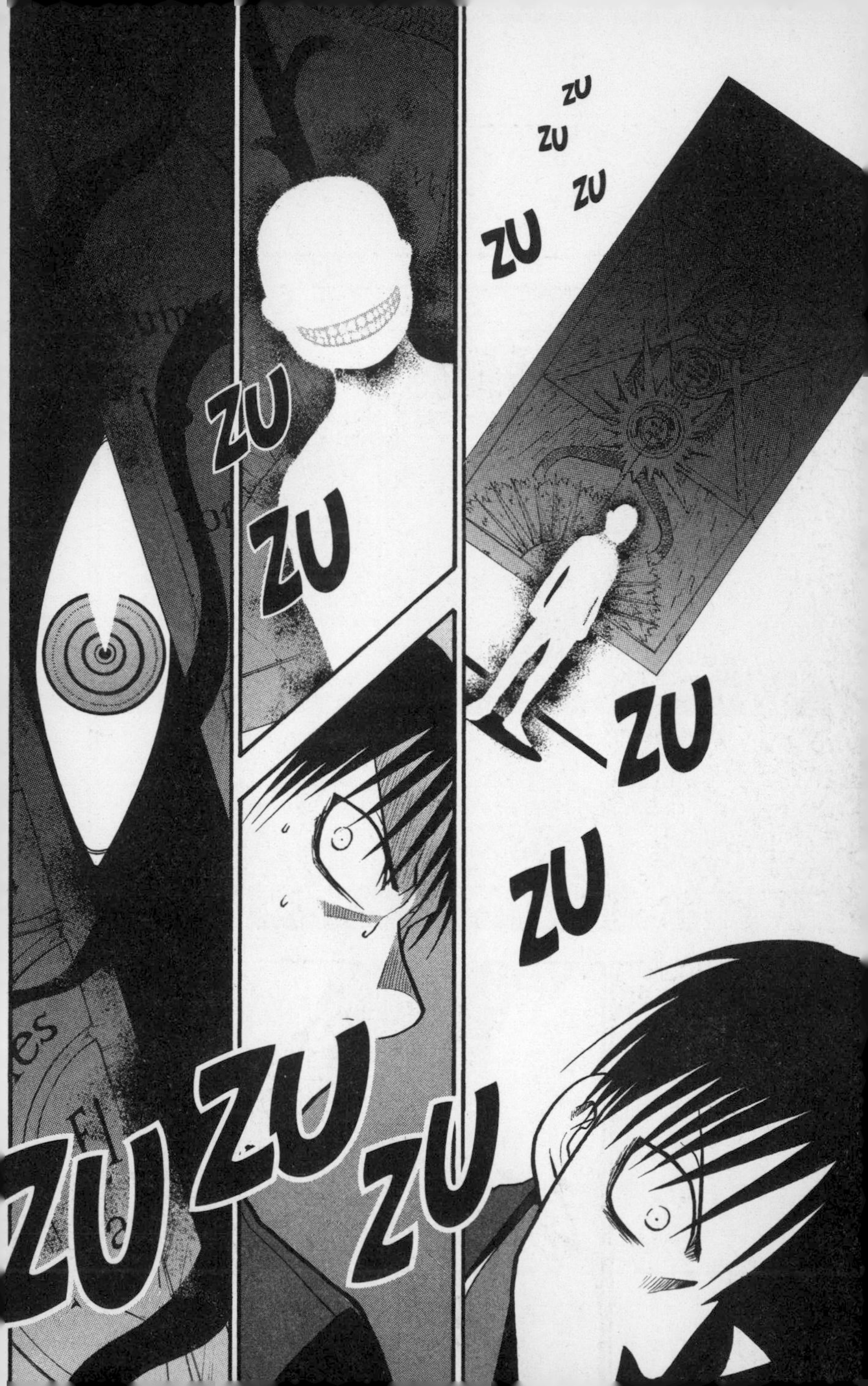
ZU
ZU
ZU
ZU
ZU
ZU
ZU
ZU
ZU
ZU
ZU
ZU

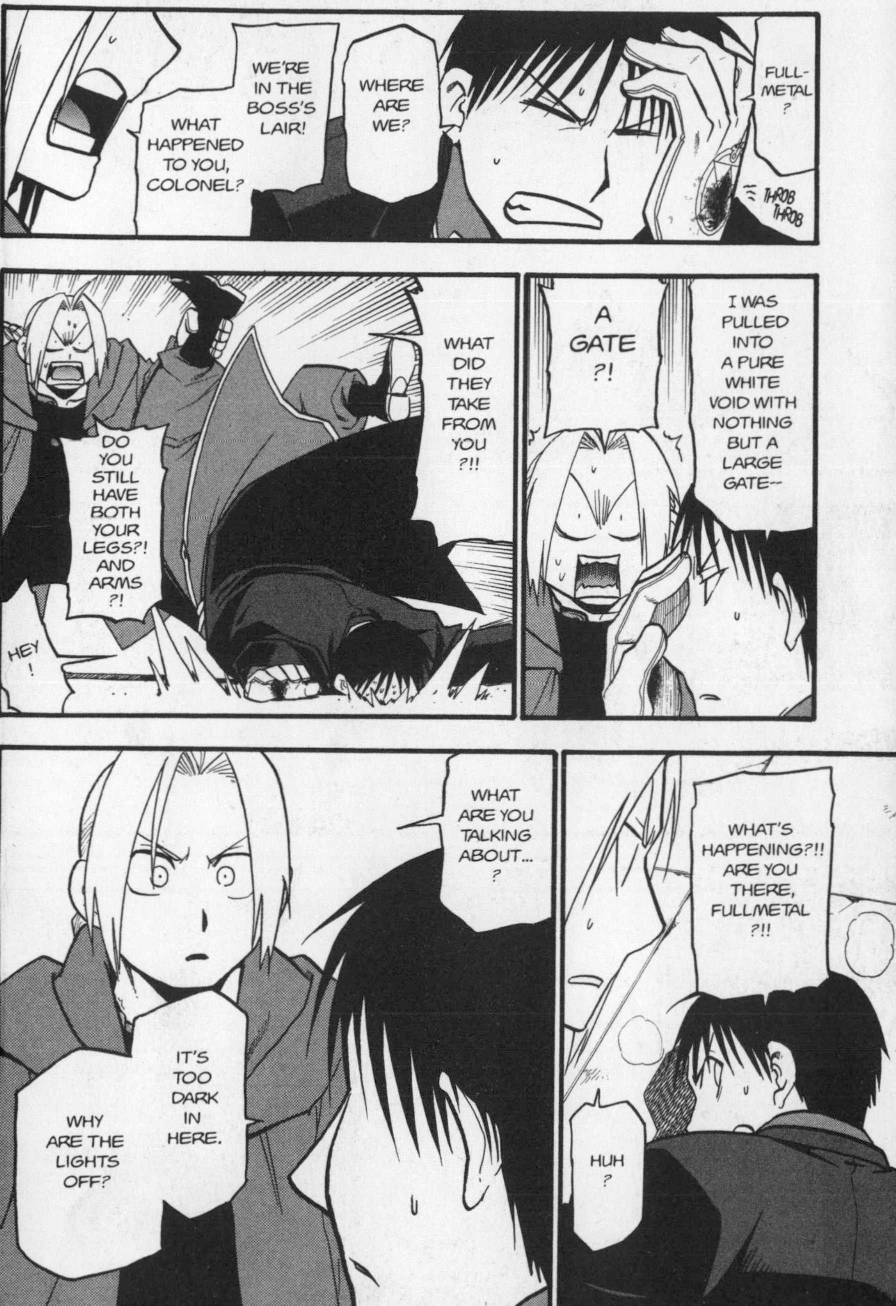
FULL-METAL ?
THROB THROB
WHERE ARE WE?
WE'RE IN THE BOSS'S LAIR!
WHAT HAPPENED TO YOU, COLONEL?
I WAS PULLED INTO A PURE WHITE VOID WITH NOTHING BUT A LARGE GATE--
A GATE ?!
WHAT DID THEY TAKE FROM YOU ?!!
DO YOU STILL HAVE BOTH YOUR LEGS?! AND ARMS ?!
HEY !
WHAT'S HAPPENING?!! ARE YOU THERE, FULLMETAL ?!!
HUH ?
WHAT ARE YOU TALKING ABOUT... ?
IT'S TOO DARK IN HERE.
WHY ARE THE LIGHTS OFF?

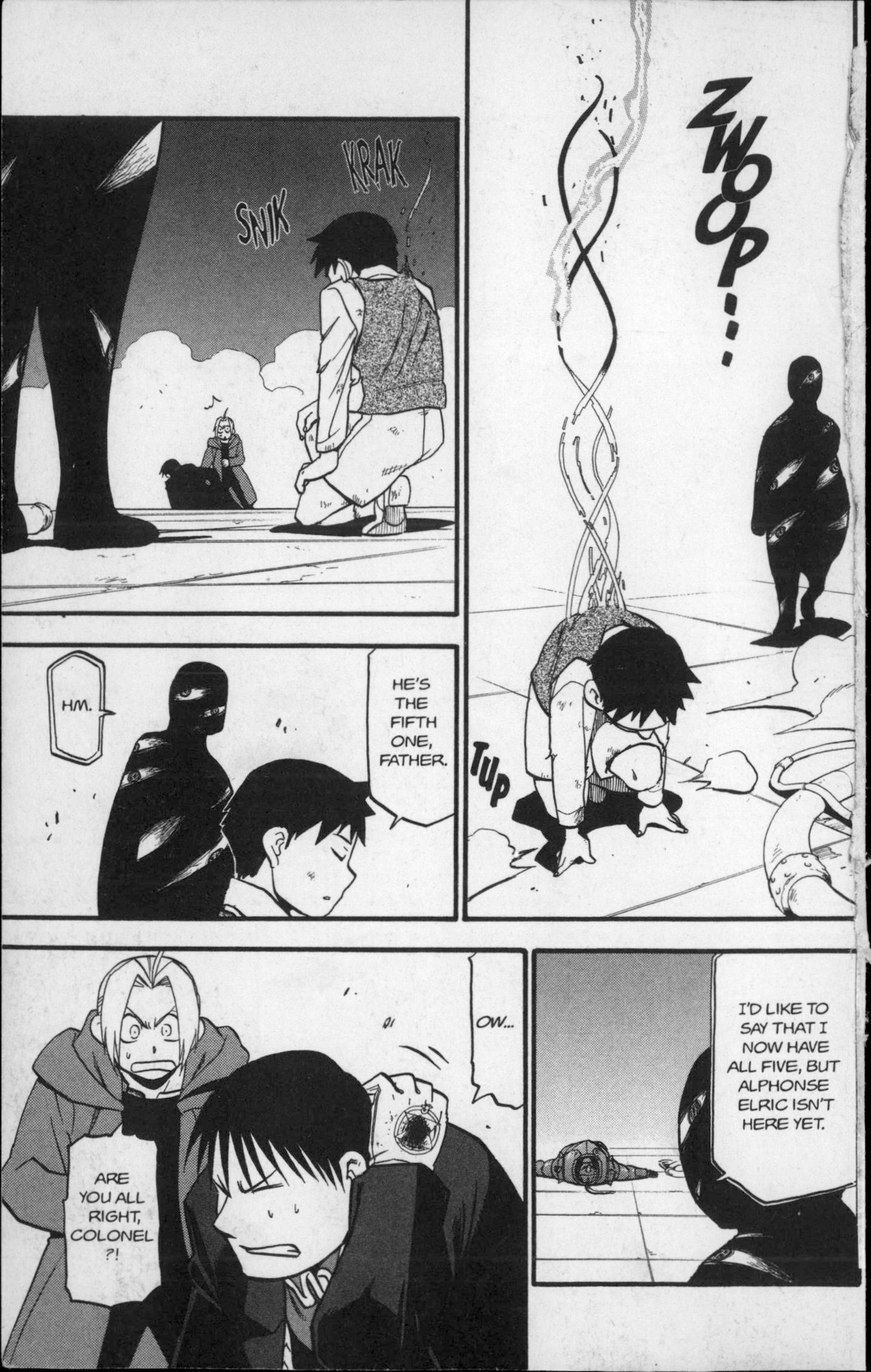
ZWOOP...
TUP
SNIK
KRAK
HE'S THE FIFTH ONE, FATHER.
HM.
I'D LIKE TO SAY THAT I NOW HAVE ALL FIVE, BUT ALPHONSE ELRIC ISN'T HERE YET.
OW...
ARE YOU ALL RIGHT, COLONEL?!

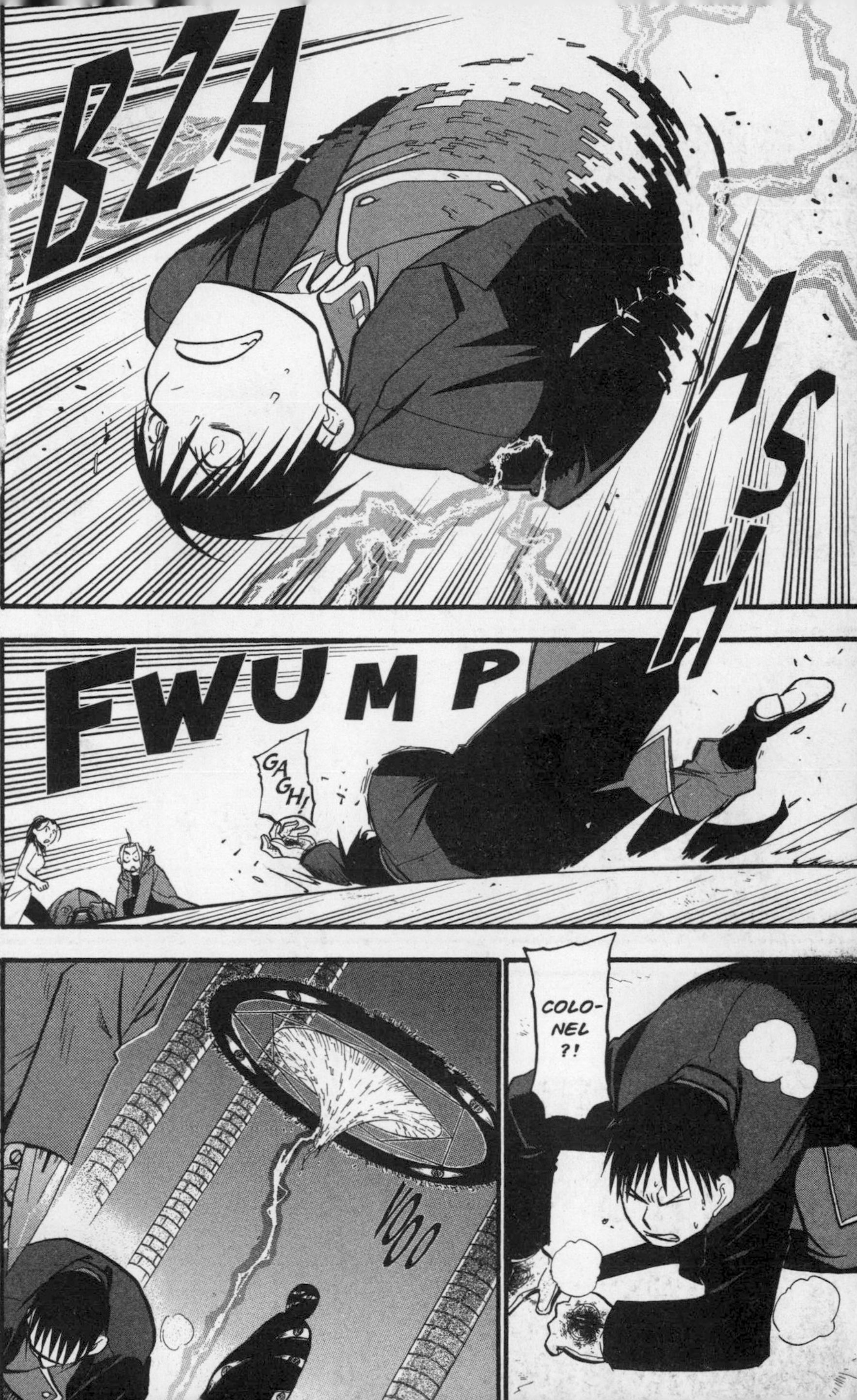
BZZA
ASH
FWUMP
GAGH!
COLO-NEL ?!

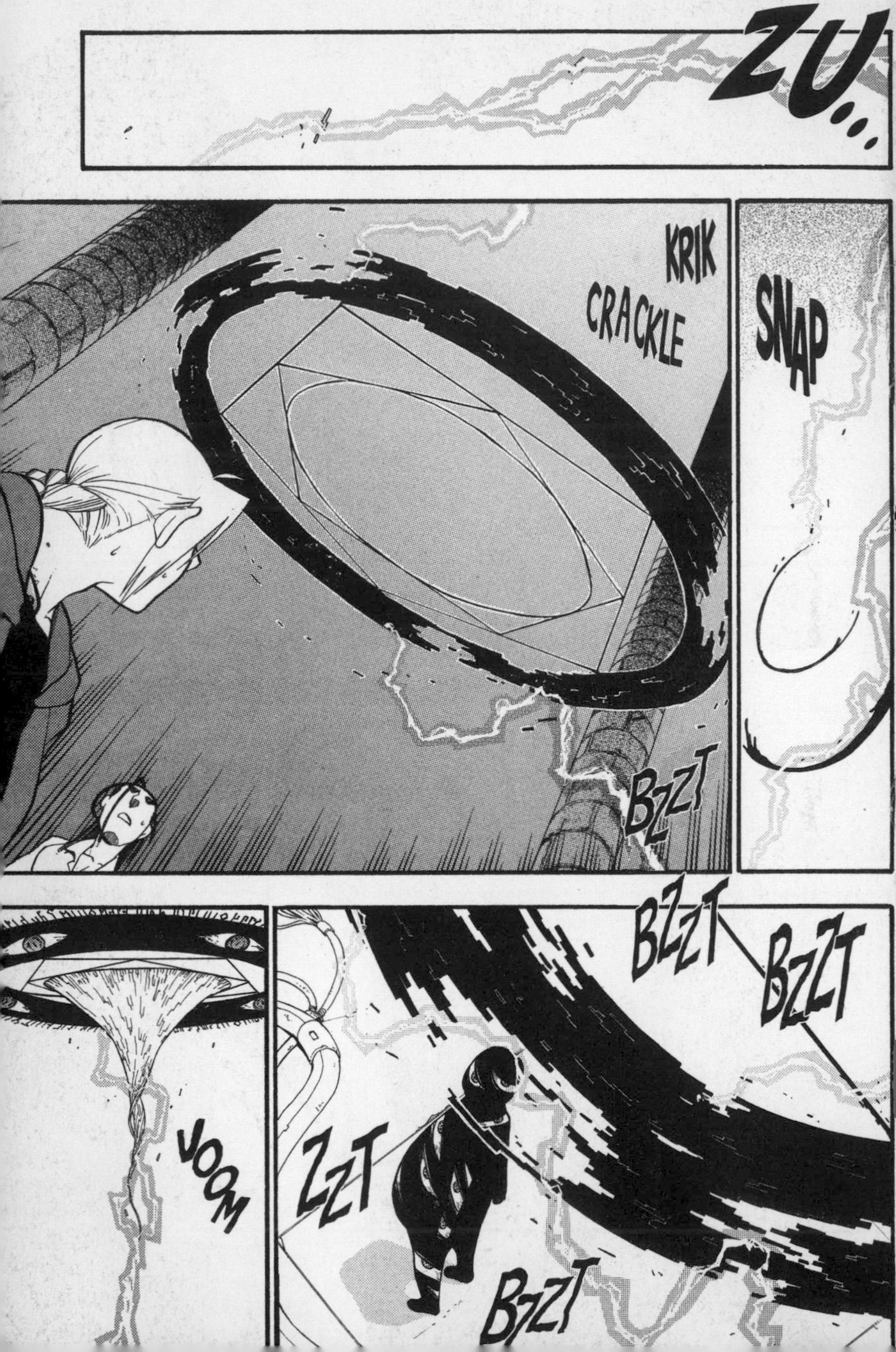
ZU...
SNAP
KRIK
CRACKLE
BZZT
BZZT
BZZT
ZZT
BZZT
JOOM

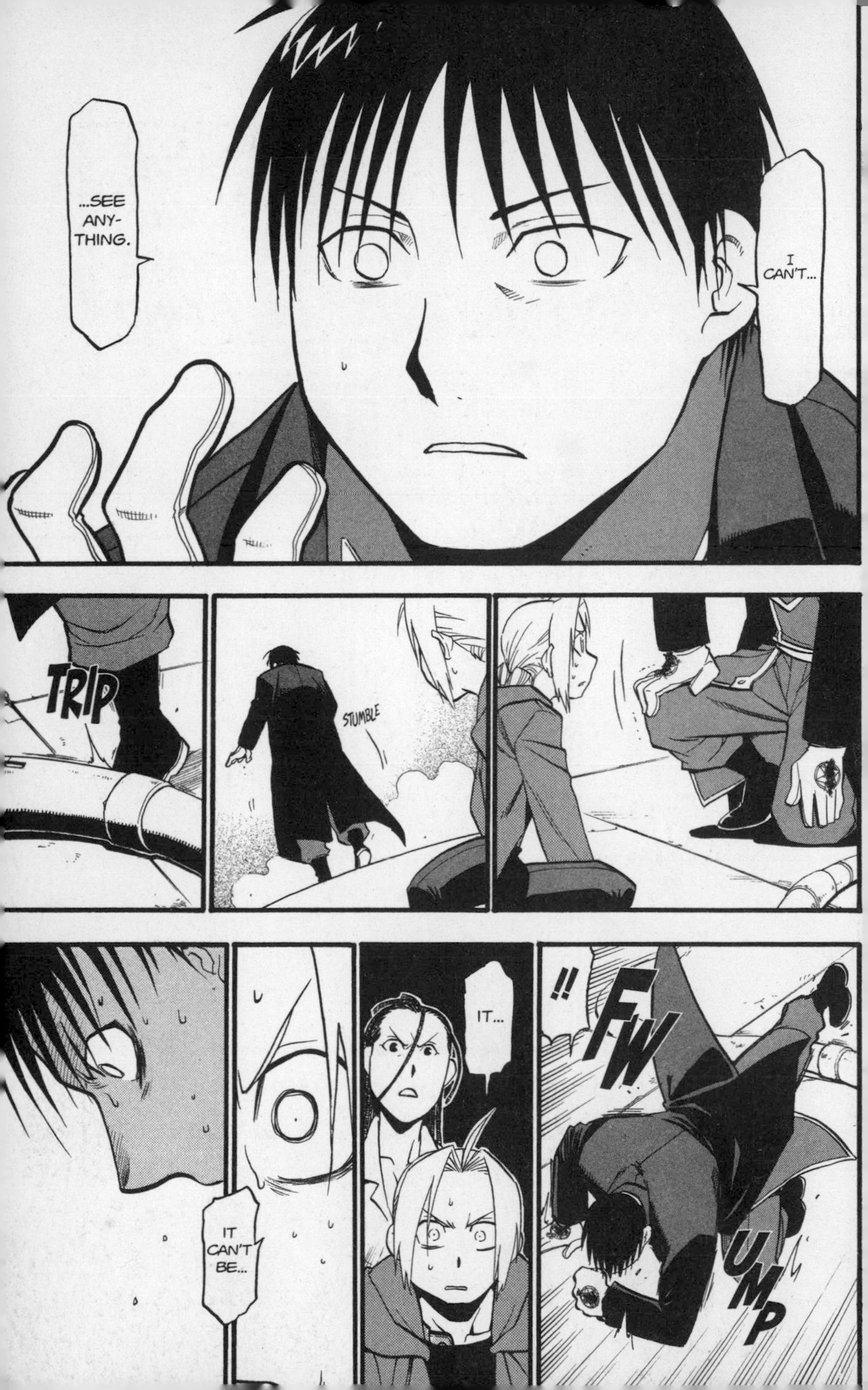

I CAN'T...
...SEE ANY-THING.
STUMBLE
TRIP
!!
FW
UMP
IT...
IT CAN'T BE...

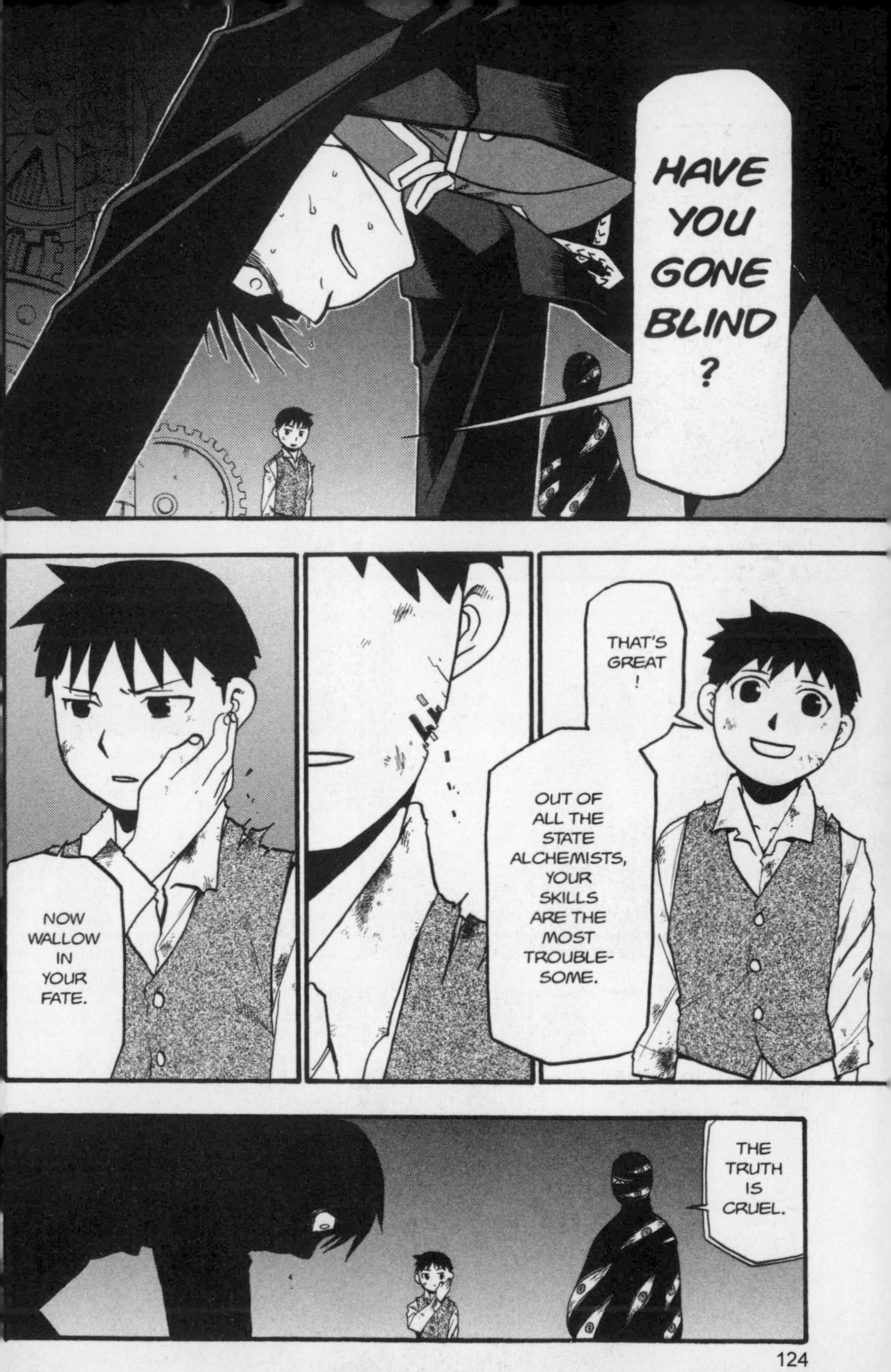
HAVE YOU GONE BLIND?
THAT'S GREAT!
OUT OF ALL THE STATE ALCHEMISTS, YOUR SKILLS ARE THE MOST TROUBLESOME.
NOW WALLOW IN YOUR FATE.
THE TRUTH IS CRUEL.

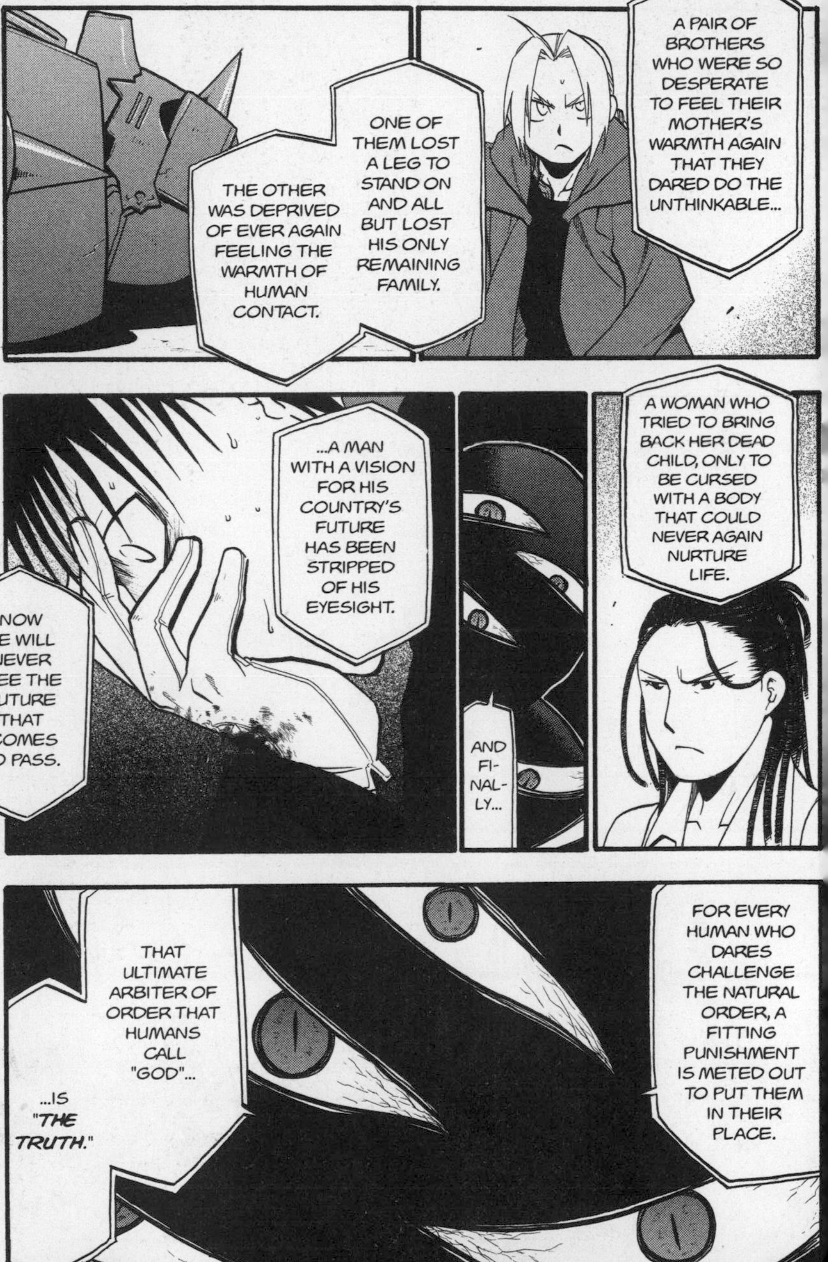

A PAIR OF BROTHERS WHO WERE SO DESPERATE TO FEEL THEIR MOTHER'S WARMTH AGAIN THAT THEY DARED DO THE UNTHINKABLE...
ONE OF THEM LOST A LEG TO STAND ON AND ALL BUT LOST HIS ONLY REMAINING FAMILY.
THE OTHER WAS DEPRIVED OF EVER AGAIN FEELING THE WARMTH OF HUMAN CONTACT.
A WOMAN WHO TRIED TO BRING BACK HER DEAD CHILD, ONLY TO BE CURSED WITH A BODY THAT COULD NEVER AGAIN NURTURE LIFE.
AND FI-NAL-LY...
...A MAN WITH A VISION FOR HIS COUNTRY'S FUTURE HAS BEEN STRIPPED OF HIS EYESIGHT.
NOW HE WILL NEVER SEE THE FUTURE THAT COMES TO PASS.
FOR EVERY HUMAN WHO DARES CHALLENGE THE NATURAL ORDER, A FITTING PUNISHMENT IS METED OUT TO PUT THEM IN THEIR PLACE.
THAT ULTIMATE ARBITER OF ORDER THAT HUMANS CALL "GOD"...
...IS "*THE TRUTH*."

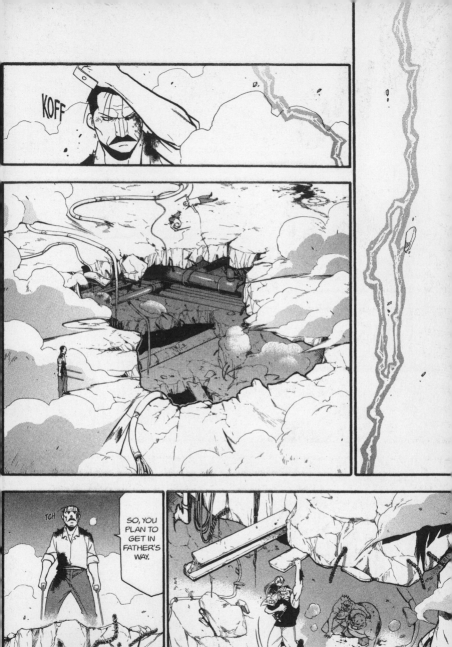

KOFF

TCH

SO, YOU
PLAN TO
GET IN
FATHER'S
WAY.

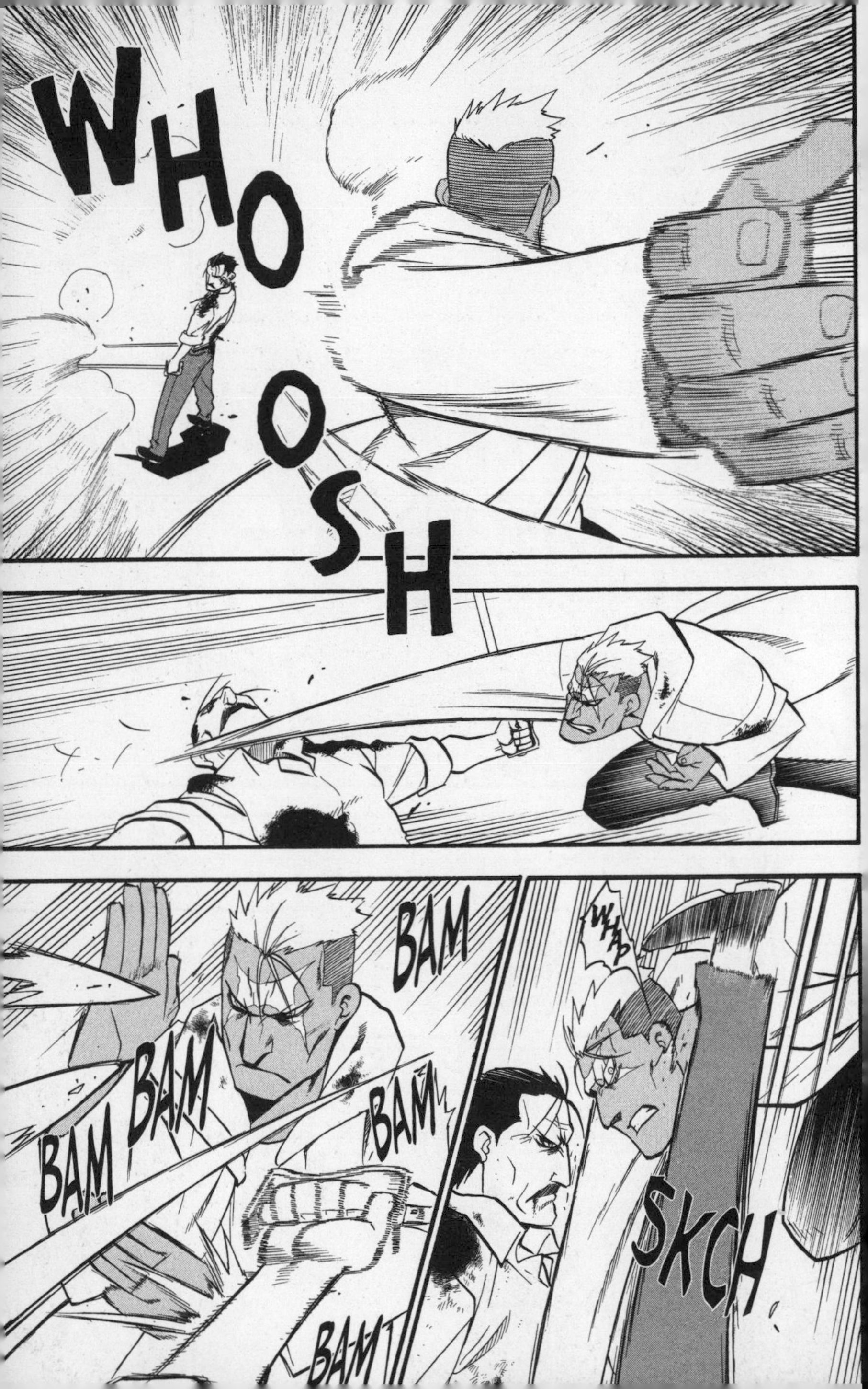
WHOOSH
WHAP
SKCH
BAM
BAM
BAM
BAM
BAM

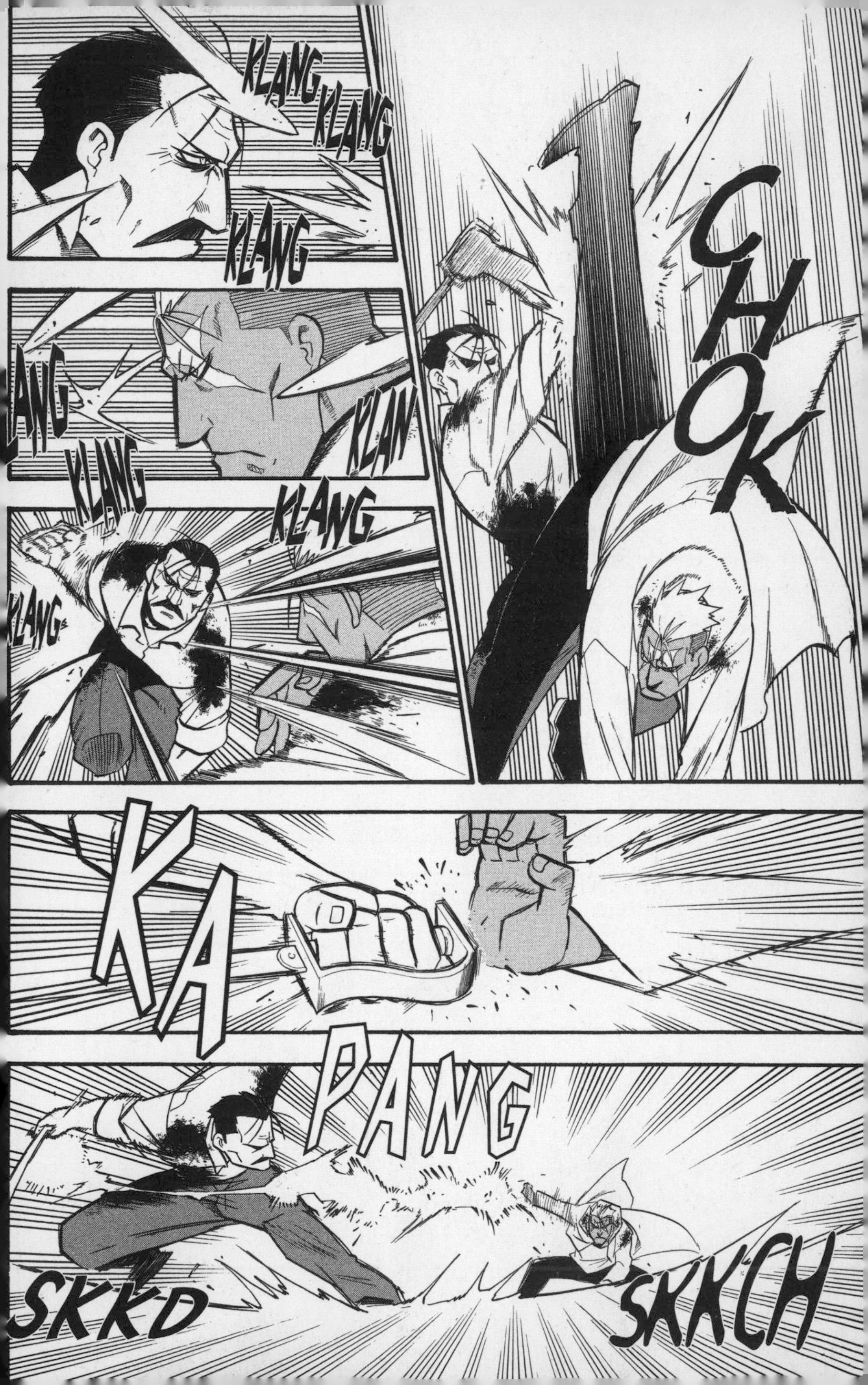
CHOK
KLANG
KLANG
KLANG
KLAN
KLANG
KLANG
KLANG
KLANG
KA
PANG
SKKCH
SKKD

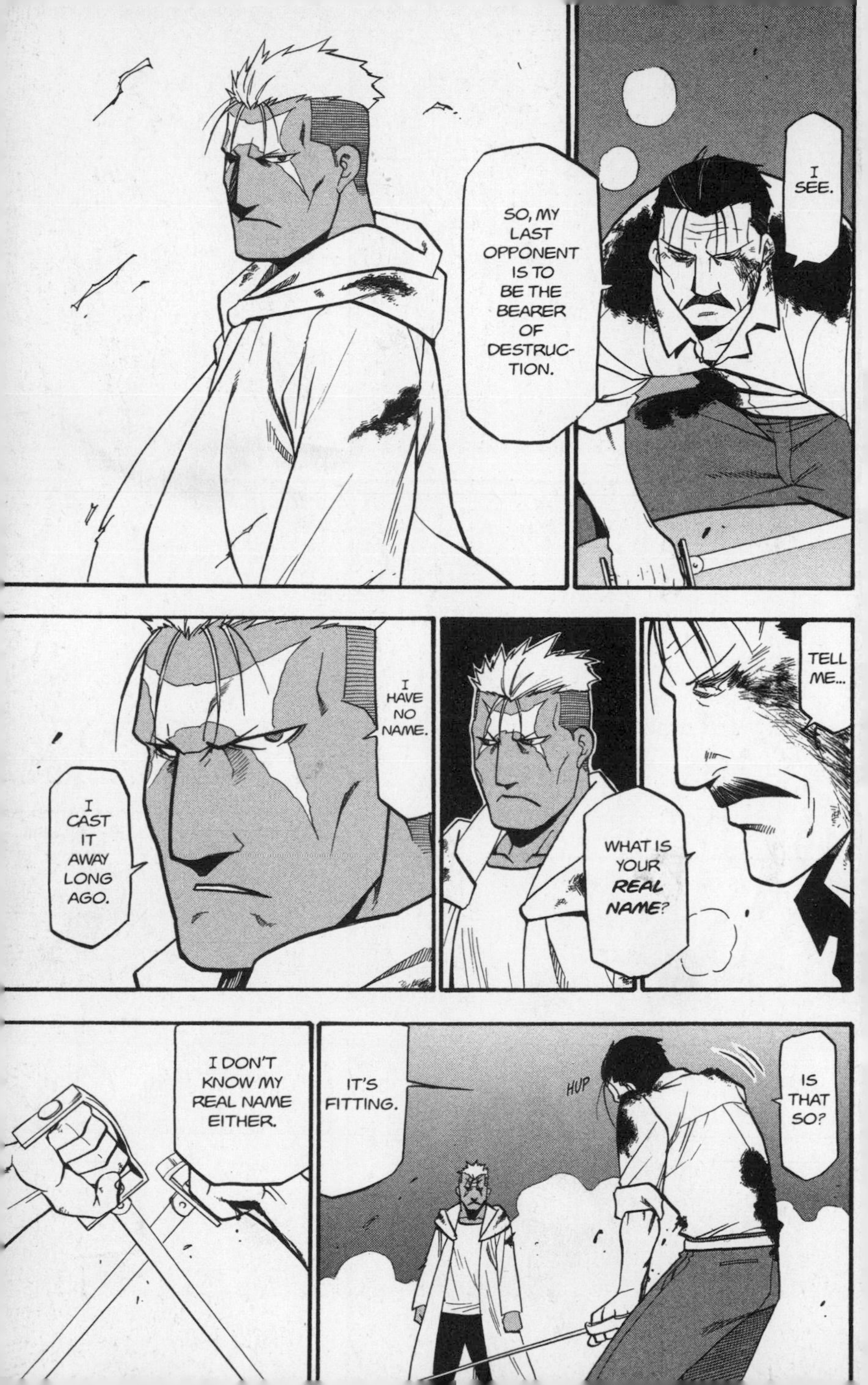
I SEE.
SO, MY LAST OPPONENT IS TO BE THE BEARER OF DESTRUCTION.
TELL ME...
WHAT IS YOUR *REAL NAME*?
I HAVE NO NAME.
I CAST IT AWAY LONG AGO.
IS THAT SO?
HUP
IT'S FITTING.
I DON'T KNOW MY REAL NAME EITHER.

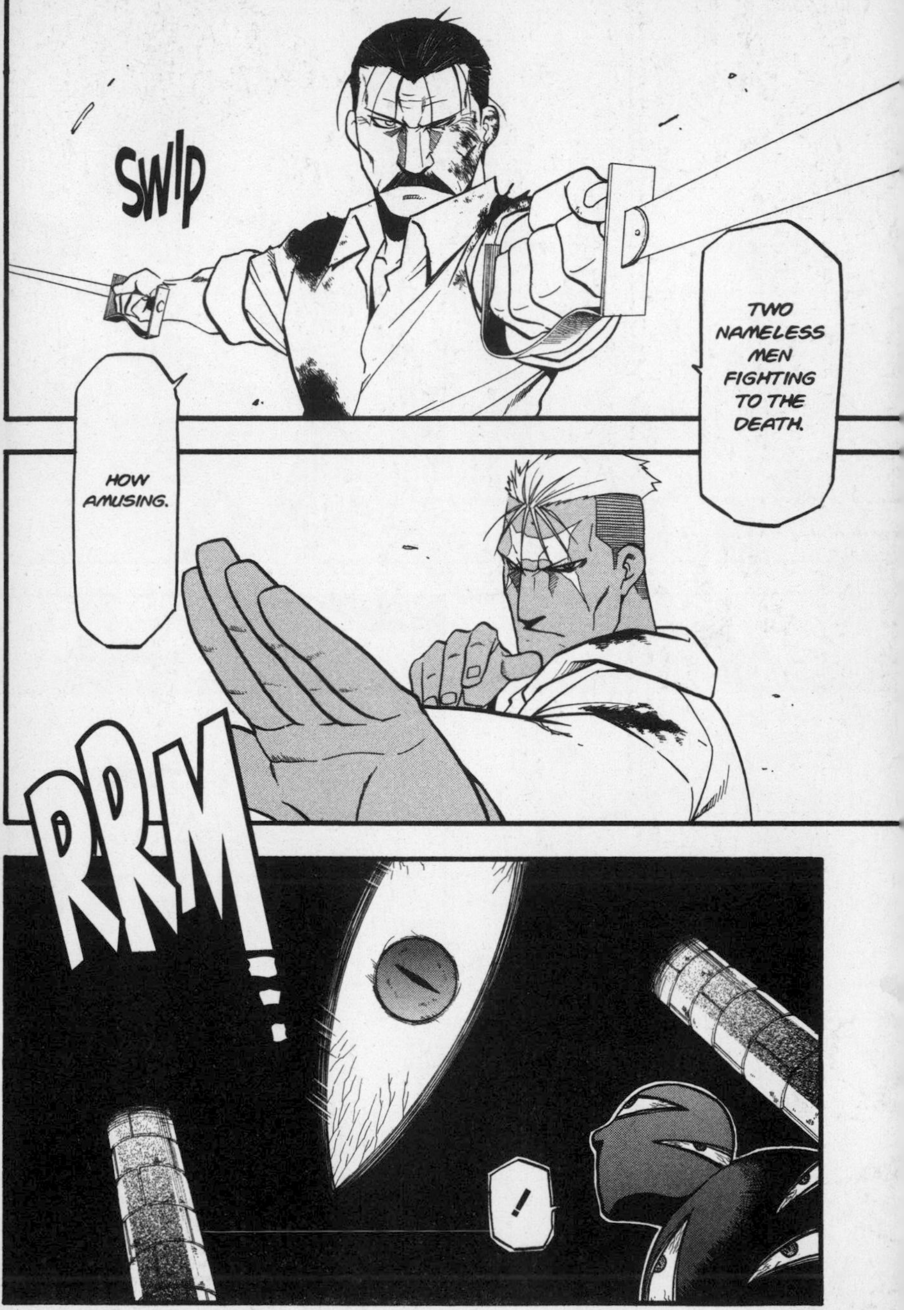
TWO NAMELESS MEN FIGHTING TO THE DEATH.
HOW AMUSING.
SWIP
RRM
!

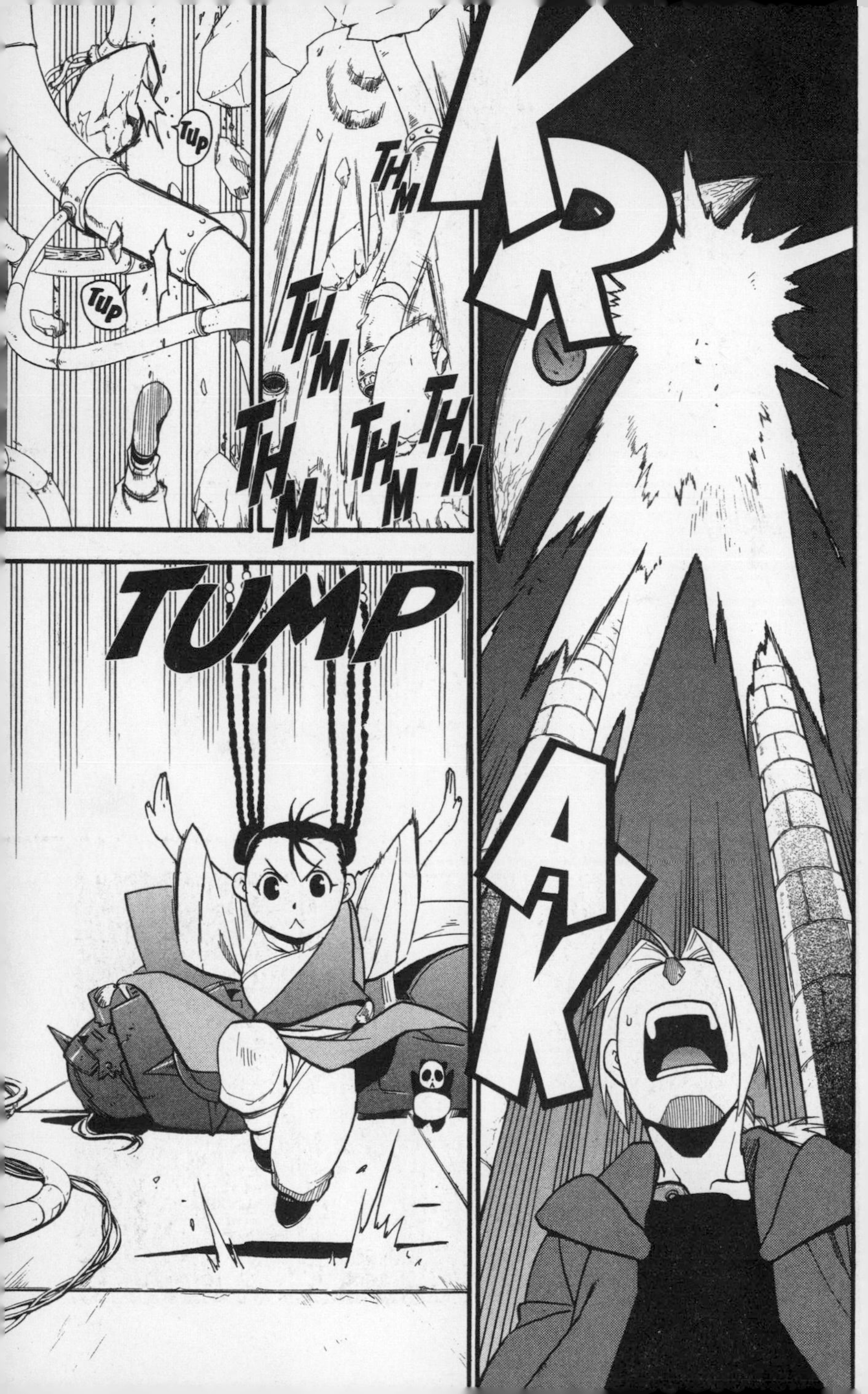
KRAK
THM
THM
THM
THM
THM
TUP
TUP
TUMP

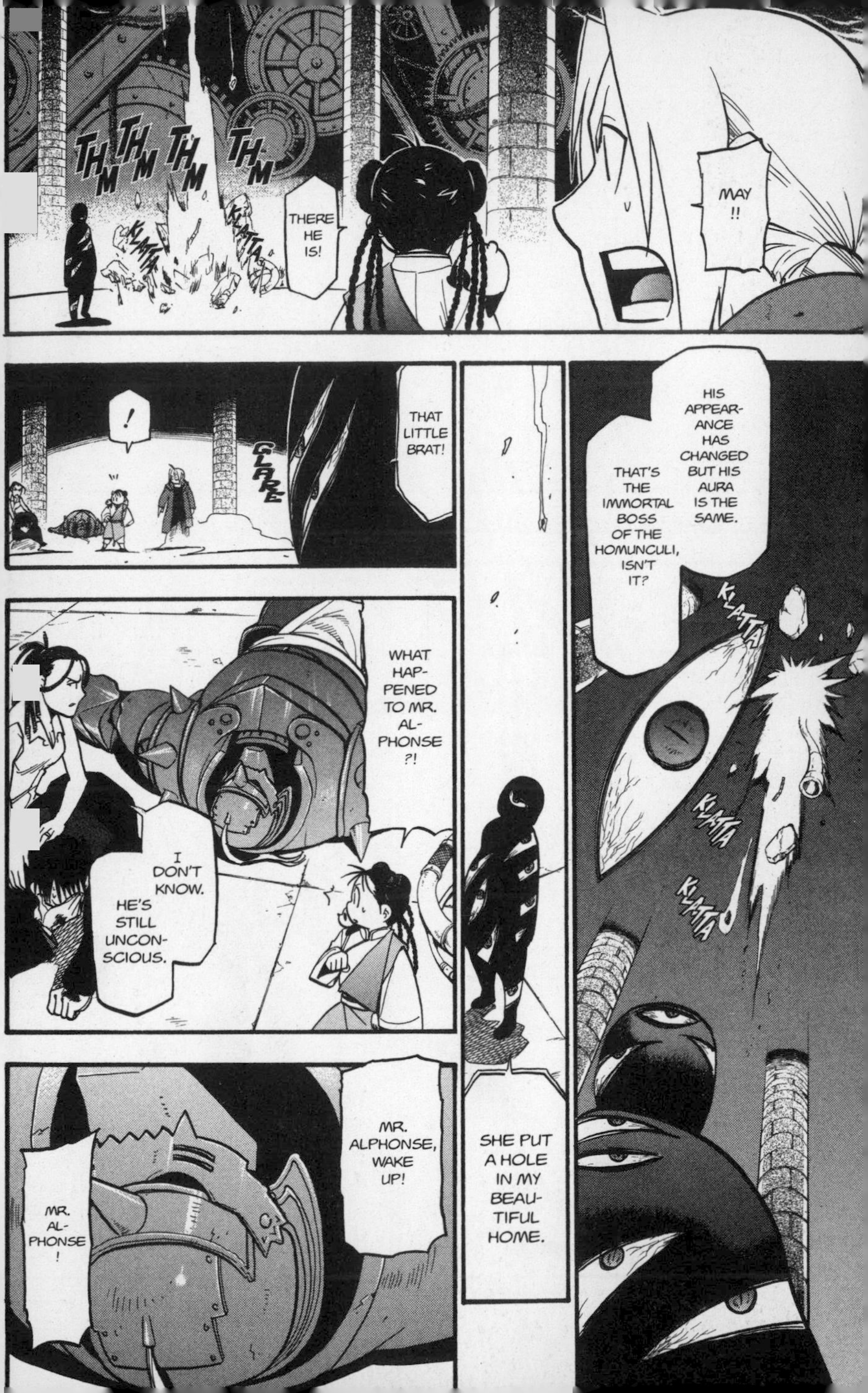
MAY!!
THERE HE IS!
THMM THMM THMM THMM
KLATTA KLATTA
HIS APPEARANCE HAS CHANGED BUT HIS AURA IS THE SAME.
THAT'S THE IMMORTAL BOSS OF THE HOMUNCULI, ISN'T IT?
KLATTA
KLATTA
KLATTA
SHE PUT A HOLE IN MY BEAUTIFUL HOME.
THAT LITTLE BRAT!
GLARE
!
WHAT HAPPENED TO MR. ALPHONSE?!
I DON'T KNOW. HE'S STILL UNCONSCIOUS.
MR. ALPHONSE, WAKE UP!
MR. ALPHONSE!

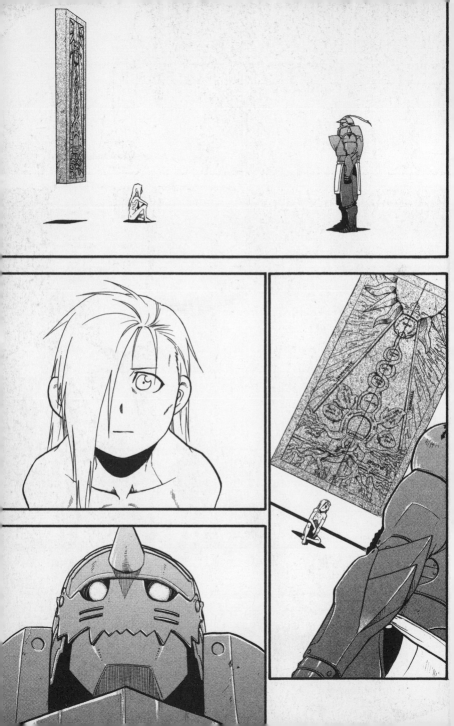

MY BODY...

STAGGER

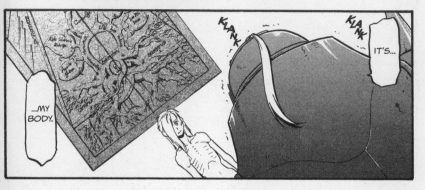

KLANK

KLANK

IT'S...

...MY BODY.

KLATUNK

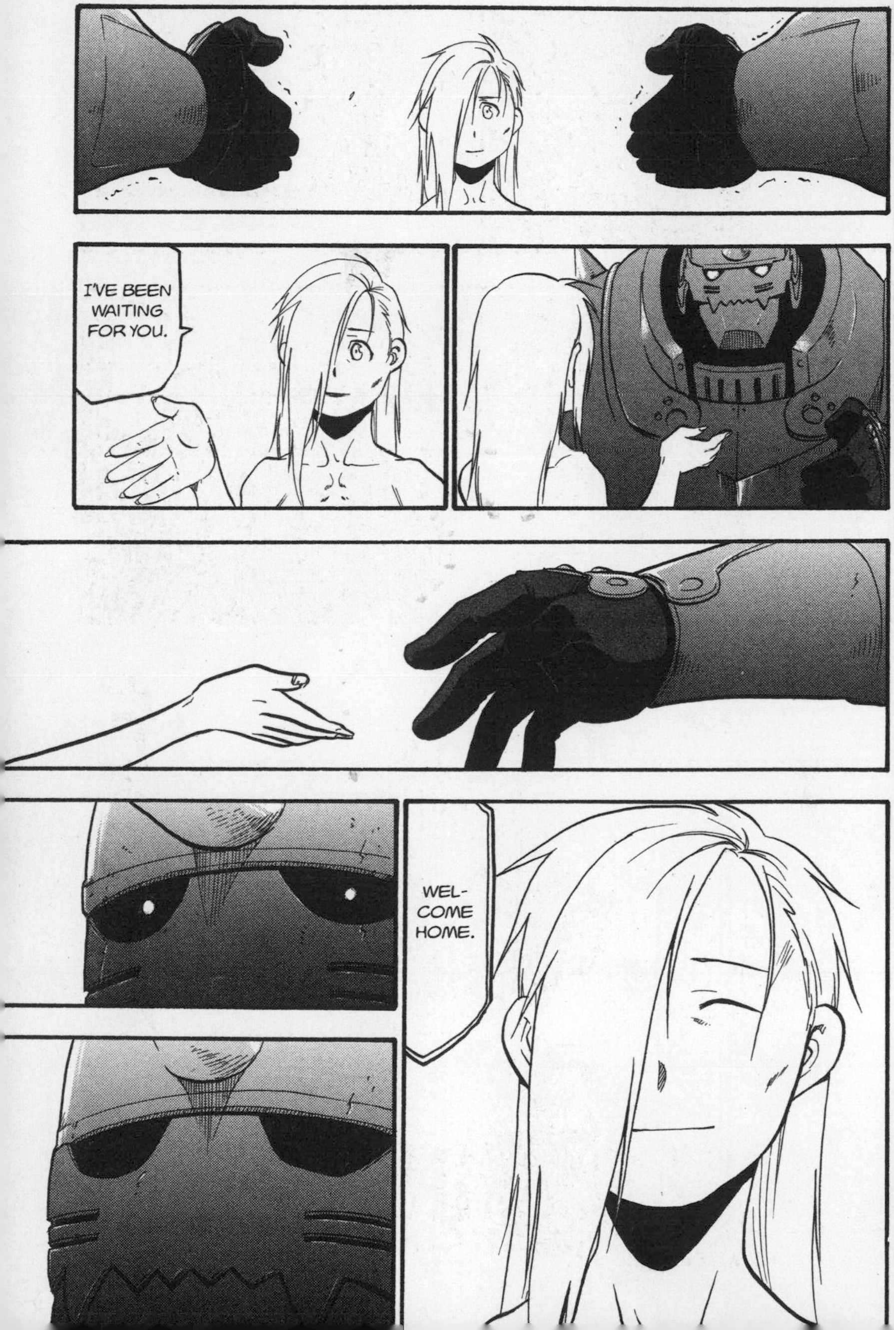
I'VE BEEN WAITING FOR YOU.
WEL-
COME
HOME.

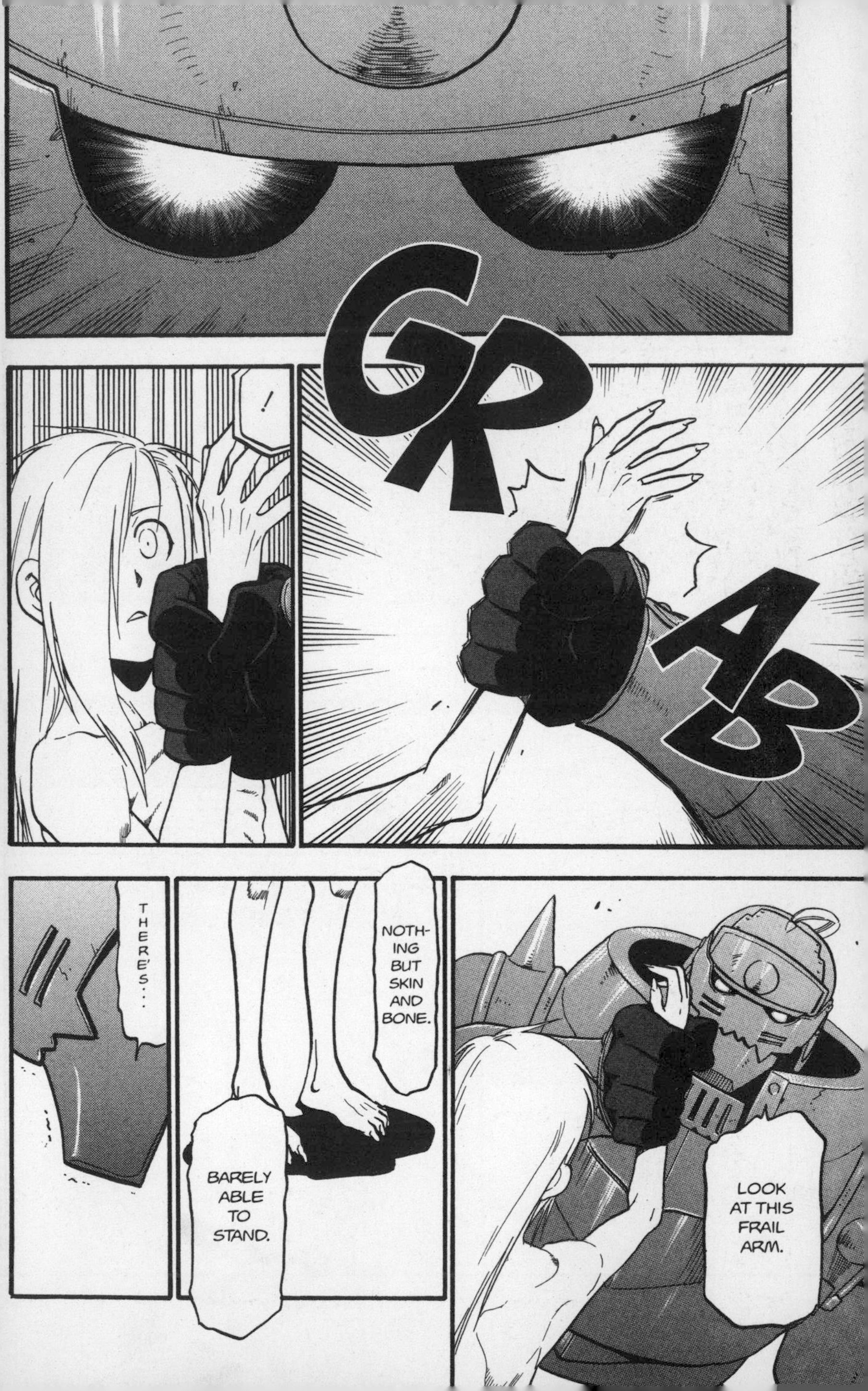
GRAB
!
LOOK AT THIS FRAIL ARM.
NOTHING BUT SKIN AND BONE.
BARELY ABLE TO STAND.
THERE'S...

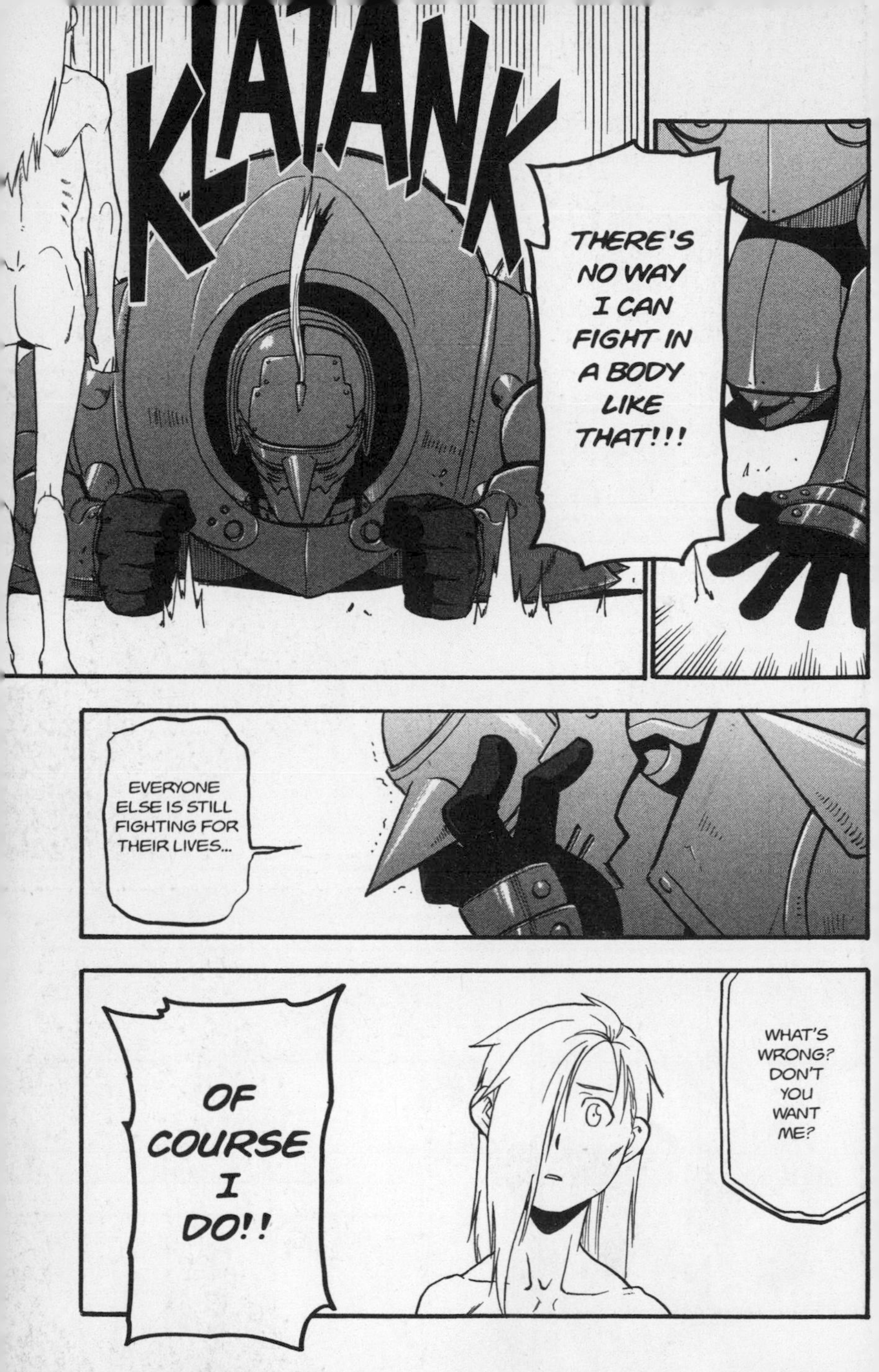
THERE'S NO WAY I CAN FIGHT IN A BODY LIKE THAT!!!
KLATANK
EVERYONE ELSE IS STILL FIGHTING FOR THEIR LIVES...
WHAT'S WRONG? DON'T YOU WANT ME?
OF COURSE I DO!!

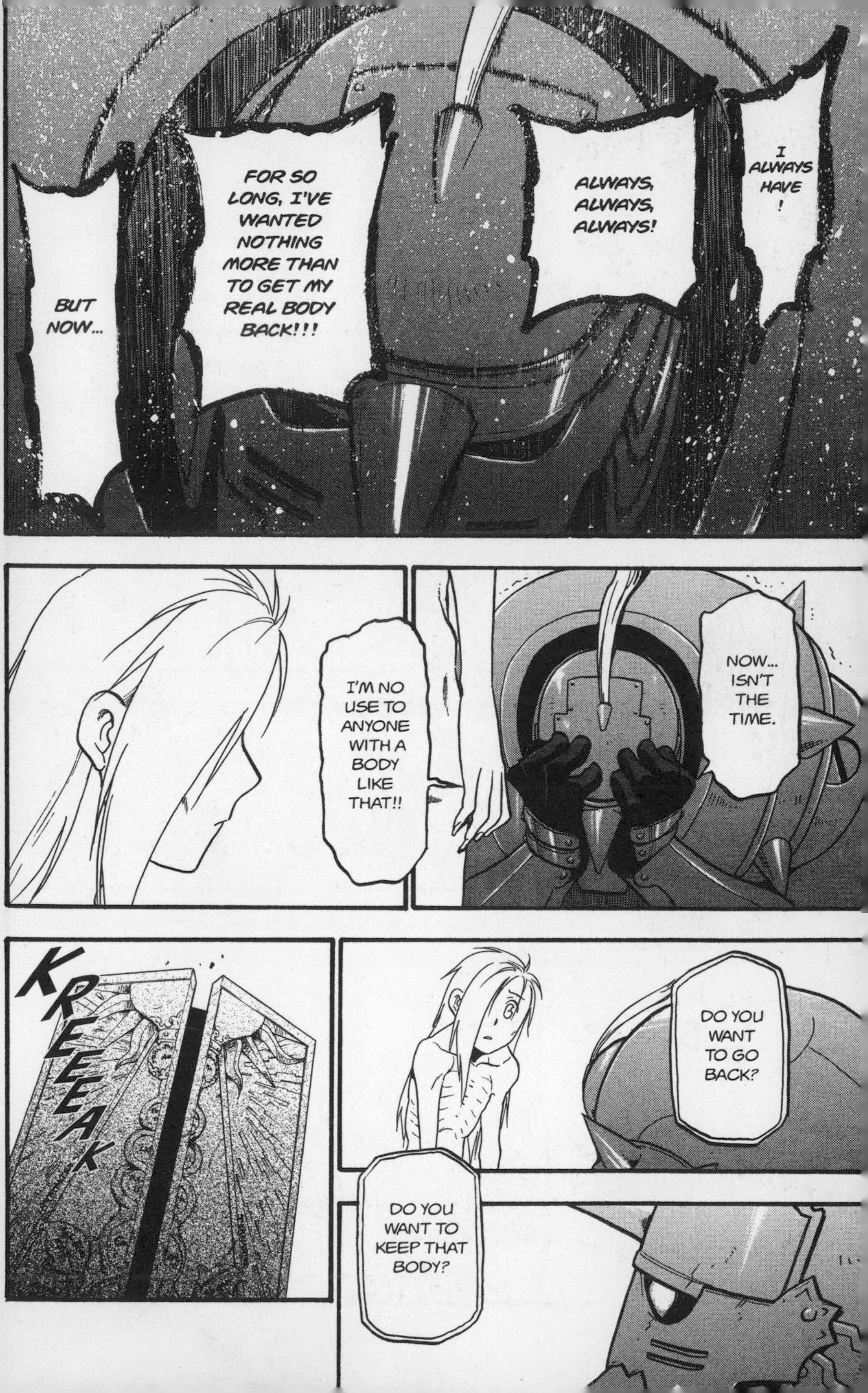
I ALWAYS HAVE!
ALWAYS, ALWAYS, ALWAYS!
FOR SO LONG, I'VE WANTED NOTHING MORE THAN TO GET MY REAL BODY BACK!!!
BUT NOW...
NOW... ISN'T THE TIME.
I'M NO USE TO ANYONE WITH A BODY LIKE THAT!!
DO YOU WANT TO GO BACK?
DO YOU WANT TO KEEP THAT BODY?
KREEEAK

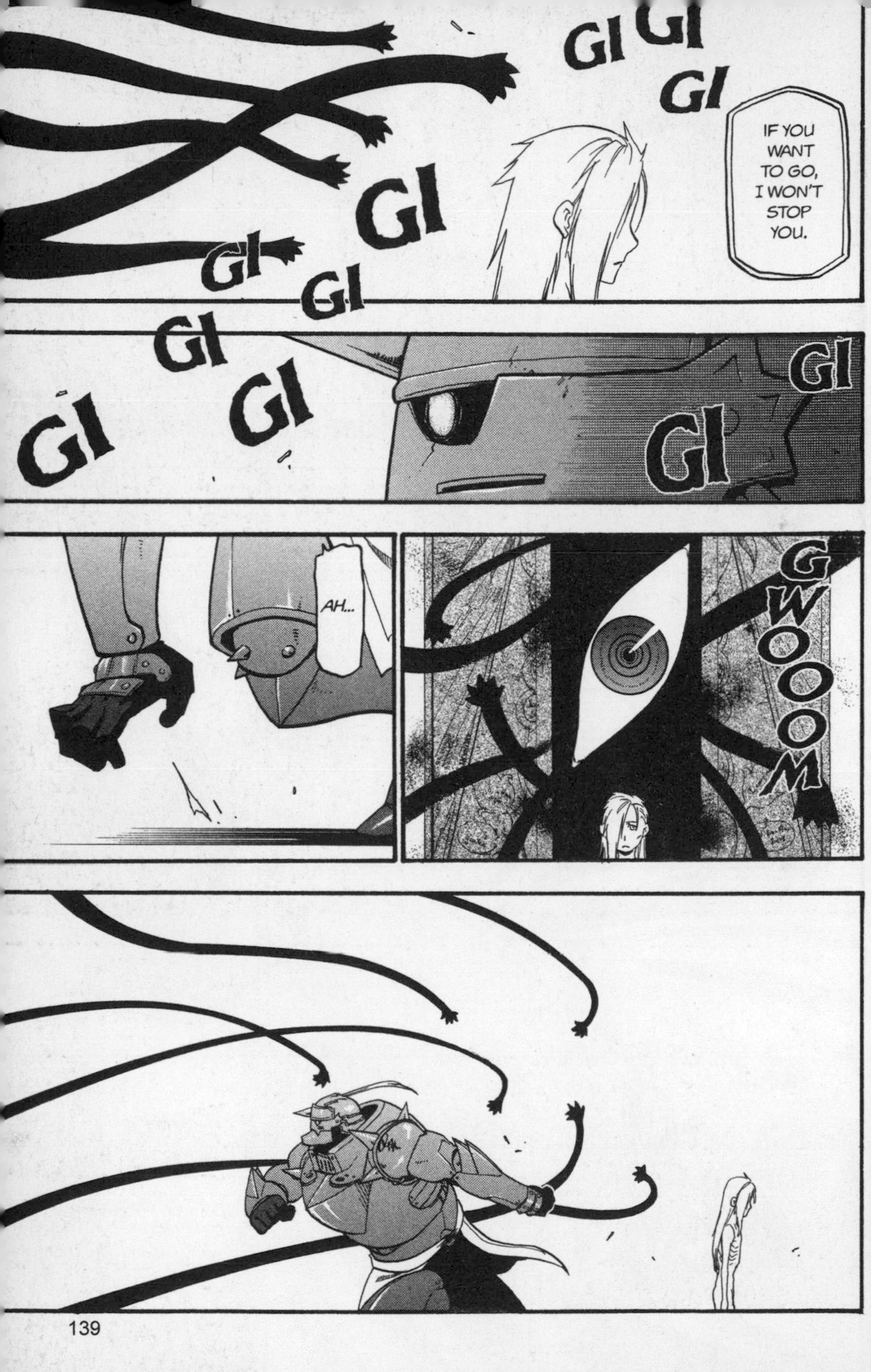
IF YOU WANT TO GO, I WON'T STOP YOU.
GI GI
GI
GI
GI
GI
GI
GI
GI
GI
GI
GWOOOOM
AH...

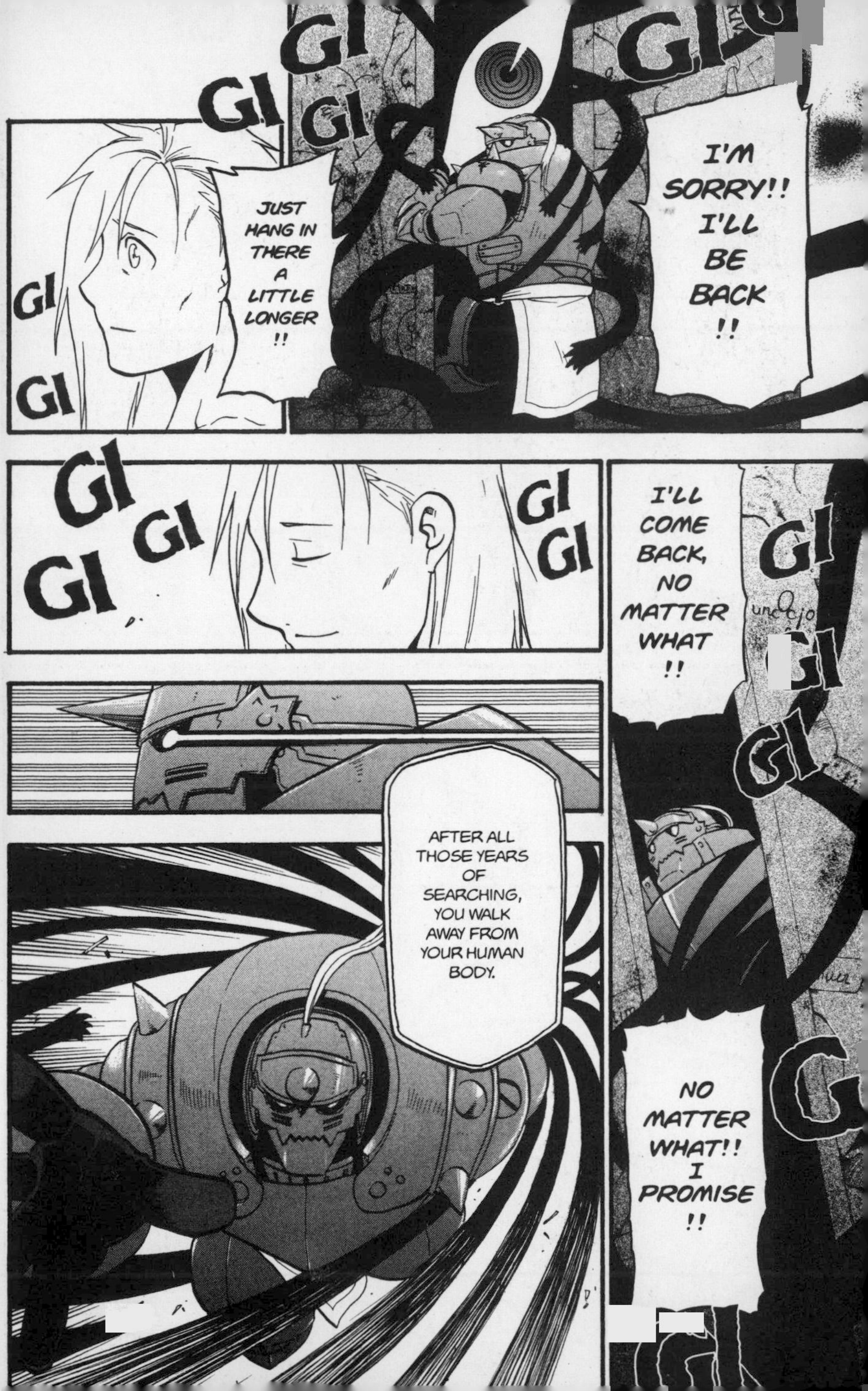
GI GI GI GLU
I'M SORRY!! I'LL BE BACK !!
JUST HANG IN THERE A LITTLE LONGER !!
GI GI
I'LL COME BACK, NO MATTER WHAT !!
GI GI GI
NO MATTER WHAT!! I PROMISE !!
G
GI GI GI GI GI
AFTER ALL THOSE YEARS OF SEARCHING, YOU WALK AWAY FROM YOUR HUMAN BODY.

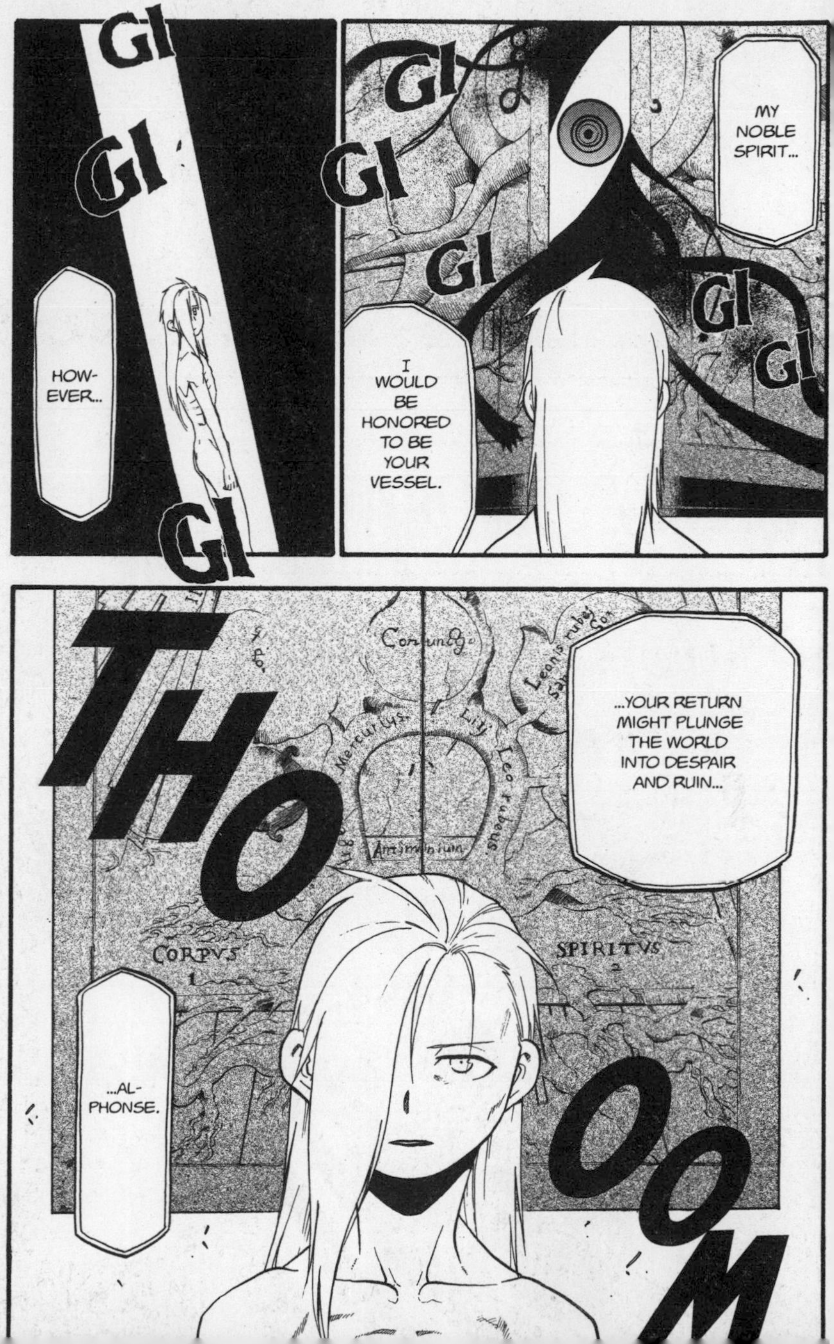
MY NOBLE SPIRIT...
GI GI
GI
GI GI
I WOULD BE HONORED TO BE YOUR VESSEL.
GI
GI
HOW-EVER...
GI
...YOUR RETURN MIGHT PLUNGE THE WORLD INTO DESPAIR AND RUIN...
THOOOOM
CORPVS
SPIRITVS
...AL-PHONSE.

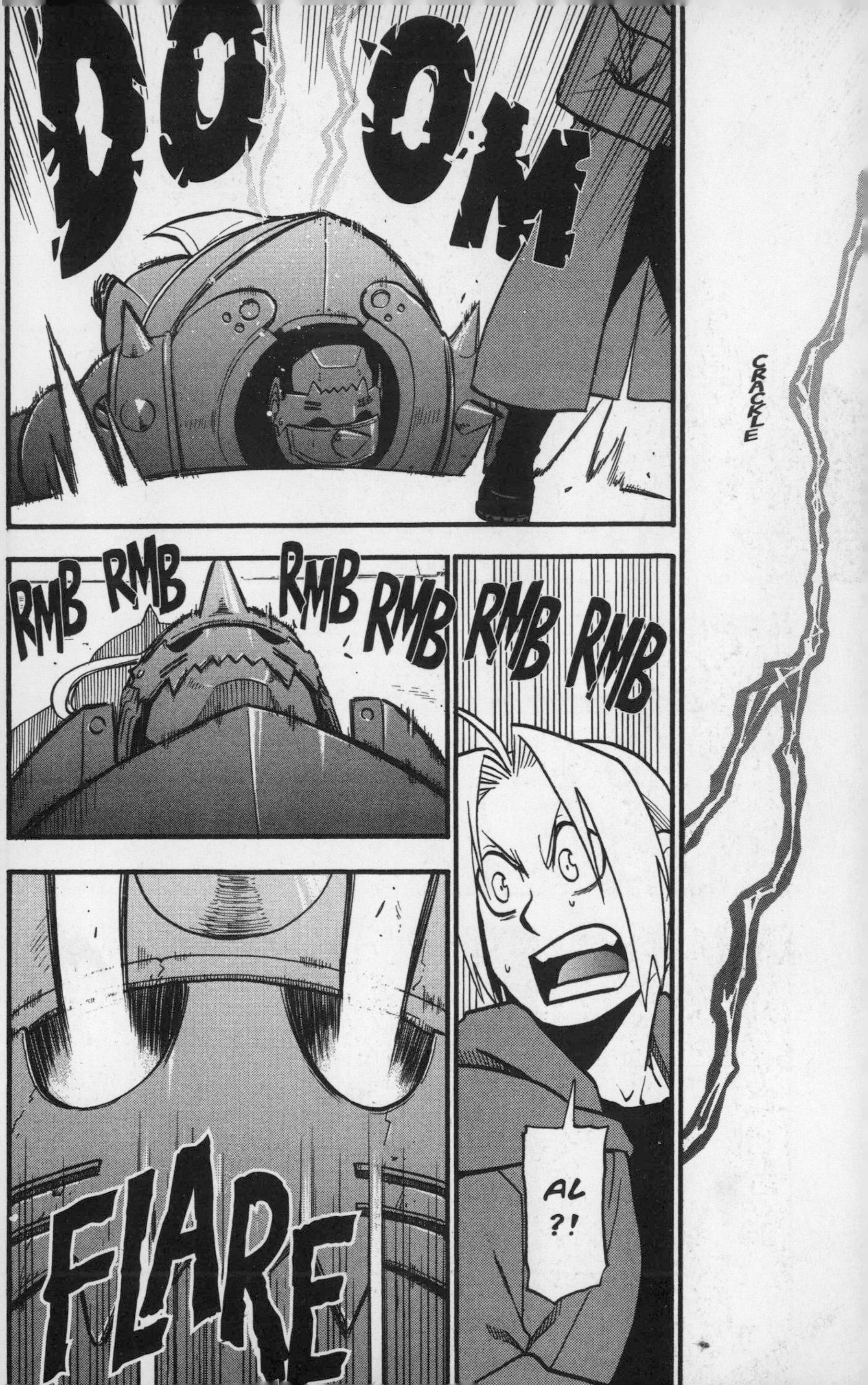
DOOM
CRACKLE
RMB RMB
AL?!
RMB RMB RMB RMB
FLARE

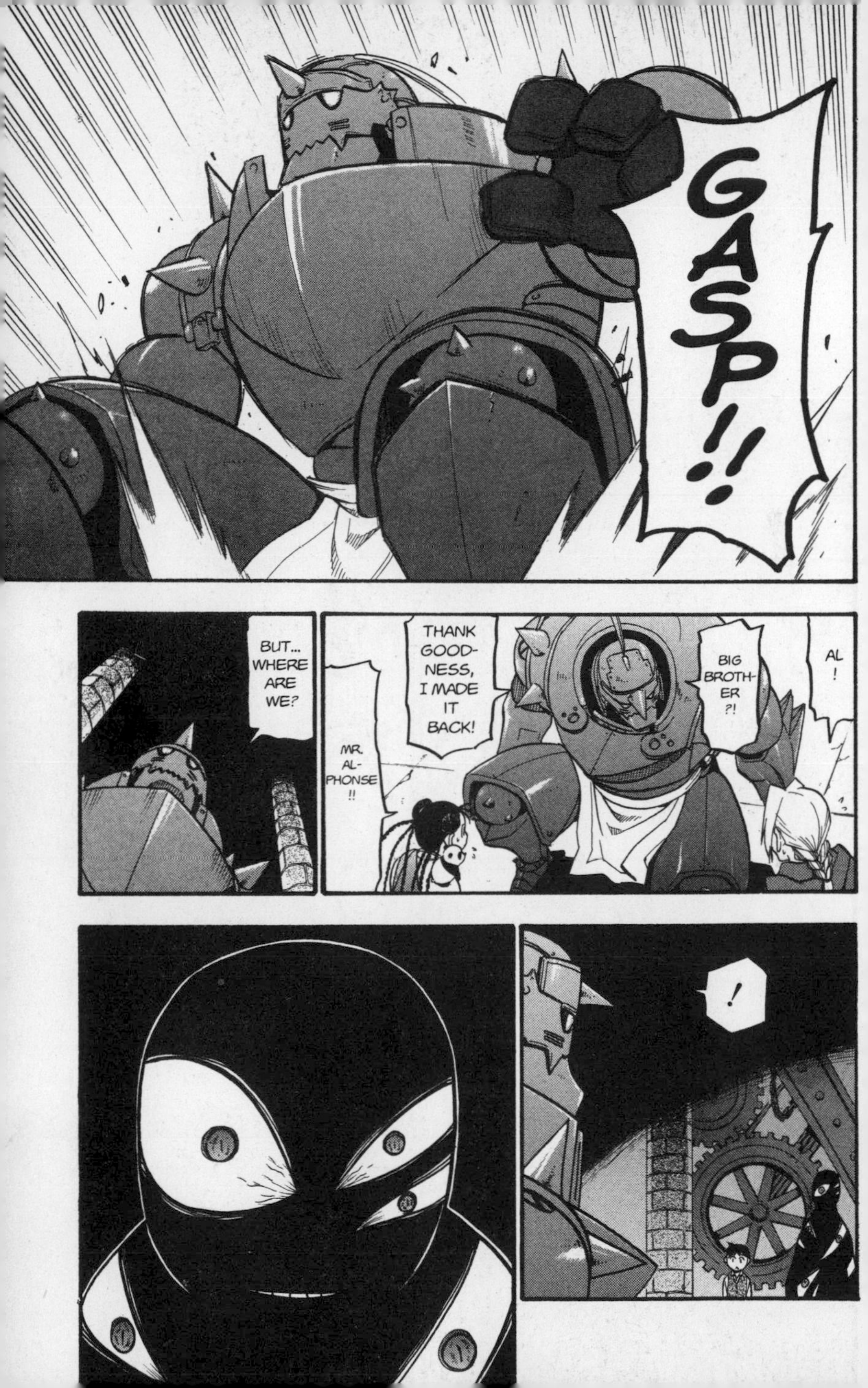
GASP!!!
AL!
BIG BROTHER?!
THANK GOODNESS, I MADE IT BACK!
MR. ALPHONSE!!
BUT... WHERE ARE WE?
!

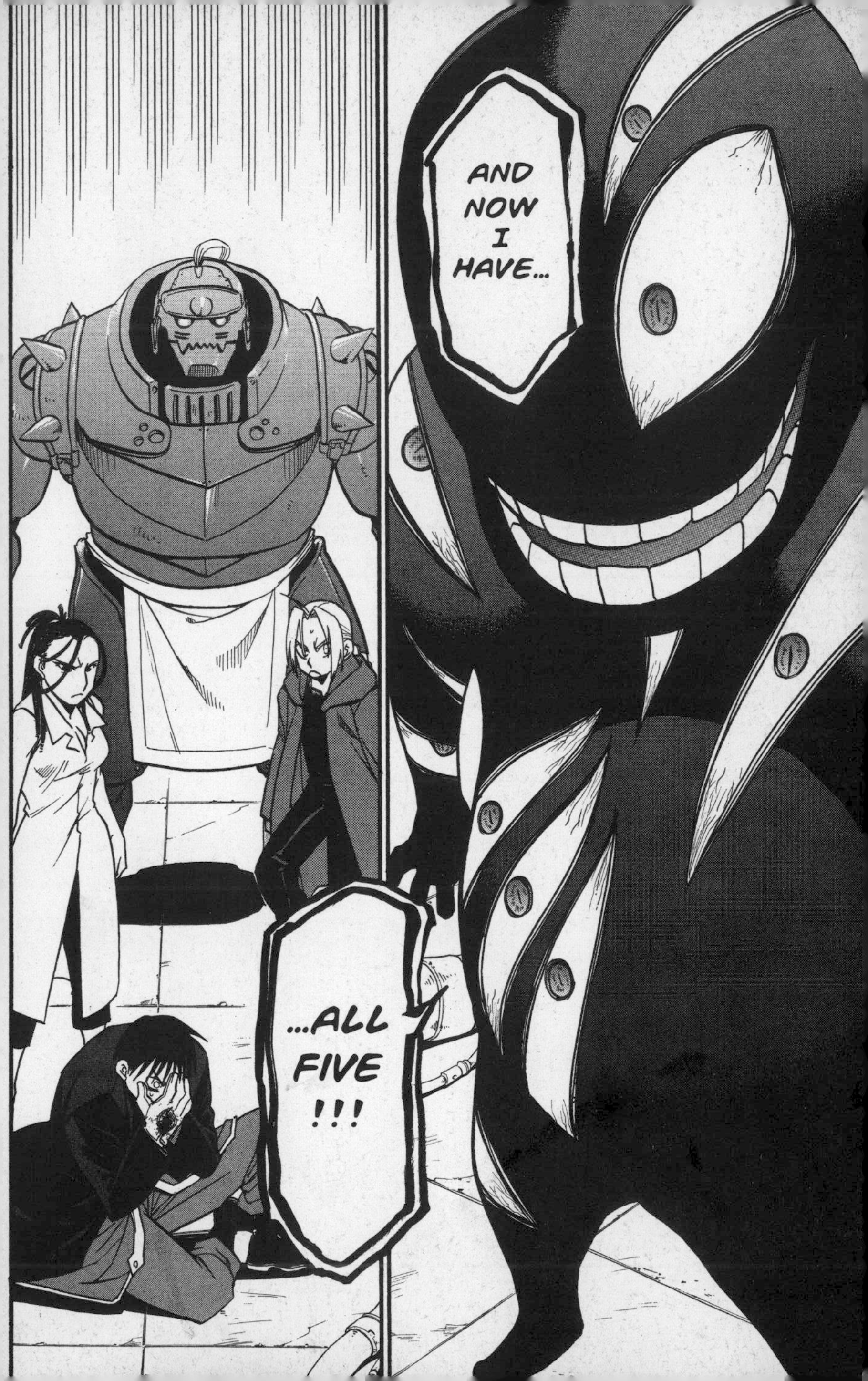
AND NOW I HAVE...
...ALL FIVE!!!

FULLMETAL
ALCHEMIST

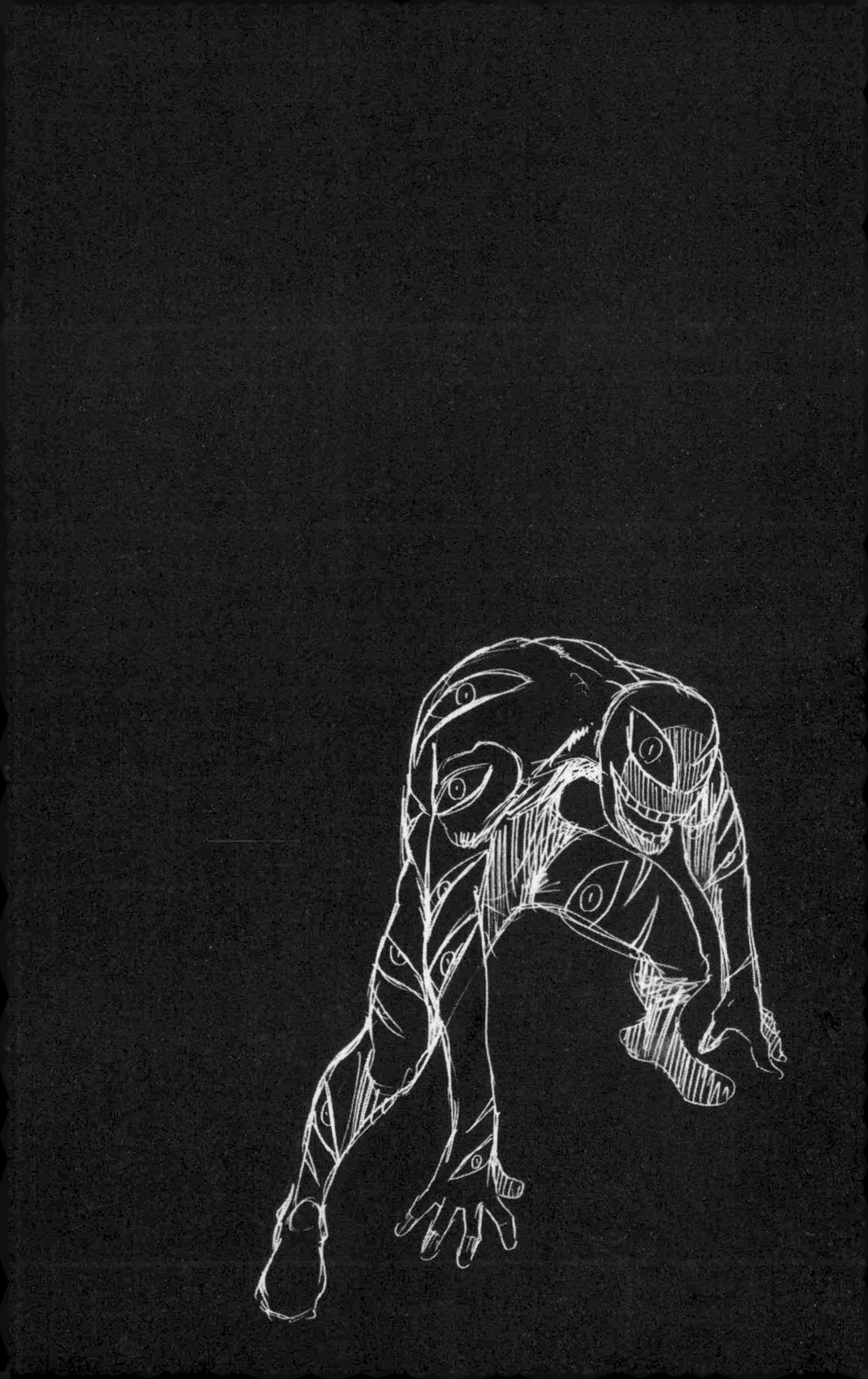

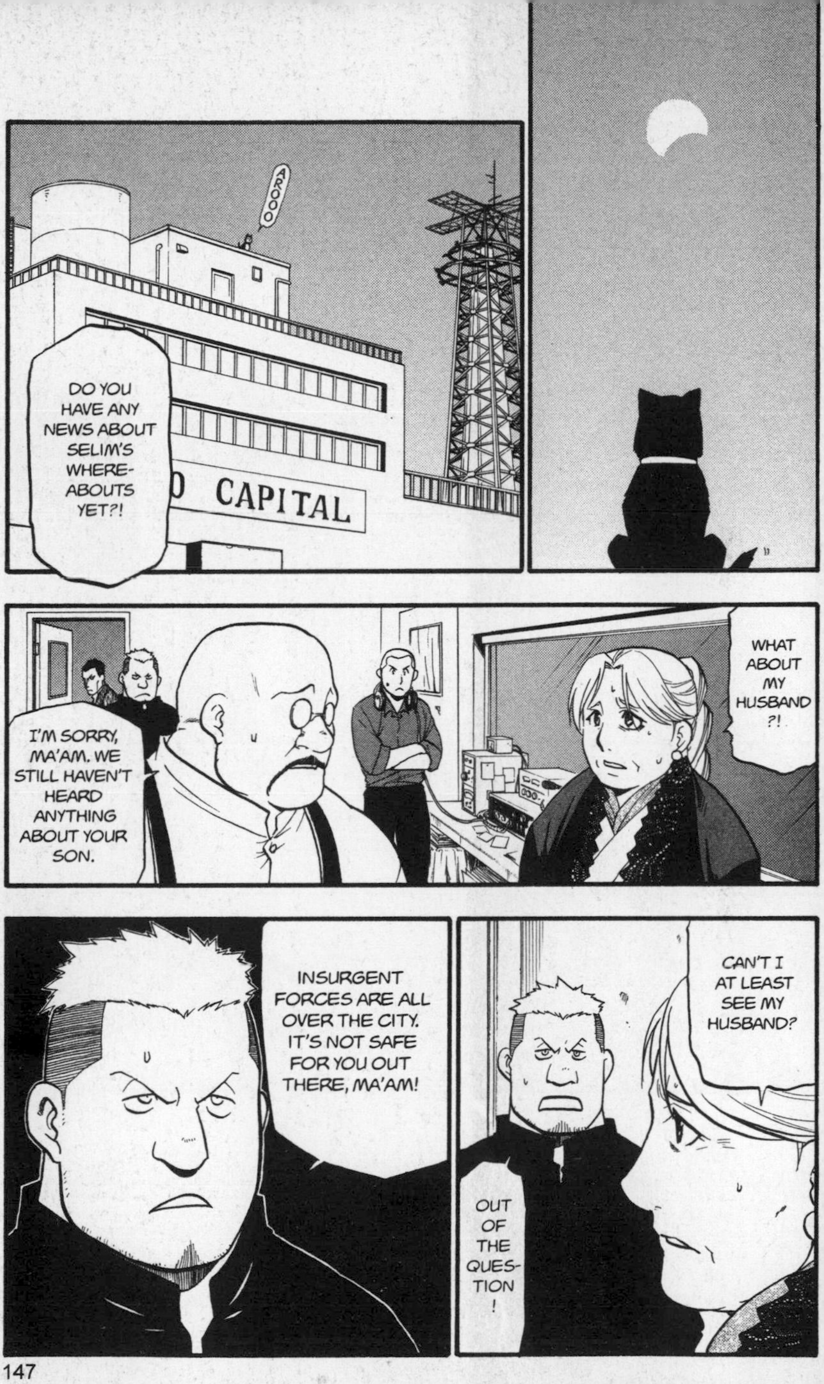
AROOO
CAPITAL
DO YOU HAVE ANY NEWS ABOUT SELIM'S WHEREABOUTS YET?!
WHAT ABOUT MY HUSBAND?!
I'M SORRY, MA'AM. WE STILL HAVEN'T HEARD ANYTHING ABOUT YOUR SON.
CAN'T I AT LEAST SEE MY HUSBAND?
OUT OF THE QUESTION!
INSURGENT FORCES ARE ALL OVER THE CITY. IT'S NOT SAFE FOR YOU OUT THERE, MA'AM!

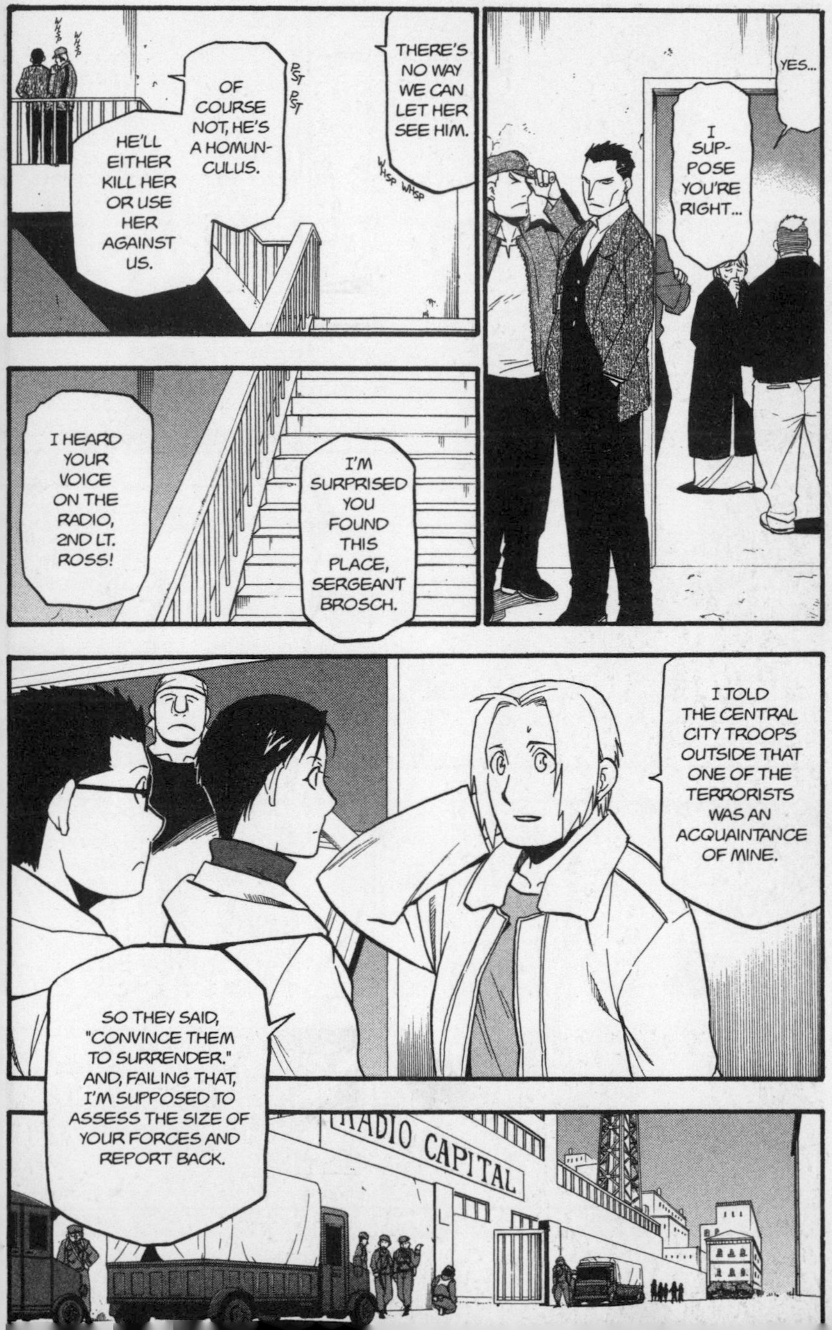
YES...
I SUP-POSE YOU'RE RIGHT...
WHSP WHSP
THERE'S NO WAY WE CAN LET HER SEE HIM.
PST PST
OF COURSE NOT, HE'S A HOMUN-CULUS.
HE'LL EITHER KILL HER OR USE HER AGAINST US.
WHSP WHSP
I'M SURPRISED YOU FOUND THIS PLACE, SERGEANT BROSCH.
I HEARD YOUR VOICE ON THE RADIO, 2ND LT. ROSS!
I TOLD THE CENTRAL CITY TROOPS OUTSIDE THAT ONE OF THE TERRORISTS WAS AN ACQUAINTANCE OF MINE.
SO THEY SAID, "CONVINCE THEM TO SURRENDER." AND, FAILING THAT, I'M SUPPOSED TO ASSESS THE SIZE OF YOUR FORCES AND REPORT BACK.
RADIO CAPITAL

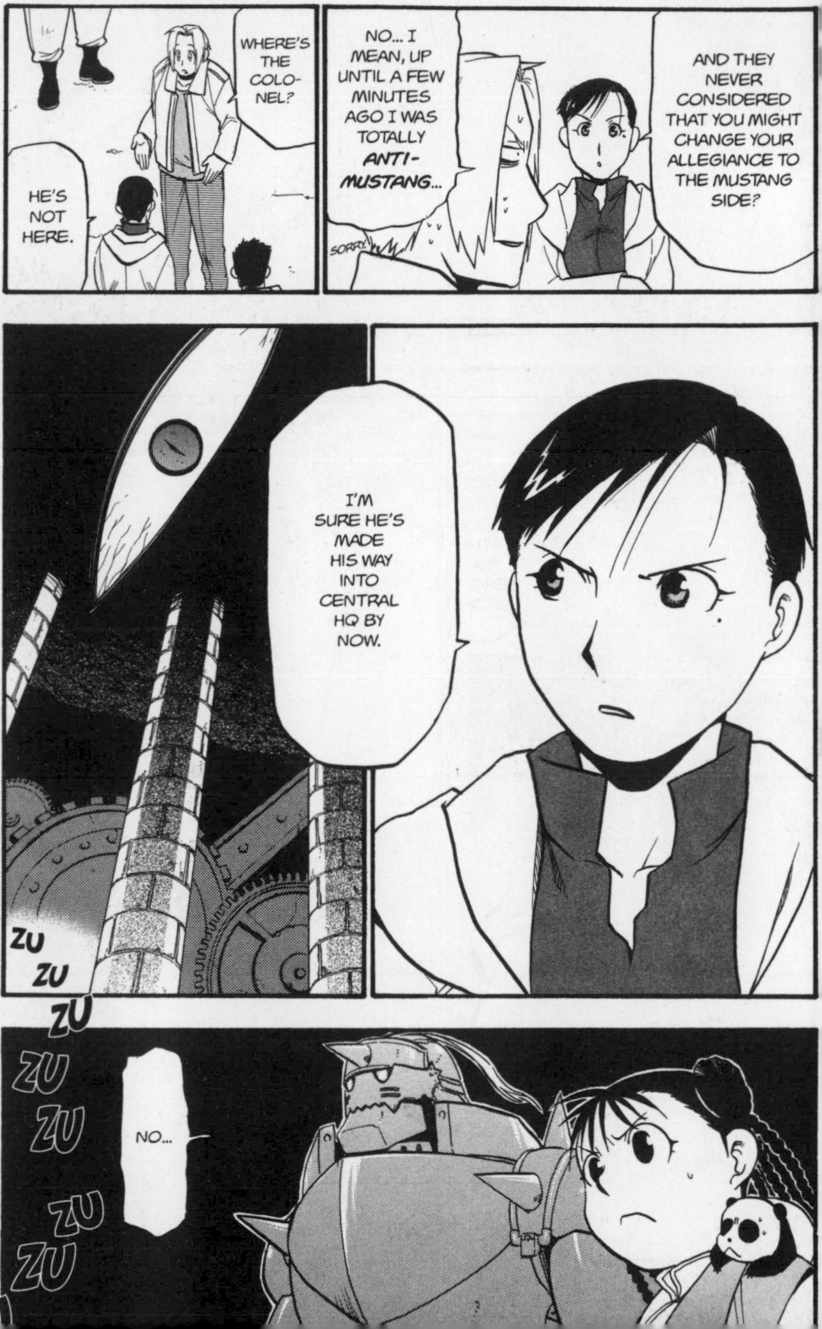
AND THEY NEVER CONSIDERED THAT YOU MIGHT CHANGE YOUR ALLEGIANCE TO THE MUSTANG SIDE?
NO... I MEAN, UP UNTIL A FEW MINUTES AGO I WAS TOTALLY ANTI-MUSTANG...
SORRY.
WHERE'S THE COLONEL?
HE'S NOT HERE.
I'M SURE HE'S MADE HIS WAY INTO CENTRAL HQ BY NOW.
ZU ZU
ZU ZU ZU ZU ZU
NO...

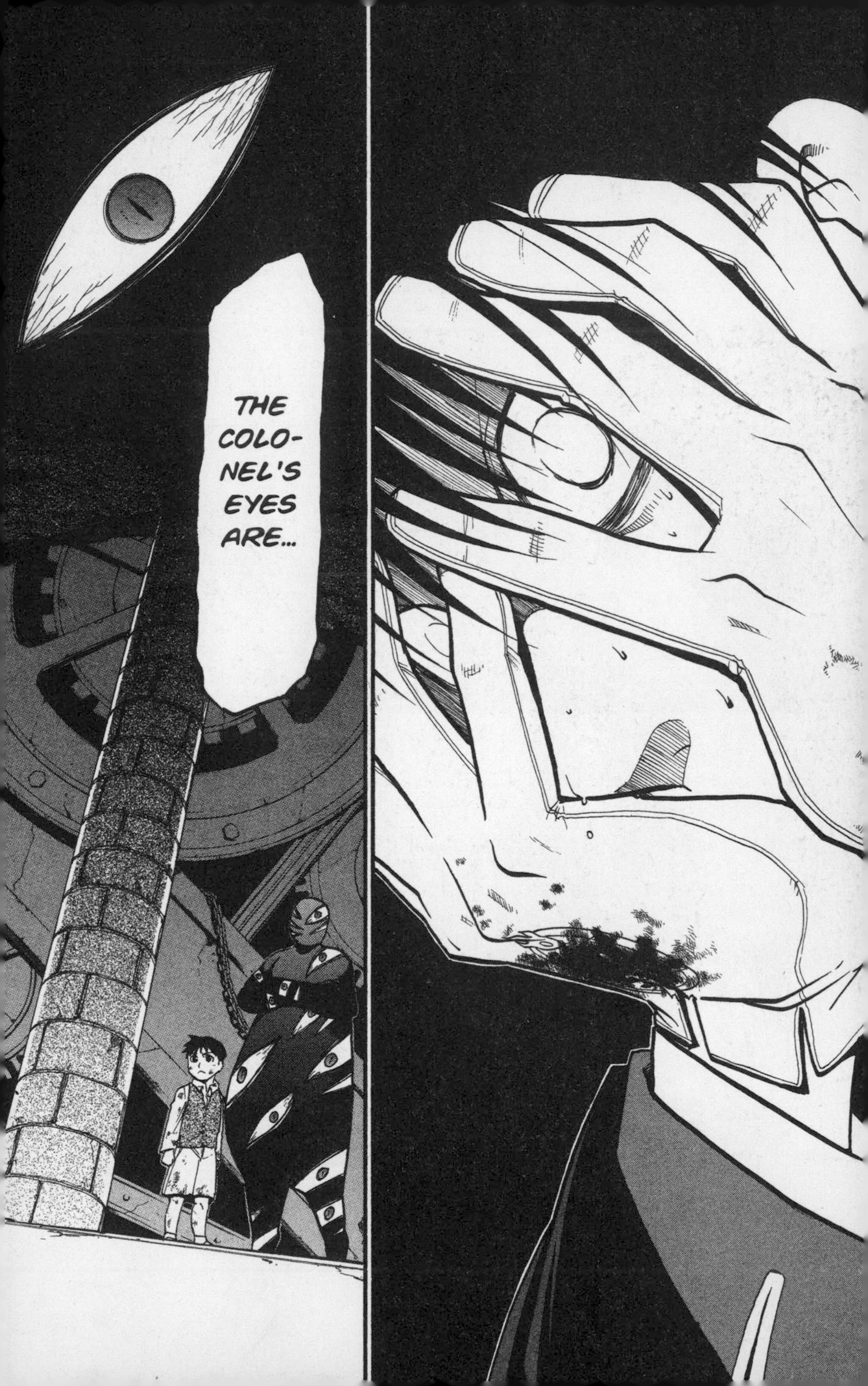
THE COLO-NEL'S EYES ARE...

Chapter 103
For Whom?

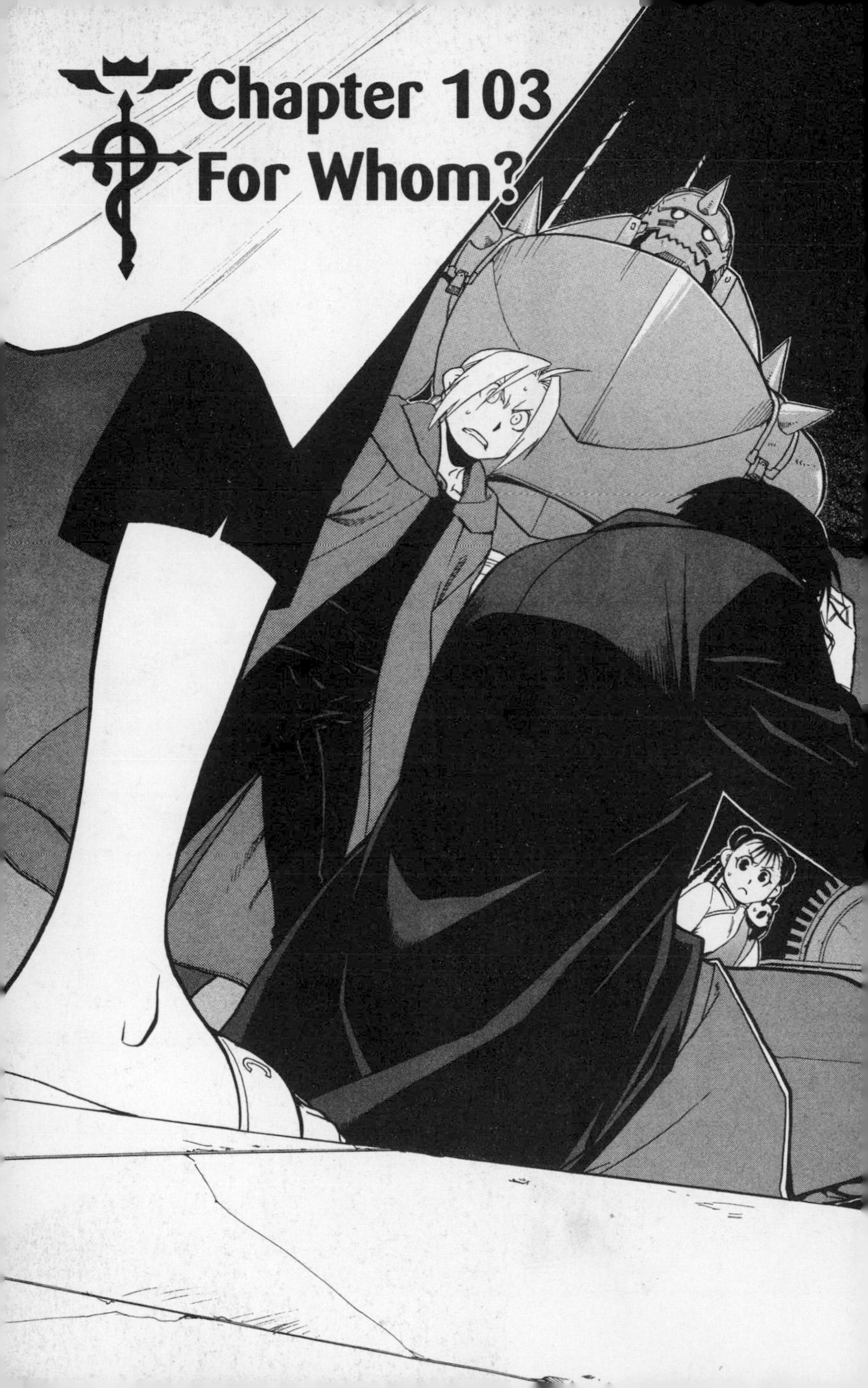

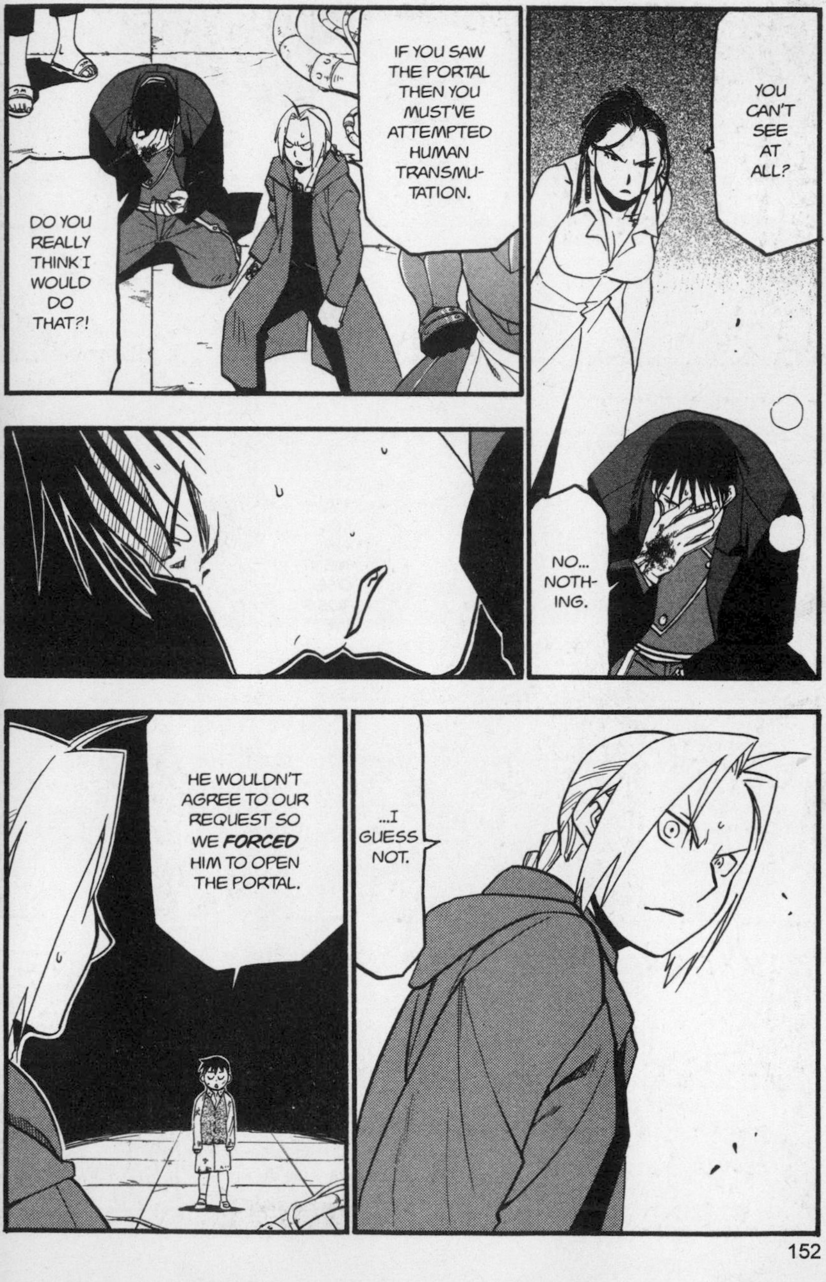
YOU CAN'T SEE AT ALL?
NO... NOTHING.
IF YOU SAW THE PORTAL THEN YOU MUST'VE ATTEMPTED HUMAN TRANSMU-TATION.
DO YOU REALLY THINK I WOULD DO THAT?!
...I GUESS NOT.
HE WOULDN'T AGREE TO OUR REQUEST SO WE **FORCED** HIM TO OPEN THE PORTAL.

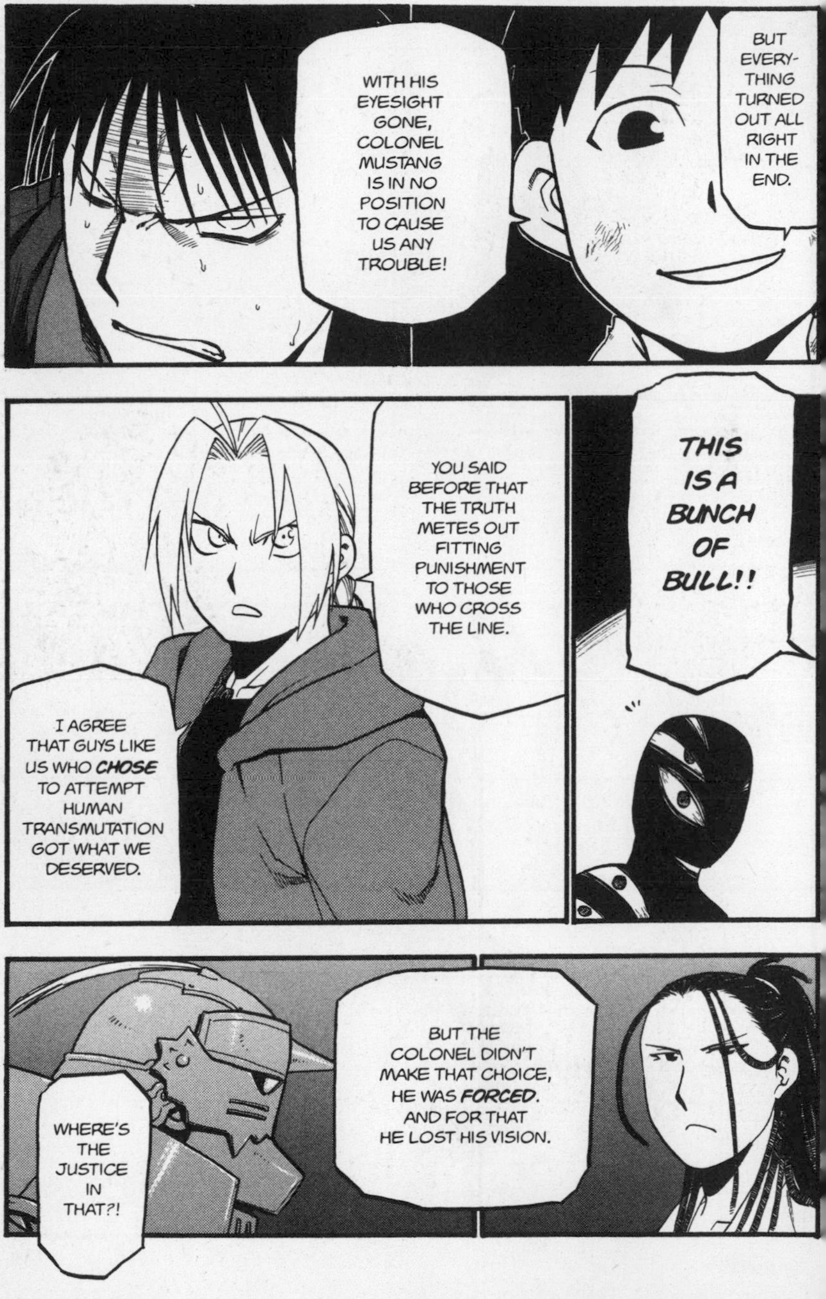
BUT EVERYTHING TURNED OUT ALL RIGHT IN THE END.
WITH HIS EYESIGHT GONE, COLONEL MUSTANG IS IN NO POSITION TO CAUSE US ANY TROUBLE!
THIS IS A BUNCH OF BULL!!
YOU SAID BEFORE THAT THE TRUTH METES OUT FITTING PUNISHMENT TO THOSE WHO CROSS THE LINE.
I AGREE THAT GUYS LIKE US WHO CHOSE TO ATTEMPT HUMAN TRANSMUTATION GOT WHAT WE DESERVED.
BUT THE COLONEL DIDN'T MAKE THAT CHOICE, HE WAS FORCED. AND FOR THAT HE LOST HIS VISION.
WHERE'S THE JUSTICE IN THAT?!

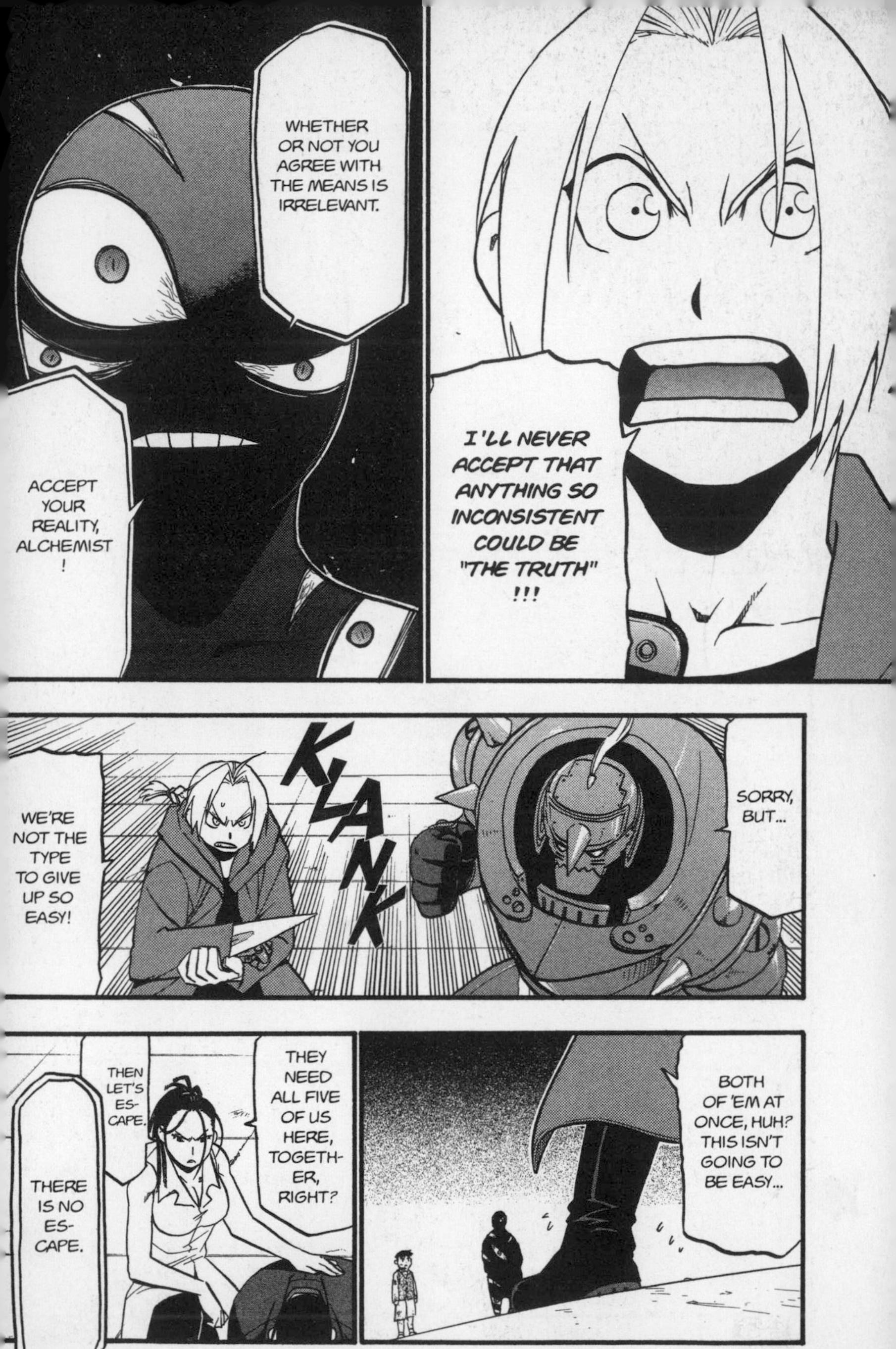
I'LL NEVER ACCEPT THAT ANYTHING SO INCONSISTENT COULD BE "THE TRUTH" !!!
WHETHER OR NOT YOU AGREE WITH THE MEANS IS IRRELEVANT.
ACCEPT YOUR REALITY, ALCHEMIST !
SORRY, BUT...
KLANK
WE'RE NOT THE TYPE TO GIVE UP SO EASY!
BOTH OF 'EM AT ONCE, HUH? THIS ISN'T GOING TO BE EASY...
THEY NEED ALL FIVE OF US HERE, TOGETHER, RIGHT?
THEN LET'S ES-CAPE.
THERE IS NO ES-CAPE.

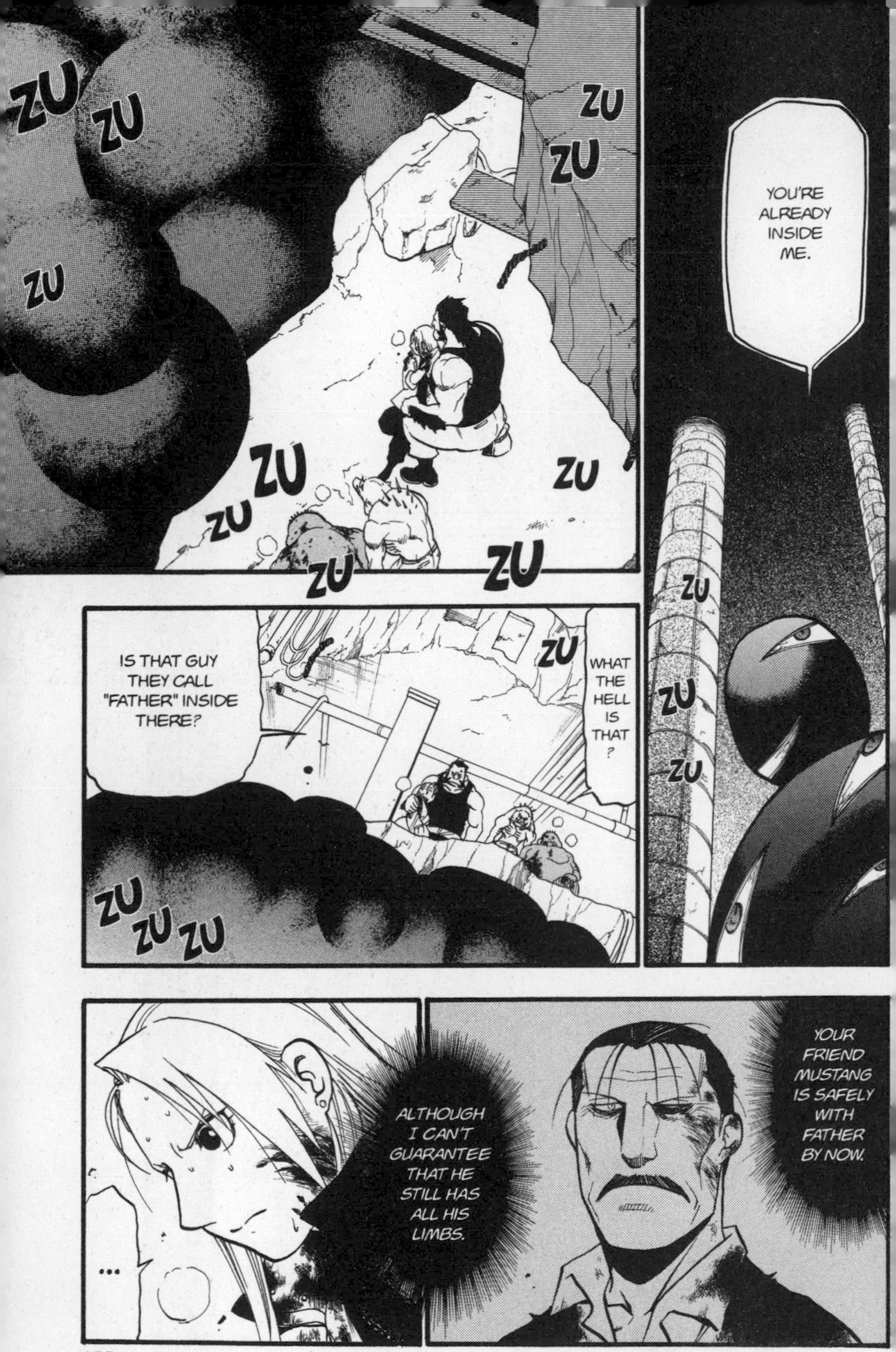
YOU'RE ALREADY INSIDE ME.
ZU
ZU
ZU
ZU
ZU
ZU
ZU
ZU
ZU
ZU
ZU
ZU
ZU
ZU
ZU
WHAT THE HELL IS THAT?
IS THAT GUY THEY CALL "FATHER" INSIDE THERE?
ZU
ZU
ZU
YOUR FRIEND MUSTANG IS SAFELY WITH FATHER BY NOW.
ALTHOUGH I CAN'T GUARANTEE THAT HE STILL HAS ALL HIS LIMBS.
...

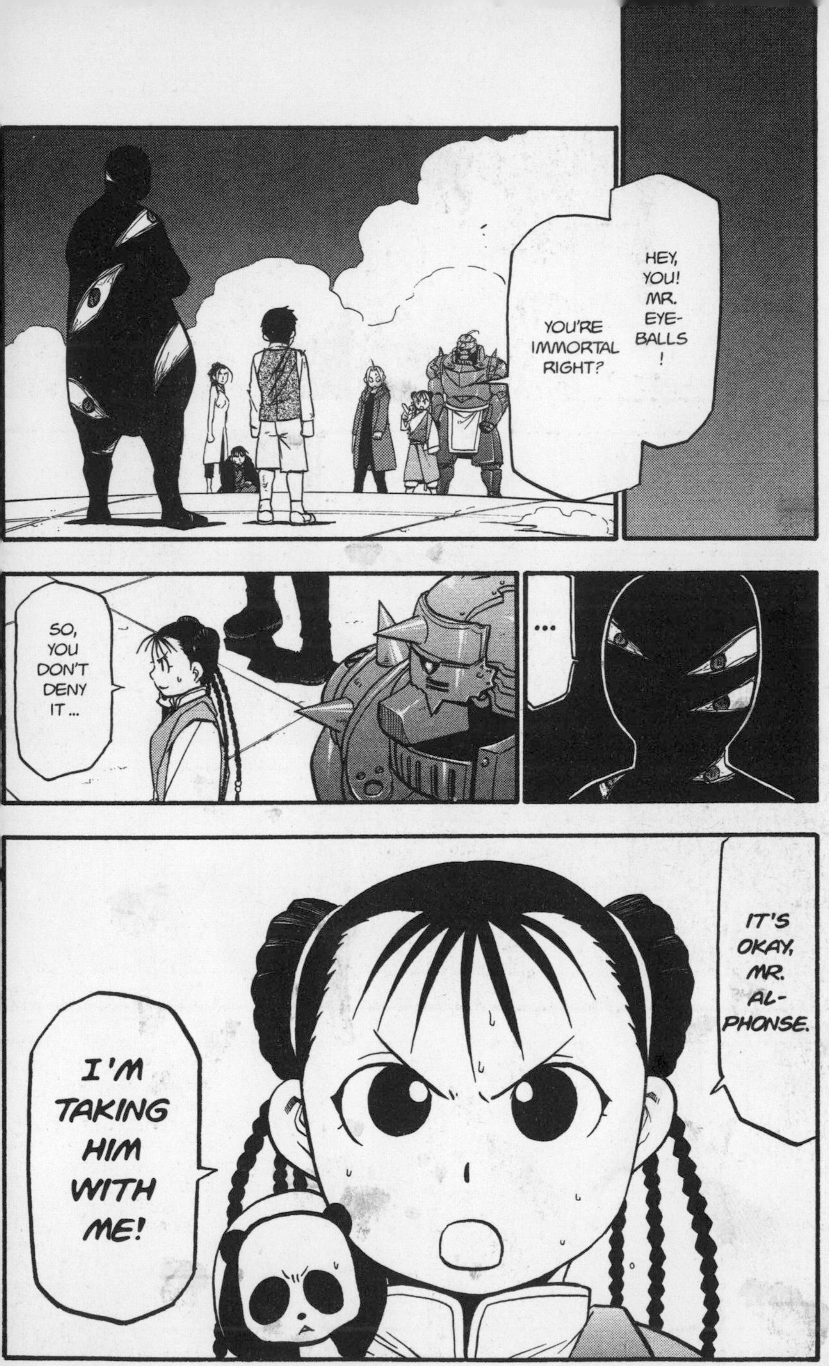
HEY, YOU! MR. EYE-BALLS!
YOU'RE IMMORTAL RIGHT?
...
SO, YOU DON'T DENY IT ...
IT'S OKAY, MR. AL-PHONSE.
I'M TAKING HIM WITH ME!

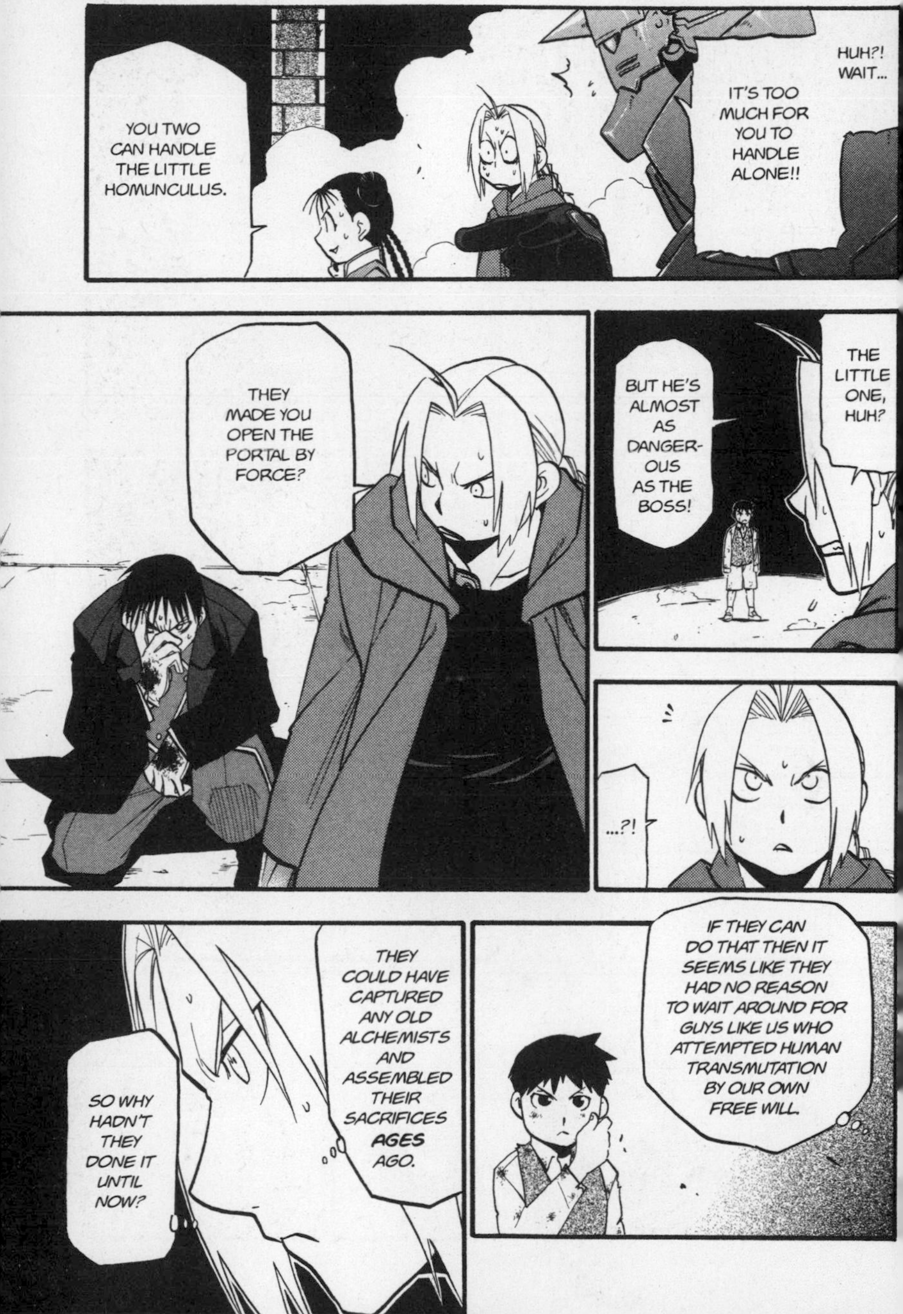
HUH?! WAIT...
IT'S TOO MUCH FOR YOU TO HANDLE ALONE!!
YOU TWO CAN HANDLE THE LITTLE HOMUNCULUS.
THE LITTLE ONE, HUH?
BUT HE'S ALMOST AS DANGER-OUS AS THE BOSS!
...?!
THEY MADE YOU OPEN THE PORTAL BY FORCE?
IF THEY CAN DO THAT THEN IT SEEMS LIKE THEY HAD NO REASON TO WAIT AROUND FOR GUYS LIKE US WHO ATTEMPTED HUMAN TRANSMUTATION BY OUR OWN FREE WILL.
THEY COULD HAVE CAPTURED ANY OLD ALCHEMISTS AND ASSEMBLED THEIR SACRIFICES **AGES** AGO.
SO WHY HADN'T THEY DONE IT UNTIL NOW?

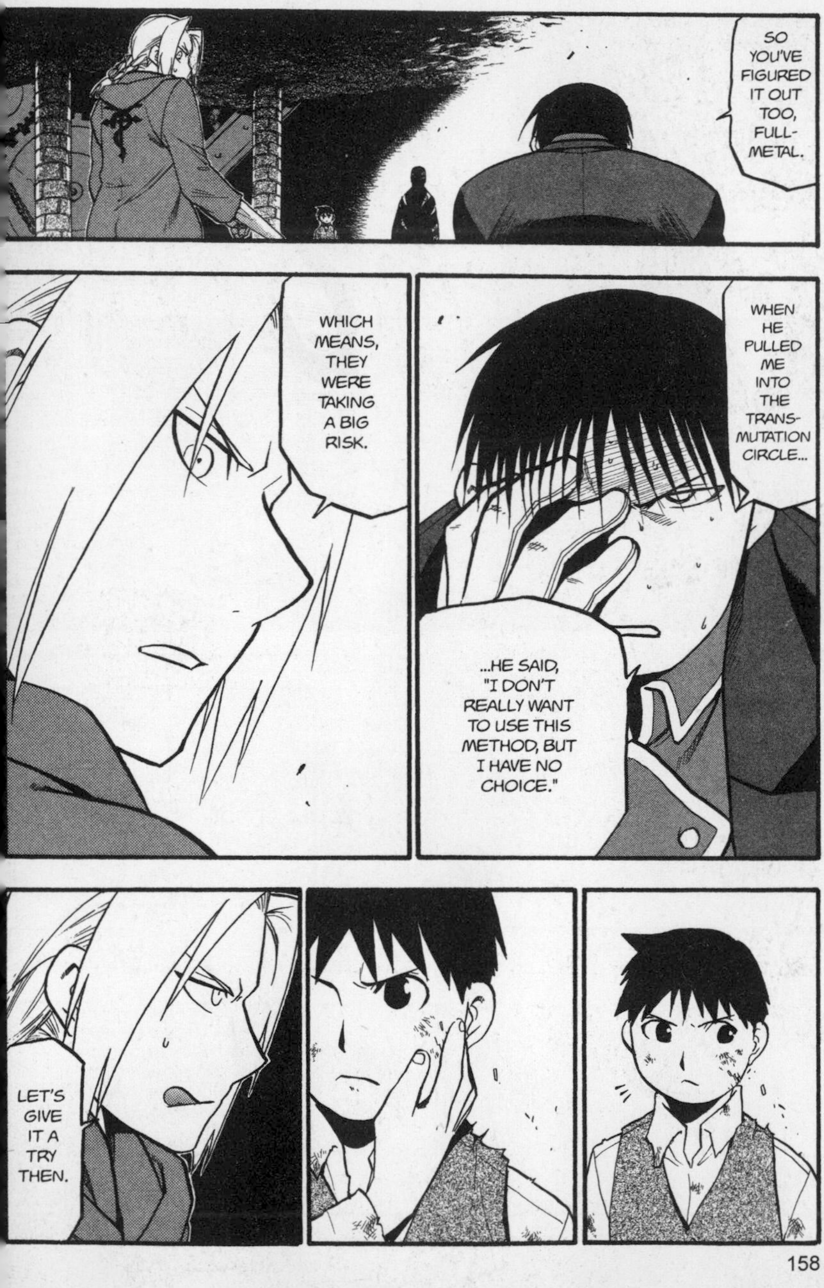
SO YOU'VE FIGURED IT OUT TOO, FULL-METAL.
WHEN HE PULLED ME INTO THE TRANS-MUTATION CIRCLE...
...HE SAID, "I DON'T REALLY WANT TO USE THIS METHOD, BUT I HAVE NO CHOICE."
WHICH MEANS, THEY WERE TAKING A BIG RISK.
LET'S GIVE IT A TRY THEN.

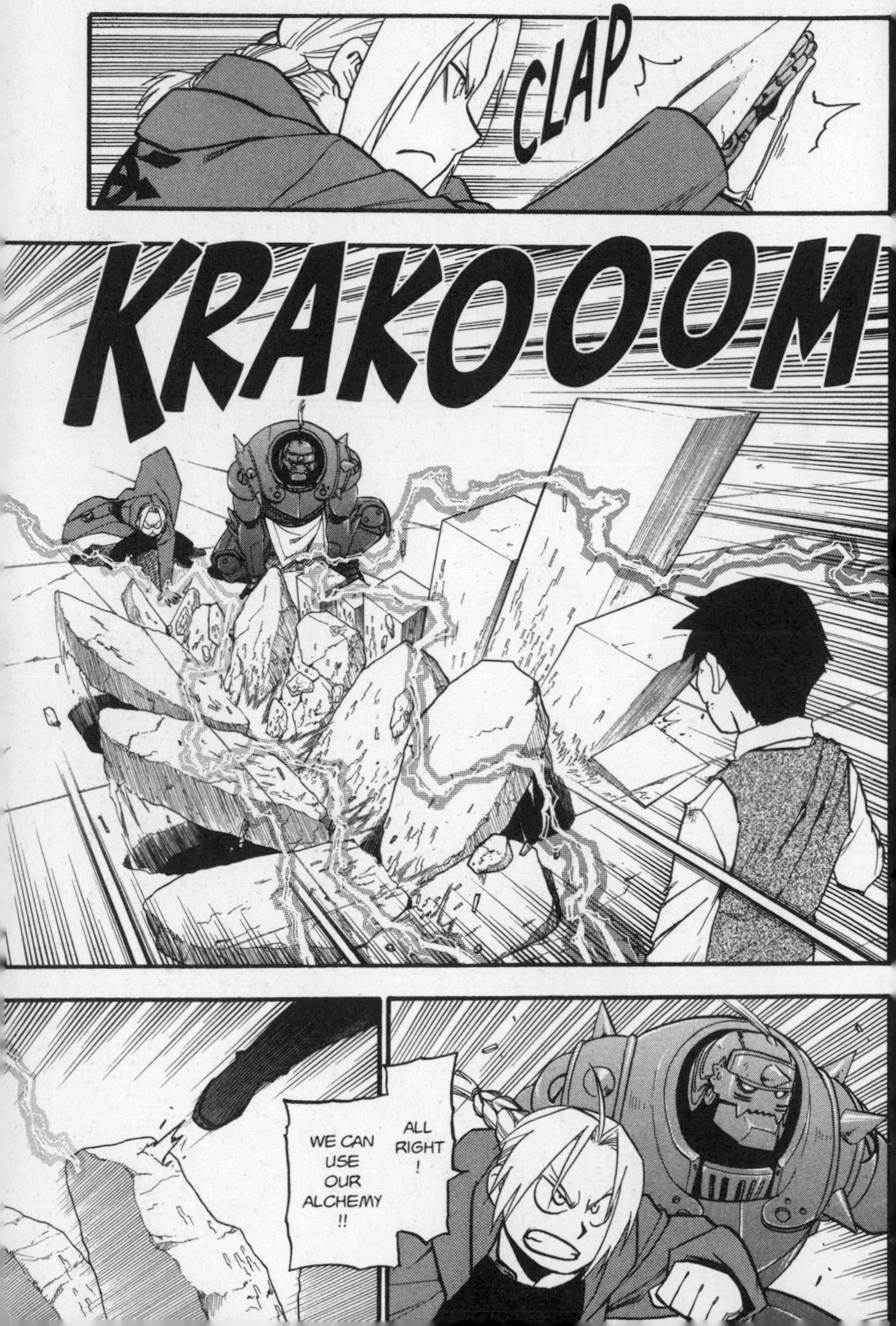
CLAP
KRAKOOOM
ALL RIGHT!
WE CAN USE OUR ALCHEMY!!

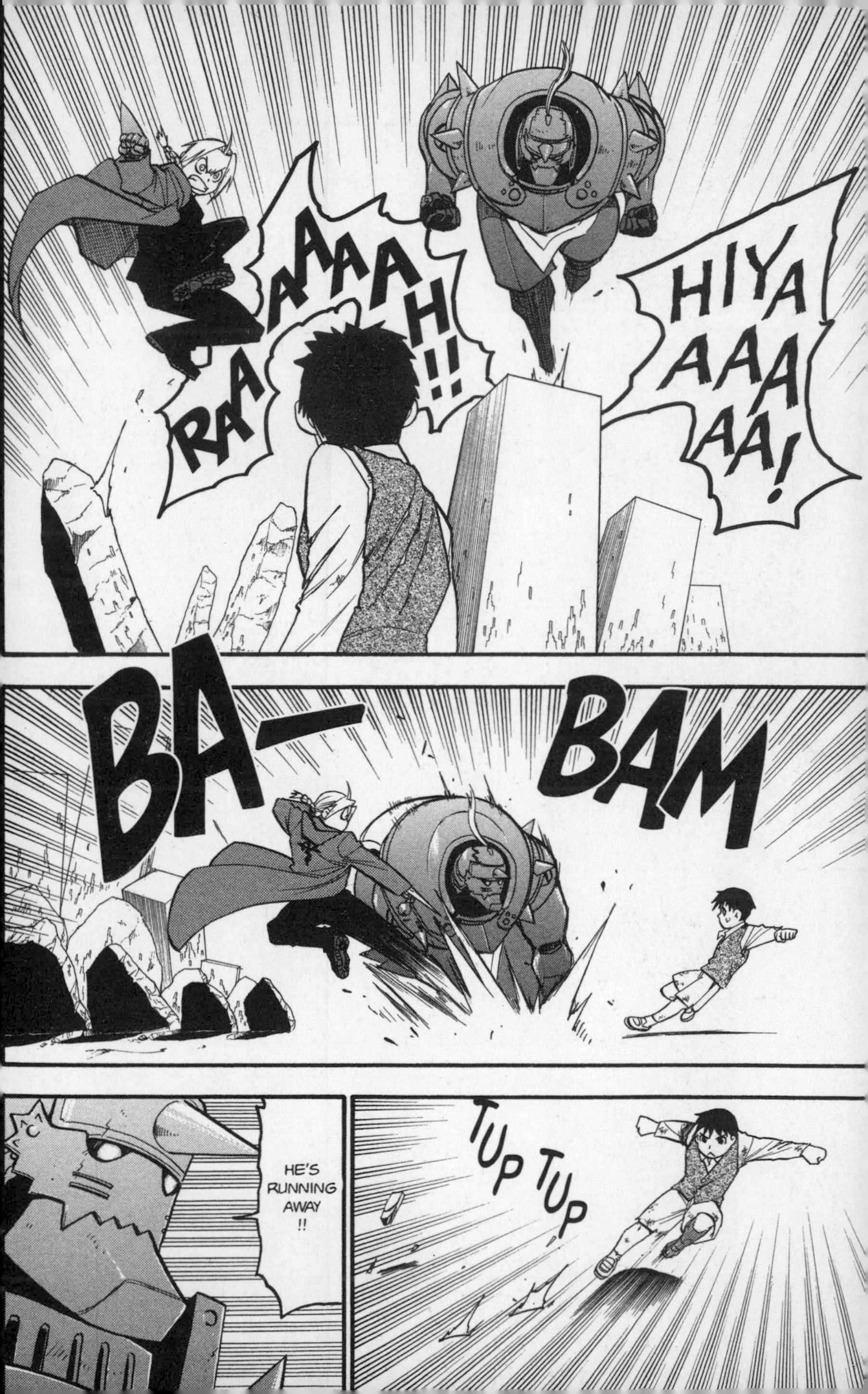
HIYAAAAAAA!
RAAAAAAH!!
BA-BAM
HE'S RUNNING AWAY !!
TUP TUP

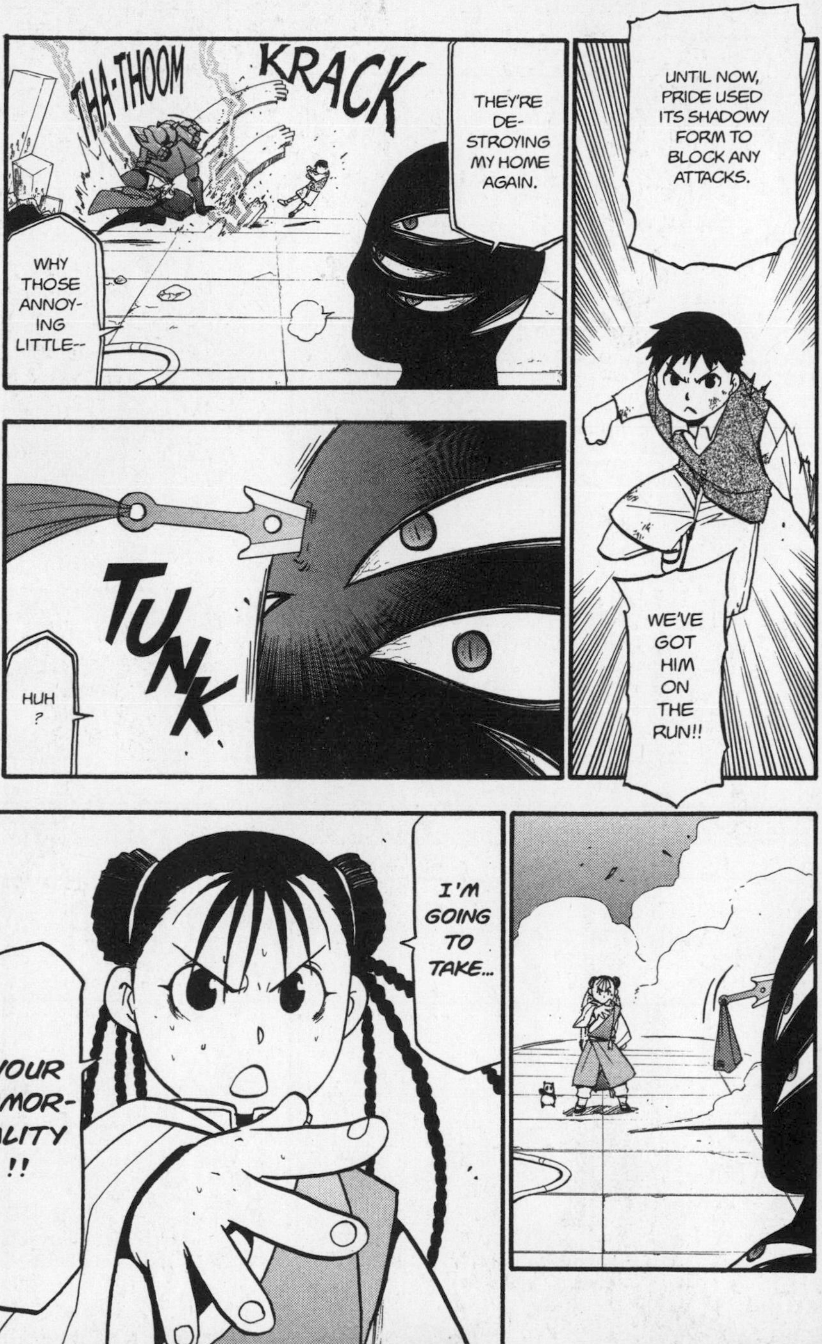
UNTIL NOW, PRIDE USED ITS SHADOWY FORM TO BLOCK ANY ATTACKS.
WE'VE GOT HIM ON THE RUN!!
KRACK
THA-THOOM
THEY'RE DE-STROYING MY HOME AGAIN.
WHY THOSE ANNOY-ING LITTLE--
TUNK
HUH?
I'M GOING TO TAKE...
...YOUR IMMOR-TALITY!!

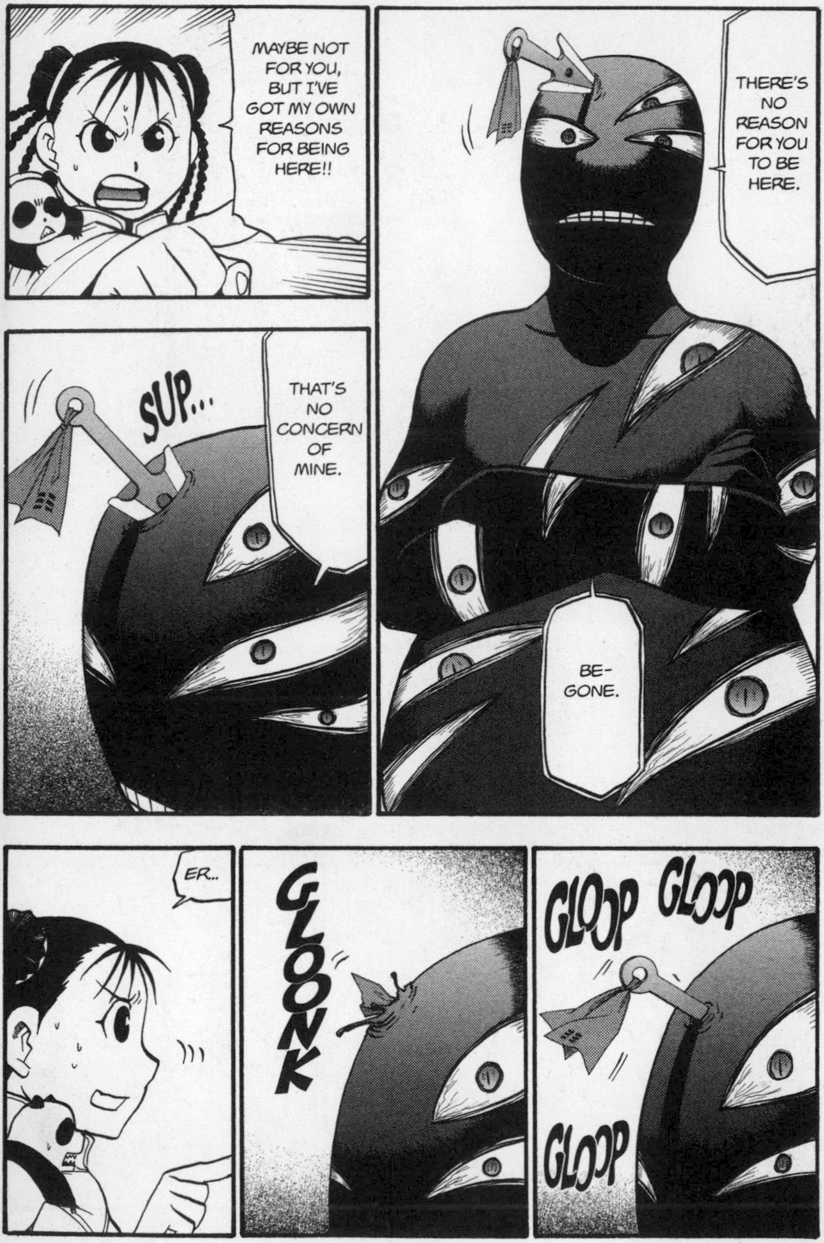
THERE'S NO REASON FOR YOU TO BE HERE.
BE-GONE.
MAYBE NOT FOR YOU, BUT I'VE GOT MY OWN REASONS FOR BEING HERE!!
SUP...
THAT'S NO CONCERN OF MINE.
GLOOP GLOOP
GLOOP
GLOONK
ER...

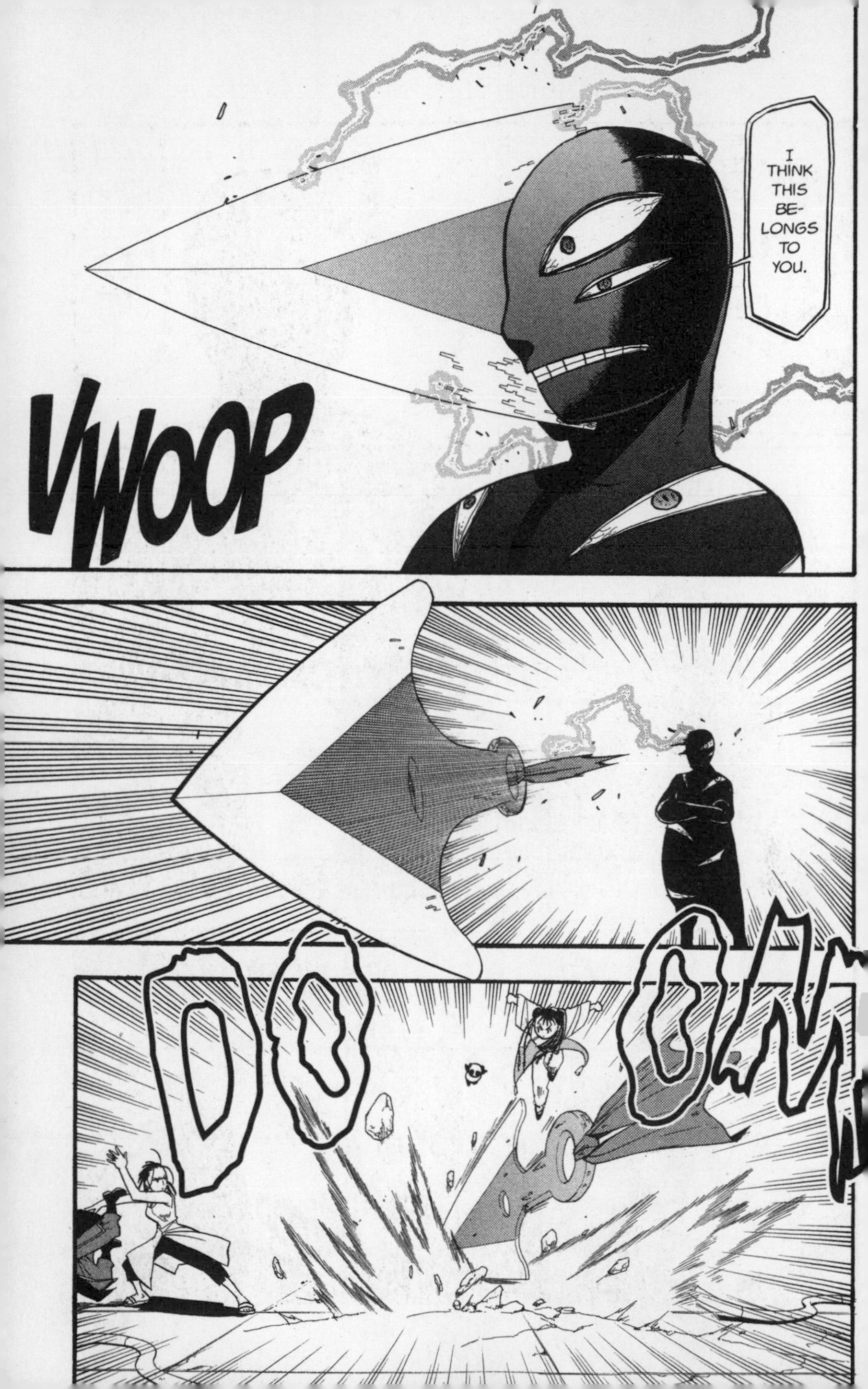
I THINK THIS BE- LONGS TO YOU.
VWOOP
DOOOM

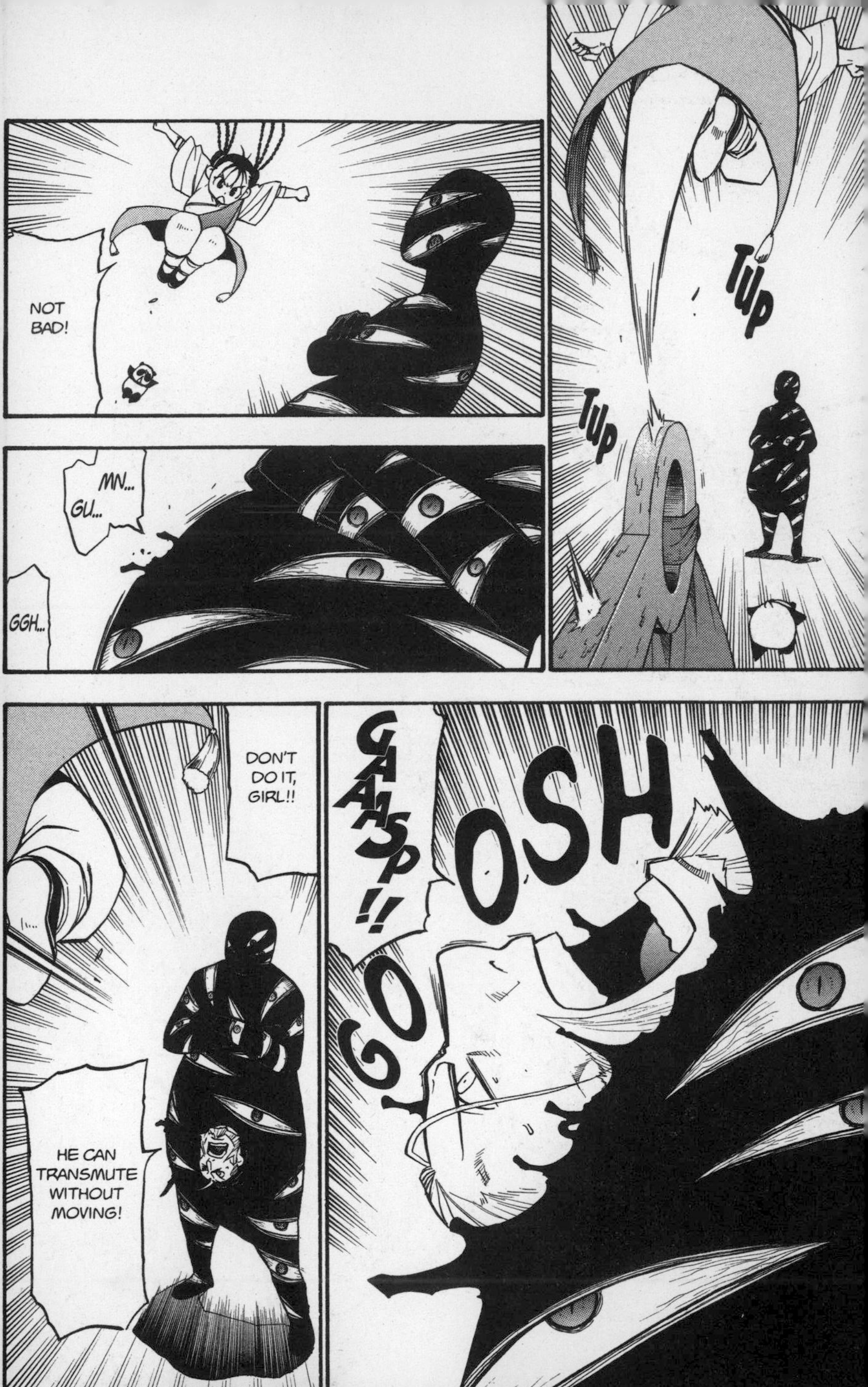
TUP
TUP
NOT BAD!
MN... GU...
GGH...
GAAASP!!
GOOSH
DON'T DO IT, GIRL!!
I...
HE CAN TRANSMUTE WITHOUT MOVING!

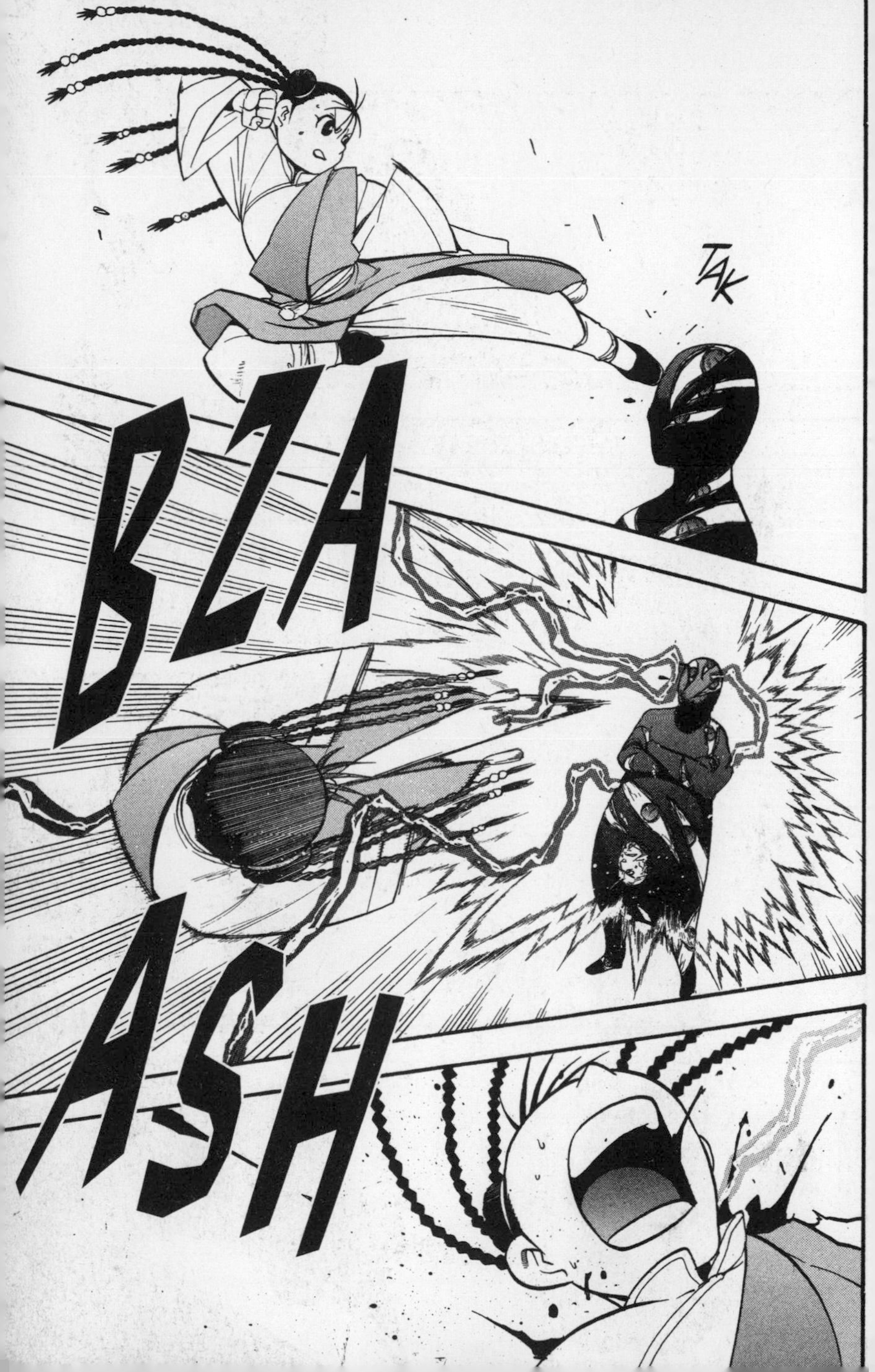
TAK
BZAASH

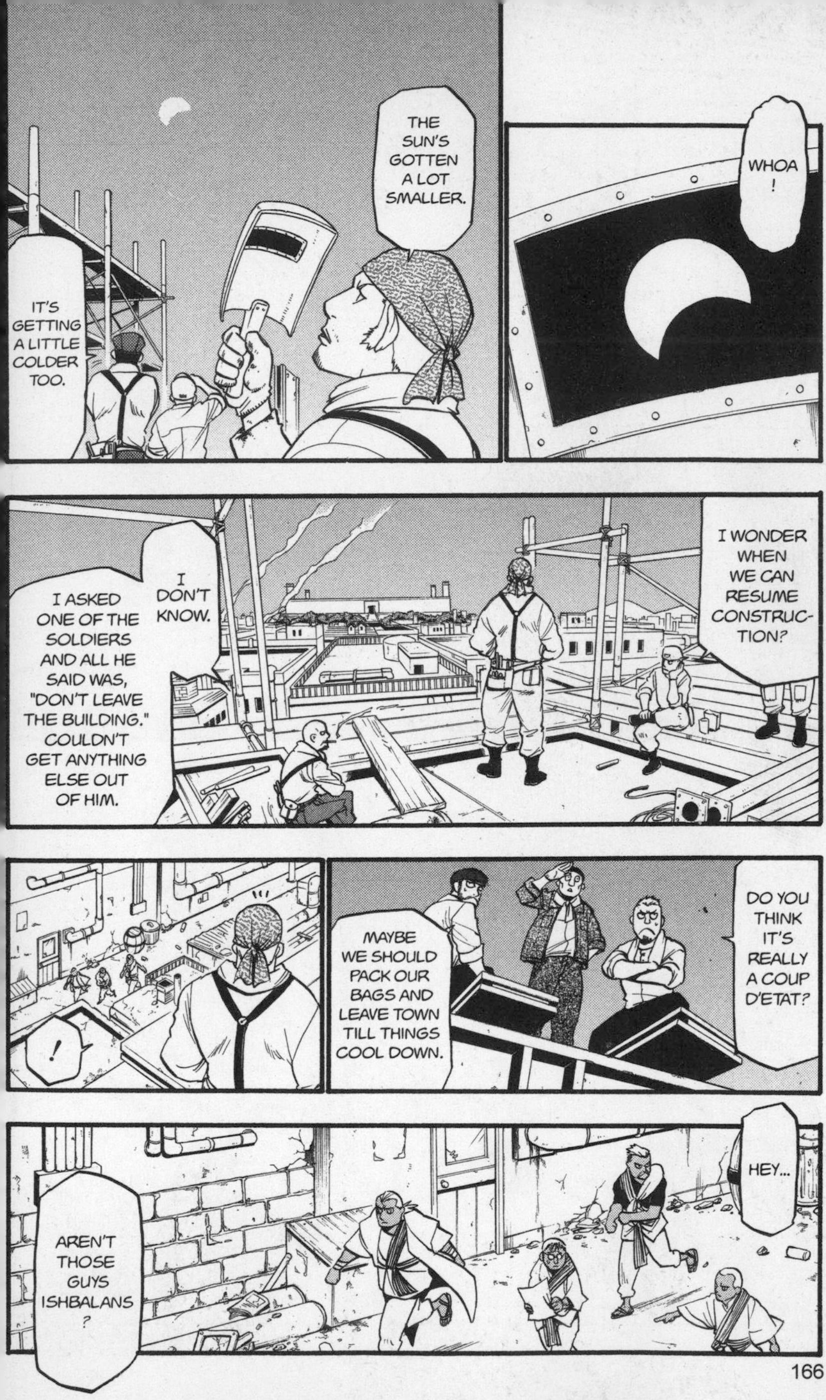
WHOA!
THE SUN'S GOTTEN A LOT SMALLER.
IT'S GETTING A LITTLE COLDER TOO.
I WONDER WHEN WE CAN RESUME CONSTRUCTION?
I DON'T KNOW.
I ASKED ONE OF THE SOLDIERS AND ALL HE SAID WAS, "DON'T LEAVE THE BUILDING." COULDN'T GET ANYTHING ELSE OUT OF HIM.
DO YOU THINK IT'S REALLY A COUP D'ETAT?
MAYBE WE SHOULD PACK OUR BAGS AND LEAVE TOWN TILL THINGS COOL DOWN.
!
HEY...
AREN'T THOSE GUYS ISHBALANS?

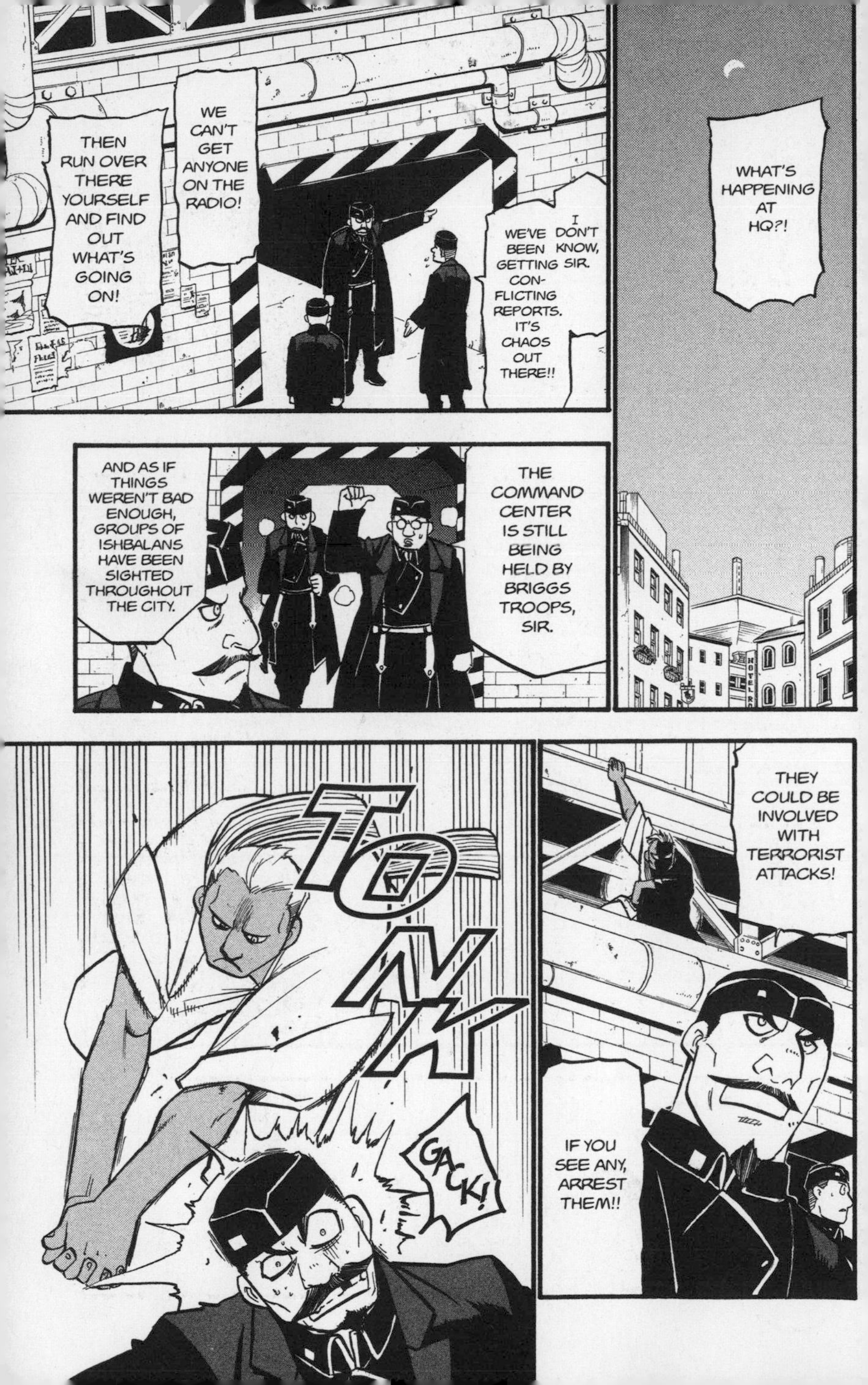
WHAT'S HAPPENING AT HQ?!
I DON'T KNOW, SIR.
WE'VE BEEN GETTING CONFLICTING REPORTS. IT'S CHAOS OUT THERE!!
WE CAN'T GET ANYONE ON THE RADIO!
THEN RUN OVER THERE YOURSELF AND FIND OUT WHAT'S GOING ON!
THE COMMAND CENTER IS STILL BEING HELD BY BRIGGS TROOPS, SIR.
AND AS IF THINGS WEREN'T BAD ENOUGH, GROUPS OF ISHBALANS HAVE BEEN SIGHTED THROUGHOUT THE CITY.
THEY COULD BE INVOLVED WITH TERRORIST ATTACKS!
IF YOU SEE ANY, ARREST THEM!!
TONK
GACK!

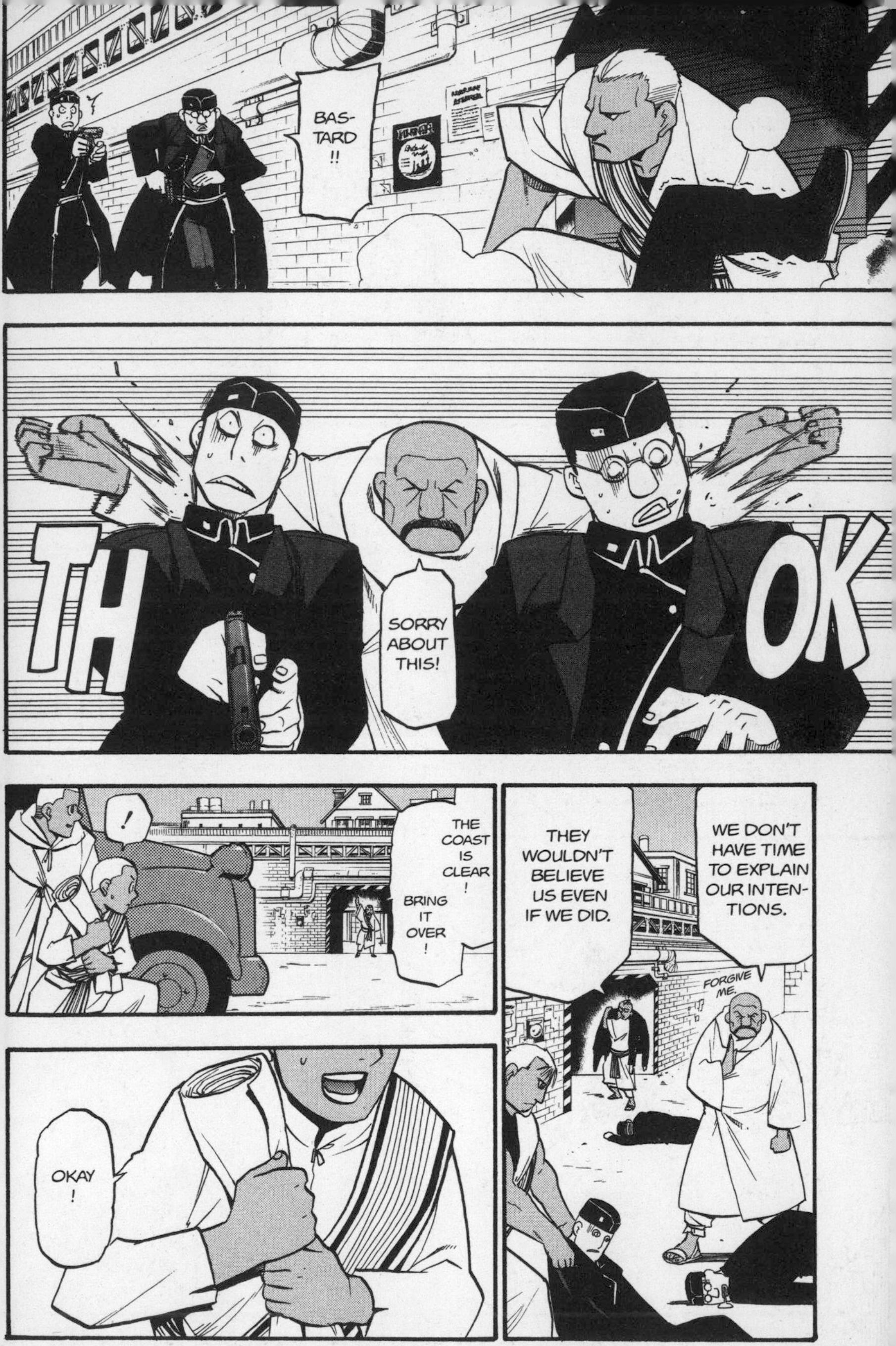
BAS-TARD !!
THOK
SORRY ABOUT THIS!
WE DON'T HAVE TIME TO EXPLAIN OUR INTEN-TIONS.
THEY WOULDN'T BELIEVE US EVEN IF WE DID.
FORGIVE ME.
THE COAST IS CLEAR! BRING IT OVER!
!
OKAY!

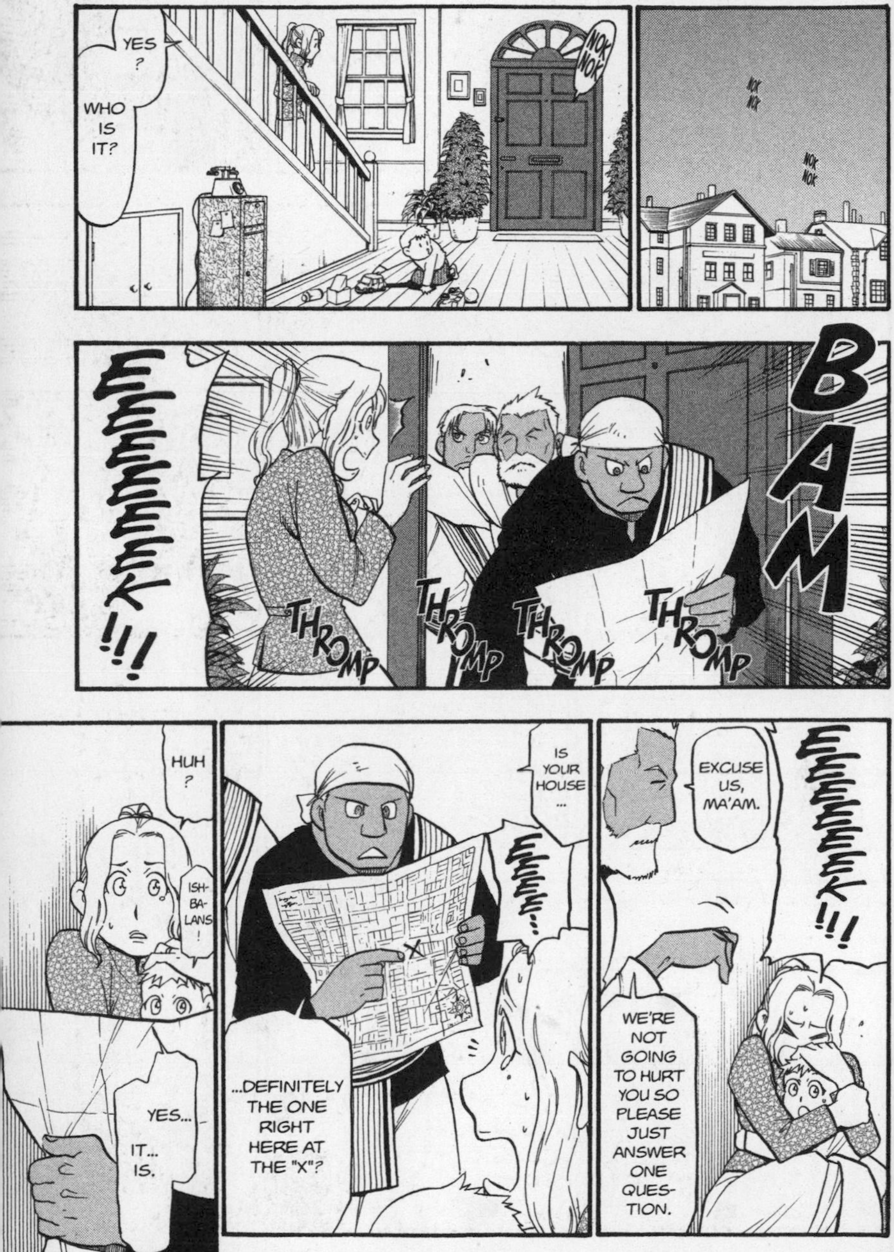
NOK NOK
NOK NOK
NOK NOK
YES? WHO IS IT?
BAM
THROMP
THROMP
THROMP
THROMP
EEEEEEEK!!!
EEEEEEEK!!!
EXCUSE US, MA'AM.
WE'RE NOT GOING TO HURT YOU SO PLEASE JUST ANSWER ONE QUESTION.
IS YOUR HOUSE...
EEEEE...
...DEFINITELY THE ONE RIGHT HERE AT THE "X"?
HUH?
ISH-BALANS!
YES... IT... IS.

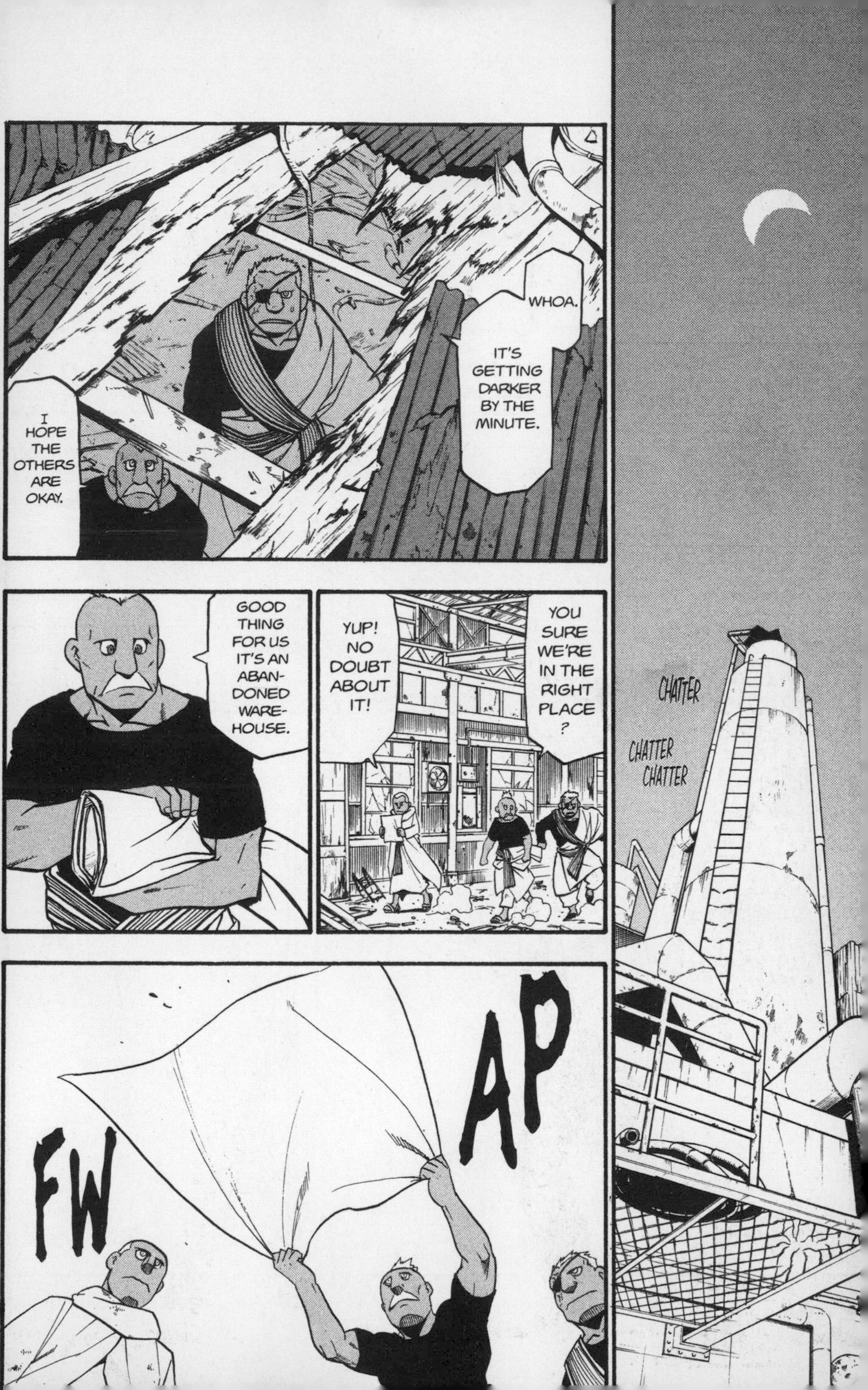
CHATTER
CHATTER CHATTER
WHOA.
IT'S GETTING DARKER BY THE MINUTE.
I HOPE THE OTHERS ARE OKAY.
YOU SURE WE'RE IN THE RIGHT PLACE?
YUP! NO DOUBT ABOUT IT!
GOOD THING FOR US IT'S AN ABANDONED WAREHOUSE.
FWAP

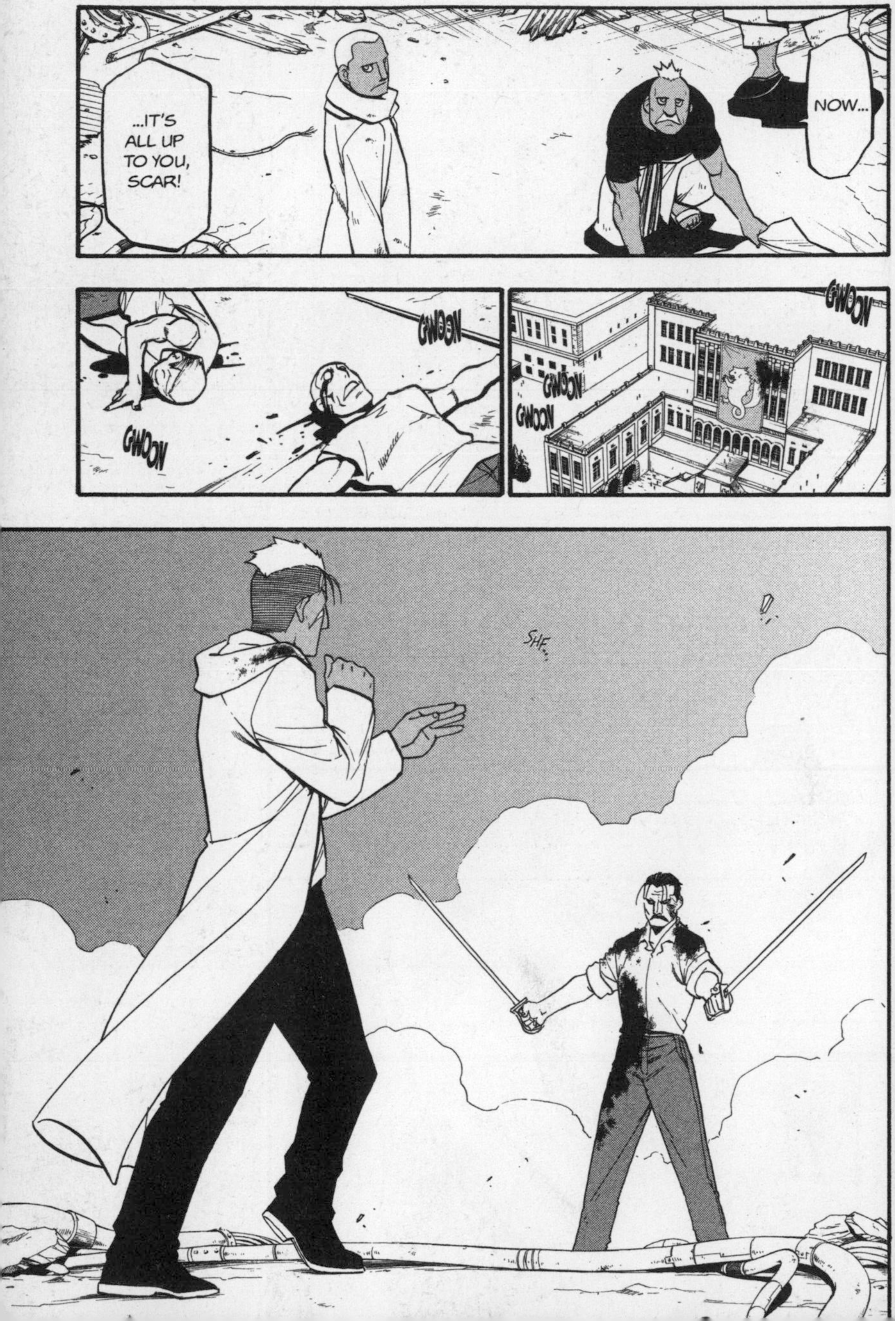
NOW...
...IT'S ALL UP TO YOU, SCAR!
GWOON
GWOON
GWOON
GWOON
GWOON
SHF

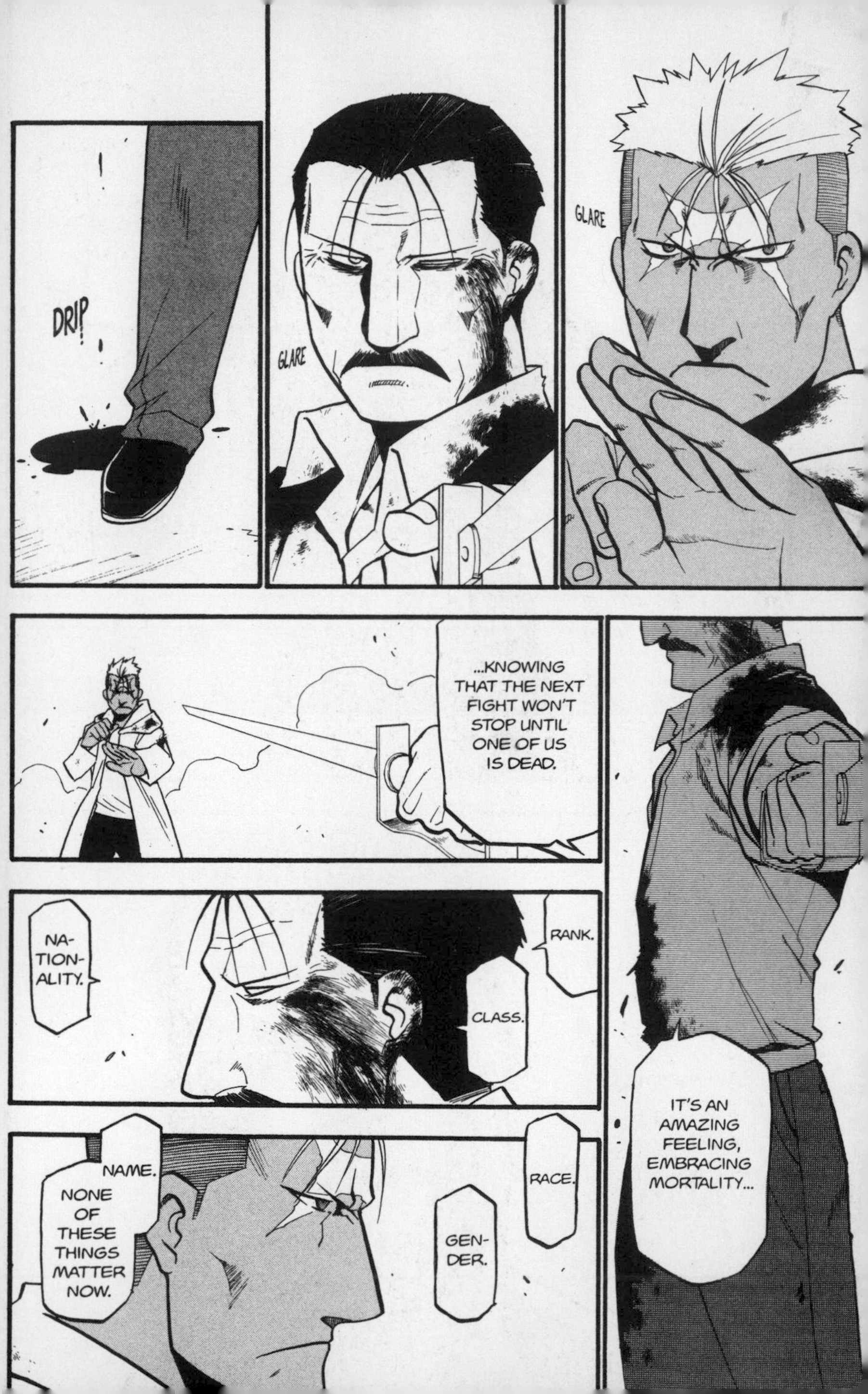
GLARE
GLARE
DRIP
IT'S AN AMAZING FEELING, EMBRACING MORTALITY...
...KNOWING THAT THE NEXT FIGHT WON'T STOP UNTIL ONE OF US IS DEAD.
RANK.
CLASS.
NA-TION-ALITY.
RACE.
GEN-DER.
NAME.
NONE OF THESE THINGS MATTER NOW.

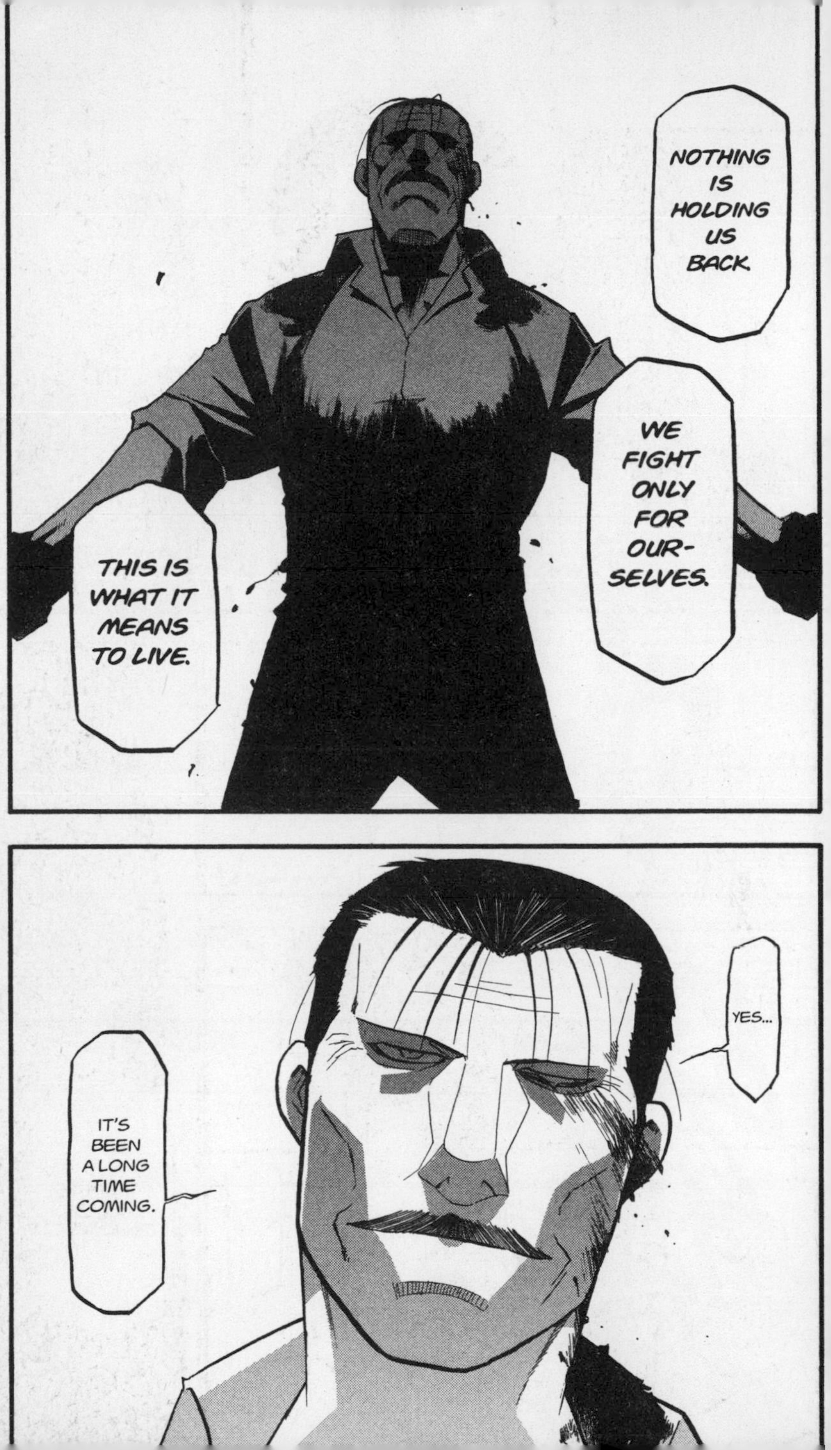
NOTHING IS HOLDING US BACK.
WE FIGHT ONLY FOR OURSELVES.
THIS IS WHAT IT MEANS TO LIVE.
YES...
IT'S BEEN A LONG TIME COMING.

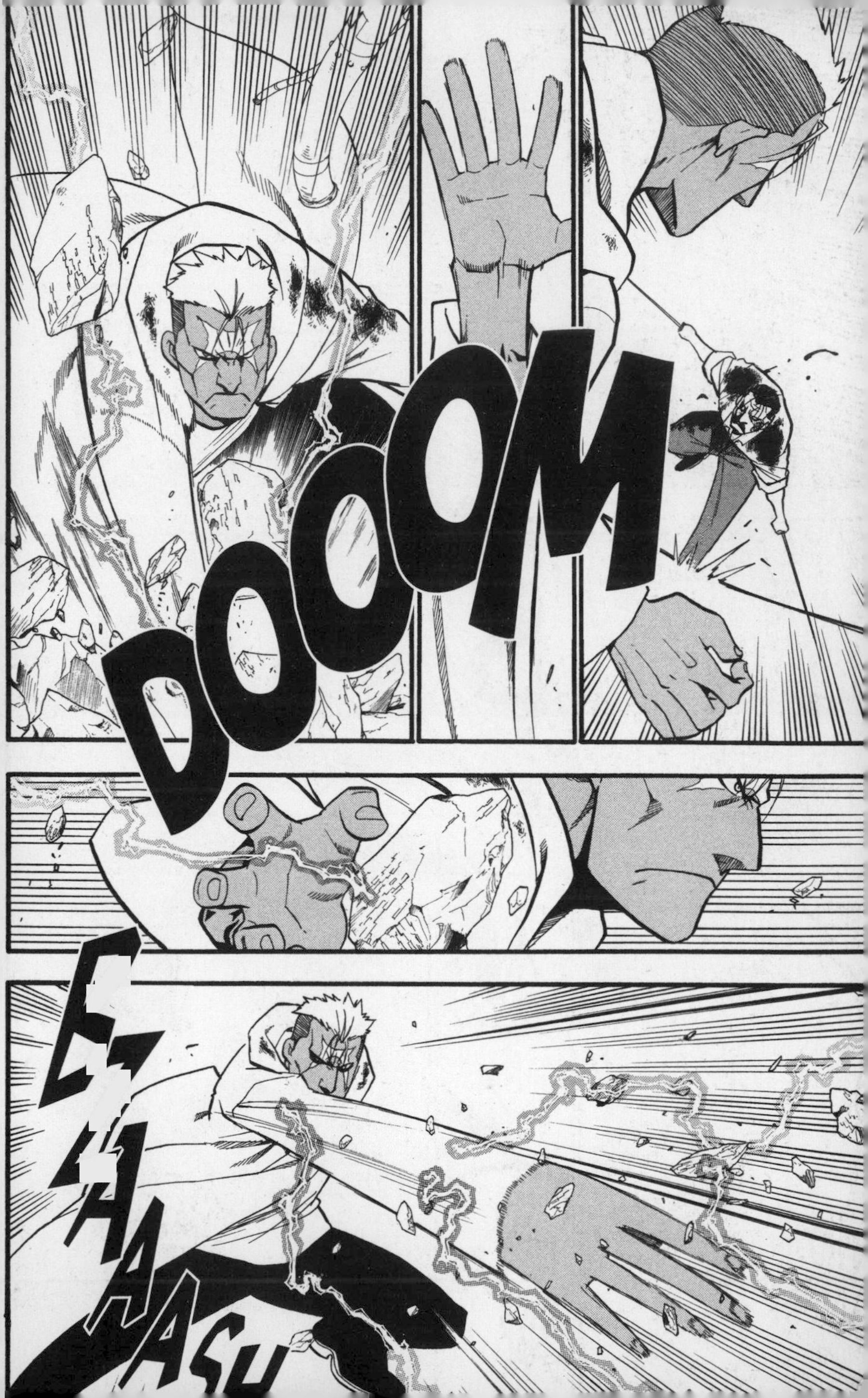
DOOOOM

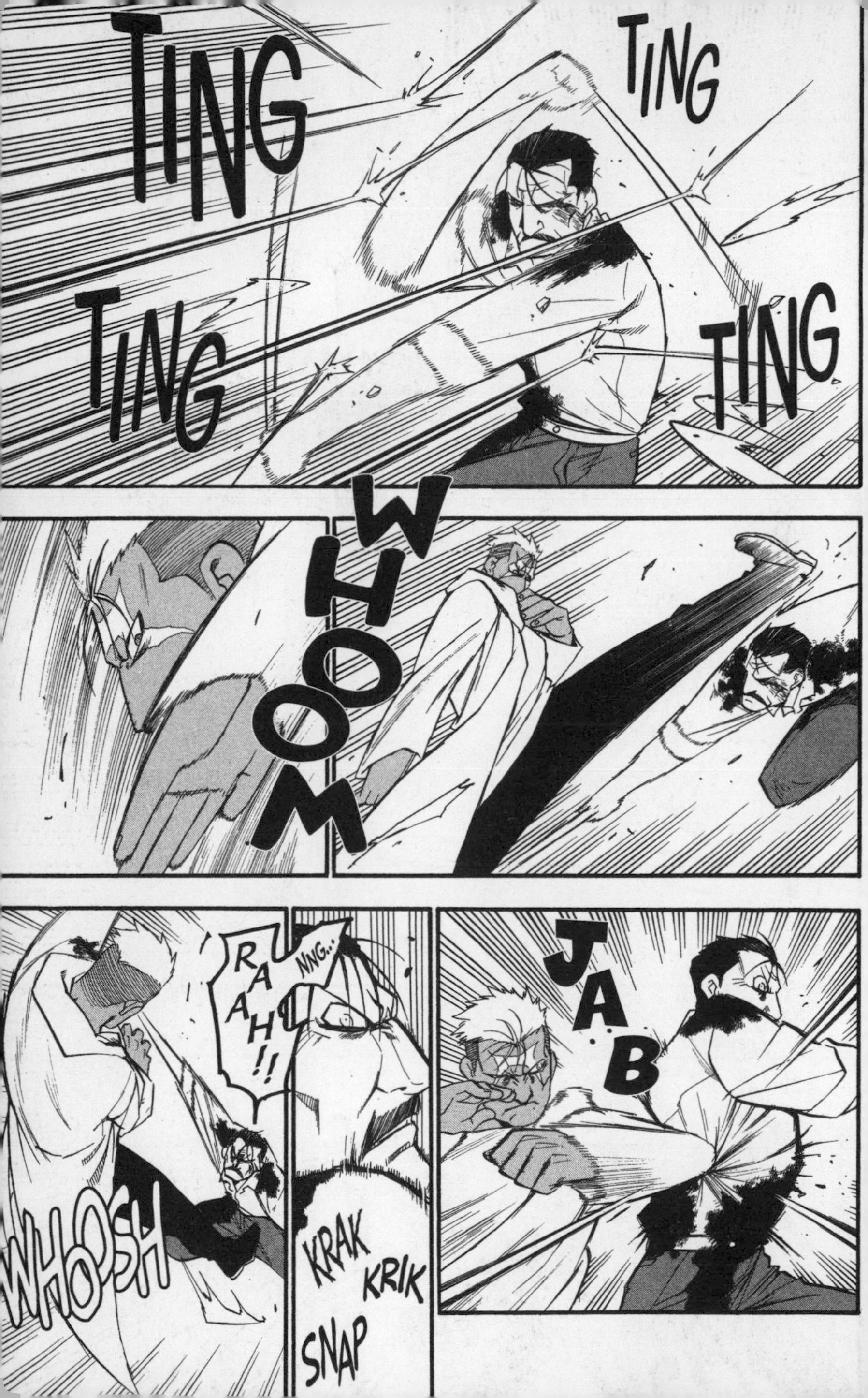

TING
TING
TING
TING
WHOOM
JAB
NNG..
KRAK
KRIK
SNAP
RAAH!!
WHOOSH

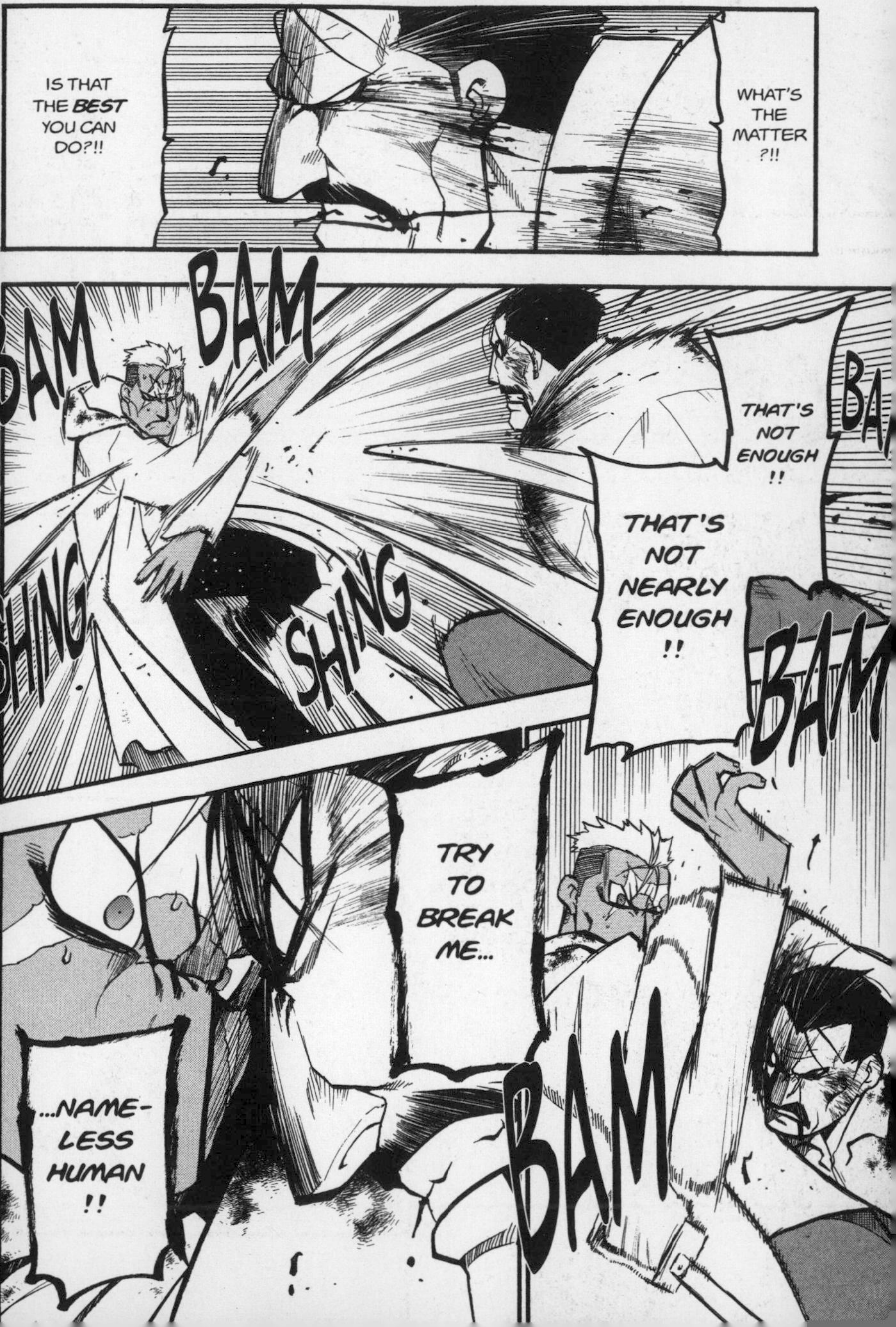
WHAT'S THE MATTER ?!!
IS THAT THE BEST YOU CAN DO?!!
BA
THAT'S NOT ENOUGH !!
THAT'S NOT NEARLY ENOUGH !!
BAM
SHING
BAM
BAM
SHING
TRY TO BREAK ME...
BAM
...NAME-LESS HUMAN !!

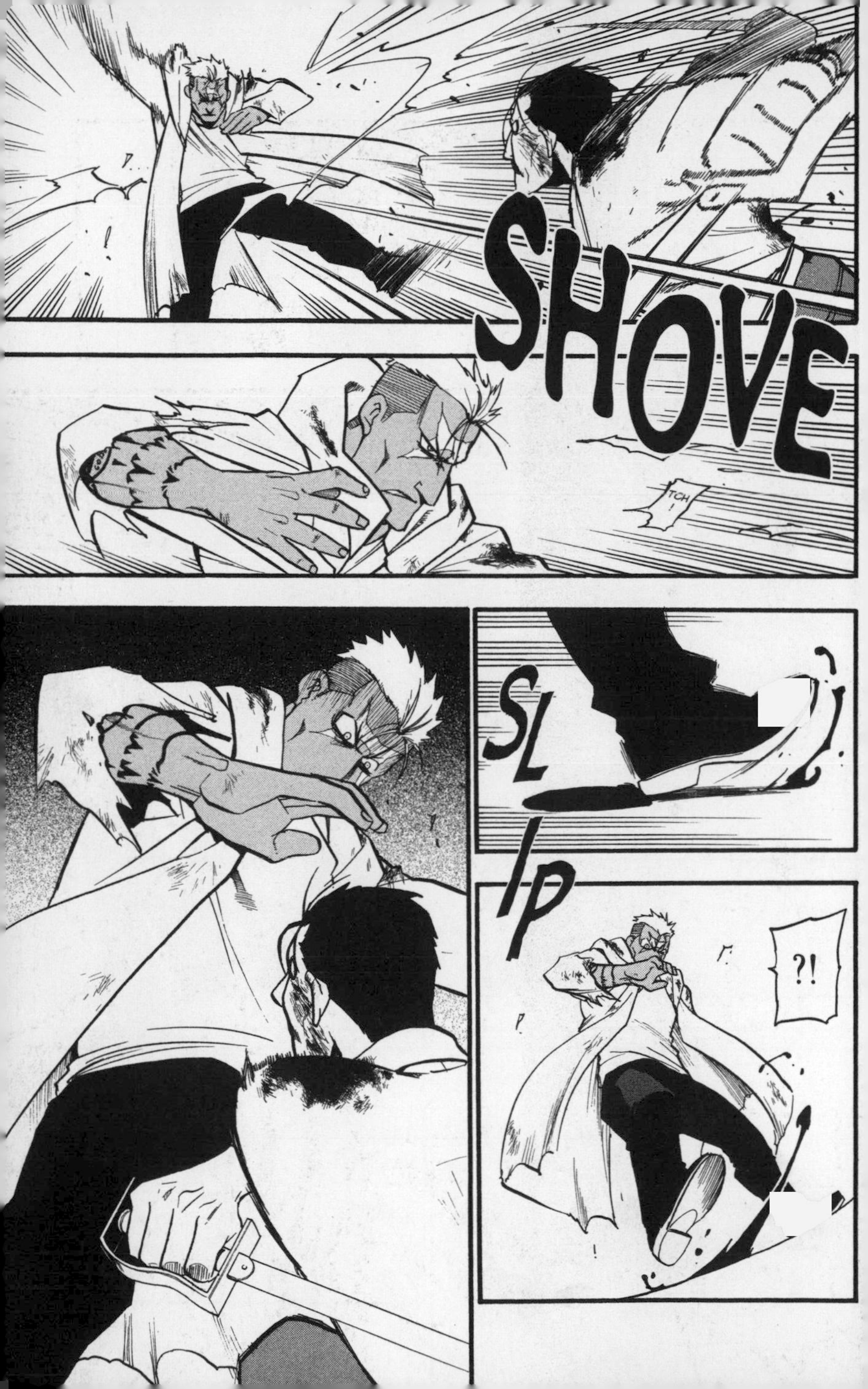
SHOVE
TCH!
SLIP
?!

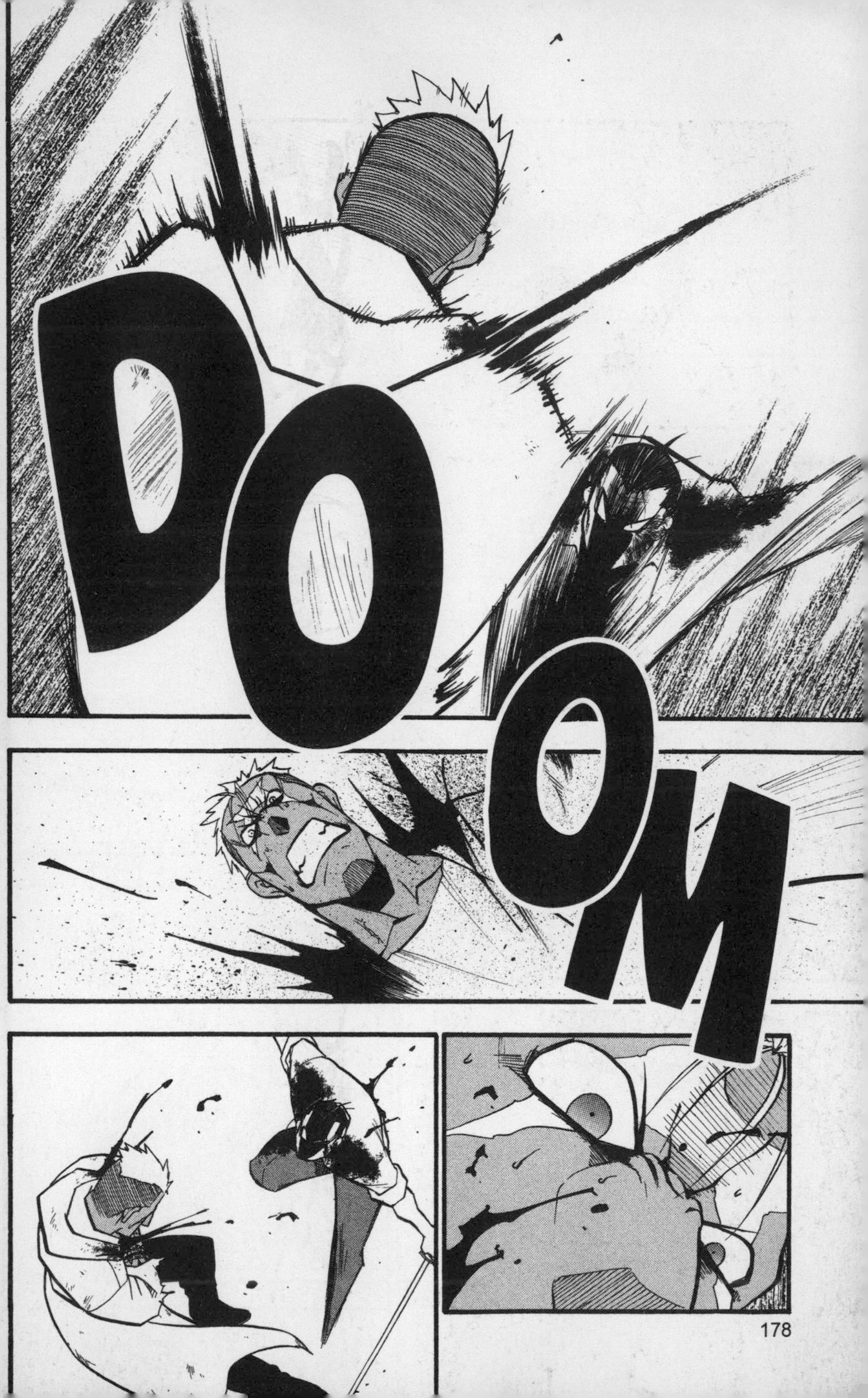
DOOOM

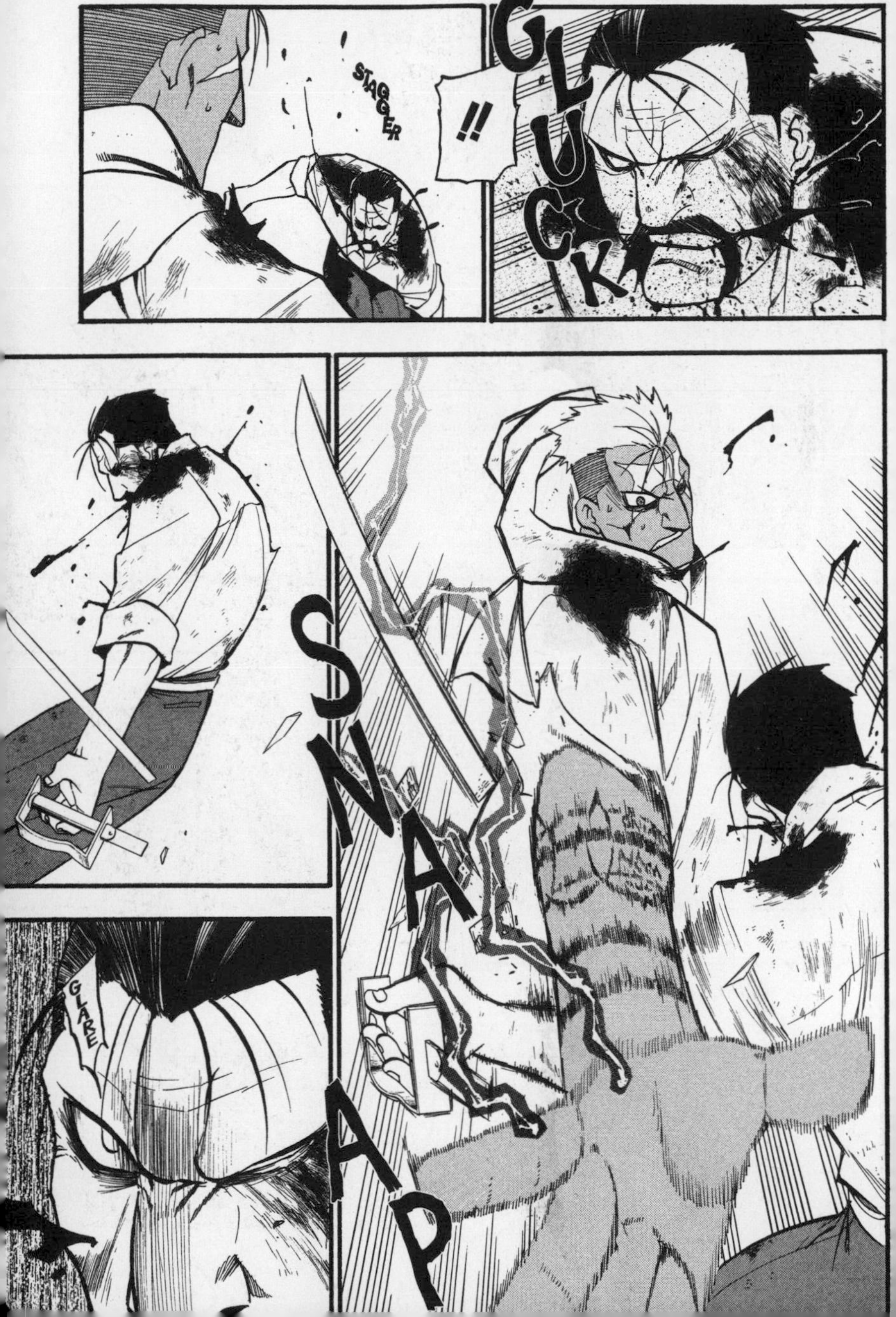
GLUCK
!!
STAGGER
SNAP
GLARE

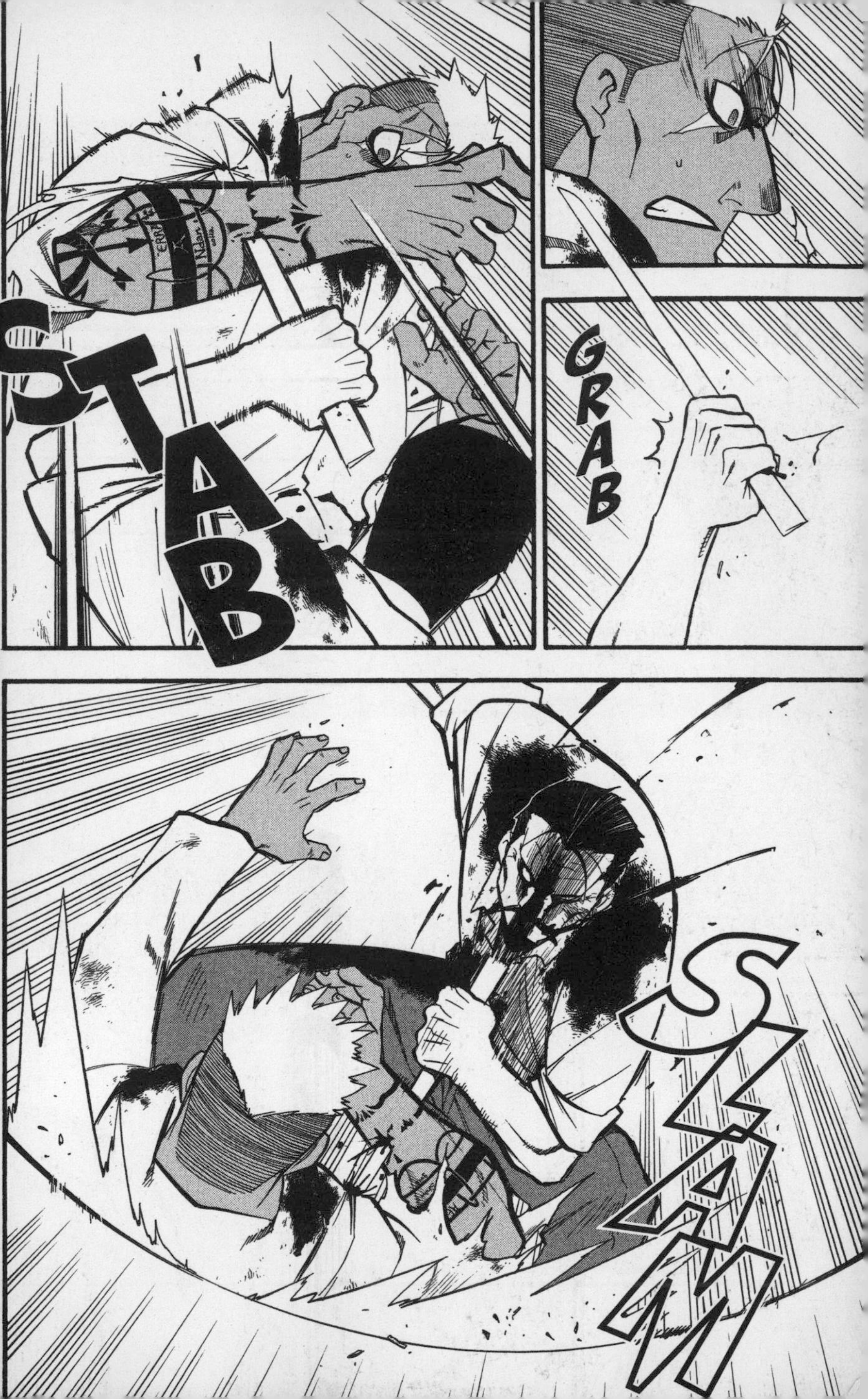
GRAB
STAB
SLAM

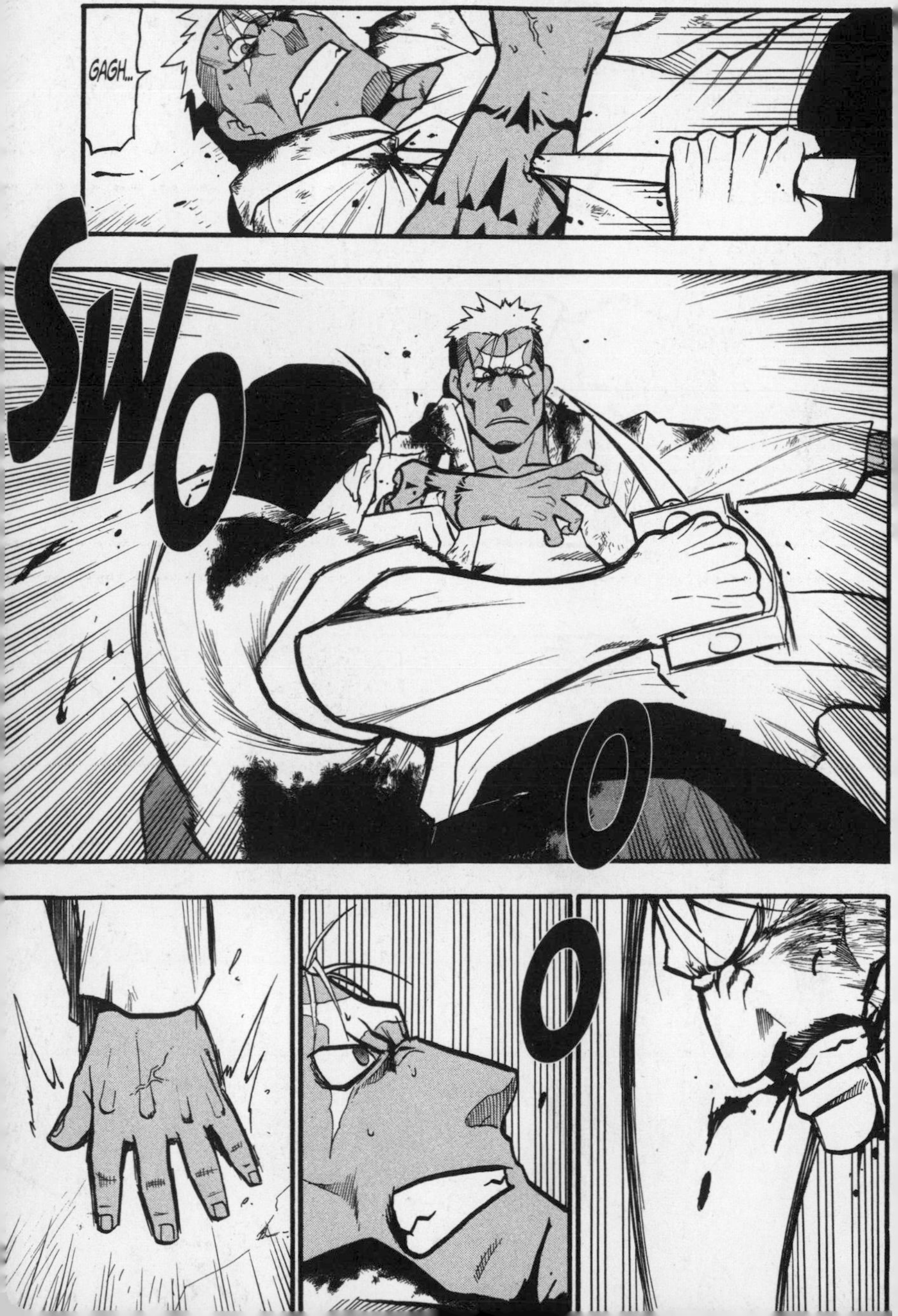
GAGH...
SWO
O
O

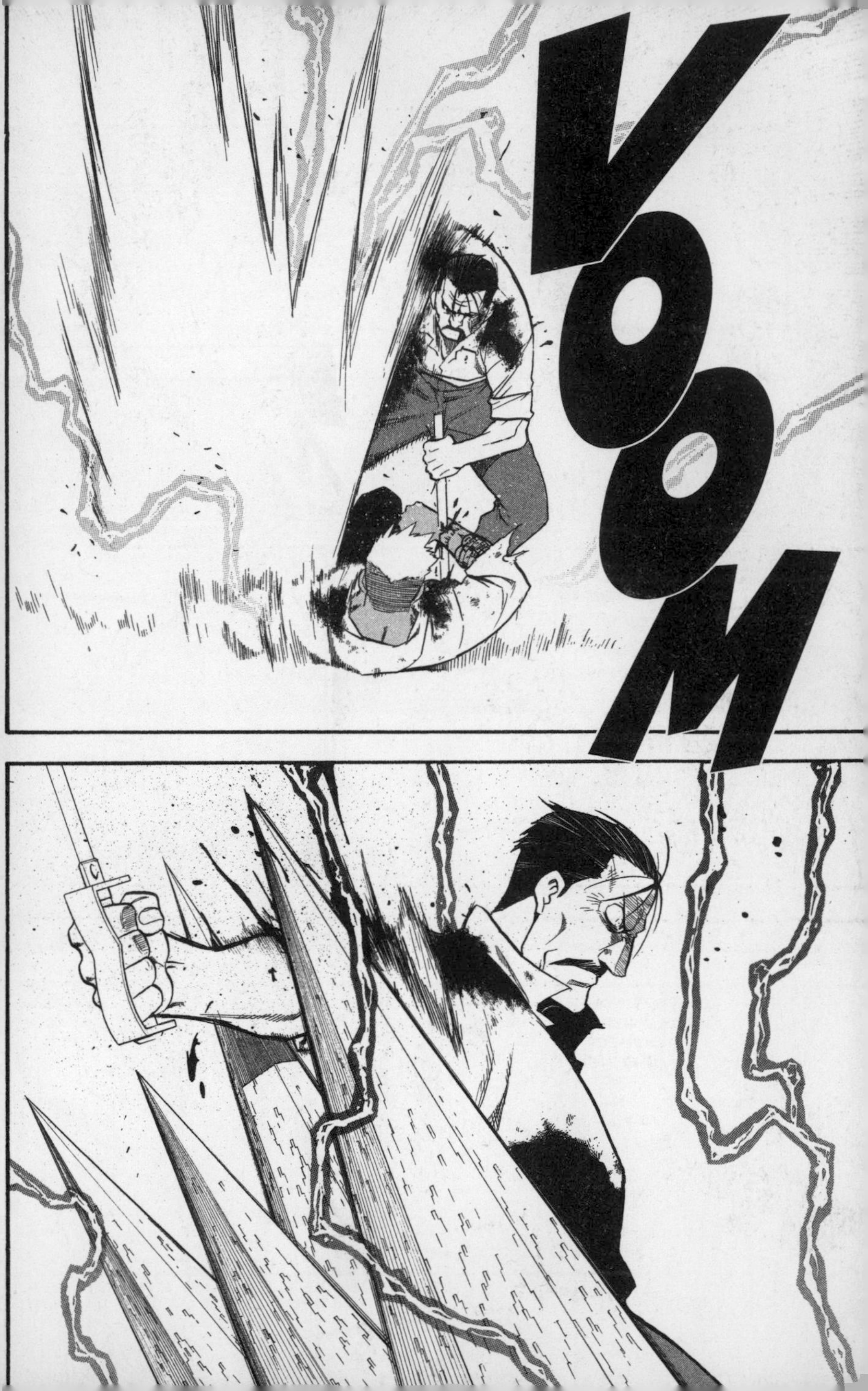
VOOM

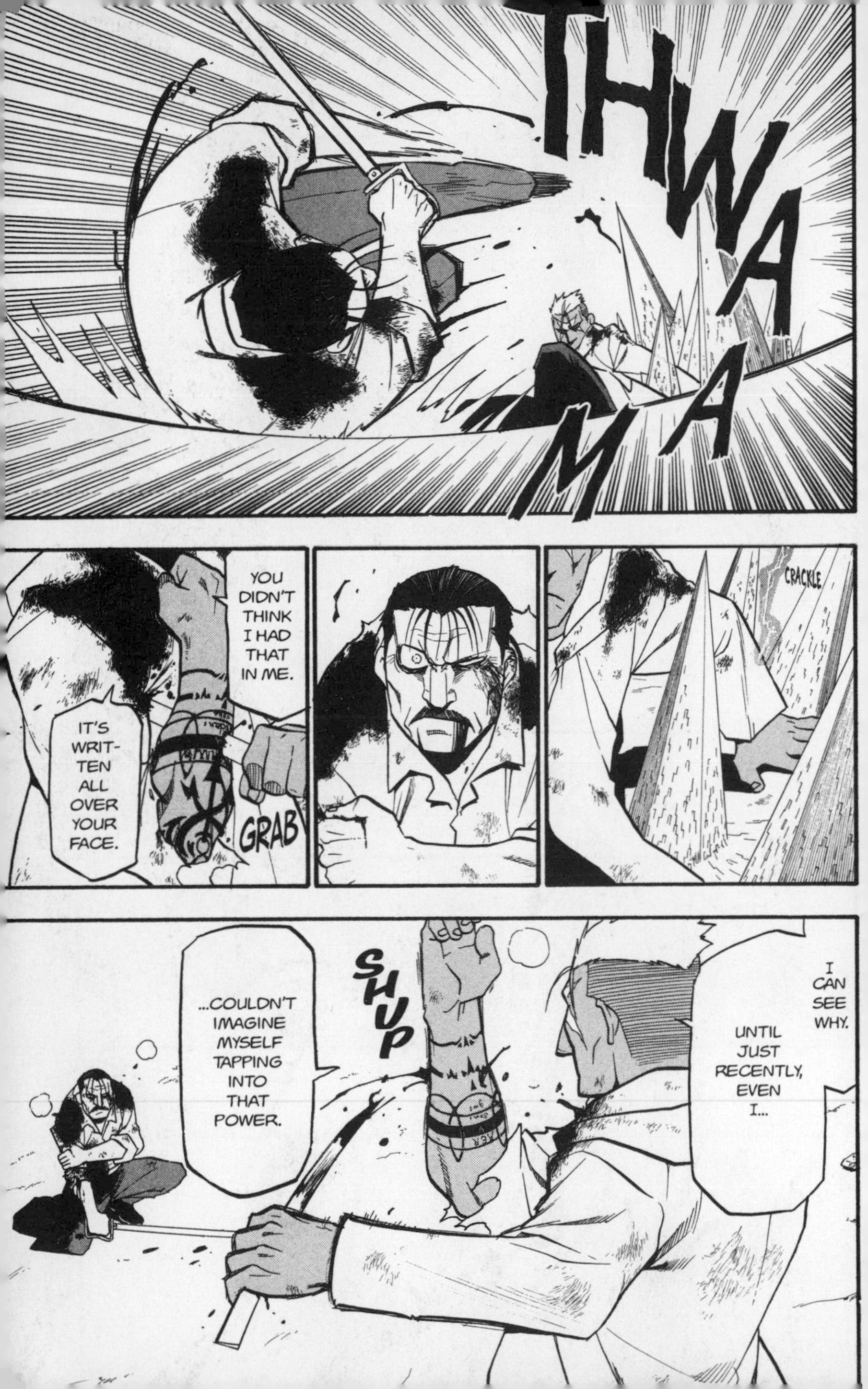
THWAAM
CRACKLE
YOU DIDN'T THINK I HAD THAT IN ME.
GRAB
IT'S WRIT-TEN ALL OVER YOUR FACE.
I CAN SEE WHY.
UNTIL JUST RECENTLY, EVEN I...
SHUP
...COULDN'T IMAGINE MYSELF TAPPING INTO THAT POWER.

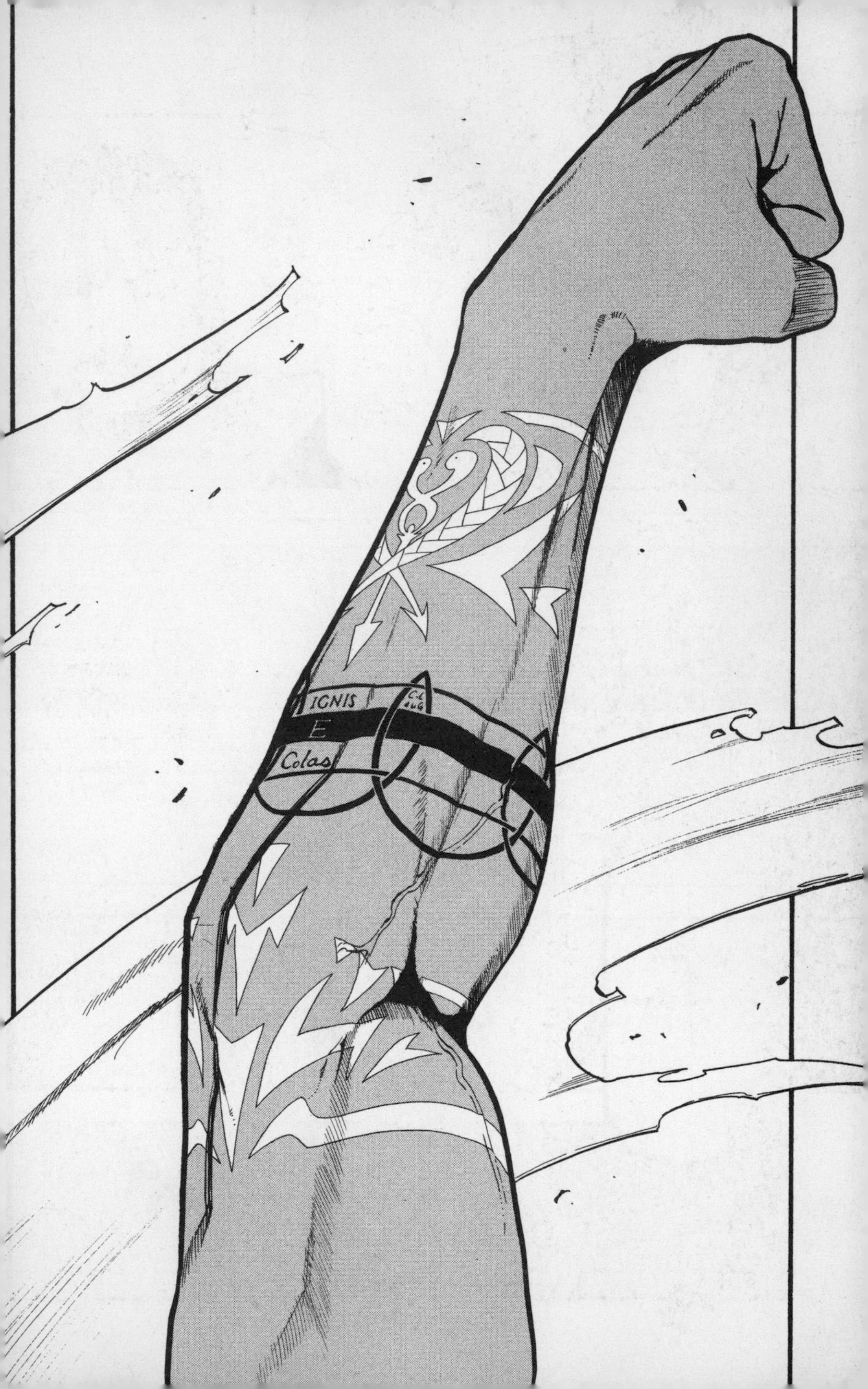
IGNIS
E
Colas

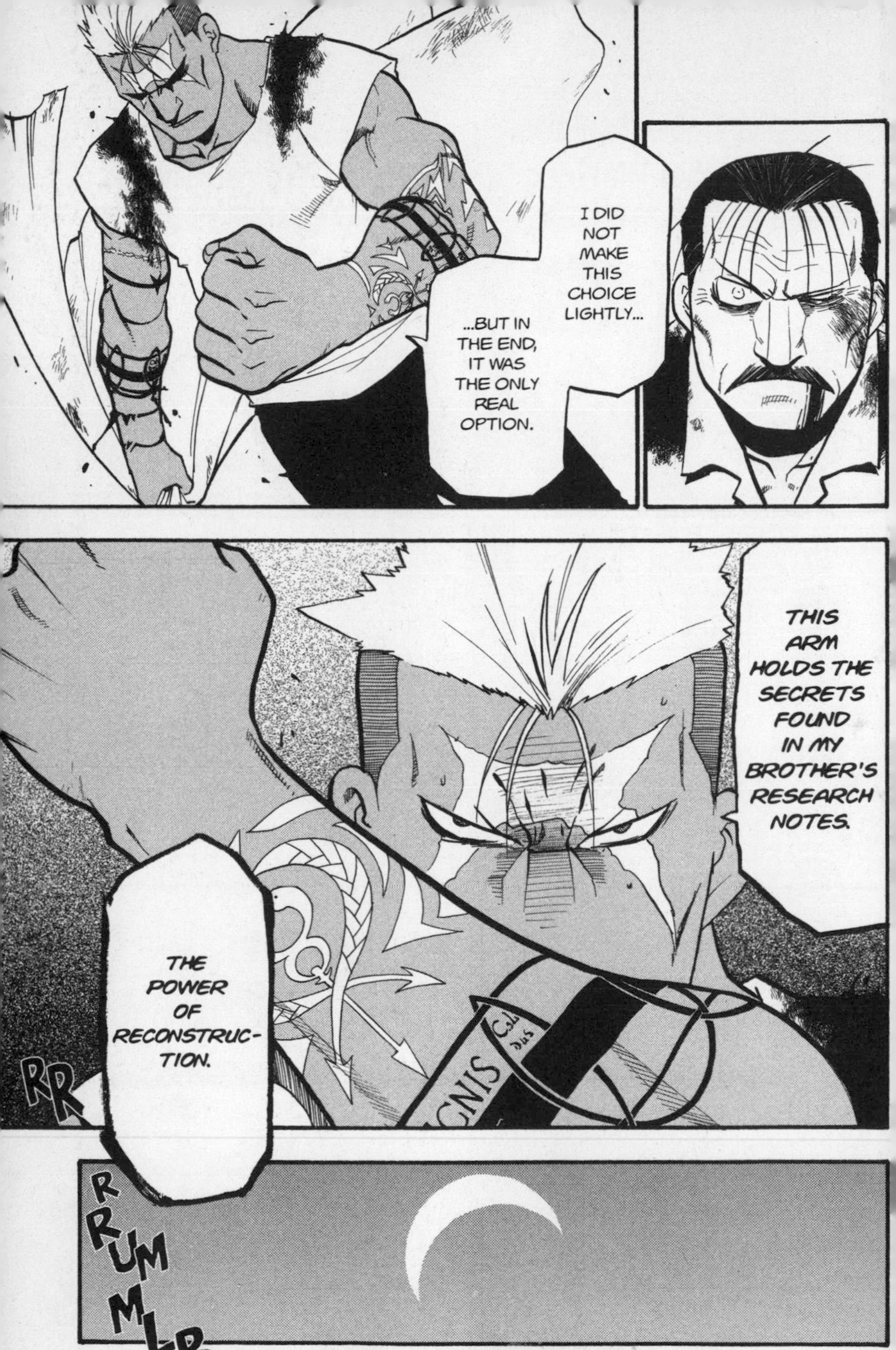
I DID NOT MAKE THIS CHOICE LIGHTLY...
...BUT IN THE END, IT WAS THE ONLY REAL OPTION.
THIS ARM HOLDS THE SECRETS FOUND IN MY BROTHER'S RESEARCH NOTES.
THE POWER OF RECONSTRUCTION.
RR
RRUMMLB

Fullmetal Alchemist 25 End

Lots of Weaknesses

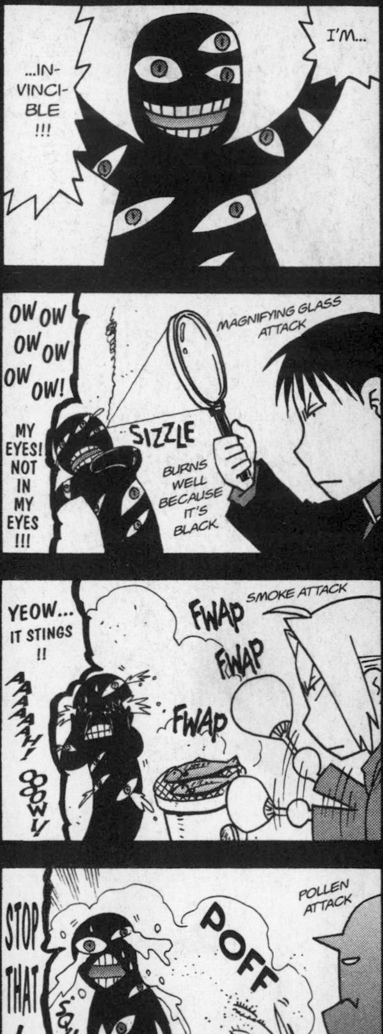
I'M...
...INVINCIBLE!!!
MAGNIFYING GLASS ATTACK
BURNS WELL BECAUSE IT'S BLACK.
SIZZLE
OW OW OW OW OW OW!
MY EYES! NOT IN MY EYES!!!
SMOKE ATTACK
FWAP
FWAP
FWAP
YEOW... IT STINGS!!
AAAAAAH! OOOOW!!
POLLEN ATTACK
POFF
POFF POFF
SQUIRT
STOP THAT!!

Psychological Warfare

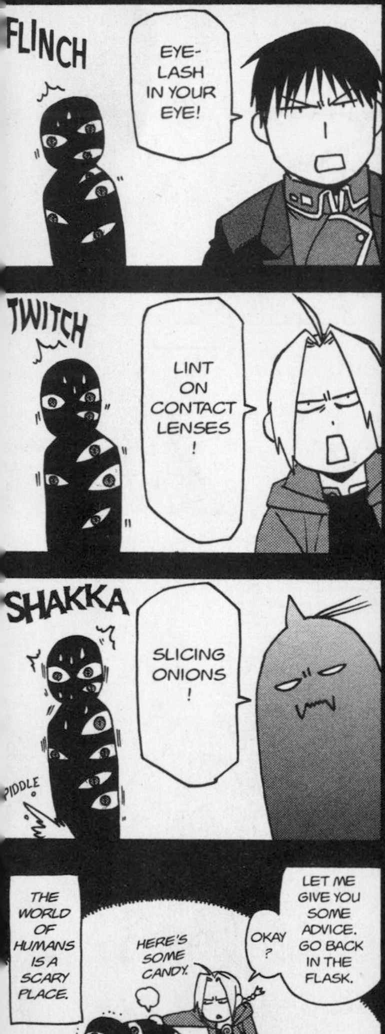
EYE-LASH IN YOUR EYE!
FLINCH
LINT ON CONTACT LENSES!
TWITCH
SLICING ONIONS!
SHAKKA
PIDDLE
LET ME GIVE YOU SOME ADVICE. GO BACK IN THE FLASK.
OKAY?
HERE'S SOME CANDY.
THE WORLD OF HUMANS IS A SCARY PLACE.
SOB SOB SOB

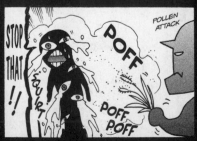

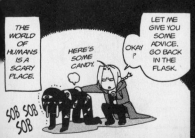

An RPG Is Coming Out For the PSP!

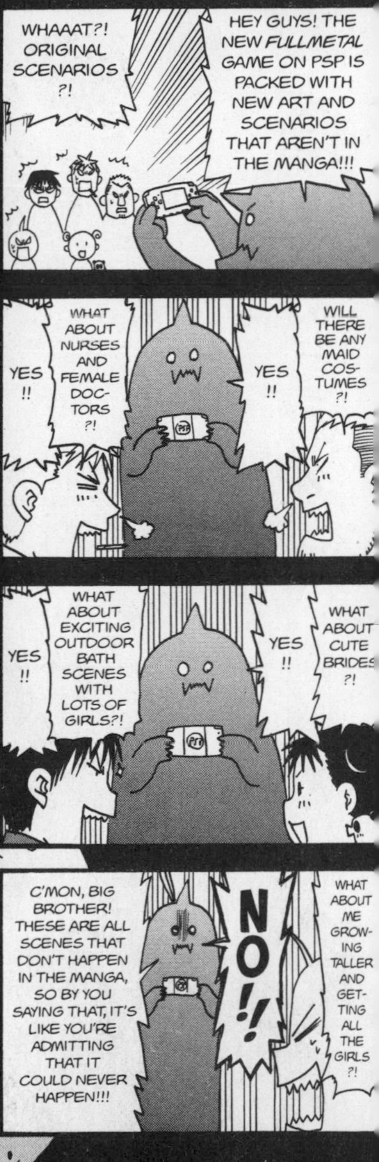
HEY GUYS! THE NEW FULLMETAL GAME ON PSP IS PACKED WITH NEW ART AND SCENARIOS THAT AREN'T IN THE MANGA!!!
WHAAAT?! ORIGINAL SCENARIOS?!
WILL THERE BE ANY MAID COSTUMES?!
YES!!
WHAT ABOUT NURSES AND FEMALE DOCTORS?!
YES!!
WHAT ABOUT CUTE BRIDES?!
YES!!
WHAT ABOUT EXCITING OUTDOOR BATH SCENES WITH LOTS OF GIRLS?!
YES!!
WHAT ABOUT ME GROWING TALLER AND GETTING ALL THE GIRLS?!
NO!!
C'MON, BIG BROTHER! THESE ARE ALL SCENES THAT DON'T HAPPEN IN THE MANGA, SO BY YOU SAYING THAT, IT'S LIKE YOU'RE ADMITTING THAT IT COULD NEVER HAPPEN!!!

SPECIAL THANKS

Jun Tohko
Masashi Mizutani
Mr. Coupon
Noriko Tsubota
Kazufumi Kaneko
Kori Sakano
Manatsu Sakura
Keisui Takaeda
My Editor, Yuichi Shimomura

AND YOU!!

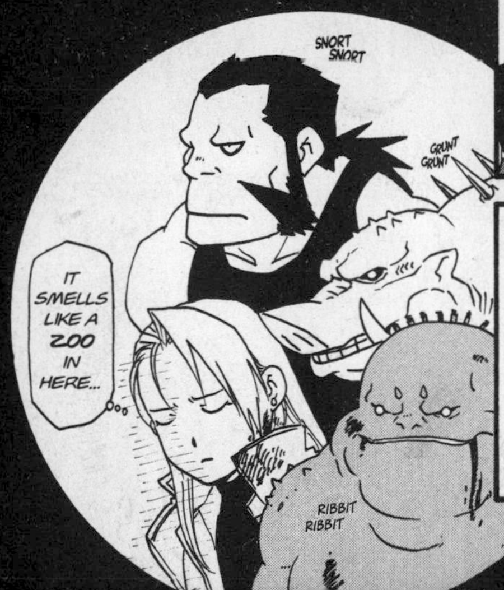
SNORT SNORT
GRUNT GRUNT
IT SMELLS LIKE A ZOO IN HERE...
RIBBIT RIBBIT

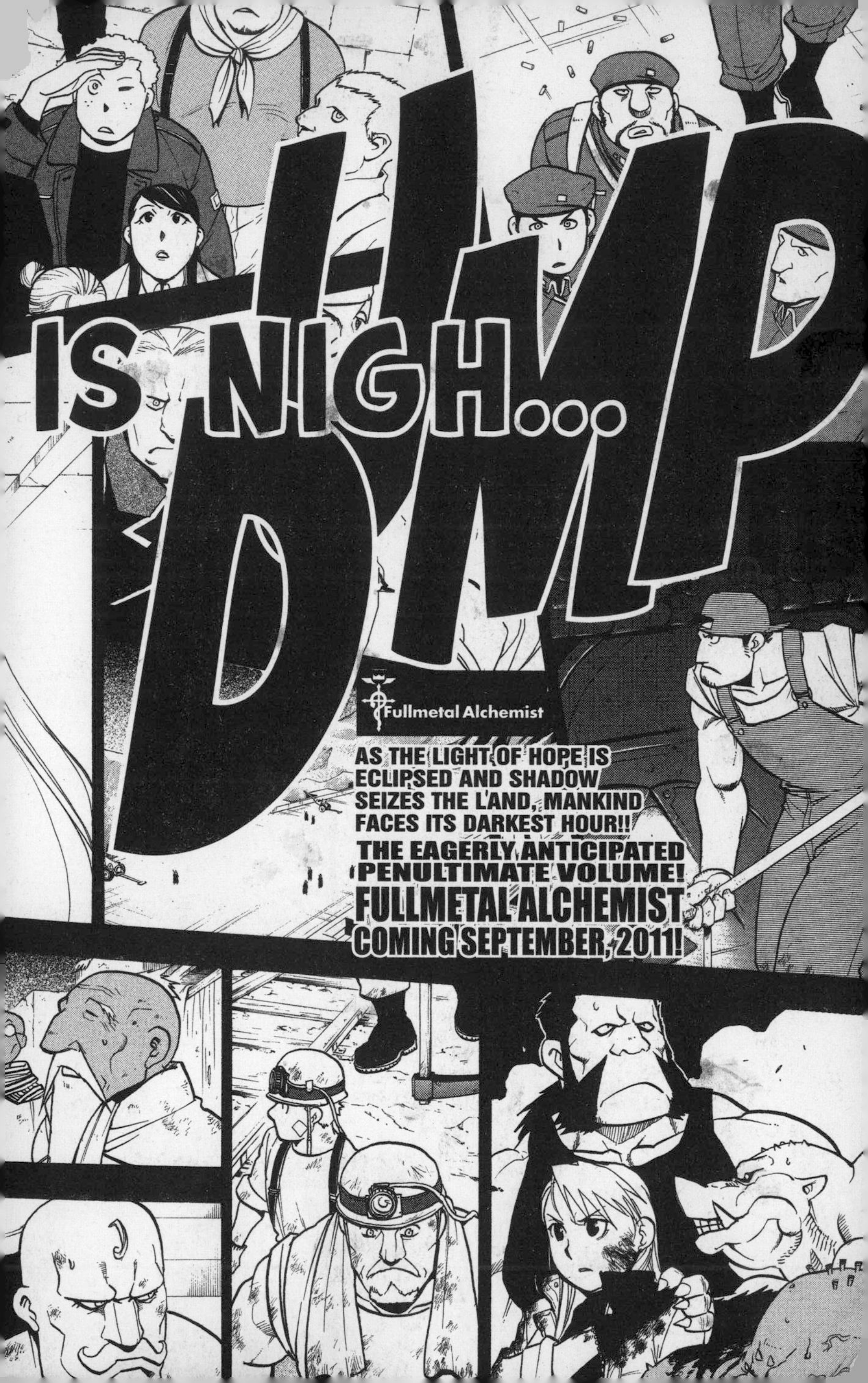

IS NIGH...
Fullmetal Alchemist
AS THE LIGHT OF HOPE IS ECLIPSED AND SHADOW SEIZES THE LAND, MANKIND FACES ITS DARKEST HOUR!!
THE EAGERLY ANTICIPATED PENULTIMATE VOLUME!
FULLMETAL ALCHEMIST
COMING SEPTEMBER, 2011!

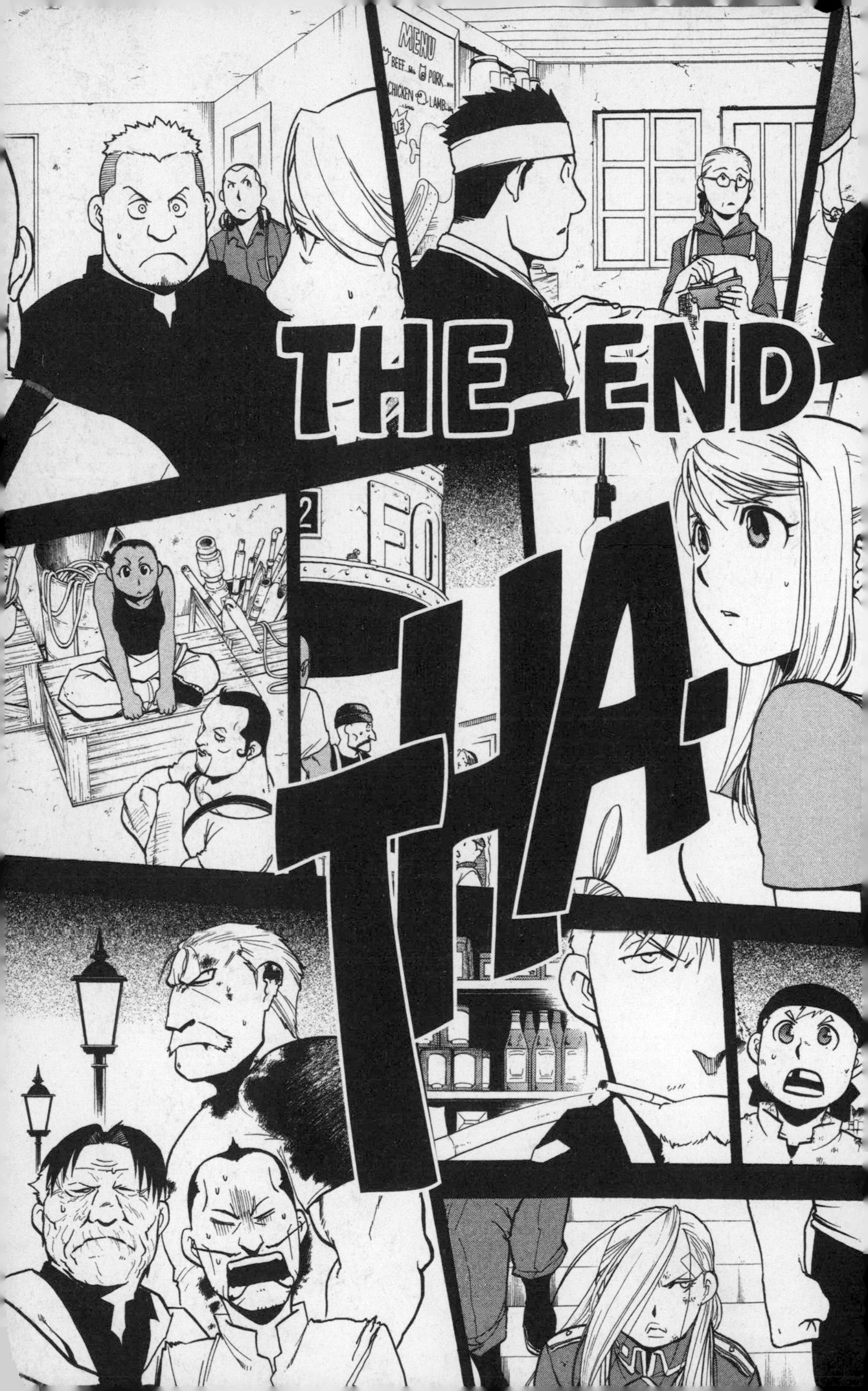
MENU
BEEF
PORK
CHICKEN
LAMB
THE END
THA-

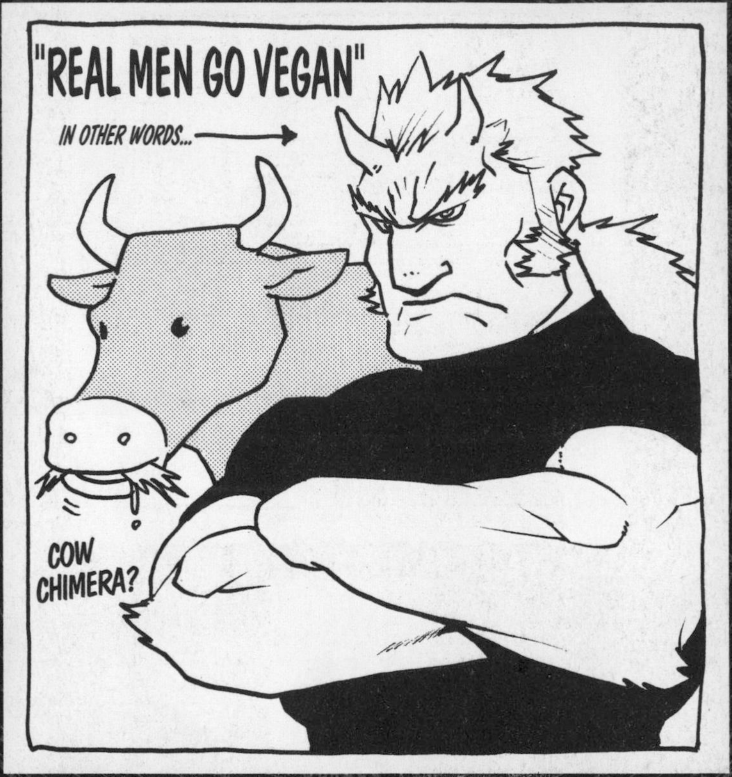
"REAL MEN GO VEGAN"
IN OTHER WORDS...
COW CHIMERA?

MY PRINCE...
BECOME THE KING YOU ARE DESTINED TO BE.
THIS OLD MAN...
...WILL NOW TAKE HIS...
BI
H
...ETERNAL REST!!!
REST TIME...
HE RAN AWAY !!
WELL, HOW THE HECK COULD I BEAT HIM ANYWAY?

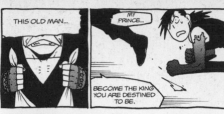

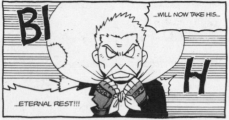

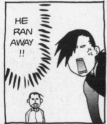

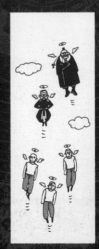

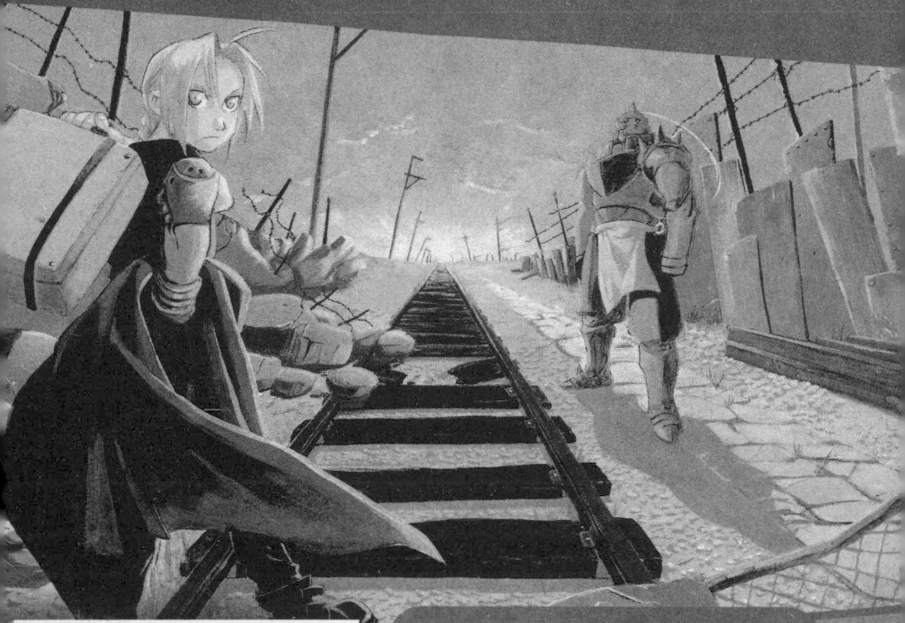

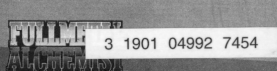

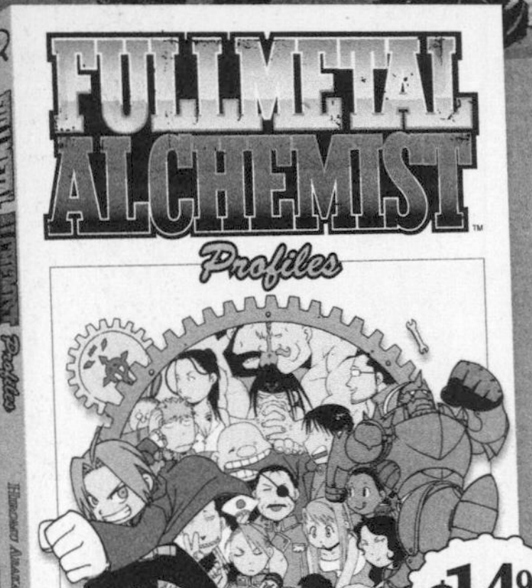
FULLMETAL ALCHEMIST
Profiles
HIROMU ARAKAWA
$14.99